Theorie s of A·   A Reade

British Film Institute Readers in Film Studies

Theories of Authorship:
A Reader/Edited by John Caughie

Routledge & Kegan Paul
London, Boston and Henley

in association with the British Film Institute
127 Charing Cross Road, London WC2H 0EA

First published in 1981
by Routledge & Kegan Paul Ltd
39 Store Street, London WC1E 7DD,
9 Park Street, Boston, Mass. 02108, USA and
Broadway House, Newtown Road,
Henley-on-Thames, Oxon RG9 1EN
Set in Linotron Sabon and Helvetica by
Input Typesetting Ltd.,
London, SW19
and printed in Great Britain by
St Edmundsbury Press
Bury St Edmunds, Suffolk

British Library Cataloguing in Publication Data

Caughie, John
Theories of authorship. − (British Film
Institute. Readers in film studies).
1. Moving-pictures − Production and direction
I. Title II. Series
791.43'0233   PN1995.9.P7   80-41575
ISBN 0−7100−0649−7
ISBN 0−7100−0650−0 Pbk

Contents

vi *Contents*

Acknowledgments

The publishers wish to thank the following for permission to reprint the copyright material listed below:
Oxford University Press for *The Mirror and the Lamp: Romantic Theory and the Critical Tradition* by M. H. Abrams. Copyright 1953 by Oxford University Press, Inc. Reprinted by permission; the author and *Screen* for Edward Buscombe, 'Ideas of Authorship', *Screen*, vol. 14, no. 3, Autumn 1973, pp. 75–85, copyright © *Screen* 1973; *Cahiers du Cinéma* for Pierre Kast, 'Des confitures pour un gendarme', *Cahiers du Cinéma* no. 2, May 1951, p. 40, Eric Rohmer, 'Renoir Américain', *Cahiers du Cinéma* no. 8, Jan. 1952, pp. 34–5, François Truffaut, 'Une certaine tendance du cinéma français', *Cahiers du Cinéma* no. 31, Jan. 1954, pp. 26–7, Eric Rohmer, 'A qui la faute?', *Cahiers du Cinéma* no. 39, Oct. 1954, pp. 6–7, Jacques Rivette, 'Notes sur une révolution', *Cahiers du Cinéma* no. 54, Christmas 1955, pp. 18–19, Fereydoun Hoveyda, 'La réponse de Nicholas Ray', *Cahiers du Cinéma* no. 107, May 1960, pp. 13–23, Luc Moullet, 'Sam Fuller: sur les brisées de Marlowe', *Cahiers du Cinéma* no. 93, March 1959, pp. 11–14, André Bazin, 'Comment peut-on être Hitchcocko–Hawksien?', *Cahiers du Cinéma* no. 44, Feb. 1955, p. 18, André Bazin, 'De la politique des auteurs', *Cahiers du Cinéma* no. 70, April 1957, pp. 9–11 (translation by Peter Graham in *The New Wave*, Secker & Warburg, 1968, reprinted by permission), Fereydoun Hoveyda, 'Autocritique', *Cahiers du Cinéma* no. 126, Dec. 1961, p. 45, Louis Marcorelles, 'Ford of the Movies', *Cahiers du Cinéma* no. 86, Aug. 1958, pp. 32–7, Jean-Louis Comolli, 'Signes de piste', *Cahiers du Cinéma* no. 164, March 1965, pp. 75–6, Jean Narboni, 'La preuve par huit', *Cahiers du Cinéma* no. 182, Sept. 1966, pp. 20–4, Jean-Pierre Oudart, 'Conclusion to "John Ford's *Young Mr Lincoln*"', *Cahiers du Cinéma* no. 223, Aug. 1970, (translation by Helen Lackner and Diana Matias in *Screen* vol. 13, no. 3, Autumn 1972, pp. 39–44, copyright © *Screen* 1972), Jean-Pierre Oudart, 'Le hors-champ de l'Auteur', *Cahiers du Cinéma* nos. 236–7, March–April 1971, pp. 86–9 – all material from *Cahiers du Cinéma* copyright les Editions de l'Etoile; English translations, except where stated, by Norman King, copyright © British Film Institute 1980; *Movie* for Ian Cameron, 'Films, Directors and Critics', *Movie* no. 2, Sept. 1962, pp. 4–6, Ian Cameron, Jim Hillier, V. F. Perkins, Michael Walker, 'The Return of *Movie*: a discussion', *Movie*

no. 20, Spring 1975, pp. 16–17; the author for Andrew Sarris, 'Notes on the Auteur Theory in 1962', *Film Culture* no. 27, Winter 1962–3, pp. 6–7; the author and E. P. Dutton for Andrew Sarris, 'Toward a Theory of Film History', in *The American Cinema: Directors and Directions 1929–68*, E. P. Dutton, New York, 1968 (first published as 'The American Cinema', *Film Culture* no. 28, Spring 1963); the author for Andrew Sarris, 'Preminger's Two Periods', *Film Comment* vol. 3, no. 3, Summer 1965; the author and *Film Comment* for Andrew Sarris, '*The Searchers*', *Film Comment* vol. 7 no. 1, Spring 1971, pp. 58–61. Copyright © 1973 by Film Comment Publishing Corporation. Reprinted by permission of The Film Society of Lincoln Center; the author and *Sight and Sound* for Lindsay Anderson, '*The Searchers*', *Sight and Sound* vol. 26, no. 2, Autumn 1956, pp. 94–5; *Film Comment* for Robin Wood, 'Shall We Gather at the River? The late films of John Ford', *Film Comment* vol. 7 no. 3, Fall 1971, pp. 8–17. Copyright © 1971 by Film Comment Publishing Corporation. Reprinted by permission of the Film Society of Lincoln Center; New Left Review Ltd. for Peter Wollen [Lee Russell], 'John Ford', *New Left Review* no. 29, Jan./Feb. 1965; Basic Books for 'The Structural Study of Myth' from *Structural Anthropology* by Claude Lévi-Strauss, translated from the French by Claire Jacobson and Brooke Grundfest Schoepf, pp. 213–17, © 1963 by Basic Books, Inc., Publishers, New York also Allen Lane, London; Martin Secker & Warburg Ltd. for Geoffrey Nowell-Smith, *Visconti*, Secker & Warburg, 1967, pp. 9–12, and for Peter Wollen, *Signs and Meaning in the Cinema*, Secker & Warburg, 1967 and 1972, pp. 93–115, 167–173, also Indiana University Press. Reprinted by permission; *Film Comment* for Charles Eckert, 'The English Cine-Structuralists', *Film Comment* vol. 9, no. 3, May/June 1973, pp. 46–54. Copyright © 1973 by Film Comment Publishing Corporation. Reprinted by permission of the Film Society of Lincoln Center; the author and *Film Quarterly* for Brian Henderson, 'Critique of Cine-structuralism Part I', © 1973 by The Regents of the University of California. Reprinted from *Film Quarterly* vol. 27, no. 1, pp. 25–34 by permission of the Regents; Routledge & Kegan Paul for Pierre Macherey, 'Literary Analysis: the Tomb of Structures', from *A Theory of Literary Production*, Routledge & Kegan Paul, London, 1978, pp. 152–6; Wm. Collins Sons & Co. Ltd. for Roland Barthes, 'The Death of the Author', from *Image/Music/Text*. Essays selected and translated by Stephen Heath. Copyright © by Roland Barthes 1977. English translation © 1977 by Stephen Heath. Collins, London, 1977, pp. 142–8; the author and *Screen* for Stephen Heath, 'Comment on "Ideas of Authorship"', *Screen* vol. 14, no. 3, Autumn 1973, pp. 86–91; the author and *Screen* for Geoffrey Nowell-Smith, 'Six authors in pursuit of *The Searchers*', *Screen* vol. 17, no. 1, Spring 1976, pp. 26–33; Lynda Myles and Macmillan for Christian Metz, 'History/Discourse: a note on two voyeurisms', from *The Imaginary Signifier*, Macmillan, London and Basingstoke, 1980 (first English translation by Susan Bennett in *Edinburgh '76 Magazine*, Edinburgh Film Festival 1976); the author for Geoffrey Nowell-Smith, 'A note on History/Discourse', *Edinburgh 76 Magazine*, Edinburgh Film Festival, 1976; the author and *Cine-Tracts* for Sandy Flitterman, 'Woman, Desire and the Look: Feminism and the Enunciative Apparatus in Cinema', *Cine-Tracts* 5, vol. 2, no. 1, Fall 1978, pp. 63–8; the author for Nick Browne, 'The Rhetoric of the Specular Text with reference to *Stagecoach*' (originally published in French in *Communications* no. 23. An expanded version published as 'The Spectator-in-the-Text: The Rhetoric of *Stagecoach*', *Film Quarterly*, vol. 29, no. 2, Winter 1975–6, pp. 26–38); the author and the British Film Institute for Pam Cook, 'The Point of Self-Expression in Avant-garde Film', *Catalogue of BFI Productions 1977–8*, BFI, 1978; the author, Basil Blackwell and La Société Française de Philosophie for Michel Foucault, 'What is an Author', from *Language, Counter-Memory, Practice*, Basil Blackwell, Oxford, 1977, pp. 121–38 (originally published in *Bulletin de la Société Française de Philosophie* vol. 63, no. 3, 1969).

Stills from *Stagecoach* by courtesy of United Artists and from *Marnie* by courtesy of Universal. The stills on the cover and jacket from *The Horse Soldiers* by courtesy of Universal.

Preface

Author and criticism have developed together over the last hundred
and fifty odd years until the achieved situation of today when the
institutionalization of 'literary criticism' (in faculties, journals,
newspaper reviews, etc.) in replacement of the discipline of rhetoric
(founded not on the 'author' but on the orders of discourse) depends
on and sustains the author (enshrined in syllabi and examinations,
interviews and television portraits). The task of criticism has been
precisely the construction of the author. It must read the author in
the texts grouped under his name. Style in this perspective is the
result of the extraction of marks of individuality, a creation of the
author and the area of his value. Criticism, in short, is the modern
hermeneutics; the passage from God to Author.

Stephen Heath[1]

This Reader attempts to do two things: using documentation and commentary, it attempts to follow the most significant stages in the development of theories of film authorship over the past thirty or so years;
and it attempts to put into play certain formulations and problems which
have to be confronted in the continuing theorization of the author's place
and function. The two aims are clearly not separate, the one determining
the reading of the other.

The challenge to the concept of the author as source and centre of
the text − as that which criticism must reveal in the text − has been
decisive in contemporary criticism and aesthetic theory; in many respects, modernist criticism and theory are founded on that challenge,
just as much of nineteenth- and twentieth-century philosophy was founded on the challenge to the centrality of God. In both instances, the result
has been a re-consideration of the text or the world as a structured play
of forces, relations and discourses, rather than as a site of final, unified
meanings, authorized by their source. Where criticism has felt the weight
of this challenge, and it is by no means universal, it has attempted to
open out (or even force open) the text as a process, obedient to a certain
history and to certain 'orders of discourse', rather than to the personality
and self-expression of its author. The function of such a criticism is, then,
not to discover, or construct, the author, but to discover the history and
the discursive organization which is foundational for the text, and which
negotiates its relationship with its historical audience. A theory of au-

1

thorship, now, involves a consideration of the position of authors within specific histories (for cinema, particularly, this involves industrial and institutional histories as well as social and political histories); and it involves a conceptualization of how the author functions as a figure within the rhetoric of the text, and of how we use this figure (fictional, constructed, actual) in our reading, and for our pleasure.

Within this context, the strategy of the Reader appears as the charting of a dissolution: by Part Three the author as a self-expressive individual has virtually disappeared, and theory is concerned with his traces in the text's discourse. This seems most clear in the little narrative of John Ford, who enters the collection as 'Ford of the Movies' and exits as a functioning look in the geography of textual authority. But while Nick Browne's article seems to me to raise more pertinent problems for film theory in the present, it is in no way my intention to construct *auteurism* or *'auteur*-structuralism' as a simple past, a background for academic study. One motivation for the Reader is the feeling that, in its reaction against a teenage romance with the *auteur*, much recent discussion of film (and teaching of film) has tended to deny its former attachment by leaving the author (or *auteur*, or director) without an adequate place in theory: if the author is not at the centre, he is nowhere; if the romance is over, I will reject him utterly. The documentation of the past of authorship theory (in so far as it is a past – many more teenage romances have blossomed in maturity into secure marriages) is functional for the present: to insert into film theory something of the fascination with the author.

The Reader is not exhaustive; it begs a number of questions of which three should be mentioned here.

First, and most noticeably, it has very little to say on the place of the author within institutions (industrial, cultural, academic), or on the way in which the author is constructed by and for commerce. Partly, this reflects a dissatisfaction with most of what has been written, which has tended to remain within the romantic concept of the artist, with its concentration on questions of artistic freedom and industrial interference, and with its continual desire to identify the true author out of the complex of creative personnel. At the same time, questions of the author's relation to institutional and commercial contexts are increasingly being recognized as crucial, particularly when one comes to consider the problems of alternative practices or the notion of independent cinema. Brecht's 1931 account of the *Threepenny Opera* trial[2] brilliantly exposes the contradiction in cinema between the commercial need to maintain the ideology of the creative artist and the simultaneous need to redefine ownership in terms of capital, rather than creative, investment. These questions are being focused now by a number of articles on copyright law, and on the way in which the author is inscribed into legal and contractual relations.[3]

Second, there is a dangerous absence of history, a lack of attention to the way in which the author's place within a particular social history is written into the text. The absence is by no means complete, and it forms the central point of J.-P. Oudart's article on Bresson; but it is worth pointing to here as a dangerous tendency within film theory: the danger is that, in placing the author as a fictional figure inside the text, we remove the most accessible point at which the text is tied to its own social and historical outside: the danger, that is, of constructing the text as an ideal essence.

Third, there is a tendency to perpetuate the concentration of authorship theory on a single cinematic practice – the classic Hollywood cinema. Again, the tendency is broken at a number of important points – Oudart on Bresson, Cook on the avant-garde, – and work on the theory of the subject clearly applies across a range of practices. But it is worth emphasizing here the point which emerges clearly from Pam Cook's essay: that work on the author has to account for widely differing, even consciously oppositional, practices – differences within, as well as between, such broad areas as popular cinema, art cinema, avant-garde cinema. While it *may* be possible to assign a relatively homogeneous function to the figure of the author if one works with a list which includes Ford, Hawks, Ray (with question marks around Hitchcock and Sirk), it becomes difficult if one extends the list to include Coppola, Altman, Bertolucci and Ozu, and impossible if one brings in Godard, Akerman, Snow, LeGrice, Mulvey and Wollen, Cinema Action or Newsreel Collective. What this impossibility does is to call into question the notion of an all-embracing, singular theory of authorship, and to suggest the need for work on authorship within specific practices.

Calling attention here to these absences and tendencies is not intended simply to ward off criticism: clearly, my excuse would be that a Reader depends on what has been written, and it reflects the absences and tendencies of its object. Rather, the intended usefulness of this preface (written after everything else was completed) is to suggest the questions which have to be put to the material in the Reader, and which have to be brought to bear on future considerations of film authorship.

One or two things should be said about the way in which the Reader is organized. I have tried to allow groups of articles to emerge which, implicitly or explicitly, speak to each other. This is clearest in the way in which Ford is inserted into the collection as a way of opening out differences of approach and methodology, and, more importantly, as a way of focusing the shifting place given to the author within film criticism and theory. The choice of Ford was motivated by the fact that he seems to have figured in theory more continuously, more centrally, and more variously than any other director. But the sense of debate, of authorship generating its own critique, emerges also in the way in which Buscombe's essay is taken up by Heath and further inflected by Nowell-Smith, or in the way in which a problematic is constituted out of the articles by Wood, Wollen, Eckert, Henderson, or out of those by Metz, Nowell-Smith and Flitterman. While the general organization is (very roughly) chronological, I would hope that the controversies within sections, and the emphases which leap-frog backwards and forwards between sections, would break down any sense of a teleological narrative in which things simply get better and better, culminating in the last article, or in the most recent issue of *Cahiers, Screen, Film Quarterly*, or whatever.

I have already implied that the position from which the selection proceeds is one of disappointment at the way in which the debate about film authorship was for a long time appropriated to the categories of traditional cultural discussions of art and creativity. Simply to reproduce the debate, featuring its high points, seemed to run the risk of allowing those categories to stand. What I have attempted to do, therefore, while representing the main areas around which discussion has clustered, is to stir up the waters a little by pulling in categories from outside the literature of film (Abrams, Macherey, Barthes), and from outside the traditional grounds on which the authorship debate has been staged (Metz, Browne). Thus, particularly in Part Three a number of articles appear which are not explicitly about film authorship, but are there to articulate problems and concepts which seem crucial if the theory of authorship is to be thought through productively.

Something should be said about the treatment of *auteurism*, since that section seems to adopt a different strategy from the others. To produce a representative selection of *auteurist* writing would, at the very least, give a considerable weighting to that section at the expense of the rest of the Reader; in fact, it would probably require a Reader of its own. Indeed, much of the material is already in circulation (*Movie Reader*, Sarris), or is coming into circulation (the forthcoming translations from *Cahiers*). Since *auteurism* is more clearly a critical practice than a theory, it seemed appropriate to indicate its operation 'in the field': hence the dossier on Ford. At the same time, as I have indicated, the choice of Ford was to provide a cross-reference with articles in other sections, and Ford is not necessarily the best choice to represent the various currents of *auteurism* (Minnelli might have done more justice to *Cahiers* and *Movie*). What I have done, therefore, is to compile dossiers mainly of extracts and short quotations from each of the main currents to indicate something of the nature of their writing.* Such extraction can only be impressionistic; but it may bring out something of the divisions and agreements within 'classical' *auteurist* writing, and construct it as some-

---

* The exception to this is *Movie*, which is represented largely by a complete article. This reflects the wishes of the editors of *Movie*, who were reluctant to have the magazine represented by extracts. A fuller selection of *Movie*'s critical writing is in any case readily available in *The Movie Reader*; see bibliography.

Part One

Auteurism

1 · Introduction

the cinema is quite simply becoming a means of expression, just as all the arts have been before it, and in particular painting and the novel. After having been successfully a fairground attraction, an amusement analogous to boulevard theatre, or a means of preserving the images of an era, it is gradually becoming a language. By language, I mean a form in which and by which an artist can express his thoughts, however abstract they may be, or translate his obsessions exactly as he does in the contemporary essay or novel. That is why I would like to call this new age of cinema the age of *caméra-stylo*.

Alexandre Astruc (1948)[1]

The *politique des auteurs* has had its day: it was only a stage on the way to a new criticism.

Fereydoun Hoveyda (1961)[2]

As a term, Astruc's *caméra-stylo* (camera-pen) failed to take root, but the association of the film artist with the 'serious' writer, and the insistence on film as individual self-expression, had a considerable polemical importance, forming the basis of the *cinéma d'auteurs* constructed in the pages of *Cahiers du Cinéma* in the 1950s. Traditionally, the reference to the *auteur* in French film criticism had identified either the author who wrote the script, or, in the more general sense of the term, the artist who created the film. In the work of *Cahiers* the latter sense came to replace the former, and the *auteur* was the artist whose personality was 'written' in the film.

Within its distinguishable currents – *Cahiers* in France, *Movie* in Britain, Andrew Sarris in America – *auteurism* shares certain basic assumptions: notably, that a film, though produced collectively, is most likely to be valuable when it is essentially the product of its director ('meaningful coherence is more likely when the director dominates the proceedings': Sarris[3]); that in the presence of a director who is genuinely an artist (an *auteur*) a film is more than likely to be the expression of his individual personality; and that this personality can be traced in a thematic and/or stylistic consistency over all (or almost all) the director's films. Most *auteurist* critics made a distinction between the *auteur* and the (mere) *metteur en scène*: the one consistently expressing his own unique obsessions, the other a competent, even highly competent, film-maker,

9

but lacking the consistency which betrayed the profound involvement of a personality. The distinction opened out energetic controversies along the borderline between the two: over Minnelli, for example, or Huston. Each of the currents had its own set of values and its own areas of privilege, and within the currents there were differences; but each seemed to assume that, if film were to be considered an art, as it quite generally was, then what they were urging inevitably followed: film is an art, and art is the expression of the emotions, experience and 'worldview' of an individual artist.

The business of introducing this section on *auteurism* is made considerably easier by the presence of Edward Buscombe's article, 'Ideas of Authorship'. Simply to repeat the points of Buscombe's critique would be redundant, and it seems more useful here to fill out something of the place of *auteurism* within the history of film criticism and theory, giving an indication of the history into which *auteurism* intervened, and the history which it initiated: the history, that is, of the before and after which is implied by the two quotations which head this introduction, and which finds a starting point in the extract from Abrams which follows.

Ironically, the intervention of *auteurism*, its critical revolution, was simply the installation in the cinema of the figure who had dominated the other arts for over a century: the romantic artist, individual and self-expressive. Established film criticism had long ago accepted that film was an art (it was the necessary justification for its own discourse), but it had meant it at the most general level, at which art has something to do with truth and beauty. Film theory had concerned itself almost exclusively with the relation between the representation and the real thing, and had not developed an aesthetic to explain the place of the artist in film art. Since the cinema which was predominantly valorized was the less apparently industrial cinema of Europe and Asia, the problem of the apparent contradiction between a commercial industry and an art was not fully confronted, and where it arose (as in the films of Ford, Welles or Griffith) it tended to be dealt with either in terms of overriding genius, or by a compromise position in which, by a combination of exceptional circumstances (a good subject, a good script, a good cast, an artist and freedom), a work of art which was personal might be produced despite the constraints of the industry. Established criticism valued as artists a small number of directors, predominantly European, who produced work which had a certain highly variable quality of 'greatness' (which was typically either a moral quality or a social penetration) and a certain 'seriousness' (which involved the apparent commitment of the artist to his theme). Art was simply a value term, and the theoretical questions which it begged went largely unanswered. *Auteur* criticism, on the other hand, proposed as artists a much larger number of directors whose work, viewed over a number of films, displayed a consistency of underlying theme and style which was surprising in the industrial and commercial system in which they worked, and which therefore, it seemed, could be ascribed to the force of the director's personality and unique obsessions expressing themselves through the film despite the constraints. In fact, the struggle between the desire for self-expression and the constraints of the industry could produce a tension in the films of the commercial cinema which was lacking in the 'art' cinema, encouraging the *auteurist* critics to valorize Hollywood cinema above all else, finding there a treasure-trove of buried personalities, and, in the process, scandalizing established criticism. Uniqueness of personality, brash individuality, persistence of obsession and originality were given an evaluative power above that of stylistic smoothness or social seriousness.

Put thus, the critical shift which *auteurism* effected within the history of film criticism can be seen as a step backwards to a romantic conception of the artist as it is described by Abrams: a regressive step precisely at the moment at which romanticism was becoming less secure in other branches of criticism, and in a medium in which an aesthetic of individual self-expression seemed least appropriate. This regression can be explained partly by the lack of definition which had been given to the notion of film art in traditional criticism, a lack of definition which allowed *auteurism* to pour cinema into the mould which was already provided by the romantic aesthetic. The relation between *auteurism* and romanticism also helps to explain the process by which, after the initial scandal, *auteurism* was easily assimilated into the dominant aesthetic mode.

But if this succeeds in explaining away Astruc's 'new age of cinema' as nothing more than the old age of romanticism, it fails to explain the relation of *auteurism* to the 'new criticism' which Hoveyda invokes. If we describe *auteurism* as nothing more than an escape into the romantic aesthetic of bourgeois criticism, away from the actual conditions of production, we pose it as simply a dead end of history, albeit one which is still with us. My argument would be that *auteurism* did in fact produce a radical dislocation in the development of film theory, which has exposed it progressively to the pressures of alternative aesthetics and 'new criticisms'. This dislocation cannot be attributed easily to a single cause, but can be associated with a number of impulses, shifts of emphasis and contradictions which were central to *auteur* criticism.

In the first place, the shift which *auteurism* effected was a shift in the way in which films were conceived and grasped within film criticism. The personality of the director, and the consistency within his films, were not, like the explicit subject matter which tended to preoccupy established criticism, simply there as a 'given'. They had to be sought out, discovered, by a process of analysis and attention to a number of films. The recognition that the director was not always able to choose the best subject matter for his own self-expression was the concession which *auteurism* made to the conditions of production. Subject matter, the story, what the film was explicitly about, could in most instances be posed as a framework given to the director by the studio, and not necessarily of his choosing. The business of the critic was to discover the director within the given framework, to find the traces of the submerged personality, to find the ways in which the *auteur* had transformed the material so that the explicit subject matter was no longer what the film was really about – 'The story of *The Criminal* centres on a race-track robbery, but this is certainly not the subject of the film.'[4] Film criticism became a process of discovery, a process which, while it remained firmly within the hermeneutics of romantic criticism, forced a more precise attention to what was actually happening within the film than had been customary for a traditional criticism which tended to be satisfied with the surfaces of popular films, assuming that the conditions of their production prevented them from having depths. More than this, *auteurism* forced an attention to what was actually happening in a lot of films. New *auteurs* were discovered like new stars in the sky; and Andrew Sarris, in particular, insisted on a rigorous and comprehensive knowledge not only of each putative *auteur*'s output, but also of as much of the total output of all cinema, and particularly of the undiscovered Hollywood, as it was physically possible to see. This attention to individual films, to groups of films, and to the whole of cinema was, of course, necessary, beneficial and, in the context of the history of film theory, progressive.

In one form, the attention involved simply a discovery of recurrent underlying themes, giving to the critic the role of interpreter, separating the true from the apparent, finding the depth below the surface, easing the object into consumption. While the awareness of recurrent themes is clearly useful, there is a continual danger in predominantly thematic approaches that they will lend themselves to a critical reductiveness: a 'eureka syndrome' in which the aim is to 'crack the code', to liberate the theme and the values from the film which contains (and conceals) them. Because of the fundamental and perpetual difficulty of quotation in film criticism (of quotation from a visual discourse in a verbal discourse) thematic analysis (which verbal discourse copes with by repressing the visual) tended more and more to establish itself in many of the currents of *auteurism*, emerging clearly in '*auteur*-structuralism'.

Elsewhere, however, *auteur* critics avoid reductiveness by a close attention to *mise en scène*, and much of the best *auteurist* criticism (Barry Boys on Minnelli,[5] Hoveyda or V. F. Perkins on Ray[6]) focuses on *mise en scène* as the stylistic 'signature' of the director, complicating a simple elaboration of themes with a constant return to the way in which they appear on the screen. The logic of this attention is clear within the *auteurist* project – given the conditions of production in which subject matter and script are likely to be in the control of the studio, style at least has the possibility of being under the control of the director, and it is there that his personality may be the most legible. *Mise en scène* has a transformative effect. It is with the *mise en scène* that the *auteur* transforms the material which has been given to him; so it is in the *mise en scène* – in the disposition of the scene, in the camera movement, in the camera placement, in the movement from shot to shot – that the *auteur* writes his individuality into the film.

While the motivation for this attention to *mise en scène* may be within the project of discovering and celebrating *auteurs*, it also raises questions of the effectivity of the visual discourse. In *auteurist* criticism *mise en scène* begins to be conceived as an effectivity, producing meanings and relating spectators to meanings, rather than as a transparency, allowing them to be seen. Luc Moullet's notorious 'Morality is a question of tracking shots'[7] appears less scandalous than it did to the critics of *Sight & Sound*[8] if it is construed to indicate an awareness of the relationship between strategies of *mise en scène* and the production of ideologies. More than that, the attention to *mise en scène* gives criticism a way of accounting for the text as pleasurable, pointing to its fascination as well as to its meaning. An almost hedonistic pleasure in visual delights is a feature of much of the writing in *Cahiers* in the mid-1950s (Hoveyda on Ray: 'if one insists on thinking that *Party Girl* is rubbish, then I proclaim: "Long live this rubbish which so pleases my eyes, fascinates my heart, and gives me a glimpse of the kingdom of heaven." '[9]), and it frequently lapses into mere formalism; but when one places *Cahiers*' development alongside that of the more soberly traditional journals, it is hard not to sympathize with Bazin when he says, 'at least in *Cahiers* we prefer this prejudice to its opposite'.[10] In many respects, the attention to *mise en scène*, even to the extent of a certain historically necessary formalism, is probably the most important positive contribution of *auteurism* to the development of a precise and detailed film criticism, engaging with the specific mechanisms of visual discourse, freeing it from literary models, and from the liberal commitments which were prepared to validate films on the basis of their themes alone.

If this is the positive contribution of *auteurism* to film criticism, the eventual theoretical dislocation which it produced is more accurately attributed to the contradictions which it exposed within the aesthetics of film. *Auteurism* was not itself a theory: *Cahiers* proposed it as a policy; Sarris was prepared to admit it was more of an attitude than a theory; and *Movie* refused theoretical elaboration. But by adopting a fairly consistent romantic position in relation to creativity, it exposed film aesthetics to the contradictions of those romantic principles of individual creativity which formed the basis of nineteenth- and twentieth-century criticism, when applied to an expressive form which was collective, commercial, industrial and popular. The contradictions of a resolutely romantic aesthetic in relation to cinema came to be generally recognized, and two modes of coping with them were developed. On the one hand, a certain inappropriateness was recognized, and the rules were relaxed to allow creativity – even creative dominance – to enter at other levels (a Paddy

Chayefsky film, a James Cagney film). This approach characterized the later work of the writers associated with *Movie*. On the same level, the critical approach could be given a greater adequacy and flexibility by introducing principles of genre and industry, situating the *auteur*, or author, as one level among several which produced meaning in the text. Such a 'liberal *auteurism*' is indeed more adequate to the conditions of cinema, and escapes much of the inappropriateness of earlier *auteurism*, but in so far as it tends to seek for alternative unifying and ordering principles, personnel or relationships, it is still closely tied to the romantic aesthetic, and causes little disruption in theory.

On the other hand, and more radically, the attempt to confront the contradictions of *auteurism* within cinema aligned an important section of theoretical work on film with a more thoroughgoing critique of the romantic conception of authorship which depended on the notion of a unified and free creative subject. It is the course of this project which the later sections of the Reader attempt to chart. The decisive intervention is perhaps that of the editors of *Cahiers*, whose work on the Ford film, *Young Mr Lincoln*, constructs the text as a play of tensions, silences and repressions, in which the author is a problematic 'inscription' rather than an intentional source of meaning, a personality or a principle of unity. No straight line can be drawn between this work, or between the work on the author as fiction and function which dominates Part Three of the Reader, and the more intuitional, impressionistic work of early *auteurism*; but it is clear that the *Cahiers* editors' text did not emerge from nowhere. The work of Comolli and Narboni on Ford in this section of the Reader seems to indicate a pull between the recognition of the *auteur* as system of consistencies and the film as site of repressions and contradictions; and Sarris, in posing 'interior meaning' as a tension between the director's personality and his material, already hints at unconscious meanings and at the authors constructed *a posteriori*, whose names Peter Wollen will later put into inverted commas. *Auteurism* was at its most productive in its contradictions, and the systematic and rigorous attempt to confront them marks a shift out of *auteurism* as a critical policy towards work on a theory of authorship.

It would be absurd to suggest that the subsequent history of film theory followed necessarily from the radical intuitions of *auteurism*. What I am suggesting is that the foundations of a number of developments in authorship theory were already present – untheorized – in the work of those *auteur* critics who were more concerned with the productivity of *mise en scène* than with the simple identification of the *auteur*'s thematic preoccupations; that the present concern with film as language or film as discourse marks a return to a more rigorous concern with the rhetorical figurations of *mise en scène*, a return which has frequently lacked the ability to account also for film as pleasure; and that other developments in film theory have followed (particularly in *Cahiers*) from the need to rationalize the massive contradictions of an untheorized and assumed romantic *auteurism*. The tendency to reject *auteurism* because it is 'hopelessly contradictory' loses sight of the extent to which subsequent authorship theories, and subsequent theories of the production of ideologies in films, were at least inflected, if not initiated, by these contradictions. Equally, the tendency to reject *auteurism* because it is 'hopelessly romantic' lends itself to an over-reaction in which the author appears as 'nothing but' an effect of the text, failing to elaborate what the effect does. The attempt to move beyond *auteurism* has to recognize the place which *auteurism* occupies, and the influence which it brings to bear. It has to recognize also the fascination of the figure of the *auteur*, and the way he is used in the cinephile's pleasure.

A final point has to be added to free *auteurism* from the historical confinement which the association of the term with a particular period of *Cahiers* implies. *Auteurism* is a critical approach which existed before Truffaut announced '*la politique des auteurs*' in 1954, and persists after the *Young Mr Lincoln* text of 1970. Lindsay Anderson, in the late 1940s in *Sequence*, was already writing about John Ford in a way which anticipated the best of *auteurism*, even to the point of distinguishing (in a *Sight & Sound* review) between Ford's *Wagonmaster* and Wise's *Two Flags West* as 'the difference between the expressive, poet's eye, and the elegant, superficial skill of the *décorateur*'.[11] And Robin Wood in 1975:[12]

> Hawks obviously isn't the sole creator of *To Have and Have Not*, but I still value it primarily as a Hawks movie: his unifying and organizing presence seems crucial to its success.

Auteurism now, even more than in the polemical situation of the 1950s and early 1960s, is a critical, rather than a theoretical, practice, fully accommodated within established aesthetics, less concerned, in its security, to defend itself or rationalize itself. Within film criticism, in fact, from being a dislocation, it has become the tradition, producing evaluations and interpretations which are frequently impressively and seductively perceptive, but which very seldom throw into question, in any rigorous way, the premises on which the cinema depends. The attention necessary to contemporary *auteurism* is not as a theory, but as a critical position within discourses about cinema, a position which is supported institutionally and ideologically by the 'received' cultural aesthetic: a position, that is, which defines the space in which other discourses about cinema take place.

Notes

1 Alexandre Astruc, 'The birth of a new avant-garde: *la caméra-stylo*', in Peter

Graham, ed., *The New Wave*, London, Secker & Warburg, 1968, pp. 17–23; first published in *Ecran français*, no. 144, 1948.

2 Fereydoun Hoveyda, 'Autocritique', *Cahiers du Cinéma*, no. 126, December 1961, p. 45.

3 Andrew Sarris, 'Toward a theory of film history', in *The American Cinema*, New York, E. P. Dutton, 1968, p. 30.

4 Letter from Ian Cameron, Mark Shivas and V. F. Perkins, editors of *Oxford Opinion*, in *Sight & Sound*, vol. 30, no. 2, Spring 1961, p. 100. The editors were responding to Penelope Houston's criticism of their position in her article 'The critical question', *Sight & Sound*, vol. 29, no. 4, Autumn 1960, pp. 160–5.

5 Barry Boys, '*The Courtship of Eddie's Father*', *Movie*, no. 10, June 1963, pp. 29–32.

6 Fereydoun Hoveyda, 'La réponse de Nicholas Ray', *Cahiers du Cinéma*, no. 107, May 1960, pp. 13–23; see extract below. V. F. Perkins, 'The cinema of Nicholas Ray', *Movie*, no. 9, May 1963, pp. 4–10; in *Movie Reader*, I. Cameron, ed., London, November Books, 1972; in Nichols.

7 Luc Moullet, 'Sam Fuller: sur les brisées de Marlowe', *Cahiers du Cinéma*, no. 93, March 1959, pp. 11–19; see extract below.

8 See Richard Roud, 'The French line', *Sight & Sound*, vol. 29, no. 4, Autumn 1960, pp. 166–71. Roud's article was a companion piece to Penelope Houston, 'The critical question' in the same volume.

9 Hoveyda, 'La réponse de Nicholas Ray'.

10 André Bazin, 'Comment peut-on être Hitchcocko-Hawksien?', *Cahiers du Cinéma*, no. 44, February 1955, pp. 17–18; see extract below.

11 Lindsay Anderson, '*Wagonmaster* and *Two Flags West*', *Sight & Sound*, vol. 19, no. 8, December 1950, p. 334.

12 Robin Wood *et al.*, 'The return of *Movie*' (an editorial discussion), *Movie*, no. 20, Spring 1975, p. 17; see extract below.

A Auteurism in theory

2 · M. H. Abrams: 'Literature as a revelation of personality' (extract)

From *The Mirror and the Lamp: romantic theory and the critical tradition*, Oxford University Press, London, 1953

Abrams's book on romantic theory and criticism is one of the classic works of literary scholarship, setting out to identify the diverse currents which informed the romantic aesthetic in the first half of the nineteenth century, and their relationship to the intellectual and philosophical background. One of the virtues of Abrams's historical approach is his attentiveness to the metaphors which characterize criticism as much as they characterize poetry: thus, the mirror and the lamp identify (p. vi):

two common and antithetic metaphors of mind, one comparing the mind to a reflector of external objects, the other to a radiant projector which makes a contribution to the objects it perceives. The first of these was characteristic of much of the thinking from Plato to the eighteenth century; the second typifies the prevailing romantic conception of the mind.

Abrams's characterization of this shift (p. 21) is interesting for the purposes of the Reader:

Through most of the eighteenth century, the poet's invention and imagination were made thoroughly dependent for their materials – their ideas and 'images' – on the external universe and the literary models the poet had to imitate; while the persistent stress laid on his need for judgement and art – the mental surrogates, in effect, of the requirements of a cultivated audience – held the poet strictly responsible to the audience for whose pleasure he exerted his creative ability. Gradually, however, the stress was shifted more and more to the poet's natural genius, creative imagination, and emotional spontaneity, at the expense of the opposing attributes of judgement, learning, and artful restraints. As a result the audience gradually receded into the background, giving place to the poet himself, and his own mental powers and emotional needs, as the predominant cause and even the end and test of art.

| The relevance of this to an understanding of the *politique* and practice of *auteurism* is striking, and the extract is placed here as a way of introducing romanticism as a specific and historical (i.e. not 'natural') aesthetic. |

Shakespeare is above all writers, at least above all modern writers, the poet of nature; the poet that holds up to his readers a faithful mirrour of manners and of life · Samuel Johnson

[Shakespeare's] works are so many windows, through which we see a glimpse of the world that was in him · Thomas Carlyle

To know a work of literature is to know the soul of the man who created it, and who created it in order that his soul should be known · J. Middleton Murry

The grand question 'usual with the best of our own critics at present,' Carlyle wrote in 1827, 'is a question mainly of a psychological sort, to be answered by discovering and delineating the peculiar nature of the poet from his poetry.'[1] There could be no more striking antithesis to the practice of critics (with the partial exception of Longinus) from the dawn of speculation about art through the greater part of the eighteenth century. So long as the poet was regarded primarily as an agent who holds a mirror up to nature, or as the maker of a work of art according to universal standards of excellence, there was limited theoretical room for the intrusion of personal traits into his product. Accordingly, practical criticism busied itself chiefly with the poem itself, its relation to the world it reflected, and its relation to the rules of writing and to the susceptibilities of the audience on which these rules were grounded. The writing of the lives of poets and artists was carried on as one branch of general biography, intended to memorialize men of note in all areas of endeavor. But once the theory emerged that poetry is primarily the expression of feeling and a state of mind – and even, in its extreme form, that poetry is the fictional gratification of desire – a natural corollary was to approach a poem as a revelation of what Carlyle called the 'individual specialties' of the author himself. Schleiermacher wrote in 1800, in the idiom of contemporary idealism:

> If the introspection of the spirit into itself is the divine source of all plastic art and poetry, and if the spirit finds within its own being all that it can represent in its immortal works: shall not the spirit, in all its products and compositions, which can represent nothing else, also look back upon itself?[2]

For good or ill, the widespread use of literature as an index — as the most reliable index — to personality was a product of the characteristic aesthetic orientation of the early nineteenth century.

Before undertaking an account of this strange innovation, which swept everything before it in applied criticism for more than a century, it will prove useful to make a few broad distinctions. We shall be concerned with three kinds of ostensibly critical activity, and although each relies on the same assumption that art and personality are correlated variables, the difference between them is important. One looks to an author for the explanation of his work; another reads an author out of his work; and the third reads a work in order to find its author in it. The first type is primarily an investigation of literary causes; *tel arbre, tel fruit*, as Sainte-Beuve, its famed exponent, put it — the attempt is to isolate and explain the special quality of a work by reference to the special quality of the character, life, lineage, and milieu of its author. The second type is biographical in aim: it sets out to reconstruct the author as he lived, and uses the literary product merely as a convenient record from which to infer something about his life and character. The third, however, claims to be specifically aesthetic and appreciative in purpose: it regards aesthetic qualities as a projection of personal qualities, and in its extreme form, it looks upon the poem as a transparency opening directly into the soul of its author. 'Where it is worth the trouble,' Herder said as early as 1778, 'this *living reading*, this divination into the soul of the author, is the *sole* mode of reading, and the most profound means of self-development.'[3] Or in F. L. Lucas's more recent and more moderate rendition of this ideal:

> I have found by spontaneous experience more and more that even the aesthetic pleasure of a poem depends for me on the fineness of the personality glimpsed between its lines; on the spirit of which the body of a book is inevitably the echo and the mould.[4]

In the critical discourse of such readers, therefore, the primary qualities of a good poem are, literally, attributes of the mind and temper of its composer: sincerity, integrity, high seriousness, shrewdness, benignity — and so on, through the whole of the characterological resources of the language.

In addition, we may profitably distinguish the level at which a critic pursues the connection between art and temperament, whether his aim is explanatory, biographical, or appreciative. First, a literary product may be taken to reflect the powers, faculties, and skill of its producer —

> Immortal flowers of poesy,
> Wherein, as in a mirror, we perceive
> The highest reaches of a human wit,

as Christopher Marlowe expressed this near-tautology long ago. On the next level, there is held to be a particularity in the style, or general cast of language, which serves as an index to the particularity of its author's cast of mind. But on the third level, the style, structure, and subject matter of literature are said to incorporate the most persistent, dynamic elements of an individual mind; the basic dispositions, interests, desires, preferences, and aversions which give continuity and coherence to a personality. In the sweeping statement of a critic of our own time, Edmund Wilson:

> The real elements, of course, of any work of fiction, are the elements of the author's personality: his imagination embodies in the images of characters, situations, and scenes the fundamental conflicts of his nature or the cycle of phases through which it habitually passes. His personages are personifications of the author's various impulses and emotions: and the relations between them in his stories are really the relations between these.[5]

The correlation of the style and certain limited attributes of a work both with the powers and general cast of the author's mind occasionally appeared in classical rhetoric and poetic; it was a prominent element in the theory of Longinus; and it became a fairly frequent subject for comment in the criticism of the seventeenth and eighteenth centuries. The distinctive characteristic in the applied criticism of many romantic critics, English and German, is the extent to which this general approach to literature superseded others, and above all, the development and exploitation of interpretation at the third of these levels. Certain of these critics even went on to distinguish between the personal attributes which an author projects directly into his work and those which he disguises and distorts in order to hide certain facts from his readers, or from himself. As a result we find the division of a work of literature into a surface reference to characters, things, and events, and a more important covert symbolism which is expressive of elements in the nature of its author. Furnished with the proper key, the romantic extremist was confident he could decipher the hieroglyph, penetrate to the reality behind the appearance, and so come to know an author more intimately than his own friends and family; more intimately, even, than the author, lacking this key, could possibly have known himself.

Notes

1 T. Carlyle, 'The State of German Literature', *Edinburgh Review*, vol. 46, no. 92, Oct. 1827, pp. 304–51.
2 Schleiermacher, *Monologen*, ed. F. M. Schiele, Leipzig, Dürr'sche Buchhandlung, 1902, p. 22.
3 J. G. von Herder 'Vom erkennen und empfinden der menschlichen Seele', Riga, J. F. Hartnoch, Sämtliche Werke, 1778, vol. VIII, p. 208.
4 F. L. Lucas, *The Decline and Fall of the Romantic Ideal*, Cambridge University Press, New York, Macmillan, 1936, p. 221.
5 Edmund Wilson, *Axel's Castle*, New York, Scribner, 1936, p. 176.

3 · Edward Buscombe: 'Ideas of authorship'

Screen, vol. 14, no. 3, Autumn, 1973

Written after the development (and into the decline) of '*auteur*-structuralism' in Britain, Edward Buscombe's article links the critique of early *auteurism* with that of the structuralist extension. In Stephen Heath's 'Comment' the critique is extended to any theory of authorship which depends on the assumption of a unified subject.

The article is a revision of a paper, 'The Idea of Authorship', given at a seminar organized by the British Film Institute and the Society for Education in Film and Television.

The *auteur* theory was never, in itself, a theory of the cinema, though its originators did not claim that it was. The writers of *Cahiers du Cinéma* always spoke of '*la politique des auteurs*'. The translation of this into 'the *auteur* theory' appears to be the responsibility of Andrew Sarris. In an essay entitled 'Notes on the Auteur Theory in 1962' he remarked, 'Henceforth, I will abbreviate "*la politique des auteurs*" as the *auteur* theory to avoid confusion.'[1] Confusion was exactly what followed when the newly christened 'theory' was regarded by many of its supporters and opponents alike as a total explanation of the cinema.

Not only was the original *politique* of *Cahiers* somewhat less than a theory; it was itself only loosely based upon a theoretical approach to the cinema which was never to be made fully explicit. The *politique*, as the choice of term indicates, was polemical in intent and was meant to define an attitude to the cinema and a course of action. In the pursuit of this course *Cahiers* did inevitably reveal some of the theory on which the *politique* was based; but usually this appeared incidentally, and at times incoherently.

One thing is clear, however. From the beginning *Cahiers*, and its predecessor *La Revue du Cinéma*, were committed to the line that the cinema was an art of personal expression. (In the second issue of *La Revue* an article appeared entitled: 'La création doit être l'ouvrage d'un seul'). At that period (the late 1940s) it was inevitable that part of the project of a new film magazine would be to raise the cultural status of the cinema. The way to do this, it seemed, was to advance the claim of the cinema to be an art form like painting or poetry, offering the individual the freedom of personal expression. The main difference at that time between *Cahiers* and other film magazines was that *Cahiers* did not feel that opportunities of this kind were to be found exclusively in the European 'art' cinema. Right from the very earliest issues there are discussions of Hollywood directors such as Welles, Ford and Lang. *Cahiers* was concerned to raise not only the status of the cinema in general, but of American cinema in particular, by elevating its directors to the ranks of the artists.

The *politique* in the sense of a line that will be rigorously pursued and provocatively expressed, really dates from an article in issue no. 31 by François Truffaut entitled 'Une certaine tendance du cinéma français'. Truffaut attacks what he calls the tradition of quality in the French cinema, by which he means the films of directors such as Delannoy, Allégret and Autant-Lara, and especially the adaptations by Aurenche and Bost of well-known novels. They are attacked for being literary, not truly cinematic, and are also found guilty of 'psychological realism'. Truffaut defines a true film *auteur* as one who brings something genuinely personal to his subject instead of merely producing a tasteful, accurate but lifeless rendering of the original material. Examples of true *auteurs* are Bresson and Renoir. Instead of merely transferring someone else's work faithfully and self-effacingly, the *auteur* transforms the material into an expression of his own personality.

So successful was Truffaut's call to arms, and so many were the *auteurs* subsequently discovered, that in all the later articles in *Cahiers* in which the '*politique*' was explicitly discussed, a great deal of space had to be devoted to dissociating the journal from the excesses committed in its name. (See, for example, issues nos 63, 70, 126, 172). Truffaut had referred only to French directors, but *Cahiers* began to give more and more space to the American cinema. In its special issue nos 150–1 on the American cinema no fewer than 120 *cinéastes* (i.e. *auteurs*) were identified.

Yet even by this late date (1964) the questions of what an *auteur* is and why the cinema should be discussed largely in terms of individual artists are ones that are only answered by implication. Clear articulations of a theory behind the practice are rare and sketchy. But a review by André Bazin of *The Red Badge of Courage* (no. 27, pp. 49f.) gives a clue. Bazin distinguishes between Hitchcock, a true *auteur*, and Huston, who is only a *metteur en scène*, who has 'no truly personal style'. Huston merely adapts, though often very skilfully, the material given him, instead of transforming it into something genuinely his own. A similar point is made by Jacques Rivette in a later issue (no. 126), in the course of a discussion on criticism. Rivette declares that Minnelli is not a true *auteur*, merely a talented director at the mercy of his script. With a bad script he makes a bad and uninteresting film. Fritz Lang, on the other hand, can somehow transform even indifferent material into something personal to him (and this, Rivette assumes, makes it interesting).

Such discussions, however, do not advance much beyond Truffaut's original position, though they serve to confirm *Cahiers'* stance on the issue of personal expression. Some attempt to modify this was made by Eric Rohmer. Rejecting the lunatic fringe who took the issue of personality to extremes, Rohmer writes, 'Le film est pour lui [the *auteur*] une architecture dont les pierres ne sont pas – ne doivent pas être – filles de sa propre chair.'[2] The comparison with architecture, another industrial art, would seem to lead in a different direction from comparisons with literature, the best known of which is, of course, Alexandre Astruc's article 'The Birth of a New Avant Garde: *La Caméra-Stylo*'.[3] But it was Astruc's article which was to prove more influential over the critics of *Cahiers*. The more romantic conception of the director as the 'only begetter' of a film was the one that dominated the journal.

One expression of this which seems particularly indebted to Romantic artistic theory is that of Rivette in issue no. 126: 'Un cinéaste, qui a fait dans le passé de très grands films, peut faire des erreurs, mais les erreurs qu'il fera ont toutes chances, a priori,* d'être plus passionantes que les réussites d'un confectionneur.'[4] What seems to lie behind such a statement is the notion of the 'divine spark' which separates off the artist from ordinary mortals, which divides the genius from the journeyman. All the articles by Truffaut, Bazin and Rivette from which I have quoted share this belief in the absolute distinction between *auteur* and *metteur en scène*, between *cinéaste* and '*confectionneur*', and characterise it in terms of the difference between the *auteur*'s ability to make a film truly his own, i.e. a kind of original, and the *metteur en scène*'s inability to disguise the fact that the origin of his film lies somewhere else.

When this is compared with a statement from early Romantic

---

* It's hard to see how this can be so *a priori* in any case; only according to the balance of probabilities.

literary theory, it is easy enough to see the derivation of this distinction.

An Original may be said to be of a *vegetable* nature; it rises spontaneously from the vital root of genius; it grows, it is not made; Imitations are often a sort of *manufacture*, wrought up by those *mechanics, art* and *labour*, out of pre-existent materials not their own.[5]

It's not surprising, therefore, to find that *auteur* critics draw others of their assumptions from Romantic theorists. For example, Coleridge makes a distinction between two kinds of literature which makes use of the metaphor of organic unity contained in the above passage: 'The plays of Beaumont and Fletcher are mere aggregations without unity; in the Shakespearean drama there is a vitality which grows and evolves itself from within – a keynote which guides and controls the harmonies throughout.'[6] This notion of the unity produced by the personality of the *auteur* is central to the *Cahiers'* position; but it is made even more explicit by their American apologist, Andrew Sarris: 'The *auteur* critic is obsessed with the wholeness of art and the artist. He looks at a film as a whole, a director as a whole. The parts, however entertaining individually, must cohere meaningfully.'[7] The work of a *metteur en scène* will never be more than the sum of its parts, and probably less. The *auteur*'s personality, on the other hand, endows his work with organic unity. The belief that all directors must be either *auteurs* or *metteurs en scène* led inevitably to a kind of apartheid, according to which, as Rivette says, the failures of the *auteurs* will be more interesting than the successes of the rest. Another formulation of what is essentially the same distinction occurs in *Cahiers* no. 172:

> l'être doué du moindre talent esthétique, si sa personalité 'éclate' dans l'oeuvre, l'emportera sur le technicien le plus avisé. Nous découvrons qu'il n'y pas de règles. L'intuition, la sensibilité, triomphent de toutes théories.[8]

Whether this zeal to divide directors into the company of the elect on the right and a company of the damned on the left owes anything to the Catholic influence in *Cahiers* is hard to say at this distance; but what can be identified, yet again, is the presence of Romantic artistic theory in the opposition of intuition and rules, sensibility and theory.

This tendency in *Cahiers* to make a totem of the personality of the *auteur* went to such extremes that every now and again the editors felt the need to redress the balance. André Bazin, writing in issue no. 70, introduces a different perspective:

The evolution of Western art towards greater personalisation should definitely be considered as a step forward, but only so long as this individualisation remains only a final perfection and does not claim to *define* culture. At this point, we should remember that irrefutable commonplace we learnt at school: the individual transcends society, but society is also and above all *within* him. So there can be no definitive criticism of genius or talent which does not first take into consideration the social determinism, the historical combination of circumstances, and the technical background which to a large extent determines it.[9]

Bazin, as Rohmer had done before, takes up the analogy of architecture:

If you will excuse yet another commonplace, the cinema is an art which is both popular and industrial. These conditions, which are necessary to its existence, in no way constitute a collection of hindrances – no more than in architecture – they rather represent a group of positive and negative circumstances which have to be reckoned with.[10]

To be fair, *Cahiers* never entirely forgot these commonplaces, and quite frequently ran articles on the organisation of the film industry, on film genres (such as Bazin's own 'The Evolution of the Western' in December 1955) and on the technology of the cinema. The development of *'la politique des auteurs'* into a cult of personality gathers strength with the emergence of Andrew Sarris, for it is Sarris who pushes to extremes arguments which in *Cahiers* were often only implicit.

Sarris, for example, rejects Bazin's attempt to combine the *auteur* approach with an acknowledgement of the forces conditioning the individual artist. Arguing strongly against any kind of historical determinism, Sarris states:

Even if the artist does not spring from the idealised head of Zeus, free of the embryonic stains of history, history itself is profoundly affected by his arrival. If we cannot imagine Griffith's *October* or Eisenstein's *Birth of a Nation* because we find it difficult to transpose one artist's unifying conceptions of Lee and Lincoln to the other's dialectical conceptions of Lenin and Kerensky, we are nevertheless compelled to recognise other differences in the personalities of these two pioneers beyond their respective cultural complexes. It is with these latter differences that the *auteur* theory is most deeply concerned. If directors and other artists cannot be wrenched

⊘from their historical environments, aesthetics is reduced to a subordinate branch of ethnography.[11]

(Pauline Kael is for once correct to write of this: 'And when is Sarris going to discover that aesthetics is indeed a branch of ethnography; what does he think it is – a sphere of its own, separate from the study of man and his environment?'[12] But her own confusion re-emerges later in the same essay when she remarks, 'Criticism is an art, not a science . . .'[13] Is ethnography, then, not a science?)

If Sarris is not saying that genius is independent of time and place, then he comes dangerously close to it. The critic's task as he sees it is to scan the cinema for signs of 'personality', and having found them to mine the film so as to bring as much as possible of it to the surface. It is not his job to explain how it got there. He is canny enough to remain aware that his position is partly determined by the need to maintain a polemic, both against those who are contemptuous of the American cinema and against the crudities of 'mass media critics'. ('*Auteur* criticism is a reaction against sociological criticism that enthroned the *what* against the *how*.'[14]) But this awareness does not save him from being driven further and further into an untenable position. That position is reached, I think, when he writes in his essay of 1962: 'The second premise of the *auteur* theory is the distinguishable personality of the director as a criterion of value. Over a group of films a director must exhibit certain recurring characteristics of style which serve as his signature.'[15] Here, surely, is a fatal flaw in Sarris's argument, and the sleight of hand he uses to cover it cannot disguise its vulnerability. He is attempting to make the *auteur* theory perform two functions at the same time. On the one hand, it is a method of classification. Sarris talks elsewhere about the value of the theory as a way of ordering film history, or a tool for producing a map of the cinema, and no one could deny that in this sense the theory has, whatever its faults, been extremely productive, as a map should be, in opening up unexplored territory. But at the same time Sarris also requires the theory to act as a means of measuring value. Films, he is saying, become valuable in so far as they reveal directorial personality. He therefore does precisely what Bazin said should not be done: he uses individuality as a test of cultural value. It's worth noting that Sarris is not consistent in practising what he preaches, for several directors whose work undoubtedly exhibits a high degree of personality do not rank very far up the league tables of *The American Cinema*. Kazan, Wilder, Dassin, even Brian

Forbes, all produce films easily recognisable as 'theirs' which are not rated by Sarris.

As one means, among others, of classifying films, the *auteur* theory has proved its usefulness. But to assert that personality is *the* criterion of value seems altogether more open to question. The assumption that individuality and originality are valuable in themselves is, as Bazin points out in 'La Politique des Auteurs', derived from Romantic artistic theory. Sarris goes further; 'the *auteur* theory values the personality of the director precisely because of the barriers to its expression.'[16] In *Culture and Society* Raymond Williams describes the way in which aesthetic theory came in the Romantic period to see the artist as essentially opposed to society, achieving personal expression in the face of a hostile environment and valuing it all the more for this.[17] Sarris is directly in this tradition.

Sarris, like *Cahiers* before him, then uses this criterion of value as a means of raising the status of American cinema. He admits that in Hollywood there are pressures which might work against individual expression. But so there are elsewhere:

All directors, and not just in Hollywood, are imprisoned by the conditions of their craft and their culture. The reason foreign directors are almost invariably given more credit for creativity is that the local critic is never aware of all the influences operating in a foreign environment. The late Robert Warshow treated Carl Dreyer as a solitary artist and Leo McCarey as a social agent, but we know now that there were cultural influences in Denmark operating on Dreyer. *Day of Wrath* is superior by any standard to *My Son John*, but Dreyer is not that much freer an artist than McCarey. Dreyer's chains are merely less visible from our vantage point across the Atlantic.[18]

Taken at face value this is unexceptionable; of course no director has total freedom, and there is no reason *a priori* why American cinema should not be as good as any other. And in fact, says Sarris, it is better:

After years of tortured revaluation, I am now prepared to stake my critical reputation, such as it is, on the proposition that Alfred Hitchcock is artistically superior to Robert Bresson by every criterion of excellence, and further that, film for film, the American cinema has been consistently superior to that of the rest of the world from 1915 through 1962. Consequently, I now regard the *auteur* theory primarily as a critical device for recording the history of the American cinema, the only cinema

in the world worth exploring in depth beneath the frosting of a few great directors on top.[19]
Again, this in itself is fair enough; the problem is that, having obtained our easy assent to the proposition that all film-makers are subject to conditions, he appears, by a sleight of hand, to proceed on the assumption that therefore conditions are unimportant. America can produce film artists in just the same way as Europe, but more of them, and of a higher standard. Film history is for Sarris the history of *auteurs*. The acknowledgement of 'conditions' turns out to be mere lip service. And it is not, I think, difficult to see why: if personality is the criterion of value, and can be achieved in the face of 'conditions', then it is not the critic's job to be much concerned with them.

One obvious objection to employing individuality as a test of value is that a director could well be highly individual, but a bad director. In the first edition of *Signs and Meaning in the Cinema* Peter Wollen does not seem wholly to avoid this trap. In the chapter on the *auteur* theory he writes:

My own view is that Ford's work is much richer* than that of Hawks and that this is revealed by a structural analysis; it is the richness of the shifting relations between antinomies in Ford's work that makes him a great artist, beyond being simply an undoubted *auteur*. Moreover, the *auteur* theory enables us to reveal a whole complex of meaning in films such as *Donovan's Reef*, which a recent filmography sums up as just 'a couple of Navy men who have retired to a South Sea island now spend most of their time raising hell.'[20]

There is no doubt that films such as *Donovan's Reef*, *Wings of Eagles* and especially *The Sun Shines Bright* (almost indecipherable to those unacquainted with Ford's work) do reveal a great deal of meaning when seen in the context of Ford's work as a whole. But does this make them 'good' films as well as interesting ones? The question is worth asking, because it seems to be just this smuggling in of one thing under the guise of another that is most responsible for the reputation in some quarters of the *auteur* theory as merely the secret password of an exclusive and fanatical sect.

Possibly people such as Pauline Kael, who are roused to fury by Sarris's version of the *auteur* theory, should simply be left to stew in their own juice. And perhaps those who won't accept that *Wings of Eagles* is a good film have a very narrow concept of what is

---

* Possibly by 'richer' Wollen does not imply 'has greater aesthetic value'; but if that is the case his terminology is a little confusing.

good and are unreasonable in demanding that all films should have
formal perfection, should be 'intelligent', 'adult', etc. But the *auteur*
theory becomes more tenable if in fact it is not required to carry
in its baggage the burden of being an evaluative criterion. And
Wollen, in the third edition of his book, dumps it along with much
else. *

At this point, it is necessary to say something about the *auteur*
theory since this has often been seen as a way of introducing
the idea of the creative personality into the Hollywood cinema.
Indeed, it is true that many protagonists of the *auteur* theory
do argue this way. However, I do not hold this view and I
think it is important to detach the *auteur* theory from any
suspicion that it simply represents a 'cult of personality' or
apotheosis of the director. To my mind the *auteur* theory
actually represents a radical break with the idea of an 'art'
cinema, not the transplant of traditional ideas about art into
Hollywood. The 'art' cinema is rooted in the idea of creativity
and the film as the expression of an individual vision. What
the *auteur* theory argues is that any film, certainly a
Hollywood film, is a network of different statements, crossing
and contradicting each other, elaborated into a final 'coherent'
version. Like a dream, the film the spectator sees is, so to
speak, the 'film façade', the end product of 'secondary
revision', which hides and masks the process which remains
latent in the film's 'unconscious'; by a process of comparison
with other films, it is possible to decipher, not a coherent
message or world-view, but a structure which underlies the
film and shapes it, gives it a certain pattern of energy cathexis.
It is this structure which *auteur* analysis disengages from the
film.

The structure is associated with a single director, an
individual, not because he has played the role of artist,
expressing himself or his own vision in the film, but because it
is through the force of his preoccupations that an unconscious,
unintended meaning can be decoded in the film, usually to the
surprise of the individual concerned. . . . It is wrong, in the
name of a denial of the traditional idea of creative subjectivity,
to deny any status to individuals at all. But Fuller or Hawks or
Hitchcock, the directors, are quite separate from 'Fuller' or

---

* The virtual obsession with aesthetic – even moral – evaluation which has characterised so much British criticism undoubtedly gave the *auteur* theory much of
its appeal. (It's hard to ascribe moral value to, say, the studio system.)

'Hawks' or 'Hitchcock', the structures named after them, and should not be methodologically confused.[21]
Wollen does not claim that this is a total theory of the cinema: *Auteur* theory cannot simply be applied indiscriminately. Nor does an *auteur* analysis exhaust what can be said about any single film. It does no more than provide one way of decoding a film, by specifying what its mechanics are at one level. There are other kinds of code that could be proposed, and whether they are of any value or not will have to be settled by reference to the text, to the films in question.[22]

There is much in this position that is attractive. It satisfies our sense that on the one hand the American cinema is the richest field for study, and on the other hand that the more one knows about its habitual methods of working the less it becomes possible to conceive of Hollywood as populated by autonomous geniuses. And certainly *a priori* evidence suggests that the themes of transferred guilt in Hitchcock, of home, and the desert/garden antithesis in Ford, for example, are almost entirely unconscious, making it inappropriate to speak, as so much *auteur* criticism does, about a director's world-view (and especially about the moral worth of that world-view). And the avoidance of the problem of evaluation is surely justified until we have an adequate description of what we should evaluate.

Structural analysis of *auteurs* has produced important results, not least in Wollen's own book. Yet there are surely problems in using techniques which were developed for the analysis of forms of communications which are entirely unconscious such as dreams, myths and language itself. For what is the exact relation between the structure called 'Hitchcock' and the film director called Hitchcock, who actually makes decisions about the story, the acting, the sets, the camera placing? It is possible to reveal structures in Hitchcock's work which are by no means entirely unconscious, such as the use of certain camera angles to involve and implicate the audience in the action. Hitchcock remarks about *The Wrong Man*:

> The whole approach is subjective. For instance, they've slipped on a pair of handcuffs to link him to another prisoner. During the journey between the station house and the prison, there are different men guarding him, but since he's ashamed, he keeps his head down, staring at his shoes, so we never show the guards.[23]

This kind of thing occurs in almost all Hitchcock's films, and so could be said to identify him as an *auteur* in the traditional sense. But it also connects to his obsessional and no doubt largely unconscious (till he read about it) concern with guilt and voyeurism, which have been revealed in structural analysis.

Earlier versions of the *auteur* theory made the assumption that because there was meaning in a work someone must have deliberately put it there, and that someone must be the *auteur*. Wollen rightly resists that. But this doesn't mean that one can only talk about unconscious structures (admittedly Wollen does say it is wrong to deny any status to individuals at all, but is there not something a little disingenuous in this concession?). The conscious will and talent of the artist (for want of a better word) may still be allowed some part, surely. But of course, that conscious will and talent are also in turn the product of those forces that act upon the artist, and it is here that traditional *auteur* theory most seriously breaks down. As Sam Rohdie says:

> *Auteurs* are out of time. The theory which makes them sacred makes no inroad on vulgar history, has no concepts for the social or the collective, or the national.
>
> The primary act of *auteur* criticism is one of dissociation – the *auteur* out of time and history and society is also freed from any productive process, be it in Los Angeles or Paris.[24]

The test of a theory is whether it produces new knowledge. The *auteur* theory produced much, but of a very partial kind, and much it left totally unknown. What is needed now is a theory of the cinema that locates directors in a total situation, rather than one which assumes that their development has only an internal dynamic. This means that we should jettison such loaded terms as 'organic', which inevitably suggest that a director's work derives its impetus from within. All such terms reveal often unformulated and always unwarranted assumptions about the cinema; a film is not a living creature, but a product brought into existence by the operation of a complex of forces upon a body of matter. Unfortunately, criticism which deals with only one aspect of the artistic object is easier to practice than that which seeks to encompass the totality. Three approaches seem possible, and each of them must inevitably squeeze out the *auteur* from his position of prominence, and transform the notion of him which remains. First, there is the examination of the effects of the cinema on society (research into the sociology of mass media, and so on). Second is the effect of society on the cinema; in other words, the operation of ideology, economics, technology, etc. Lastly, and this is in a sense only a sub-section of the preceding category, the effects of films on other films; this would especially involve questions of genre, which only means that some films have a *very* close relation to other films. But all films are affected by the previous history of the cinema. This is only one more thing that traditional *auteur* theory could not cope with. It identified the code of the *auteur*; but was silent on those codes intrinsic to the cinema, as well as to those originating outside it.

Notes

1 *Film Culture*, no. 27 (Winter 1962–3); reprinted in *Perspectives on the Study of Film*, ed. John Stuart Katz, Boston, Little, Brown, 1971 (p. 129). Sarris later conceded, 'Ultimately, the *auteur* theory is not so much a theory as an attitude, a table of values that converts film history into directorial biography.' *The American Cinema*, New York, Dutton, 1968, p. 30.

2 'For the *auteur*, the film is a piece of architecture whose bricks are not – must not be – the children of his own body.' *Cahiers du Cinéma*, no. 63, October 1956, p. 55.

3 Alexandre Astruc, 'The Birth of a New Avant-Garde: "La Caméra-Stylo." ', reprinted in *The New Wave*, ed. Peter Graham, London, Secker & Warburg, 1968.

4 'A *cinéaste* who has made great films in the past may make mistakes, but his mistakes will have every chance of being, *a priori*, more impressive than the successes of a "manufacturer" '. *Cahiers*, no. 126, p. 17. The same idea is to be found in Sarris, in *The American Cinema*, p. 17: 'the worst film of a great director may be more interesting than the best film of a fair to middling director.'

5 Quoted in Raymond Williams, *Culture and Society 1780–1950*, Harmondsworth, Penguin, 1961, p. 54.

6 S. T. Coleridge, *Lectures and notes on Shakespeare and other English poets* (1818), London, Dent, 1951.

7 Sarris, *American Cinema*, p. 30.

8 *Cahiers*, no. 172, November 1965, p. 3: 'a man endowed with the least aesthetic talent, if his personality "shines out" in the work, will be more successful than the cleverest technician. We discover that there are no rules. Intuition and sensibility triumph over all theories.'

9 André Bazin, 'La Politique des Auteurs', trans. in *The New Wave*, p. 142.

10 ibid.

11 Sarris, in Katz, op. cit., pp. 132–3.

12 Pauline Kael, 'Circles and Squares: Joys and Sarris', in Katz, op. cit., p. 154.

13 ibid., p. 142.

14 Sarris, *American Cinema*, p. 36.

15 Sarris, in Katz, op. cit., p. 137.

16 Sarris, *American Cinema*, p. 31.

17 See Williams, op. cit., pp. 48–64 and *passim*.

18 Sarris, *American Cinema*, p. 36.

19 Sarris in Katz, op. cit. p. 134.
20 Peter Wollen, *Signs and Meaning in the Cinema*, 3rd edn, London, Secker & Warburg, 1972, p. 102.
21 ibid., pp. 167–8.
22 ibid., p. 168.
23 François Truffaut, *Hitchcock*, London, Panther edn 1969, p. 296.
24 Sam Rohdie, 'Education and Criticism', *Screen*, vol. 12, no. 1, p. 10.

B The theory in practice

4 · Cahiers du Cinéma

Cahiers du Cinéma: revue mensuelle du cinéma et du télécinéma began publication in April 1951 under the editorship of Lo Duca and Jacques Doniol-Valcroze, joined in the second issue by André Bazin. François Truffaut's polemical article, 'Une certaine tendance du cinéma français', which threw down the gauntlet of '*la politique des auteurs*', appeared in issue no. 31 in January 1954. Truffaut's article was essentially a fierce attack on the '*Tradition de la Qualité*' which was currently dominant in French cinema, a tradition which gave the central creative role to the writers – notably Aurenche and Bost – whose work was mainly adaptation of 'quality' novels, leaving to the director the secondary role of implementing their scenarios. In opposition to this, Truffaut proposed the *cinéma d'auteurs*, in which the creative role was given to the director as *auteur*, whose commitment to the film was something more than an implementation of someone else's creation. The appeal was for more than a shift in creative responsibility; in asking that cinema be given over to the true *hommes de cinéma*, Truffaut was rejecting a novelistic, psychologically realistic cinema (however socially conscious it might be) and appealing for a cinema that was truly cinematic. The directors he pointed to as exemplary *auteurs* for the French cinema were Renoir, Bresson, Cocteau, Becker, Gance, Ophuls, Tati and Leenhardt.

In his history of *Cahiers* in issue no. 100, Doniol-Valcroze identifies Truffaut's article (published with some hesitation by himself and Bazin) as a turning point, the 'real point of departure' – 'From then on there was one doctrine, the *Politique des auteurs*, even if it did lack flexibility. . . .' At the same time, while Truffaut's article may have initiated *auteurism* as a critical policy for the magazine, it did not invent the idea of *auteurism*. This idea seems rather to have been foundational for *Cahiers*, informing a number of the earliest articles, most notably Rohmer's 1952 essay,

'Renoir Américain'. Historically and internationally, an idea of *auteurism* seems also to have informed the project of the earlier *Revue du Cinéma* which provided *Cahiers* with much of its inspiration and some of its personnel, and which, in its first editorial in 1946, identified itself as 'the home of inventors and poets' (vol. 1, no. 1, p. 5), and in Britain much of the writing of Lindsay Anderson and his colleagues in *Sequence* was informed by Anderson's belief (expressed in 1950) that the director was 'the man most in a position to guide and regulate the expressive resources of the cinema' ('The director's cinema?' *Sequence* no. 12, p. 37). Anderson sees in Wyler (pp. 11, 37),

> a perfect example of the director . . . who seeks with honesty, artistry and technical skill of the very highest order to make his films a true and perhaps enriched realisation of their authors' intentions. What Wyler does not attempt to do – the declaration is his own – is to use the cinema to express his own feelings or his own ideas; and as a result there is about them a certain impersonality which marks them as the work of a brilliant craftsman rather than a serious artist.

The anticipation of *Cahiers*' distinction of *auteur* and *metteur en scène* indicates that, while *Cahiers* carried the implications of *auteurism* to conclusions which were resisted elsewhere, it did not invent *auteurism* in a vacuum.

The role of the *Cahiers* critics as the directors of the New Wave cinema in France in the late 1950s achieved for *Cahiers* the same sort of cultural currency as the 'Angry Young Men' in Britain. Internationally, the mid-1950s saw the emergence of an oppositional culture which took various forms, but which invariably involved a generational clash, a rebellion against old values and a disappointment with the sterile conventionality of the post-war society from which so much had been hoped. *Cahiers* participated in this in contradictory ways. Much of its writing was conservative, if not reactionary, in its implications at least. (Truffaut's rejection of 'psychological realism' echoes with the scandalized prudishness which greeted the 'smut' of Zola's naturalism: 'In one single reel of the film, towards the end, you can hear in less than ten minutes such words as: "tart", "whore", "bitch", and "bullshit". Is that realism?' – François Truffaut, 'Une certaine tendance du cinéma francais'). But its 'tone' was rebellious, albeit in a way which had very little to do with a conscious politics. This lack of politics irritated 'committed', socially conscious criticism, while the extension of 'art' to popular and commercial cinema (and to its lowest echelons) constituted an erosion of the traditional field of art which was equally disturbing to 'bourgeois' criticism. In fact, *Cahiers* critics seemed to delight in the polemical situation in which they found themselves, scandalizing both the bourgeoisie and the committed.

But this has a serious side, the most fundamental point of which is the refusal to valorize films on the basis of their subject matter, preferring instead to discover the audacities of the *mise en scène*, and the marks of the *auteur*'s unique personality. Again the search was for the purely filmic, but it lead *auteurism* into a formalism which not only brought down the scorn of its detractors but also worried its elder statesman, Bazin, whose reservations on the question of subject matter appear over and over again in his writing. In an important article written in 1974 ('La Politique des auteurs', *Jump Cut*, nos 1 and 2) John Hess identifies the *politique* as (no. 1, p. 19),

a justification, couched in aesthetic terms, of a culturally conservative, politically reactionary attempt to remove film from the realm of social and political concern, in which the progressive forces of the Resistance had placed all the arts in the years after the war.

There is no doubt that *auteurism* as practised in the *politique* was formalist, or that *Cahiers* swung between a-politicism, political confusion and downright political reaction. At the same time, its rivals in the field, *Positif*, say, or *Sight & Sound*, expose the opposite danger of a contentism in which a film is valued on the basis of the correctness or relevance of its sentiments. Fereydoun Hoveyda, in his 'Autocritique', in *Cahiers*' December 1961 special issue on criticism accepts the condemnation of formalism, but adds (p. 45):

But they forget that, far from overvaluing form, [formalism] mistakes it by separating it from meaning. This formalism meets up with the cinema of 'subject-matter' which ignores form. It can't be enough to judge Stanley Kramer or Autant-Lara on their intentions alone, however worthy they may be. It's not enough to protest against atomic suicide or war: it's also necessary to produce a work of art capable of shifting the spectator and of making him ask himself questions.

John Hess attributes something of *Cahiers*' cultural conservatism to its association with Personalism, a movement of Catholic intellectuals, including Bazin and Leenhardt, initiated in the 1930s around the magazine *Esprit*. But Personalism itself is something of a mish-mash: a quasi-philosophical attempt to align anti-capitalism with a belief in the importance of spiritual development, appropriating terms from socialism and early existentialism; and it's a mish-mash which tended to characterize *Cahiers*' intellectual background in the 1950s, a variable confusion of religious moralism, existential anxiety, absurdist nihilism, Angry Young Man polemics and beatnik rejection of convention. Alongside this should be placed the fascination which American culture had traditionally exerted on French intellectual life, a fascination which had been intensified by the cultural deprivation of the Occupation. The toughness and brashness associated with American culture was a quality to be valued, and in *Cahiers* it appears supported by such terms of approval as spontaneity, originality, roughness, primitiveness, violence and virility.

It is this diversity of stimuli, rather than a singular philosophical source, which seems to account for the confusion of positions in early *Cahiers*.

At the same time, a certain ideological profile can be discerned in the confusion, a certain privileging of those films which focused the themes of solitude, aimlessness, introspection, aggression and failure, leaving little room for the political concerns of *Positif*, or for the liberal social values of *Sight & Sound*.

Cahiers' function in the history of film criticism appears as a shaking loose of established modes. Not necessarily progressive in itself, *Cahiers* seemed to enable progress. In so far as there was a 'critical revolution' it was a revolution within bourgeois film criticism, which made other critical revolutions possible and necessary.

In the selection of extracts, which concentrate on the period 1951–61, I have tried to preserve something of the confusion of voices. It is tempting to present the principles of the *politique* as a set of rules: the late work of an *auteur* is necessarily more interesting than the earlier work, the worst work of an *auteur* is necessarily worth more than the best work of a *metteur en scène*, etc.; but such a schematization, though it has a substantial foundation, avoids the seductiveness of *Cahiers'* auteurist practice, with its celebration of *mise en scène* and its ability to account for pleasure and excitement: it misses the variety and dissensions in the writing, and, most seriously, it situates the *politique* as an aberration outside any tradition of criticism, rather than as an attempt to bring the principles of romantic criticism to bear on cinema, as they had been brought to bear on the other arts.

Extract from Pierre Kast, 'Des confitures pour un gendarme'
Cahiers du Cinéma, no. 2, May 1951

The film *auteur* who thinks that, in the current system of production it is possible to *express himself* is not only massively deluding himself but is also, however pure his intentions may be, defending and protecting the mystifications which the cinema generously distributes to its spectators.

Extract from Eric Rohmer (Maurice Schérer), 'Renoir Américain'
Cahiers du Cinéma, no. 8, January 1952

The history of art, as far as I know, contains no example of an authentic genius who has experienced, at the end of his career, a period of real decline. Rather history encourages us to discover, under the apparent awkwardness or poverty of these films [Renoir's American films], the traces of that willingness to lay oneself bare which characterizes the 'late period' of a Titian, a Rembrandt, a

Beethoven or, nearer home, of a Bonnard, a Matisse or a Stravinsky. Having once cited those great names, I would wish then to propose a form of criticism which would not concern itself with 'beauties' or 'faults', but which would uncover the rationale underlying a development whose thread has eluded us, and would discover, under its 'pseudo-faults', the true brilliance which a cursory glance had only been able to tarnish. Such a proposal involves a certain overturning of commonly accepted values, and I believe that our time is more ready than any other to recognize that it is the property of all masterpieces to suggest a new definition of the beautiful.

Extract from François Truffaut, 'Une certaine tendance du cinéma français'

Cahiers du Cinéma, no. 31, January 1954
(the article appears in full in Nichols, see bibliography)

'But why', they will say to me, 'why couldn't we have the same admiration for all those film-makers who do their best to work within this Tradition and within the Quality which you deride so flippantly? Why not admire Yves Allégret as much as Becker, Jean Dellanoy as much as Bresson, Claude Autant-Lara as much as Renoir?' ('Taste is made up of a thousand distastes' – Paul Valéry.)

Well, I can't believe in the peaceful co-existence of the *Tradition de la Qualité* and a *cinéma d'auteurs*.

Basically, Yves Allégret and Dellanoy are only *caricatures* of Clouzot, and of Bresson.

It isn't the desire to create a scandal that leads me to deprecate a cinema so praised elsewhere. I remain convinced that the exaggeratedly long life of *psychological realism* is the cause of the public's incomprehension when faced with works as new in their conception as *Le Carosse d'or* [Renoir], *Casque d'or* [Becker], not to mention *Les Dames du bois de Boulogne* [Bresson], and *Orphée* [Cocteau].

Long live audacity, certainly, but it's still necessary to discover it where it really is. In terms of this year, 1953, if I had to draw up a balance sheet of the audacities of the French cinema, there wouldn't be a place on it for the vomiting in *Les Orgueilleux* [Allégret], nor for Claude Laydu's refusal to be sprinkled with holy water in *Le Bon Dieu sans confession* [Autant-Lara], nor for the homosexual relations of the characters in *Le Salaire de la peur* [Clouzot], but instead it would have the gait of *Hulot* [Tati], the maid's soliloquies in *La Rue de l'estrapade* [Becker] the *mise en scène* of *Le Carosse d'or*, the direction of the actors in *Madame de . . .* [Ophuls], and also Abel Gance's experiments in Polyvision. You will have understood that these are the audacities of *hommes de cinéma*, and no longer of scenarists, *metteurs en scène*, or *littérateurs*.

Extract from Eric Rohmer, 'A qui la faute?'
Cahiers du Cinéma, no. 39, October 1954
(the article introduces a special issue on Hitchcock)

Is it our fault, can those of us who like Hitchcock and think him the equal of the greatest creators in the history of the cinema be blamed, if, simply because he can perform with greater assurance on that difficult instrument called the motion picture camera, one is supposed to consider him as a mere virtuoso, as a man with a clever but superficial touch? Is it our fault if it isn't possible to speak of profundity without using profound terms, or if the whole essence of profundity consists of not revealing itself on the surface? . . .

It is well known that the *Cahiers* team is divided on the Hitchcock case, as it is on many others. Since Jacques Doniol-Valcroze has given an advantage to the defence by entrusting the presentation of this issue to one of the most fervent Hitchcockians, I will gladly return the compliment by not launching from the outset into a sectarian apologetic. I willingly concede to Hitchcock's critics that our author is indeed a formalist. Even so, we still need to determine whether this appellation is as pejorative as they like to think it is. What, for example, is a formalist painting: a painting without soul, purely decorative, in which the play of lines and colours seems to have been imposed by a preconceived design on the part of the artist rather than born directly from a perception of things? Does it mean, on the contrary, that the painter can express nothing except through the intermediary of spatial relations? I see nothing in that undertaking which is incompatible with the very essence of his art, and it is clearly a difficult task, one which only the very greatest have been able to accomplish, while the more superficial artists, on the other hand, express their emotion in ways which have nothing to do with plasticity. In this sense, the film director could never be too formalist.

Extract from Jacques Rivette, 'Notes sur une révolution'
Cahiers du Cinéma, no. 54, Christmas 1955: special issue on
American cinema

After the existential *coup de force* of Griffith, the first age of the
American cinema was that of the actor; then came that of the
producers. If we declare that this is at last the age of the *auteurs*,
I know quite well that I will provoke sceptical smiles. I won't put
up wise theories against them, but four names. They are those of
film-makers, Nicholas Ray, Richard Brooks, Anthony Mann, Robert Aldrich, whom criticism had scarcely accounted for, when it
didn't purely and simply ignore them. Why four names? I would
have liked to have added others (those for example of Edgar Ulmer,
Joseph Losey, Richard Fleischer, Samuel Fuller, and still others
who are only promises, Josh Logan, Gerd Oswald, Dan Taradash),
but these four are *for the moment* incontestably at the front of the
queue.

It's always ridiculous to wish to unite arbitrarily under a single
label creators with different affinities. At least you can't deny them
this trait in common: youth (the kiss of death for a director),
because they possess its virtues.

Violence is their prime virtue; not that easy brutality which
constituted the success of a Dmytryk or a Benedek, but a virile
anger, which comes from the heart, and lies less in the scenario or
the choice of events, than in the tone of the narrative and the very
technique of the *mise en scène*. Violence is never an end, but the
most effective means of approach, and these fist fights, these
weapons, these dynamite explosions have no other purpose than
to make the accumulated debris of habit jump, to drill an opening:
in short, to open the shortest routes. And the frequent resort to a
technique which is discontinuous, halting, which refuses the conventions of cutting and continuity, is a form of that 'superior
madness' which Cocteau speaks about, born out of the need for
an immediate expression which accounts for and shares in the
primary emotion of the *auteur*.

Violence is still a weapon, a double-edged weapon: physically
touching an insensible public with something new, imposing oneself as an individual, if not a rebel, unsubdued. Above everything,
it's a question for them all of refusing, more or less freely, the
dictates of the producers, and of trying to make a personal work
– and these are all *liberal* film-makers, some of them openly men
of the left. The throwing out of the traditional rhetoric of the
scenario and of the *mise en scène*, of this limp and anonymous

dough imposed by the *executives* since the beginnings of the talkies as a symbol of submission, has primarily the value of a manifesto. In short, violence is the external sign of rupture.

Extract from Fereydoun Hoveyda, 'La réponse de Nicholas Ray'
Cahiers du Cinéma, no. 107, May 1960

The subject of *Party Girl* is idiotic. So what? If the substratum of the cinematic opus was made up simply of the convolutions of the plots which are unravelled on the screen, then we should just annex the Seventh Art to literature, be content with illustrating novels and short stories (that, moreover, is exactly what happens in a great many films which we do not admire), and hand over *Cahiers* to literary critics. I am not attempting to reopen here an old debate which is both pointless and without interest. But, with the regularity of a clock, some critics keep harping back to how necessary it is not to neglect the importance of the screenplay, of the acting, of the production system. While they are about it, why not take into account as well the influence of celestial bodies?

Of course cinema is at the same time a technique, an industry and an art, and like all art, it borrows from other arts. But to my knowledge, the diversity of production systems and of types of subject has not stopped masterpieces reaching us from every latitude. This digression doesn't really take me away from the point I am making. Precisely because *Party Girl* comes just at the right moment to remind us that what constitutes the essence of cinema is nothing other than *mise en scène*. It is through this that everything on the screen is expressed, transforming, as if by magic, a screenplay written by someone else and imposed on the director into something which is truly the film of an *auteur*. . . .

I said at the beginning of this article that Nicholas Ray's new film is in its way a continuation of the interview which *Cahiers* published in 1958. *Party Girl* does indeed reply, in colours on celluloid, to the *big* question: the ultimate meaning of an already extensive body of work. Should we be looking for this meaning in Ray's thematics? I have already talked about the subjects he uses. Solitude, violence, moral crises, love, struggle against oneself, self-analysis, the common features of the characters and their preoccupations in the different films, in a word, the constants of this universe, present nothing which is original, and belong to an arsenal shared by all the film-makers whom we admire. Where then can we locate the deep meaning of his work? *Party Girl* shows us in the clearest possible way: we must look for it purely and simply in the *mise en scène*: not in the apparent answer that Ray gives to the mystery of the world and of people, but in the way in which he interrogates this world and imitates life. It is not by examining immediate significance that we can come into contact with the best films, but by looking at the personal style of each author. It is obvious why I think that *Party Girl* is Ray's most interesting film to date.

Extract from Luc Moullet, 'Sam Fuller: sur les brisées de Marlowe'

Cahiers du Cinéma, no. 93, March 1959

Young American film directors have nothing at all to say, and Sam Fuller even less than the others. There is something he wants to do, and he does it naturally and effortlessly. That is not a slight compliment: we have a strong aversion to would-be philosophers who get into making films in spite of what film is, and who just repeat in cinema the discoveries of the other arts, people who want to express interesting subjects with a certain artistic style. If you have something to say, say it, write it, preach it if you like, but don't come bothering us with it. . . .

Could Fuller really be the fascist, the right-wing extremist who was denounced not so long ago in the communist press? I don't think so. He has too much the gift of ambiguity to be able to align himself exclusively with one party. Fascism is the subject of his film, but Fuller doesn't set himself up as a judge. It is purely an inward fascism he is concerned with rather than with any political consequences. That is why Meeker's and Steiger's roles [*Run of the Arrow*] are more powerfully drawn than Michael Pate's in *Something of Value* [Richard Brooks]: Brooks is far too prudent to feel directly involved, whereas Fuller is in his element: he speaks from experience. And on fascism, only the point of view of someone who has been tempted is of any interest.

It is a fascism of actions rather than of intentions. For Fuller does not seem to have a good head for politics. If he claims to be of the extreme right, is that not to disguise, by a more conventional appearance, a moral and aesthetic attitude which belongs to a marginal and little respected domain?

Is Fuller anti-communist? Not exactly. Because he confuses, partly no doubt for commercial reasons, communism and gangsterism, communism and Nazism. He invents the representative of Moscow, about whom he knows nothing, on the basis of what he does know, through his own experience, about Nazis and gangsters. We must not forget that he only talks about what he knows. When he depicts the enemy (and in *The Steel Helmet, Fixed Bayonets* and *Hell and High Water*, he usually tries just to avoid doing so), it is a very abstract conventional enemy. Only the dialogue dots the i's, and it is really unfortunate that *Pickup on South Street* and *China Gate* should remain *verboten* to us for such unjustified reasons.

Morality is a question of tracking shots. These few characteristic features derive nothing from the way they are expressed nor from the quality of that expression, which may often undercut them. It would be just as ridiculous to take such a rich film [as *Run of the Arrow*] simply as a pro-Indian declaration as it would be to take Delmer Daves for a courageous anti-racist director because there is a clause in each of his contracts which stipulates that there will be love affairs between people of different races. The unsuspecting public is taken in and he always ends up on the right side of the fence.

Extract from André Bazin, 'Comment peut-on être Hitchcocko– Hawksien?'
Cahiers du Cinéma, no. 44, February 1955

I for my part, in common with many others, deplore the ideological sterility of Hollywood, its growing timidity when it comes to dealing with 'big subjects' with any freedom, and this is why *Gentlemen Prefer Blondes* makes me long for *Scarface* or *Only Angels Have Wings*. But I am grateful to the admirers of *The Big Sky* and of *Monkey Business* for discovering with passionate perception that, in spite of the explicit stupidity of the screen-writers, the formal intelligence of Hawks's *mise en scène* conceals an actual intelligence. And if they are wrong not to see, or to wish to ignore, the stupidity, at least in *Cahiers* we prefer this prejudice to its opposite.

Extract from André Bazin, 'La politique des auteurs'
Cahiers du Cinéma, no. 70, April 1957
(translated in Peter Graham, *The New Wave*, and in forthcoming translations from *Cahiers*)

(This short extract simply attempts to focus Bazin's position on the issue of subject matter; it does not do justice to the breadth of Bazin's critique, which is available elsewhere in English, and is taken up in Edward Buscombe's article.)

To its supporters *Confidential Report* is a more important film than *Citizen Kane* because they justifiably see more of Orson Welles in it. In other words, all they want to retain in the equation *auteur plus subject = work* is the *auteur*, while the subject is reduced to zero. Some of them will pretend to grant me that, all things being equal as far as the *auteur* is concerned, a good subject is naturally better than a bad one, but the more outspoken and foolhardy among them will admit that it very much looks as if they prefer small 'B' films, where the banality of the scenario leaves more room for the personal contribution of the author.

Of course I will be challenged on the very concept of *auteur*. I admit that the equation I just used was artificial, just as much so in fact as the distinction one learnt at school between form and content. To benefit from the *politique des auteurs* one first has to be worthy of it, and as it happens this school of criticism claims to distinguish between true *auteurs* and directors, even talented ones: Nicholas Ray is an *auteur*, Huston is supposed to be only a *metteur en scène*; Bresson and Rossellini are *auteurs*, Clément is only a great *metteur en scène*, and so on. This conception of the *auteur* is not compatible with the *auteur*/subject matter distinction, because it is of greater importance to find out if a director is worthy of entering the select group of *auteurs* than it is to judge how well he has used his material. To a certain extent at least, the *auteur* is always his own subject matter; whatever the scenario, he always tells the same story, or, in case the word 'story' is confusing, let's say he has the same attitude and passes the same moral judgments on the action and on the characters. Jacques Rivette has said that an *auteur* is someone who speaks in the first person. It's a good definition; let's adopt it.

The *politique des auteurs* consists, in short, of choosing the personal factor in artistic creation as a standard of reference, and then of assuming that it continues and even progresses from one film to the next. It is recognized that there do exist certain important films of quality that escape this test, but these will systematically be considered inferior to those in which the personal stamp of the *auteur*, however run-of-the-mill the scenario, can be perceived even minutely. . . .

The American cinema is a classical art, but why not then admire in it what is most admirable, i.e. not only the talent of this or that film-maker, but the genius of the system, the richness of its ever-vigorous tradition, and its fertility when it comes into contact with new elements – as has been proved, if proof there need be, in such films as *An American in Paris, The Seven Year Itch* and *Bus Stop*. True, Logan is lucky enough to be considered an *auteur*, or at least a budding *auteur*. But then when *Picnic* or *Bus Stop* get good reviews the praise does not go to what seems to me to be the essential point, i.e. the social truth, which of course is not offered as a goal that suffices in itself but is integrated into a style of cinematic narration just as pre-war America was integrated into American comedy.

To conclude: the *politique des auteurs* seems to me to hold and defend an essential critical truth that the cinema needs more than the other arts, precisely because an act of true artistic creation is more uncertain and vulnerable in the cinema than elsewhere. But its exclusive practice leads to another danger: the negation of the film to the benefit of praise of its *auteur*. I have tried to show why mediocre *auteurs* can, by accident, make admirable films, and how, conversely, a genius can fall victim to an equally accidental sterility. I feel that this useful and fruitful approach, quite apart from its polemical value, should be complemented by other approaches to the cinematic phenomenon which will restore to a film its quality as a work of art. This does not mean that one has to deny the role of the *auteur*, but simply give him back the presupposition without which the noun *auteur* remains but a halting concept. *Auteur*, yes, but what *of*?

Extract from Fereydoun Hoveyda, 'Autocritique'
Cahiers du Cinéma, no. 126, December 1961; special issue on criticism

This leads me to clarify my ideas on the function of criticism. In many respects, it resembles that of the psychoanalyst. Must it not, in effect, re-establish across the film the discourse of the *auteur* (subject) in its continuity, bring to light the unconscious which supports it, and explain its particular 'joints'? The unconscious, as Lacan would say, is indeed marked by a gap; it constitutes in some way the censored sequence. But, as in psychoanalysis, the truth can reveal itself: it is written somewhere other than in the 'apparent' chain of the images: in that which we call the 'technique' of the *auteur*, in the choice of actors, in the decor and the relationship of the actors and objects with this decor, in the gestures, in the dialogue, etc. A film is, in some ways, a rebus, a crossword puzzle. Better still: it is a language which inaugurates a discussion, which doesn't end with the viewing of the film, but incites a genuine research.

5 · Movie

The influence of the *politique des auteurs* was felt most in Britain in the pages of *Movie*, which was first published in 1962 under the editorship of Ian Cameron, Mark Shivas, Paul Mayersberg and Victor Perkins. *Movie* appeared, at first regularly and then intermittently, until 1972, disappeared, and then reappeared with issue no. 20 in 1975. Its origins lay in the film criticism written by Cameron, Shivas and Perkins in the university magazine, *Oxford Opinion*: 'In *Oxford Opinion* we tried to write criticism that was actually about films' (letter in response to editorial criticisms, *Film Quarterly*, vol. 14, no. 4, Summer 1961, p. 64).

As a 'position', and much of its importance is in the position which has been constructed for it and by it, *Movie* can be related to three currents in film criticism and in cultural criticism at large.

1 *Cahiers*   While *Movie* was careful to keep a critical distance from the 'extremities' of the *politique*, and engaged less in polemical and partisan excesses, it shared with *Cahiers* the general principle that the director was central to the work (with admitted exceptions) and that the work expressed his personality; it shared the close attention to the film's *mise en scène*; and it displayed a similar (though never exclusive) commitment to the American popular cinema and its undiscovered *auteurs*. Looking at the two magazines together, what is most immediately striking is the difference in their mode of writing, from the excited, frequently over-heated subjectivism which typifies *Cahiers*, to the more controlled, academic writing of *Movie*, which seems to speak 'common sense'. The distinction, and a certain difference in privileged values, can obviously be attributed to distinct cultural situations.

2 *British film criticism*   However much more 'respectable' than *Cahiers* *Movie* seems now, it did not protect it from the suspicion and hostility of the established film criticism in which it intervened. In the late 1940s the film magazine *Sequence*, edited by Lindsay Anderson and also coming out of Oxford, had already anticipated many of the principles which *Movie* was to build on; but by 1962 the vigour of *Sequence* had disappeared (the magazine had ceased publication in 1950), and the energy of the debate about 'commitment' which had been released with the publication, in *Sight & Sound*, of Lindsay Anderson's 1956 article, 'Stand Up! Stand Up!' (a plea for a cinema and a criticism which made clear its social and political commitment) had been for the most part absorbed in the vague

and self-effacing moral, social and cultural liberalism of *Sight & Sound* – the perpetual background to British film criticism. Criticism tended to be neither very committed nor particularly rigorous. Within that context, in the 1960s, *Movie*'s attention to 'style', to the way the film was constructed, to the movement of the *mise en scène*, its focus on '*how* a film should be made, rather than on *why*' (V. F. Perkins, 'British Cinema', *Movie Reader*, p. 10), constituted and produced a radical shift in British film criticism. That the extent of the shift tends to be ignored is a mark of the extent to which *Movie*'s practice and principles have, in their turn, been absorbed into the main stream. In the 1970s 'the *Movie* position' was constructed as one of cultural and critical conservatism by those writers, notably in *Screen*, who were attempting to develop a more theoretically founded account of cinema.

3 *Leavis* The particular critical tradition in which *Movie* placed itself (or found itself) is both important and difficult to define. Sam Rohdie, writing in 1972 when he was editor of *Screen* (Review, '*Movie Reader* and *Film as Film*', *Screen*, vol. 13, no. 4, p. 138):

If *Movie* inscribed the Hollywood film into discourse about cinema in Britain, and if, in doing so, it called attention to the structure of the text, *Movie* nevertheless carried out that inscription within, rather than opposed to, a critical tradition already familiar and easily relatable to the work of F. R. Leavis.

In general terms, 'the Leavis position' is identified by its close reading of the text (the literary magazine which Leavis edited in the 1930s was aptly named *Scrutiny*); by a refusal of theory; by a realist aesthetic which favours texts in which the personality and values of the author emerge from an implicit relationship between text and author (the author concealed in the story), rather than being uttered as an explicit discourse; by a view of the text as a coherence, a harmony, a 'living organism'; by a view of culture and tradition, where it has not been debased by mass industrial society, as potentially enriching; and by a system of humanistic values which resists a classifying name, but which can be suggested by a list of privileged critical terms: integrity, wholeness, experience, life, intensity, organic, ethical, truth, moral, honesty, personal, individual, vision, profound. The description is selective, but it throws into relief certain points of intersection with the *Movie* project: an intersection which the *Movie* critics, and particularly Robin Wood, would probably describe in a much more complex way, but would not absolutely reject. In many ways, it is more useful to relate *Movie*'s critical approach to this tradition within academic literary studies than to the influence of *Cahiers*. Which is not to say *Movie* was academic or literary in its approach to cinema; far from it, its criticism was highly specific, deriving from Leavis the detailed attention to 'what is actually there' ('The function of criticism', in *The Common Pursuit*). Perhaps the most important, and ultimately the most limiting, point of contact with Leavis was the refusal of theory, which seemed to allow the *Movie* critics to make their judgments from a position which was never itself called into question, a position which seemed to depend on an appeal to an undefined 'common-sense'. This refusal of theory not only provoked the challenges of the alternative position represented by *Screen*, but, more importantly for the history of *Movie*, may also account for a certain lack of development in the *Movie* position: a lack of development, that is to say, relative to the shifting conjuncture of film and cultural criticism.

Movie's writing is less various than that of *Cahiers du Cinéma*, tending, within the fluctuations of taste and preference, towards a homogeneity. Ian Cameron's essay, which is included here in full, represents almost the only sustained reflection on the magazine's critical practice, and while it does not give a full impression of the best of *Movie*'s critical writing (Barry Boys on *The Courtship of Eddie's Father* in *Movie* no. 10, say, or V. F. Perkins on Nicholas Ray in *Movie* no. 9 – reprinted in Nichols; see bibliography) it does offer a clear statement of the early *Movie* position. It is accompanied here by an extract from an editorial discussion which was published in the first issue produced when the magazine reappeared in 1975 (*Movie* no. 20) and which offers a more recent view of *Movie*'s reflections on authorship.

Ian Cameron, 'Films, directors and critics'

Movie, no. 2, September 1962

Why does the camera go up now?
Because he's watching the sky.

This question and answer, printed in an interview with Vincente Minnelli from the first *Movie*, have excited more comment than anything else in the magazine. Derek Hill in *The Financial Times* found them so absurd that he used them to dismiss the whole of *Movie* as an expensive joke. I suspect that there were a number of causes behind Mr. Hill's mirth: the idea of asking such questions on minute detail to a director would have seemed pointless to him, particularly when the answer was so simple that he probably took it at once to explode the grandiose theories which the foolish young critics were doubtless hatching about the director's intentions and to stamp him as ambitionless or simple.

Had we found Minnelli's answers stupid, we would obviously not have printed them in *Movie*. And if they were in flat contradiction to our theories about his work, we would certainly have hesitated to use them without comment. Where we differ from Mr. Hill, then, is in our attitude to directors. Apparently our assumptions are still sufficiently strange to need explanation. In aiming to fill that need here, I do not want to say anything particularly new or to provide a defence of our views. Our only defence is that our approach seems to work when actually applied to films. Before starting to recapitulate our assumptions, though, I would like to say a little more about the Minnelli business.

In *The Four Horsemen of the Apocalypse*, the shot in question occurs just after the death of Lee J. Cobb. Shattered by the discovery that one of his grandsons is a Nazi, he has rushed out into the garden, haunted by the destructive vision of the Four Horsemen. As he collapses to the ground and dies of a heart attack, another grandson (Glenn Ford) rushes out to him, kneels down on the ground and cradles the body in his arms. As he looks up at the sky, sobbing, and sees the vision of the horsemen, the camera cranes up and moves in. Our question and its answer may look a little less rudimentary if one bothers to think of other reasons why the camera might have craned up. Thus: (1) Emotional: the camera moves up to leave him cowering before the vision. (2) Symbolic: the camera looks down on him in judgment because he feels himself (or the director feels him) responsible in some way for the old man's death. (3) As a way of linking the shot to its successor, which shows the Horsemen in the sky. (4) As orchestration, taking up the bravura of the camera movements which have preceded it. That Minnelli cranes up simply because of the movement of his actor is indicative of his whole method (and confirms what was said elsewhere in the magazine). The camera moves so that we can see Ford's face as clearly as possible. The reason is neither inevitable nor foolish.

The motive for interviewing directors at all is to see how far their ideas of their aims square with the critics' rationalisations from the films. When the director disagrees with the critics this does not mean that the critics are wrong, for, after all, the value of a film depends on the film itself, and not on the director's intentions, which may not be apparent from the finished work.

For talking about one small section of a film in great detail, whether in an interview or in an article, we have been accused of fascination with technical *trouvailles* at the expense of meaning. The alternative which we find elsewhere is a *gestalt* approach which tries to present an overall picture of the film without going into 'unnecessary' detail, and usually results in giving almost no impression of what the film was actually like for the spectator.

The film critic's raw materials – apart from his own intelligence – are his observations in the cinema: what he sees, hears and feels. By building up our theses about films from these observations, we are going through the same processes as the audience although, of course, our reactions are conscious whereas those induced in the cinema, particularly at the first viewing of a film, tend to be reached unconsciously. We believe that our method is likely to produce criticism which is closer, not just to objective description of the film itself but to the spectator's experience of the film.

The assumption which underlies all the writing in *Movie* is that the director is the author of a film, the person who gives it any distinctive quality it may have. There are quite large exceptions, with which I shall deal later. On the whole we accept this cinema of directors, although without going to the farthest-out extremes of *la politique des auteurs* which makes it difficult to think of a bad director making a good film and almost impossible to think of a good director making a bad one. One's aesthetic must be sufficiently flexible to cope with the fact that Joseph Pevney, having made dozens of stinkers, can suddenly come up with an admirable western in *The Plunderers*, or that Minnelli, after years of doing wonders often with unpromising material, could produce anything as flat-footed as *The Bells Are Ringing*.

Everyone accepts the cinema of directors for France, Italy, Japan, India, Argentina, Sweden and Poland – everywhere, in fact, that the Art is easily identifiable. Critics will talk happily about a Bergman film, or a Mizoguchi film, or even a Carol Reed film. It is only over American movies that the trouble starts, and reviews are likely to end with a desultory 'George Cukor directed efficiently.' The reasons are easy enough to find. Hollywood pictures are not so much custom-built as manufactured. The responsibility for them is shared, and the final quality is no more the fault of the director than of such parties as the producer, the set designer, the cameraman or the hairdresser. Only by a happy accident can anything good escape from this industrial complex. The good American film comes to be regarded as the cinematic equivalent of a mutant.

Now there are qualities superimposed on most big studio films (these days there are very few of them indeed) that depend not on the director but on the studio: the look of colour films is particularly prone to this sort of control. An extreme example is Fox films in the late forties and early fifties which are almost immediately identifiable by their photography and music, particularly if these are by the leading exponents – photographers Joseph la Shelle and Joe MacDonald and composers Leigh Harline and David Raksin. However, these qualities are rather peripheral, and one common accusation of this sort, that Gregg Toland effectively directed the films he photographed so remarkably, has been disposed of by Andrew Sarris in *Film Culture*: 'Subtract Gregg Toland from Welles and you still have a mountain; subtract Toland from Wyler and you have a molehill.'

The closer one looks at Hollywood films, the less they seem to be accidents. There is a correlation between the quality of the films and the names of their directors. When one notices that such masterpieces as *Scarface, Bringing Up Baby* and *Gentlemen Prefer Blondes* were all directed by the same man, one begins to wonder whether the merits of these otherwise dissimilar films might not be explained by this man's talent. On a slightly closer look, one finds that he was also responsible for such generally admired movies as *Twentieth Century, Sergeant York, Red River* and *Monkey Business*, not to mention *Rio Bravo*, a film which gained little attention on its release and is now accepted as a masterpiece, even by *Sight and Sound*, which greeted its appearance with a singular lack of enthusiasm.

Hawks is just beginning to be accepted in Britain and the US. Raoul Walsh, on the other hand, is virtually unknown. Yet if one looks at Walsh's films (or some of them – he has made 200 since he started directing in 1913), one can identify the same talent and highly sympathetic personality behind a British cheapie of 1937, *Jump for Glory*, a 1945 racecourse movie, *Salty O'Rourke*, and more recent works like *Blackbeard the Pirate* (1952), *The Lawless Breed* (1952), *Battle Cry* (1955), *Esther and the King* (1960) and *Marines Let's Go* (1961). The similarity of these movies made in three different countries over a period of 25 years by a director whose name does not spell prestige, who will thus not have an exceptional degree of freedom, should leave no doubt that, provided he has any talent, it is the director, rather than anyone else, who determines what finally appears on the screen.

Part of the neglect of American directors comes from the simple fact that it is easier to accept foreign films as Art: a status word to indicate that the film is worth the critic's serious attention. In foreign language movies, one of the biggest obstacles has been limited: the dialogue. Even if they are bad, subtitles provide a shock-absorber between the dialogue and the audience. Everyone knows that laughable subtitles do not necessarily indicate defects in the original language. But two lines of ill-written dialogue in an

American picture will put the critics on their guard. Almost invariably it is duff dialogue that alienates them, not unconvincing motivation, or false movements of actors or pointless camerawork. A recent victim is *The Four Horsemen*, which did have rather more than a couple of bad lines.

When a *Sight and Sound* critic does manage to work up some enthusiasm for an American film, it is usually self-limiting: 'very good . . . of its kind.' So we are treated to dimly remembered sections of John Russell Taylor's childhood erotic fantasies about Maria Montez and Veronica Lake as a picture of the Forties. Reviews of American films tend to link them together in remarkably ill-assorted pairs. One would be amazed at the current review of *The Man Who Shot Liberty Valance* and *Guns in the Afternoon* (both 'so consciously old-fashioned and nostalgic that, appearing in 1962, they seem almost esoteric') if one had not already been treated to such unlikely joint reviews as *Exodus* plus *The Guns of Navarone* and *Psycho* plus *The Apartment*. If the writers of these pieces were literary critics, which, barring a certain illiteracy, they very nearly are, one imagines that they would happily review *Tender Is the Night, Miss Lonelihearts* and *Manhattan Transfer* together entirely in terms of American *mal-de-siècle* in the twenties. Any other qualities would be written off in a well-chosen sentence: 'Mr. Dos Passos's narrative technique of intertwining a number of almost unconnected stories does not make for easy comprehension.' *Sight and Sound* has just produced the most accurate piece of unconscious self-criticism in its most recent and most desperate attempt to be hip: a column in which the glad hand of John Russell Taylor is hidden behind the name of Arkadin. 'Why,' he opens brightly, 'don't we take horror films more seriously? Well, not seriously seriously . . .'

The worst sufferer from restricted admiration has been Hitchcock. *Psycho* was passed over as one big laugh. As a joke it could not possibly be anything else. *Psycho*'s joke-content is very large, but that doesn't mean it is only joke. Example: the scene of Janet Leigh and Anthony Perkins getting acquainted is both an ingeniously extended *double entendre* on stuffing birds and a very real and touching picture of two people, isolated from others by their actions, voluntary or otherwise, trying to talk to each other.

The great weakness of *la politique des auteurs* is its rigidity: its adherents tend to be, as they say, totally committed to a cinema of directors. There are, however, quite a few films whose authors are not their directors. The various film versions of Paddy Chayefsky's works are all primarily Chayefsky movies rather than Delbert

Mann, or John Cromwell or even Richard Brooks movies. Given a weak director the effective author of a film can be its photographer (Lucien Ballard, *Al Capone*), composer (Jerome Moross, *The Big Country*), producer (Arthur Freed, *Light in the Piazza*) or star (John Wayne, *The Comancheros*). None of those films was more than moderately good. Occasionally, though, something really remarkable can come from an efficient director with magnificent collaborators. Such a film was Michael Curtiz's *Casablanca*, which contained Humphrey Bogart, Ingrid Bergman, Paul Henreid, Claude Rains, Sidney Greenstreet, Conrad Veidt, Peter Lorre and Marcel Dalio, and was somehow missed from John Russell Taylor's knee-high panorama of the forties. More recently we have had *The Sins of Rachel Cade*, which, although directed by the excellent Gordon Douglas, was above all an Angie Dickinson movie, being entirely shaped by her personality and deriving all its power, which was considerable, from her performance.

Many films have also an iconographical interest, which is something quite apart from any aesthetic merits they may have. This interest comes from their relationship either to conditions external to their making (things as diverse as the discovery of the H bomb or current trends in automobile design, which influenced the design of the submarine in *Voyage to the Bottom of the Sea*) or to other films. Joseph Newman's *Spin of a Coin (The George Raft Story)* is fascinating because of its similarity to other period gangster movies: the sequences are built in the same way towards a climax of slaughter – only in this case the burst of gunfire is replaced by equally staccato laughter, for instance, as Al Capone (played by Neville Brand, who was Capone in Karlson's *The Scarface Mob*) tells George (Ray Danton, whose performance is an extension of his previous *Legs Diamond* in Boetticher's film) how much he liked his performance as Capone in *Scarface*, the climactic scene of which has been reconstructed for us. This sort of kick is also available even more lavishly in Vincente Minnelli's amazing new *Two Weeks In Another Town*, where faded movie star Kirk Douglas sits in a viewing theatre watching a film he has previously made with the director for whom he is now working in the dubbing room. The film is *The Bad and the Beautiful*, which Minnelli made ten years ago with Douglas, as well as the same writer, producer and composer (Charles Schnee, John Houseman and David Raksin). In another Joseph Newman movie, *The Big Bankroll (Arnold Rothstein, King of the Roaring Twenties)*, it is assumed that the audience has seen the earlier movies which found it necessary to explain how boot-legging and protection worked. *The Big Bankroll* (in spite of 26 missing minutes in the British version one of the very best of its kind) builds on the knowledge it assumes to tell the story of Arnold Rothstein, who turned the mechanics of corruption to his own ends.

A few films are interesting for a related reason: the picture of their audience which they provide. The best example is Delmer Daves, who makes movies for stenographers and provides them with just what they wish to see. His pictures may be trivial, dishonest, immoral – Daves' movies have every fault in the book except bad production values – but they do provide a picture of the girl Daves is aiming his films at (very successfully, it seems). However irritating one may find Suzanne Pleshette in *Lovers Must Learn (Rome Adventure)*, one has to admit that her performance is brilliantly pitched at just the right level of gush.

While one can appreciate films for their iconographical significance or as a critique of their audience, any merit they may have still comes from the director, much more than from any other source. Although finally our belief in the cinema of directors can only be justified through continuous application of our ideas in *Movie*, I want to conclude this article with an extended example of the part played by the director, based on three films, two of them well-liked, more or less, British offerings, J. Lee Thompson's *The Guns of Navarone* and David Lean's *Bridge on the River Kwai*, the third a much less respected American film, Don Siegel's *Hell Is for Heroes*.

All three contain the simple moral that war is futile and degrading; all three use one of the basic war film stories: the strategic action of considerable importance which devolves on a very few men. *Navarone* sets out with the obvious intention of telling a rattling good yarn about the way our chaps heroically battled against almost impossible obstacles to knock out the Jerry guns. Even this it almost fails to do by disastrously overplaying its suspense potential in a lengthy sequence of spurious thrills as the team crawl up a crumbling cardboard cliff so early in the movie that everyone will need to survive to justify their billing on the credits. However, its worst sin is stopping off at least twice in the course of the narrative for dialogue meditations on the nastiness of war, which the audience is meant to accept and which would in themselves be perfectly sympathetic, if slightly superfluous, in a film that refused to present war as enjoyable. But here their effect is completely vitiated by the rest of the action, and in context they seem almost hypocritical. I have a feeling that the failure is not inherent in the script but comes from the lack of any firm control in the direction. Even the one moment which could hardly help having some force, the shooting of Gia Scala as a collaborator, in the film has none. Here admittedly the script does side-step by letting Irene Papas, who is Greek and only a secondary character, forestall Peck and Niven in shooting her, when they are both more directly affected by the responsibility for her death. But even allowing for this, the lack of conviction is total.

Hell Is for Heroes is based on a story by Robert Pirosh which could easily have been turned into the sort of plug for the gallantry of the American fighting man which William Wellman made 13 years ago from a Pirosh story in *Battleground* (recently re-released with Anthony Mann's remarkable ex-3D western *The Naked Spur*). I am not concerned here with the central theme in the film which is embodied in the Steve McQueen character, the psychopath who makes an ideal soldier but goes to pieces outside the field of combat. Two sequences are particularly relevant to my purpose here as they could easily have degenerated to the same level as *Kwai* and *Navarone*. In the first, three soldiers set out at night on a manoeuvre to trick the enemy into thinking that they are sending out large patrols and therefore have the front well-manned. The idea is to take empty ammunition tins out into no-man's land, fill them with stones and rattle them by remote control from their position by means of lengths of telephone wire. The noise of these would be picked up by the enemy's ground microphones and all hell would be let loose to greet the ghost patrol. Siegel does not tell us what they are doing until their mission is almost completed. We take the episode seriously, which is right because it is serious and no less dangerous than a real patrol. If he had shown us beforehand exactly what they were doing, the episode would have been invested for us in the safety of our cinema seats with a feeling of fun, of fooling the enemy. Never once in the film do we get this feeling.

The last sequence for once does sum up the whole film by its picture of the contribution an individual can make to the action. In serious trouble after leading an abortive attack on the crucial pillbox, which has resulted in the death of his two companions, McQueen takes it upon himself to put the pillbox out of action. He manages by a suicidal charge to get close enough to lob a satchel charge into the mouth of the box. Inevitably he is shot. Seeing the charge thrown out of the pillbox, he staggers forward, grabs it and rolls into the mouth of the box with it as it explodes. A flame-thrower is played on the mouth of the pillbox to make sure it is out of action. The last shot of the film is a longshot of a general advance beginning along the section of the front around the pillbox. The advance is obviously going to be very costly. The camera zooms into the mouth of the pillbox and the end title is superimposed. The zoom in from the general view to the detail emphasises the smallness of the gain from McQueen's death. One pillbox has been put out of action, and as the advance continues that pillbox ceases to have any significance. It is left behind a dead, almost abstract object. Unlike *Navarone*, there is no conflict between the intended content and the form which expresses it.

Contrast with the last shot of *Hell Is for Heroes* the end of *Bridge on the River Kwai*. James Donald stands surveying the wreckage after the destruction of the bridge. 'Madness, madness,' he says, and the camera soars back away from him in a mood of triumph which is taken up by the martial music on the soundtrack. In the contradiction between the sentiments expressed by the dialogue and the meaning contained in the treatment, critics have noticed only the former. *Bridge on the River Kwai*'s anti-war content is widely accepted to be impeccable. But *Hell Is for Heroes*, where the ideas are expressed by the whole form of the film, can pass nearly unnoticed and even be described as equivocal in its attitude to war. The lack of perception which results in this sort of fuzzy thinking is the best argument for a detailed criticism.

Extract from Ian Cameron, Jim Hillier, V. F. Perkins, Michael Walker and Robin Wood, 'The return of *Movie*: a discussion'
Movie, no. 20, Spring 1975

JH What, then, does the word *auteur* imply?
MW I suppose it's insight into the creator: the sense of being able to identify certain elements in a film as personal to the director, scriptwriter or whoever.
RW It takes one back to the films with one more tool for understanding their qualities.
JH But are we talking about Cukor as a man or some critical abstraction called Cukor?
VFP It would be very dangerous to take your 'man behind the camera' line literally, because it is Cukor the artist rather than Cukor the man – an interaction in which Cukor the man is only one part and which inevitably accommodates, and is allowed to accommodate, only some aspects of the man Cukor.
JH So is the *auteur* a critical construct?

VFP Yes, as long as you're not implying by that a degree of unreality. It doesn't make it a 'fabrication'.

JH Isn't the distinction important? With Hawks, for example, there's often a very strong impulse to appeal to the actuality of the man, a confused attempt to merge that with Hawks as an *auteur*. Maybe it's more appropriate with Hawks.

VFP Do you feel that you know about the actuality of the man? I think that we should stick to helpfulness rather than appropriateness, because one cannot know about that. I find Hawks as a personality a baffling commodity to speculate upon – the great friend of a rather difficult novelist, the man who turned out *Rio Bravo*, the fashion plate melodramatist described by Ben Hecht, etc. It's not a simple case. And always there are the evasions and the image-mongering of the director, the whole projection business. In this sense, Preminger is an even more difficult case: is there a real Otto Preminger?

IAC It's worth emphasising that the view which got summarised as the *auteur* theory was a much more extreme and rudimentary one than any of us ever *felt* we represented.

MW There was a search for *auteurs* – not necessarily directors. Ian's piece in *Movie 2* spoke of a number of movies in terms of the *dominant personalities* in each – *The Sins of Rachel Cade* as an Angie Dickinson movie or *The Big Country* as a Jerome Moross movie. You could say that *Movie* was inhibited by looking only for the dominant personality behind a particular film, where there were obviously lots of things coming into play which were never properly disentangled.

IAC We had to wade in somewhere, and we chose to limit ourselves, possibly to make the task simpler.

JH It was also largely a historical thing: finding yourself in a situation in which the American cinema is not valued and having to find a strategy. The strategy was to talk about Hawks, Preminger, etc., as artists like Bunuel and Resnais.

VFP What's interesting is how far in the current, much less polemical situation on that front one would choose to operate in the same way. To a large degree, I would, getting rid if possible of the aberrations and occasional stupidities.

JH One of the requirements is to be conscious of the problems of writing about film in a certain way. This has to be tentative – an understanding of some of the limitations without being at all sure how to overcome them, but the awareness is vital.

RW It seems clearer now that the great Hollywood films are the products of multiple determinants rather than of a single personality. At the same time, it is also true that we value these films still for the role played in them by that personality while acknowledging the other factors.

JH For, or because of?

RW Both. That *To Have and Have Not* is so much finer and more successful than *Sergeant York* can't simply be attributed to Hawks as director, though it's closely bound up with the question of the appropriateness of material to a given artist. Factors of genre, casting, script and subject-matter all enter in. The question of collaboration is part of it: Hawks/Furthman/Bogart versus Hawks/Huston/Cooper. Hawks obviously isn't the sole creator of *To Have and Have Not*, but I still value it primarily as a Hawks movie: his unifying and organizing presence seems crucial to its success.

The business of introducing a variant of the *politique des auteurs* into American film criticism is largely associated with an individual critic, Andrew Sarris, rather than a magazine. In the 1950s and 1960s, Sarris contributed regularly to *Film Culture*, the magazine, edited by Jonas Mekas, of the East Coast avant-garde film-makers; a magazine in which increasingly Sarris's articles (and those, notably, of Peter Bogdanovich) on the popular commercial cinema seemed compatible with the rest of the contents only in their insistence that even that kind of cinema was an art form. The wider dissemination of the debate around *auteurism* in America was helped by the West Coast magazine, *Film Quarterly*, whose initial contribution was the dramatization of the hostilities between Pauline Kael and almost anyone who mentioned *auteurism* in English.* Kael's principal target was Sarris, but salvoes were fired at *Movie*, and at the relatively innocent *Film Quarterly* itself. Subsequently, *Film Quarterly* featured a series of articles which developed debate of *auteurism* and '*auteur*-structuralism' at a more theoretical level.

Although Sarris's writing operates at a much more journalistic level than that of, say, *Movie*, his contribution to the development of a theory of authorship was probably more significant. In the first place, he seemed to recognize the industrial structure of the cinema as something more than an 'interference' on the *auteur*'s freedom of creativity; he saw it rather as something which produced a 'tension' between the *auteur* and his material, a tension which structured the 'interior meaning' of the film. Following from this, there is a sense in which, while the personality of the director remains crucial for Sarris, the notion of directorial intention is called into question. His comments on Preminger below suggest a 'personality', which is no longer simply expressions from intentions, but is constructed out of the tensions and gaps in the text. This opens the way (in a sense, whether Sarris likes it or not) for the '*auteur*-structuralist' shift from John Ford and Sam Fuller to 'John Ford' and 'Sam Fuller'.

Sarris's critical practice seems principally motivated by the desire to

---

* e.g., 'Circles and squares', *Film Quarterly*, vol. 16, no. 3, Spring 1963, pp. 12–26 (extracted in Mast and Cohen); Andrew Sarris, 'The *auteur* theory and the perils of Pauline', *Film Quarterly*, vol. 16, no. 4, Summer 1963, pp. 26–32; editors of *Movie*, '*Movie* vs Kael' and reply by Kael, *Film Quarterly*, vol. 17, no. I, Fall 1963, pp. 57–64.

construct a history of the American cinema on an evaluative basis, placing directors within a hierarchical system – the 'Pantheon' system being his most immediately identifiable, most regressive, and possibly (though never explicitly) most applied contribution to film criticism. In the end, perhaps, his most decisive intervention has been the naturalization of *'politique'* as 'theory'. It's worth noting that Luc Moullet, in his article on Fuller written in *Cahiers* in 1959, had already referred to 'Truffaut's celebrated *auteur* theory' (*Cahiers*, no. 93, p. 15), whereas Sarris claims that his first use of the term was in 1962. This suggests that the boundaries between policy and theory were less clearly defined in *Cahiers'* *auteurist* practice than has sometimes been assumed, and modifies the enormity of Sarris's apparent mis-translation. What Sarris did, though, at least for Anglo-American criticism, was to establish *auteurism* in critical discourse (and in general, non-specialized discourse about cinema) with the clothing, if not the substance, of a theory. The currency of the notion of an *auteur* theory preceded its theoretical formulation. Sarris, in a sense, begged the question of theory.

Extract from Andrew Sarris, 'Notes on the auteur theory in 1962'

> *Film Culture*, no. 27, Winter 1962–3
> (reprinted in Mast and Cohen; see bibliography)

(Henceforth, I will abbreviate *la politique des auteurs* as the *auteur* theory to avoid confusion.) . . .

What is the auteur *theory?*

As far as I know, there is no definition of the *auteur* theory in the English language, that is, by any American or British critic. Truffaut has recently gone to great pains to emphasize that the *auteur* theory was merely a polemical weapon for a given time and a given place, and I am willing to take him at his word. But, lest I be accused of misappropriating a theory no one wants anymore, I will give the *Cahiers* critics full credit for the original formulation of an idea that reshaped my thinking on the cinema. First of all, how does the *auteur* theory differ from a straightforward theory of directors. Ian Cameron's article, 'Films, Directors, and Critics,' in *Movie* of September, 1962, makes an interesting comment on this issue: 'The assumption that underlies all the writing in *Movie* is that the director is the author of a film, the person who gives it any distinctive quality. There are quite large exceptions, with which I shall deal later.' So far, so good, at least for the *auteur* theory, which even allows for exceptions. However, Cameron continues: 'On the whole, we accept the cinema of directors, although without going to the farthest-out extremes of *la politique des auteurs*, which makes it difficult to think of a bad director making a good film and almost impossible to think of a good director making a bad one.' We are back to Bazin again [see extract above], although Cameron naturally uses different examples. That three otherwise divergent critics like Bazin, Roud [*Sight and Sound*, vol. 29, no. 4], and Cameron make essentially the same point about the *auteur* theory suggests a common fear of its abuses. I believe there is a misunderstanding here about what the *auteur* theory actually claims, particularly since the theory itself is so vague at the present time.

First of all, the *auteur* theory, at least as I understand it and now intend to express it, claims neither the gift of prophecy nor the option of extracinematic perception. Directors, even *auteurs*, do not always run true to form, and the critic can never assume that a bad director will always make a bad film. No, not always, but almost always, and that is the point. What is a bad director, but a director who has made many bad films? What is the problem then? Simply this: the badness of a director is not necessarily considered the badness of a film. If Joseph Pevney directed Garbo, Cherkassov, Olivier, Belmondo, and Harriet Andersson in *The Cherry Orchard*, the resulting spectacle might not be entirely devoid of merit with so many subsidiary *auteurs* to cover up for Joe. In fact, with this cast and this literary property, a Lumet might be safer than a Welles. The realities of casting apply to directors as well as to actors, but the *auteur* theory would demand the gamble with Welles, if he were willing.

Marlon Brando has shown us that a film can be made without a director. Indeed, *One-Eyed Jacks* is more entertaining than many films with directors. A director-conscious critic would find it difficult to say anything good or bad about direction that is nonexistent. One can talk here about photography, editing, acting, but not direction. The film even has personality, but, like *The Longest Day* and *Mutiny on the Bounty*, it is a cipher directorially. Obviously, the *auteur* theory cannot possibly cover every vagrant charm of the cinema. Nevertheless, the first premise of the *auteur* theory is the technical competence of a director as a criterion of value. A badly directed or an undirected film has no importance in a critical scale of values, but one can make interesting conversation about the subject, the script, the acting, the color, the photography, the editing, the music, the costumes, the decor, and so forth. That is the nature of the medium. You always get more for your money than mere art. Now, by the *auteur* theory, if a director has no technical competence, no elementary flair for the cinema, he is automatically cast out from the pantheon of directors. A great director has to be at least a good director. This is true in any art. What constitutes directorial talent is more difficult to define abstractly. There is less disagreement, however, on this first level of the *auteur* theory than there will be later.

The second premise of the *auteur* theory is the distinguishable personality of the director as a criterion of value. Over a group of films, a director must exhibit certain recurring characteristics of style, which serve as his signature. The way a film looks and moves should have some relationship to the way a director thinks and feels. This is an area where American directors are generally superior to foreign directors. Because so much of the American cinema is commissioned, a director is forced to express his personality through the visual treatment of material rather than through the literary content of the material. A Cukor, who works with all sorts of projects, has a more developed abstract style than a Bergman, who is free to develop his own scripts. Not that Bergman lacks personality, but his work has declined with the depletion of his ideas largely because his technique never equalled his sensibility. Joseph L. Mankiewicz and Billy Wilder are other examples of writer-directors without adequate technical mastery. By contrast, Douglas Sirk and Otto Preminger have moved up the scale because their miscellaneous projects reveal a stylistic consistency.

The third and ultimate premise of the *auteur* theory is concerned with interior meaning, the ultimate glory of the cinema as an art. Interior meaning is extrapolated from the tension between a director's personality and his material. This conception of interior meaning comes close to what Astruc defines as *mise en scène*, but not quite. It is not quite the vision of the world a director projects nor quite his attitude toward life. It is ambiguous, in any literary sense, because part of it is imbedded in the stuff of the cinema and cannot be rendered in noncinematic terms. Truffaut has called it the temperature of the director on the set, and that is a close approximation of its professional aspect. Dare I come out and say what I think it to be is an *élan* of the soul?

Lest I seem unduly mystical, let me hasten to add that all I mean by 'soul' is that intangible difference between one personality and another, all other things being equal. Sometimes, this difference is expressed by no more than a beat's hesitation in the rhythm of a film. In one sequence of *La Règle du Jeu*, Renoir gallops up the stairs, turns to his right with a lurching movement, stops in hop-like uncertainty when his name is called by a coquettish maid, and, then, with marvelous postreflex continuity, resumes his bearishly shambling journey to the heroine's boudoir. If I could describe the musical grace note of that momentary suspension, and I can't, I might be able to provide a more precise definition of the *auteur* theory. As it is, all I can do is point at the specific beauties of interior meaning on the screen and, later, catalogue the moments of recognition.

Extract from Andrew Sarris, 'Toward a theory of film history'
The American Cinema: Directors and Directions, 1929–68,
New York, E. P. Dutton, 1968. (first published as 'The American cinema', *Film Culture*, no. 28, Spring 1963; reprinted in Nichols)

Ultimately, the *auteur* theory is not so much a theory as an attitude, a table of values that converts film history into directorial autobiography. The *auteur* critic is obsessed with the wholeness of art and the artist. He looks at a film as a whole, a director as a whole. The parts, however entertaining individually, must cohere meaningfully. This meaningful coherence is more likely when the director dominates the proceedings with skill and purpose. . . .

Even the vaunted vulgarity of the movie moguls worked in favour of the director at the expense of the writer. A producer was more likely to tamper with a story line than with a visual style. Producers, like most people, understood plots in literary rather than cinematic terms. The so-called 'big' pictures were particularly vulnerable to front-office interference, and that is why the relatively conventional genres offer such a high percentage of sleepers. The culturally ambitious producer usually disdained genre films, and the fancy dude writers from the East were seldom wasted on such enterprises. The *auteur* theory values the personality of a director precisely because of the barriers to its expression. It is as if a few brave spirits had managed to overcome the gravitational pull of the mass of movies. The fascination of Hollywood movies lies in their performance under pressure. Actually, no artist is ever completely free, and art does not necessarily thrive as it becomes less constrained. Freedom is desirable for its own sake, but it is hardly an aesthetic prescription. . . .

To look at a film as the expression of a director's vision is not to credit the director with total creativity. All directors, and not just in Hollywood, are imprisoned by the conditions of their craft and their culture. The reason foreign directors are almost invariably given more credit for creativity is that the local critic is never aware of all the influences operating in a foreign environment. The late Robert Warshow treated Carl Dreyer as a solitary artist and Leo McCarey as a social agent, but we know now that there were cultural influences in Denmark on Dreyer. *Day of Wrath* is superior by any standard to *My Son John*, but Dreyer is not that much freer an artist than McCarey. Dreyer's chains are merely less visible from our vantage point across the Atlantic.

The art of the cinema is the art of an attitude, the style of a gesture. It is not so much *what* as *how*. The *what* is some aspect of reality rendered mechanically by the camera. The *how* is what the French critics designate somewhat mystically as *mise en scène*. *Auteur* criticism is a reaction against sociological criticism that enthroned the *what* against the *how*. However, it would be equally fallacious to enthrone the *how* against the *what*. The whole point of a meaningful style is that it unifies the *what* and the *how* into a personal statement. Even the pacing of a movie can be emotionally expressive when it is understood as a figure of style. . . . Of course, the best directors are usually fortunate enough to exercise control over their films so that there need be no glaring disparity between *what* and *how*. It is only on the intermediate and lower levels of film-making that we find talent wasted on inappropriate projects.

Extract from Andrew Sarris, 'Preminger's two periods'
Film Comment, vol. 3, no. 3, Summer 1965

What's art to Preminger or Preminger to art? Preminger's champions on *Movie* and *Cahiers du Cinéma* would retort that Preminger's art is of the highest order. I find myself in a dangerous middle position that I would like to explain in some detail. To do so, I must begin with a very personal definition of *mise en scène*.

For me, *mise en scène* is not merely the gap between what we see and feel on the screen and what we can express in words, but it is also the gap between the intention of the director and his effect upon the spectator. Serious film criticism of Hollywood movies is always impaled upon the point that Hollywood directors are not profoundly articulate about their alleged art. How can one possibly compare John Ford to Michelangelo Antonioni, for example? Antonioni talks like an intellectual, albeit a middle-brow intellectual, while Ford talks like an old prospector cut off from civilization. American critics travel abroad bemoaning the fact that American directors are unable to conduct festival seminars on the Pressing Problems of Our Time. Certainly any three Polish directors you might pick up in the street would undoubtedly outpontificate and outparadox the legions of Hollywood directors from time immemorial.

In this respect, Preminger is not a 'good' interview. He will freely concede that more is read into his films by some critics than he consciously put there. He neither abuses his detractors nor embraces his defenders. He seems to enjoy the effect he creates with his outrageous personality, a personality that serves also as a mask. To read all sorts of poignant profundities in Preminger's inscrutable urbanity would seem to be the last word in idiocy, and yet there are moments in his films when the evidence on the screen is inconsistent with one's deepest instincts about the director as a man. It is during these moments that one feels the magical powers of *mise en scène* to get more out of a picture than is put in by a director.

C Dossier on John Ford

As I indicate in the Preface, the reason for privileging Ford as 'case-study' for this dossier is partly that he seems to appear as a privileged figure in theoretical writing elsewhere in the Reader. There are limitations to using Ford in this way: he was not 'discovered' by the *auteurist* critics, but was already accepted as a film artist in the early 1940s (particularly after *Grapes of Wrath*); he was not the object of an *auteurist* cult, provoking less passionate controversy; consequently, in early *Cahiers* and early *Movie* he appears less frequently than favoured *auteurs* like Ray or Minnelli. In some ways, for an understanding of the *politique* and its descendants, Minnelli, as a director who lived on the border-line between *auteur* and *décorateur*, might have been a more obvious choice. What the choice of Ford does, however, is allow for an extension of *auteurism* beyond the immediate and limiting context of the *politique*, emphasizing it as a more subtle and extensive critical practice. The particular attention paid to Ford's later films in the dossier brings out something of the development of *auteurism* into the 1960s and 1970s when it is less clearly contained within specific currents or magazines, and, importantly, it exposes the divisions which were opened up by films like *The Searchers, Cheyenne Autumn, Donovan's Reef* and *Seven Women*.

7 · Louis Marcorelles: 'Ford of the movies'

Cahiers du Cinéma, no. 86, August 1958

In the first ten years of *Cahiers* (1951–61) there were relatively few general articles (as opposed to reviews) devoted to Ford. This is by far the most extensive, the others being an interview with Jean Mitry (*Cahiers*, no. 45, March 1955), and two translations of articles by Michael Killanin and Lindsay Anderson, which accompanied this article by Marcorelles.

> I hate pictures. . . . Well, I like making them. . . . But it's no use asking me to talk about art.
>
> John Ford

Using grand words, waxing lyrical or lapsing into a kind of verbal delirium in the face of Ford's films would be to betray the simple, straightforward nature and the great sincerity of the work of a man who, with Jean Renoir, is the greatest director alive today. We can admire Bergman or Welles for their high ambitions and their single-minded quest for lucidity. But only Ford gives us that feeling of complete euphoria created by the perfect matching of the thing to be expressed and its expression. Here cinema is King, the enemy of all literature, of tormented minds, of self-indulgent sophisms. Cinema, a new, untried technique, becomes ethics, a new way of apprehending the world. People are from now on defined purely by their actions, by their situation in time and space. Suddenly an ideal equilibrium seems to be established between men as they are and men as they ought to be. The poet's vision transports reality beyond all realism, while preserving enough of the secret essence of civilizations to make us believe in the original, fundamental beauty of existence. Essence of the cinema, of the earth, of Ireland, Ford is a living summary of one of the most noble humanisms of our time.

Ford has been working in cinema for more than forty years, having begun to make Westerns as far back as 1917. The first of the glorious three musketeers (the two others being Dwan and

69

Walsh; the fourth, Vidor), he grew up with that primitive American cinema which inspired all other schools. His approach to cinema was never in the slightest theoretical. He set about making films as the blacksmith at his anvil forges tools, one after the other. Western after Western, two-, three-, four-, ten-reelers, shot from one day to the next, often in the heat of improvization and with subjects pinched from the next man, established a mastery whose primary concern was invariably respect for the appearance of people and things. The shot, that new divinity of contemporary criticism, never ceased in Ford's eyes to be the very foundation of cinema. The truth of a character or a scene must be immediately apparent to the wide-eyed, almost enraptured spectator (whence the dangerous excesses of *The Informer* and *The Fugitive*). Life exists first and foremost in plastic form, not the heavy-handed plasticity of a Figueroa[1] or of some central European cameraman, whose facile contrasts and search for chiaroscuro effects become an end in themselves, but that more noble kind which comes from the gradual appreciation of corporeal values, of the sovereign weight of reality. One can sense in Ford such a love for everything that lives and shimmers in the sunlight that one can understand his reluctance to use special effects in shooting or editing. His camera, apart from a few discreet pans, is almost always stationary. It rarely tracks for more than a few yards. Every action thus looks like a party, like a group of peaceful men gathered around the hearth or the campfire in the evening to tell each other some good stories. In contrast, when violence breaks out it is implacable, with nothing superfluous. Even in his earliest films, Ford makes extensive use of depth of field, because man cannot live by close-ups alone, with suffused background lighting and other visual gimmicks. More importantly, as often as possible, the Fordian eye cuts through space – wide open spaces – bringing us prodigious shots in which we can pick out a character who is miles away from the principal action.

Ford's art pushes its roots right down into the tilled soil, with the result that the fixed shot becomes a kind of value judgment. Filmic genius is inseparable from a certain conception of the world, a conception that has to be called paternalistic but which is directly inherited from the harsh experience of the pioneers who, hardly more than fifty years ago, were still in the process of building what was to become the greatest nation of modern times. Let us hope that, one day soon, the French public will discover or rediscover those prodigious epics *Drums Along the Mohawk, Young Mr Lincoln, Wagonmaster, She Wore a Yellow Ribbon*, films in which

Ford, with neither great stories nor a declared position, defines a virile ideal that our witch-hunters will of course call fascist but which is in fact the spontaneous vision of an artist who chooses to dally in a period he really cares about. Spelled out in black and white, this paternalistic idealism would warm the hearts of readers of *Le Figaro*[2] or of *Aspects de la France*.[3] But on the screen it acquires the innocent virtue of primitive societies. Since, in addition, he has so successfully espoused the essence of this art-form we love so much, he is suddenly endowed with qualities that we wouldn't accept in a novel or on the stage. Like his friend Howard Hawks, but in a more impetuous way, John Ford preaches a morality of pure action, of continuous creation. The dialectic, that crystallization of contemporary schizophrenia, that refuge for all uneasy consciences, has no place in a self-evident world in which there's only one way to throw a punch or ride a Western trail.

Ireland, which isn't in fact Ford's native country (it was his father who was born somewhere in the region of Galway), is at the heart of his work and of his mentality. Ireland is the land of Synge's *Playboy of the Western World*, of O'Flaherty, of eternal revolt. It isn't so much a revolt against any particular oppression as against human stupidity in general, bigotry and intolerance in all its forms. It's the defence of the imagination, of the right to love as freely as you breathe; to feud, to fight as and when you please. The blood-relationship with Synge seems to me indisputable: the same love for off-beat humour, for incredible legends, for the fantastic lying just below the surface. Life is an enormous farce that shouldn't be taken too seriously. For once, comparisons with Shakespeare, or rather with Homer, have some justification. To admit this is to recognize the artful ingenuousness in the eye of our author. The heroes who typify his *Weltanschauung*: Casey, the unfrocked priest in *The Grapes of Wrath*, Michaeleen O'Flynn, the crooked bookmaker in *The Quiet Man*, the modest Judge Priest in *The Sun Shines Bright*. This world-view inevitably seems esoteric to our Cartesian public. We love to classify, to 'embalm' famous people and, as much as possible, to elicit complacent explanations from them. Since Ford usually dismisses the importunate with a high hand, even if they appear in the guise of the sophisticated Left Bank intellectual or of the declared progressive, the critics, left without a leg to stand on, have had to fall back on reassuring clichés. Hence errors of perspective.

Ford has suffered immensely in France from an over-estimation of his 'classic' films, *The Informer*, *Stagecoach*, *The Long Voyage Home*, to the detriment of works judged to be minor but which time has shown to be infinitely closer to his real temperament. With a complacency that seems to know no bounds, the critics have already classified our author in that category of second-rate formalists which includes Marcel Carné and Sternberg (as opposed to the really great visual stylists like Dreyer and Eisenstein). It would be absurd to ignore his pronounced liking for what are clearly formalistic show-pieces which, combined on occasion with a propensity for a very literary symbolism, have given us the movies referred to above. In a sense these films are exemplary, in that the methodical analysis of the exegetist can dissect them with matchless precision; but they are stunted by a too-manifest concern to find equivalences between two radically antagonistic modes of expression, the word and the image. Dudley Nichols, Ford's accredited collaborator during the 1930s, has quite openly admitted (in the preface to *Twenty Best Filmplays* and in a long letter addressed to Lindsay Anderson) how fundamental his role was in the preparation of *The Informer*, in that heavy-handed attempt to find literary and visual symbols which, while they make the film an ambitious one, also condemn it to remain on the surface of things, a decorative piece trapped in its own formalism. The curious thing is that, immediately after *The Informer*, Ford made for Fox – the humble Fox of before Darryl F. Zanuck and the era of super-productions – a slight work, as unpretentious as it is inspired, *Steamboat Round the Bend* – a film not released in France – in which we see an eccentric steamboat captain rescue an abandoned girl, moralize jauntily reel after reel and get involved in an incredible race along the Mississippi with two other boats. Will Rogers, the idol of the great American public of the time, is the perfect summing-up of that homespun wisdom which informs so many of Ford's later films; Barton Churchill, a stock actor frequently used by Ford (the corrupt banker in *Stagecoach*), posits himself in a quite unforgettable way as a kind of prophet, 'the new Moses', striving without respite to regenerate his fellow men and convert them to a religion born solely of his imagination. Inventiveness abounds in every sequence. Apparently without the slightest effort, we are projected into an original, intensely poetic but familiar world which can only be compared to Mark Twain. To ignore that versatility which enables our director to pass from the austere aestheticism of *The Informer* to the unfettered fantasy of *Steamboat Round the Bend* would be a complete and utter distortion of the perspectives of Fordian creation. With time, Ford has learned to take the best of his plastic achievement in the 'classic' films and combine it with the immensely free treatment seen in *Steamboat*. From this point of view, *My Darling Clementine* reveals a marked progress compared with *Stagecoach*. Ford ditches all his psychological pretensions and instead is content to draw a loving caricature of his characters. As a result, he makes them so much more alive than the puppet-like imitations of Maupassant that Nichols invented for *Stagecoach*.

Ford's weakness lies to a great extent in his inability to control his lyrical outbursts. Ford lacks ideological rigour and is in a sense at the opposite extreme from Marxist or pseudo-Marxist filmmakers. When sentimentalism wins out over every other consideration, we have the lachrymose movies like *The Long Grey Line* and *Wings of Eagles*, in which our US Navy admiral cannot help displaying the 'affection' (in English it's the much more suggestive word, 'fondness') which he has always felt for the armed services. Unable to disguise his emotions beneath a mask of elegant sophistry, Ford simply serves us up (with a visual genius which I find as real here as anywhere else) an undoctored portrait of military life which, however idealized it may be, seems to me exact. At the height of the Second World War he had been able, with more restraint and true greatness, to express his admiration for his friends in the US Navy in the moving *Battle of Midway*, not released in France, and in *They Were Expendable*. This continual lack of consistency on the part of the director of *The Searchers* has resulted in his being devalued in the eyes of many critics and especially young critics. Ford is rarely equivocal: on the one hand there are the films he makes to earn a living; on the other there are those he can really put his heart into. In both instances there is the same love for his job and for individuals. Sometimes one category overflows into the other: an 'art' film like *The Informer* doesn't have the qualities of a 'studio picture' like *Steamboat*. Ford, whose creativity is instinctive rather than the product of reason, is quite certainly his own worst judge. And we, like him, must always expect to see sudden falls followed by extraordinary resurrections.

In a splendid letter to John Ford published in the *Revue du Cinéma* in the spring of 1947, Jean George Auriol wrote: 'Don't hesitate to make another Western if you're short of a subject.' And he added: 'Go on not admiring yourself, but go on making us admire films which are as violent and healthy as the leap of an athlete in full possession of his youth, who doesn't need to get drunk in order to live out a life which is only bearable if you get up and live it.' Ford remains an exception in an industry given over to success at all costs, to ambivalent declarations of intent. In my experience, no living film-maker has succeeded in recreating with such fidelity a world which seems to be such an integral part of his own *Weltanschauung*. One takes it or leaves it, as a piece, in the same way as one categorically accepts or rejects the specific genius of the greatest art of our time. If Ford identifies himself so entirely with the art of moving pictures, it is because he has the continual ability to reconstitute for us all that is best in the moral values which characterize civilisations in the making. It's a sham, illusory world, as art always is, but it's a world so impregnated with a love of appearances, that with each film of our Irish joker, we have the impression of being reborn into a purer and more generous universe, a universe truly worthy of mankind. 'All that lives is sacred', says one of Steinbeck's heroes somewhere in the novel on which Ford based his great film *The Grapes of Wrath*.

Translator's notes

1 Cameraman on *The Fugitive*; also on Bunuel's *Los Olvidados* and *Simon of the Desert*.
2 The leading French right-wing daily.
3 A periodical produced by the French government information services for distribution abroad.

8 · Lindsay Anderson: *'The Searchers'*

Sight and Sound, vol. 26, no. 2, Autumn 1956

Ford's reputation flourished in the late 1930s and early 1940s around
the period of *Grapes of Wrath* and *Young Mr Lincoln*, and then went into
a decline.
  Only the Lindsay Anderson–Gavin Lambert generation of *Sequence*
and *Sight & Sound* kept Ford's reputation alive in the period
beginning with *They Were Expendable* in 1945 and ending with *The
Sun Shines Bright* in 1954. The British critics could appreciate Ford
for the flowering of his personal style at a time when the rest of the
world (this critic included) were overrating Carol Reed and David
Lean for the efficient, impersonal technicians they were.
                           Andrew Sarris, *The American Cinema*.
Anderson had championed Ford particularly in his 1950 *Sequence* article,
'They Were Expendable and John Ford'. In 1955 he wrote a monograph
on Ford for the BFI Index Series, which was subsequently published in
Cinema (USA) (vol. 6, no. 3, Spring 1971, pp. 23–36). This later review
of *The Searchers* indicates something of the difficulty which one of the
post-1954 films of Ford created for a critic who had previously celebrated
him as a poet of the cinema.

Great men who fail habitually achieve more than lesser men who
succeed; and films by great directors that miss their mark are often
more interesting – more meaningful – than spotless but commonplace successes. We saw this recently with Mark Donskoi's new
version of *Mother*, a film obviously worked on with the greatest
care by a fine director, with beautiful and characteristic things in
it. Yet the parts did not coalesce and the essential theme never
came alive. How so? we ask; and in asking we come to understand
Donskoi better: and perhaps the cinema as well.
  It is the same with *The Searchers* (Warners). As Donskoi's return
to Gorki whetted our expectations, so does Ford's return to the
West, to Monument Valley, to those beloved mesas which domi-
nate the landscapes of *Stagecoach, My Darling Clementine* and *She
Wore a Yellow Ribbon*. We are back again in that beautiful but

daunting world of isolated frontier farms, marauding Indians, hardy pioneers. Surely Ford has only to be set at liberty here for him to give us something memorable, something heartening, another glimpse of that unique vision? *The Searchers* certainly begins with a promise: the camera tracking out of the dark homestead interior, following the hesitant figure of a woman, out into sunshine, a vast sandy desert world, blue sky, distant rocks, and an approaching horseman. As the lonely rider draws nearer, the whole family emerge and stand watching with anxious curiosity: how many weeks – months – is it since they saw a stranger? The scene is presented with Ford's familiar incisiveness and dignity of composition, made vivid by human detail: the panting mongrel dog, the wind blowing the women's skirts, the hand held up against the glare of the sun. And yet somehow, curiously, the effect is cold. . . .

It is a difficult effect to analyse; and perhaps impossible. Absence of feeling, of inner conviction, is just a fact, whatever the cause. Again and again in *The Searchers* there are moments, incidents even, that recall past splendours: the Jorgensen family grouped in front of their farm stand like Muley's family in *The Grapes of Wrath* before the tractor comes crashing through. The shadow that falls across the child hiding from the Indians by her grandmother's grave recalls a similar shadow falling across Nathan Brittles in *She Wore a Yellow Ribbon*. There is a farcical fight that takes us back to *The Quiet Man*. But a lack of intensity in all these echoes reminds us that it is not enough just to set Ford down among the mesas with a large budget: he has to have a story – or at least a theme. And the story of *The Searchers* (based on a novel by Alan LeMay) does not turn out to be a good one for him. In the first place there is too much of it. The pictures Ford has himself produced in the last ten years (and they comprise all his important work since *My Darling Clementine*) have relied less and less on narrative, concentrated more and more on mood. *The Searchers* is a long and complicated story, spread over eight or nine years. Moreover its hero, Ethan Edwards, is an unmistakable neurotic, devoured by an irrational hatred of Indians and half-breeds, shadowed by some mysterious crime. His search for his little niece who has been abducted by Comanches seems, indeed, to be inspired less by love or honour than by the obsessive desire to do her to death, as a contaminated creature. Now what is Ford, of all directors, to do with a hero like this? One is reminded of his previous failure, in *Fort Apache*, to make anything of a story centred on a bitter and obsessed character. And here similarly disjointed rhythm and uneven playing betray the director's unease with his subject.

The only way, one would have thought, that Ford could give such a story significance was to make its hero not Edwards but Martin Pawley, the young half-breed, adopted son of the slaughtered family, who doggedly accompanies him on the search, determined to save the girl's life. At least here is a character who stands for something, and it is likeably played by Jeffrey Hunter; but the direction gives the boy no stature. It is John Wayne, as Edwards, who stands firmly at the centre of the film; and his performance lacks either complexity or consistency. Instead of complexity, we get occasional nastiness alternating with guarded but essentially genial humour. The moods of the film are equally uneven. The drama of the girl's discovery is followed by a slapstick fight which completely destroys any tension in the situation or characters. Pawley's Indian 'wife', delightfully introduced, is suddenly sent rolling down a hillside by a violent kick in the back (a particularly, and unnecessarily, coarse touch). Any excitement there might have been in the climax is punctured by a lot of good-natured, quite unserious fooling with a green young cavalry officer (played by John Wayne's son). The acting is very up-and-down: Vera Miles is a spirited but rather modern heroine, Hank Worden as the pathetic half-crazed Mose is frankly amateurish, and for the first time (to my knowledge) an Indian chief in a Ford picture is played by a white actor in make-up. The only really authentic performance is that of Olive Carey as a brave and hardy frontier wife.

The Searchers in fact shows very clearly how Ford is a director with whom things are either right or wrong. When the feeling is true, it is also deep, powerful and suggestive. When belief is lacking, not all the technique in the world can hide the fact. There is even a certain pride in him which refuses to simulate: when his story reaches a point where only dishonesty can conceal an essential falsity – he simply films it, throws it in our faces, saying, 'If this is what you want – take it!' All the climax of *The Searchers*, with its preposterous rescue and Edwards' unbelievable change of heart, is like this. The extraordinary thing is that he gets away with it. 'The finest Western since *Stagecoach*', someone writes; or 'Joins *Stagecoach* and *Shane* in my list of classic Westerns'. The Old Man's smile must be rather wry if he ever reads his press cuttings.

Film Comment, vol. 7, no. 1, Spring 1971

This was one of a series of essays in *Film Comment* in which critics re-assessed classic movies. The essay appears as part of Sarris's subsequent book on Ford, *The John Ford Movie Mystery*.

The Searchers was generally misunderstood by American reviewers in 1956. Adapted from the Alan LeMay novel by Ford's family scenarist Frank S. Nugent, *The Searchers* represents Ford's ultimate divergence from the dramatic ironies of Dudley Nichols to the epical directness of Nugent. The Fifties marked the breakdown of traditional dramatic forms by a new surge of stylistic ambitiousness. 1956 was the year also of such official big pictures as George Stevens' *Giant*, John Huston's *Moby Dick*. William Wyler's *Friendly Persuasion* and Laurence Olivier's *Richard III*. But even to the conventional reviewers of the period, there was something flawed, unwieldy and heavy about these preconceived classics. And so the critical consensus settled upon *Around the World in 80 Days*, a producer's package of highly publicized cameo vaudeville bits glossed over with the superciliousness of an alleged S. J. Perelman script that later became the cause of litigation with two other screenwriters. Between the official classics and Michael Todd's camp classic there were a group of genuinely picaresque movies which were fully appreciated only in France. Among these were *The Searchers*, Alfred Hitchcock's *The Man Who Knew Too Much*, George Cukor's *Bhowani Junction*, Budd Boetticher's *Seven Men from Now*, King Vidor's *War and Peace* and even Cecil B. De Mille's *The Ten Commandments*. And the best of these is still *The Searchers*, which manages to sum up stylistically all the best of what Ford had been with all the best of what he was to be.

The innate pictorialism of Ford's style, evident as early as 1917 in *Straight Shooting*, finds in *The Searchers* a majestically familial context in the very first shot of a door opening onto the screen and the world and the past, extending outward to a solitary figure inching his way forward to the enclosure, the sanctuary, the long-lost home, the full measure of his aching aspirations. However, Ford's pictorialism is just angular enough and windswept enough to avoid the too contrivedly concentric compositions of George Stevens' *Shane* in which an antelope turns its head at that precise moment that its antlers will frame the mysterious horseman (Alan Ladd) in the distance. But then *Shane* is storybook (and storyboard) myth par excellence whereas *The Searchers* is lived-in epic with the kind of landscaped pastness across which the characters hang up their laundry and other hang-ups.

The Searchers is concerned as much with a peculiarly American madness and wanderlust as with anything else. Some of the characters start out mad, some achieve madness, and some have madness thrust upon them. Ford's world accommodates madness as it accommodates everything else, and with madness there is wisdom and robust humor, as with Mose Harper (Hank Worden), a certified lunatic who asks only to while away his last days in a rocking chair by a fireplace, and who gains his rocking chair for services rendered (to Ford as well as to John Wayne's Ethan Edwards.)

There is a fantastic sequence in *The Searchers* (I wrote some years ago) involving a brash frontier character played by Ward Bond. Bond is drinking some coffee in a standing-up position before going out to hunt some Comanches. He glances toward one of the bedrooms, and notices the woman of the house tenderly caressing the Army uniform of her husband's brother. Ford cuts back to a full-faced shot of Bond drinking his coffee, his eyes tactfully averted from the intimate scene he has witnessed. Nothing on earth would ever force this man to reveal what he had seen. There is a deep, subtle chivalry at work here, and in most of Ford's films, but it is never obtrusive enough to interfere with the flow of the narrative. The delicacy of emotion expressed here in three quick shots, perfectly cut, framed and distanced, would completely escape the dulled perception of our more literary-minded film critics even if they deigned to consider a despised genre like the Western. The economy of expression that Ford has achieved in fifty years of filmmaking constitutes the beauty of his style. If it had taken him any longer than three shots and a few seconds to establish this insight into the Bond character, the point would not be worth making. Ford would be false to the manners of a time and a place bounded by the rigorous necessity of survival.

Yet when Peter Bogdanovich asked Ford 'Was the scene, toward the beginning, during which Wayne's sister-in-law gets his coat for him, meant to convey silently a past love between them?' Ford answered somewhat gruffly (in *John Ford* by Peter Bogdanovich, London, *Movie* Paperback, 1967): 'Well, I thought it was pretty obvious – that his brother's wife was in love with Wayne; you couldn't hit it on the nose, but I think it's very plain to anyone with any intelligence. You could tell from the way she picked up his cape and I think you could tell from Ward Bond's expression and from his exit – as though he hadn't noticed anything.'

The scene may be 'obvious' now that we have been alerted to the larger implications of *The Searchers*, but in its own time, the scene, like Poe's purloined letter, was overlooked because of rather than in spite of its very obviousness. The intended emotion seems early and misplaced. We have just met the characters involved, and we have no inkling that this will be absolutely the last opportunity for a faded frontierswoman (Dorothy Jordan) to express, however covertly, the forbidden feelings of a lost love. We are dealing here with lives that are almost over, and the dreadful constriction of time running out is felt in the pinched awkwardness and cramped closeness of the domestic scenes involving a group of people variously doomed to slaughter, captivity, revenge before the final moments, two hours (screen time) and several years (narrative time) later when a man picks up a girl in his arms and is miraculously delivered of all the racist, revenge-seeking furies that have seared his soul.

Jean-Luc Godard once observed that as much as he despised the reactionary politics of John Wayne he could never help but be moved by the emotional sweep of the awesomely avuncular gesture with which Wayne gathers up Natalie Wood after having given every indication that he wished to kill her for defiling his sacred memories of a little girl accepting his medal as a token of his chivalric devotion to her mother. Deep down we don't really expect him to kill her, any more than we expect Wayne to kill Montgomery Clift in Hawks's *Red River*, but nonetheless the *dénouement* of *The Searchers* is infinitely more moving and artistically satisfying than that of *Red River*, even discounting the intrusion of Joanne Dru's *dea ex machina* in the latter film. Part of the disparity of emotional effect can be attributed to the philosophical distinction between two visual styles – Hawks the eye-level vision of man as the measure of all things, Ford the double vision (through classical editing) of an event in all its vital immediacy and yet also in its ultimate memory image on the horizon of history.

Hence, the dramatic struggle of *The Searchers* is not waged between a protagonist and an antagonist, or indeed between two protagonists as antagonists, but rather within the protagonist himself. Jeffrey Hunter's surrogate son figure in *The Searchers* is the witness to Wayne's struggle with himself rather than a force in resolving it. The mystery of the film is what has actually happened to Wayne in that fearsome moment when he discovers the mutilated bodies of his brother, his beloved sister-in-law, his nephew, and later his niece. Surly, cryptic, almost menacing even before the slaughter, he is invested afterward with obsessiveness and implacability. We in the audience never see the bodies or the actual slaughter, only the smoke passing across Wayne's face at the moment of discovery, a cosmic composition of man ravaged by revenge-seeking emotions in the aftermath of an atrocity, but that cosmic composition reprinted so often in specialized film magazines never breaks the flow of action, but instead accelerates the development of characters, and cracks open, as violence traditionally does in drama, all their massively encrusted psychological secrets.

The Searchers is rich in the colors and substances of the seasons and the elements, from the whiteness of winter snows to the brownness of summer sands. When Wayne pledges his implacable presence at the last hiding place of his niece's Comanche captors 'as sure as the earth turns,' the film switches seasons with a swiftness that augments the metaphysical majesty of Wayne's turn of phrase. And with the change of seasons, come changes in the searchers, changes of costume, mood and even silhouette. The startling sight of Wayne in a sombrero is the final confirmation of psychological adaptability obliterating the conventions of a genre. The mere *littérateurs* who still infest the field of film reviewing may tend to overlook *The Searchers* as just another Western. The fact remains that few Westerns even in the so-called modern mold are so resolutely untraditional in their trappings. Ward Bond's head Texas ranger wears a stovepipe derby, and the rifles are sensibly if tackily sheathed to keep out the dust. The only bona fide gun fight between good guys and bad guys ends with the bad guys shot in the back and robbed besides. Ford and Wayne tried back as long ago as *Stagecoach* (1939) to introduce suspenders to the standard Western costume, and they failed miserably.

Ford's humor is something else again. I must confess I found it eminently resistible back in the Forties and Fifties in that period when I, like most of the critical establishment, was unable to adjust to and discern the emotional connections in the new direction that Ford had taken. Nowadays I welcome the rugged frontier slapstick in *The Searchers* as a necessary humanizing modification of characters otherwise too excruciating to watch in their more serious pursuit. The community involvement, to which Ford's slapstick tends (with the help of reaction shots, that banal bugaboo of modern *cinéastes*), reduces some of the overwhelming solitude felt by the protagonist, and thus intensifies our own awareness of feelings that are all the more vivid for being momentarily relieved. It is much easier to see now than it was in 1956 that if Ford had been more solemn, *The Searchers* would have been less sublime.

It is our misfortune as film critics that we must discuss a film one-thing-at-a-time when on a screen so many things are happening and reverberating at the same time. How to evoke, for example, the conjunction of a geometric convergence of three columns of horsemen, two Indian, one Texan, with the evocative magnificence of Monument Valley, Ford's own slice of stylized Nature. All we can suggest is that Ford began filmmaking as a painter and added drama and music as he went along. In these terms, *The Searchers* is his greatest symphony.

10 · Robin Wood: 'Shall we gather at the river?; the late films of John Ford'

Film Comment, vol. 7, no. 3, Fall 1971

Of the writers associated with British *auteurism* and with *Movie*, Robin Wood is probably the best known internationally, and is the one whose writing seems most consistently to represent a 'held position' within film criticism, a position which has frequently been described, attacked and defended in terms of 'Leavis-ism'.* In his published work, he has been drawn more to Hawks than to Ford, this article being one of very few in which he has specifically addressed himself to Ford.

The Man who Shot Liberty Valance seems to me John Ford's last successful movie; yet most of Ford's admirers appear to place a very high value on the three features that followed it, finding sustained significance in *Donovan's Reef*, explaining away the weaknesses of *Cheyenne Autumn* in terms of studio interference, and acclaiming *Seven Women* as a masterpiece. Of these three films only *Cheyenne Autumn* strikes me as deserving any great effort of critical attention, the other two seeming thin and perfunctory; and I have yet to find any convincing case made out for them by their professed admirers – a case that doesn't simply take their value for granted and concentrate on the kind of peripheral felicities one can expect *any* Ford to offer. This article is at once an attempt to account for the failure of these films as I see it, and an open challenge to reasoned disagreement, to a demonstration of their substance or stature.

One way of defining the relationship of Ford's late films to his previous work would be to compare *The Man Who Shot Liberty Valance* with *My Darling Clementine*. One's immediate reaction

---

* See particularly Alan Lovell, 'Robin Wood: a dissenting view', *Screen*, vol. 10, no. 2, March–April 1969, pp. 47–55; Robin Wood, 'Ghostly paradigm and HCF: an answer to Alan Lovell', *Screen*, vol. 10, no. 3, May–June 1969, pp. 25–48; Alan Lovell, 'The common pursuit of true judgement', *Screen*, vol. 11, nos. 4–5, August–September 1970, pp. 76–88; and Robin Wood, *Personal Views*, London, Gordon Fraser, 1976.

to the juxtaposition may at first seem paradoxical: that the later film is more complex but less rich. In fact, the sense that *Clementine* is the less complex work proves on reflection to be illusory: the impression derives simply from the fact that its complexities are experienced as resolvable in a constructive way, the different positive values embodied in East and West, in civilization and wilderness, felt to be ultimately reconcilable and mutually fertilizing. There is, it is true, as in all of Ford's Westerns a pervading note of nostalgia to be taken into account. But the tone of the opening and close of *Liberty Valance* is more than nostalgic: it is overtly elegiac.

It is, however, the long central section of *Liberty Valance* that most invites comparison with *Clementine*, and the difference of tone here is very marked. It is partly determined by the movement away from location shooting to studio work in the later film, and partly by the characterization: both tend strongly towards stylization. The sense of community is certainly there in *Liberty Valance* – in the restaurant, the school-room scene, the political meeting – but it is sketched rather than lovingly created. It is not that there is an absence of detail; what is lacking in the later film and present in the earlier is something much less tangible, something perhaps only describable in loose terms such as 'aura' but palpably *there* in *Clementine*. One sees this, I think, if one asks where in *Liberty Valance* there is an equivalent of the Sunday morning sequence where Earp and Clementine join and dignify the dance on the newly dedicated floor of the unbuilt church. The schoolroom scene in *Liberty Valance*, though it has something of the same *thematic* value – the development of civilization within a primitive community – seems in itself relatively cursory, as if Ford were by now content with establishing what was necessary where earlier a major element in the creative impulse had been an outgoing love and tenderness for the thing itself. The characterization in the later film is very much broader, two-dimensional, verging in several cases on the comic-grotesque. Fonda's Wyatt Earp is a far more detailed creation than either Stewart's or Wayne's performance in the later film. The grotesquerie of the minor parts is immediately striking if one compares Marvin's Valance with Walter Brennan's Clanton, or Edmond O'Brien's editor with Alan Mowbray's Shakespearean actor: this latter comparison offers the difference between an essentially straight character-part rendered into caricature by the performance and an inherently grotesque role given a naturalistic roundness and complexity. It is difficult to make these distinctions without suggesting that *Liberty Valance* is the inferior film, and this is not my aim (I think both reach a level of achievement where discriminations of the A-is-better-than-B kind become merely petty and academic). All I want is to establish here, as starting point, the different natures of the two films, and to suggest that there is more than one possible explanation: one could argue that Ford in his old age had the right to take his previous work for granted, that no one should ask him to do again what he did in *Clementine* when he wants, perhaps using *Clementine* as a reference-point, to go on to do something quite different; or one could argue that something very important in his earlier work had been undermined or whittled away, leaving a gap the new developments, while very interesting in themselves, cannot fill. Far from being incompatible, these two explanations can co-exist, suggesting in their juxtaposition something of the complexity of the issues involved in confronting late Ford.

In fact, *Liberty Valance* makes perfect artistic sense. The main body of the film has something of the nature of the morality play, the characters conceived more in terms of their functions than in terms of naturalistic characterization: Ford had undoubtedly by then developed a much sharper consciousness of the thematic level of his work. Before one accuses Edmond O'Brien, Lee Marvin, Andy Devine of over-playing or crudity, one should pause to consider the homogeneity of tone of which their histrionic hyperbole constitutes a major element: it is above all what distinguishes the main body of the film from the framework, where this quality is totally absent. The distinction is most obvious in the playing of Devine, since (unlike Marvin and O'Brien) he appears in both framework and flashback: the Link Appleyard of the film's 'present,' though an entirely convincing development of the character, appears thoroughly subdued and demoralized beside the Link Appleyard of the film's past; he has become sadder and more sensitive, the inherent pathos has become manifest. In his development is epitomized the whole relationship between framework and flashback. The Old West, seen in retrospect from beside Tom Doniphon's coffin, is invested with an exaggerated, stylized vitality; in the film's 'present' (still, of course, *our* past, but connected to our present, as it were, by the railroad that carries Senator Stoddard and Hallie away at the end) all real vitality has drained away, leaving only the shallow energy of the news-hounds, and a weary, elegiac feeling of loss. What is lost for the characters is defined in concrete, dramatic terms in the film – but there is beyond this a sense that the loss is also Ford's. What Ford had lost becomes steadily clearer, I think, through a close examination of the three post-*Liberty Valance* films; for the moment, suffice it to say that it is what was so abundantly and pervasively present in *Clementine*, in the texture and spirit of the film as much as its thematic structure.

Of Ford's nine feature films from *The Searchers* to *Liberty Valance* all but two (*The Rising of the Moon* and *Gideon of Scotland Yard*) are set in America and are concerned to varying degrees with episodes and epochs in American history; of the three made since, only *Cheyenne Autumn* is set in America, the other two in very remote parts of the world, and a fourth film started by Ford and abandoned because of illness (*Young Cassidy*) is set in Ireland. Coincidence, perhaps, but I find the simple fact in itself suggestive. The course of Ford's flight from his own country – I think in artistic terms it amounts to that – to the Pacific, to China, or back to Ireland, is interrupted only by his account of the desperate trek of the Cheyenne back to their native country. The relationship of *Cheyenne Autumn* to the cavalry trilogy (*Fort Apache, She Wore a Yellow Ribbon, Rio Grande*) parallels that of *Liberty Valance* to *Clementine* and is even more richly suggestive. The failure of *Cheyenne Autumn* as a work of art is due less to studio interference than to Ford's inability – after so many years working with Indians, and despite scrupulous care in research – to create a really convincing Cheyenne life: his actors may be going through all the correct motions but they remain wooden Indians. This failure of the imagination relates significantly to much else in Ford (indeed to many of his imaginative successes) and I shall return to it. The film becomes intensely moving only, I think, when one sees it in relation to the earlier cavalry films, and thinks of Ford rather than of his characters.

That Ford himself wanted us to be aware of a connection is suggested by a number of cross-references, some of which at least can hardly have been unconscious. *She Wore a Yellow Ribbon* was the first Ford film in which Ben Johnson appeared and the second in which Harry Carey Jr appeared (the first was *Three Godfathers*, a year earlier). In it, Johnson is a sergeant and Carey a lieutenant. They are both cavalrymen again (though now mere troopers) in *Rio Grande*, having also appeared together in the intervening *Wagonmaster*. *Cheyenne Autumn* not only reunites them as troopers but nostalgically gives to Johnson his two recurring catchphrases from *Yellow Ribbon*: 'That ain't in my department,' and 'I don't get paid for thinking.' What's more, Johnson did not appear in any of Ford's intervening films and had become largely overlooked in Hollywood movies, so his casting in *Cheyenne Autumn* constitutes one in the long line of Fordian 'resurrections' of forgotten or passed-over actors; it is also a resurrection of the earlier character, though he now has a different name.

This reminder is sufficient to alert us to a number of specific reversals of motifs from the cavalry trilogy (especially *Yellow Ribbon*). In *Yellow Ribbon* the Indians' horses are stampeded by the cavalry; in *Cheyenne Autumn* the Indians stampede the cavalry horses. In *Yellow Ribbon* a solitary white man (Johnson, in fact) is pursued by a party of Cheyenne, and escapes by urging his horse over a chasm which the Indians' horses can't leap; in *Cheyenne Autumn* a solitary Cheyenne is pursued by a party of white men, and escapes in precisely the same manner (here, even the movement within the image is reversed, right to left in the earlier film, left to right in the later). One of the most touching, and thematically central scenes in *Yellow Ribbon* is the nocturnal burial, with full honors, of General Clay, the Confederate general re-enlisted as a trooper after the Civil War; one of the most visually impressive scenes in *Cheyenne Autumn* is the ceremonial burial of the Indian chief, in which the Cheyenne warriors move on horseback against the skyline in a way that strikingly recalls certain of Ford's favorite heroic cavalry images.

Such specific reversals point of course to far more general reversal-patterns in *Cheyenne Autumn*. There is a significant transference of Christian imagery. The best reference point here is the climax of *Rio Grande*. There, troopers Johnson and Carey (with Claude Jarman Jr) protect the white children they have rescued from the Indians in a church. A little girl summons the cavalry by ringing the church bell, and the troopers actually shoot down Indians through a cross-shaped aperture in the church door. In *Cheyenne Autumn* it is shells from Cavalry cannons that kill and injure Indian children who are under the protection of Quaker Deborah Wright (Carroll Baker), the film's chief representative of Christianity. What is striking is not merely the reversal but the weakening of the Christian imagery. Church, bell and cross in *Rio Grande* are integrated in a climax of triumphant force and power; Deborah in *Cheyenne Autumn* is largely ineffectual, unable to do anything amid the chaos of the battlefield but wind a rag as a bandage around a child's injured leg without even removing the blood-soaked clothing already covering the wound.

Ford clearly made *Cheyenne Autumn* with the deliberate intention of righting the balance of sympathies and allegiances in the earlier cavalry westerns, and the intention is partly realized in the reversal-patterns. At the end of *Fort Apache* John Wayne, having adopted Henry Fonda's dress, mannerisms and persona, and having contributed to the white-washing of his character, is about to depart on the mission of herding the last rebel Indians back into the reservations. The film seems to me – quite astonishingly, in view of what has gone before – to be at that point solidly behind him. At least, it is extremely difficult to detect any irony in the tone of the last scene, Wayne's abrupt (as presented) capitulation to the kind of fascist policy and outlook the rest of the film seemed to have been criticizing being linked unequivocally with that continuity of tradition which Ford consistently endorses in his work: a complete analysis of the scene would reveal, I think, the intimate interconnection of its every detail, relating the attitude to the Indians to the naming of Shirley Temple's baby ('Michael Thursday Yorke O'Rourke'). Those who see irony and ambiguity here must concede, I think, that they are arguing against the tone of the scene and trusting the tale, not the artist. Certainly, the ending does violence to the previous development of the Wayne character and to the whole drift of the preceding narrative. *Cheyenne Autumn* undoubtedly reverses Ford's decision there, at least as far as the Indians are concerned.

In fact, diverse pulls and impulses have always existed in Ford. At times they can give rise to a rich complexity (*My Darling Clementine*) or carefully defined ambivalence (*The Man Who Shot Liberty Valance*), at others to confusion and self-contradiction as at the end of *Fort Apache*. An artist need not necessarily be a clear thinker, but Ford's self-contradictions can sometimes be very disconcerting. Peter Bogdanovich questioning him as to whether the men should have obeyed Fonda in *Fort Apache* knowing that he was wrong, elicited the following forthright response: 'Yes – he was the colonel, and what he says goes; whether they agree with it or not, it still pertains. In Vietnam today, probably a lot of guys don't agree with their leader, but they still go ahead and do the job.'* The interview was made during the filming of *Cheyenne Autumn*, which contains, in the Karl Malden sequence, one of the most devastating attacks on blind obedience the cinema has given us. (It's not a pleasant thought, but I can't escape the feeling that the fact that Malden plays a foreigner – a sort of Prussian archetype – was crucial in enabling Ford to denounce the character and his reliance on orders unequivocally: he is somehow not quite the US army, not quite 'one of us'). This is not a marginal point: concepts such as duty and obedience are integral to the Fordian value-complex. In *She Wore a Yellow Ribbon* – greatest of the cavalry

---

* *John Ford*, by Peter Bogdanovitch. *Movie* Paperback, p. 86

trilogy and one of Ford's most deeply satisfying movies – the conflicts inherent in his attitude to duty, to the 'book of rules' are treated in a beautifully complex and flexible way. He is always at his greatest as an artist when he (or his material) can allow his central traditionalist values to be challenged without being radically undermined. The attempt to 'tell it the other way' in *Cheyenne Autumn* is quite another matter. The rich and complex ethic of the cavalry trilogy is built on interlocking and interdependent concepts of civilization, of the Indians, and of the cavalry itself; its structure collapses in ruins if the values invested in those concepts are undermined or reversed.

Ford's Westerns have always implicitly acknowledged that American civilization was built on the subjugation of the Indians; it is his attitude to that fact that changes. It is obvious that Indians in Westerns are not just a people but a concept: they have a basic mythic meaning on which individual directors ring many changes but which remains an underlying constant. As savages, they represent the wild, the untamed, the disruptive, the vital forces that remain largely unassimilable into any civilization man has so far elaborated: in psychological terms, the forces of the Id. James Leahy has drawn a parallel (in *Movie* 14) between Major Dundee's fanatically dedicated campaign against the Indians in Peckinpah's film and Captain Ahab's mission to destroy the White Whale. The psychological attitudes of directors who have made Westerns can usually be found accurately epitomized by or implicit in their treatment of Indians, as one sees if one examines the role of Indians in, say, *The Big Sky, Run of the Arrow* and *Little Big Man* and works outward from that to apply one's findings to the total *oeuvres* of Hawks, Fuller and Penn. In Ford's Westerns of the late Thirties and early Forties, the role of the Indians is relatively simple and not far removed from this pure archetype. The presentation of the Indians in *Stagecoach* and *Drums Along the Mohawk* is almost entirely untroubled by any sense of them as individual human beings. The allegorical overtones of the stagecoach journey in the former help define the Indians' role. There are three coach-stations, each more primitive than its predecessor. At the first there are no Indians; at the second the supposedly friendly Indians defect in the middle of the night; the third has been burnt down. When the Indians at last attack, Ford produces that stunning visual effect of the coach suddenly emerging into the great arid sandy waste; it is stunning not only because of its visual power but because of the symbolic overtones, the association of the Apache with barren desert. In *Drums Along the Mohawk* the Indians are again screaming, destructive savages, a concept rather than characters, but a new and very important component is added to this by way of modification: Ford's paternalism, which continues basically unchanged right through to *Cheyenne Autumn*. As well as supplying Henry Fonda and Claudette Colbert with a devoted Indian servant, the film culminates in a poetic vision of integration that invariably (and understandably) evokes jeers from contemporary audiences, but which is rather touching in its naïveté: Indian and Negro, accepted in their subservient roles, joining in the salutation of the American flag.

An Indian makes a brief but significant appearance in *Clementine*: 'Indian Joe,' shooting up the town in a drunken frenzy, disturbing Wyatt Earp's first 'civilizing' visit to the barber's. Earp knocks him around a bit and wants to know why he's been let out of the reservation: in racial terms the scene is obviously very unpleasant, but in mythic terms very meaningful, civilization conceived as demanding the rigorous suppression of the untamed forces Indian Joe represents.

The paternalist attitude dominates the treatment of the Indians in the cavalry trilogy: the noble and dignified Cochise in *Fort Apache*, and John Wayne's old friend Pony-that-Walks in *Yellow Ribbon* (the scene of their conference is perhaps the best involving an individual Indian in all Ford's Westerns), are in terms of presentation but two sides of the same coin. As in *Drums Along the Mohawk*, the contrariness of Indians is typically attributed (in differing ways and to differing degrees) to the influence or interference of evil white men; which is a way of at once excusing the Indians and condescending to them. The presentation of the Indians in *Fort Apache* reveals characteristic confusion (rather than complexity – for the divergent attitudes are not held in any meaningful balance): the loathsome Meacham, purveyor of bad liquor, refers to them cynically as 'children' and we are clearly meant to find the remark offensive. But Ford's own attitude isn't altogether clearly distinguishable from its inherent paternalism – Meacham is a nasty father, Ford supports kind ones – and one is left reflecting that, after all, it is only the cynicism in the remark that is supposed to be offensive. But Ford is too intelligent, too honest, and too generous to be quite content with that; and he builds up Cochise into a figure of considerable dignity and moral weight (though he remains very much the 'noble savage,' with the implication that he would behave himself if the white men were nice to him). He is sufficiently a presence to lead us to question not only Colonel

Thursday's obviously monstrous attitudes and errors, but the whole validity of building a civilization at his expense. It is already the problem of the Indians that constitutes a potential threat to the stability of the whole structure of values elaborated in the cavalry films.

Comparisons between Ford and Hawks are usually mutually illuminating, nowhere more so than in their treatment of Indians. In *Red River* the Indians merely fulfil a plot function and the presentation of them is conventional and non-personal; it is *The Big Sky* that provides the basis for comparison. Hawks is scarcely more successful than Ford in creating a convincing Indian life on the screen, but the implicit attitude is radically different from Ford's. When Ford's heroes move out into the wilderness, they carry the frontier with them, extending it, establishing civilization. The whole movement of *The Big Sky* is a movement beyond the frontier, into the uncultivated wilds, away from what Boone (Dewey Martin) succinctly describes as 'stinking people.' Boone ends up accepting his marriage with an Indian girl and at least partial integration in her tribe: a denouement unambiguously endorsed by the film and unimaginable in Ford (compare the treatment of Martin Pawley's Indian 'marriage' in *The Searchers*!). Most striking of all, perhaps, is the famous scene of the finger amputation, one of Hawks's favorite examples of his fondness for using violence or pain as material for robust humour. Jim (Kirk Douglas) knows the Indian superstition that you can't enter heaven if you don't die physically complete; and so, riotously drunk on whisky, he crawls in the dust around the camp-fire with his friends, searching for the severed finger which has been casually tossed aside. The white man becomes an Indian (just as, earlier, in the town, he picked up and adopted a Negro dance-step), quite unselfconsciously and without the slightest hint of condescension: there is no suggestion in Hawks' treatment of the scene that Jim is debasing himself. Can one imagine such a sequence in Ford?

The corollary of this opposition lies in the two directors' responses to civilization. Hawks' work, in fact, offers very little by way of constructive attitude to civilization: most typically, his movies tend to become celebrations of all that civilization can't contain. Metaphorically, his heroes are always moving outside the frontier, either (in the adventure films) to form their own primitive societies with their own strictly functional rules for survival, or (in the comedies) into an exhilarating and perilous chaos and anarchy. Ford, on the contrary, is the American cinema's great poet of civilization. Where Hawks' world is dominated by the Id, Ford's is dominated by the Superego – though, in the best films of both, the domination is not unchallenged.

The ambivalence of Ford's attitude to civilization that reaches full explicitness in *Liberty Valance* is implicit in all his work. It is already very clear in *Stagecoach*. There, at one extreme, are the Apache, like an incarnation of the spirit of the wilderness, savage and irreducible; but the opposite pole is represented by the Purity League ladies who are (according to Claire Trevor) 'worse than the Apache.' Between the two unacceptable extremes come characters embodying partially conflicting values between which one feels Ford's allegiances to be divided. The luncheon scene at the first coach station, for example, sets the artificial southern gallantry of the fallen gentleman Hatfield against the natural courtesy of the outlaw Ringo; and sets the 'cultivated' sensibility of cavalry wife Lucy Mallory against the natural sensitivity of the fallen Dallas. At the end of the film, as Ringo and Dallas drive away to start a new life together, Doc Boone comments, 'Well, they're saved from the blessings of civilization.' But Ringo and Dallas are setting out to start a farm and raise a family: their proposed future embraces precisely the fundamentals on which civilization is built.

The values that are in conflict in *Stagecoach* are partly reconciled in *Clementine*, Ford's most harmonious vision of a primitive but developing civilization. When Wyatt Earp and Clementine dance together on the church floor, it is as if Ringo were united with Lucy Mallory (except that Earp is the new marshall and Clementine sweeter, and more generous and open, than Lucy): the union of the natural with the cultivated. At the end of the film Clementine – without the flowered bonnet that marks her out as the girl from the East, and wearing a simple dress of the kind becoming her environment – is planning to stay on as a schoolteacher, while Earp hopes to pass that way again sometime: it is touchingly tentative rather than triumphant, but rich in a sense of potentiality.

The Girl from the East turns up again in *Fort Apache*, in the person of Shirley Temple, and adds a further problem to that dense but problematic film: if civilization is adequately embodied in Miss Temple, with her relentless dimpled affectations, is it really worth defending? Everyone in the film coos over her effusively, and there is little indication that Ford realized that we might not fall in line and do the same. The partial answer is that the film's dramatization of the concept of civilization does not depend exclusively on her: there is the deeply affectionate and detailed portrayal of the 'civilization' of the fort: the cavalry itself, and their wives and homes. The role of the cavalry in Ford's value-system is a complex one. It is the defender of civilization, but it also embodies within itself what are for Ford civilization's highest values – honor, chivalry, duty, the sense of tradition – so that it almost comes to stand for civilization itself. Yet, clearly, it can never quite do this: the cavalry life is in obvious respects too specialized, too much a thing apart, and what is basic to Ford's (and most other people's) concept of civilization – marriage, home, family – is necessarily marginal to it.

Central to Ford's work is the belief in the value of tradition. This is clearly what attracts him so much to the cavalry – *his* cavalry, for, despite the authenticity of material details of dress, ritual, etc., it is obviously a highly personal creation. In the trilogy, the cavalry becomes Ford's answer to mortality and transience. Individuals come and go, but the continuity of tradition is unbroken, the individual gaining a kind of immortality through the loss of his individuality and assimilation into the tradition. The emphasis is on continuity rather than development: indeed, the moral objection to the end of *Fort Apache* is that it deliberately and perversely eschews the possibility of development by insisting that nothing in the tradition must change. The civilized values embodied in the cavalry – honor and duty – are essentially superego values, expressed through the ever-recurring rituals and ceremonies that continue without modification. This is the most important difference between the concepts of civilization enacted in the Tombstone of *Clementine* and the cavalry of the trilogy, and it perhaps explains why Ford, wishing to affirm a belief in the continuity of civilized values, in a world changing radically and with alarming rapidity, turned from a developing community to an unchanging military body for an embodiment of his ideals.

The treatment of love relationships in Ford forms an entirely consistent part of this pattern: one could easily relate it, in psychological terms, to the presentation of the Indians on the one hand and the cavalry values on the other. Suffice it to say here that Ford tends to sublimate sexual attraction into either gallantry or heartiness: the relationships positively presented are always strictly 'wholesome' and honorable. Romance and courtship have their own rules and rituals, and sexual love is never regarded by Ford as a value in itself. It becomes one only when subordinated to the concept of marriage and family, conceived less as the relationship of individual to individual than as the establishment of continuity within a civilized tradition. He never treats sensuality positively: he can only tolerate Chihuahua in *Clementine* when she is shot and dying, whereupon he promptly sentimentalizes her (the char-

acter is the film's one major weakness). It is symptomatic also that
he is so ill at ease when forced to depict sexual abnormality: the
rapist in *Sergeant Rutledge* is conceived and acted in the crudest,
most conventional terms; and Ford's direction of Margaret Leighton's Agatha Andrews in *Seven Women* looks as if someone had
explained to him what a lesbian was five minutes before shooting
and he hadn't had time to recover from the shock. Again, Hawks
provides an illuminating contrast. The incestuous relationship of
Tony and Cesca in *Scarface* becomes, in the last scenes, the most
positive force in the film: the catastrophe is provoked not by the
'abnormal' feelings but by the characters' refusal to confront and
accept them, acceptance coming as a triumphant (if short-lived)
release – Hawks anticipating Bertolucci by over thirty years!
Hawks' treatment of sexual relationships has, of course, its own
inhibitions and oddities; with his 'primitive' lack of interest in
tradition goes – again in sharp opposition to Ford – an apparent
lack of interest in marriage except in the most superficial sense of
the term. Yet the positive relationships in his films can incorporate
eroticism more easily than can those in Ford. The Wayne/Dickinson
relationship in *Rio Bravo*, for example, has a strong, if muted,
erotic charge: in the Doc Holliday/Chihuahua relationship in *Clementine* the eroticism (very crudely and untenderly handled) is seen
merely as part of Holliday's degeneration, as against the purity
offered by Clementine.

In Ford's presentation of a growing civilization in *Clementine*
and a 'permanent' civilization in the cavalry films, nostalgia plays
a key role. It is a paradox of the cavalry films, in fact, that 'the
army' is regarded as at once unchanging and in the past – it isn't
the modern army. Ford's respect for the past works on various
levels, in his casting as much as in the lovingly detailed re-creation
of time and place. In a profoundly characteristic scene of *Fort
Apache*, Dick Foran is let out of the jailhouse to sing 'Genevieve'
to an audience that includes Guy Kibbee, George O'Brien, Anna
Lee, and Shirley Temple (also in the film are Pedro Armendariz,
Ford's old friends Ward Bond and Victor McLaglen, and Mae
Marsh). The scene is like an old stars' reunion. The words of the
song beautifully evoke the spirit of the cavalry trilogy, with its
intermingling of historical reality and deeply personal fantasy: 'But
still the hand of *mem'ry* weaves/The blissful *dreams* of long ago.'
Of Ford's thirty-four feature films since *Stagecoach*, at least
twenty-four are set in the past, and nowhere does he show either
the inclination or the ability to confront the realities of contemporary American life in his work.

It is easy to argue that, in *Clementine, Wagonmaster* and the cavalry trilogy, Ford is primarily concerned with constructing a value system, only secondarily with depicting various stages in American civilization. Yet the two impulses are so closely interwoven as to be really inseparable. For his vision to retain its vitality, it was necessary for him to feel at least a possible continuity between the civilization depicted in his films and that of contemporary America. Already in the Forties this must have been difficult; by the Sixties it had clearly become impossible. What can Ford possibly be expected to make of contemporary American society – whether one calls it disintegrating or permissive – where no values are certain or constant, all traditions questioned and most rejected, all continuity disrupted, and where the army is a dirty word? Yet how could he possibly remain unaffected by it, unless his art became finally petrified and sterile? What is lost in *Liberty Valance* that was triumphantly present in *Clementine* is faith; hence the film's elegiac tone, and the sad, and very saddening, lack of conviction in the subsequent films.

Returning at last to *Cheyenne Autumn*, we can now clearly see the effect on Ford's structure of values of the reversal-patterns: it is, quite simply, undermined, and falls in ruins. The change in Ford's attitude to American civilization can be vividly illuminated by juxtaposing his two Wyatt Earps and the communities for which they are spokesmen: Fonda in *Clementine*, James Stewart in *Cheyenne Autumn*. The very concept of civilization has dwindled from its rich and complex embodiment in the church-floor dance of *Clementine* to the later Earp's desire to be allowed to finish his poker-game undisturbed. An obvious weakness in *Cheyenne Autumn* is Ford's failure to define a coherent response to Deborah (Carroll Baker). Part of the trouble may lie in the reported studio interference with the casting. Ford told Peter Bogdanovich: 'I wanted to do it right. The woman who did go with the Indians was a middle-aged spinster who finally dropped out because she couldn't take it any more. But you couldn't do that – you have to have a young, beautiful girl.' One can explain his failure with the character in terms of a clash between his original concept and the conventional noble heroine. The problem is that Deborah most of the time *seems* silly and ineffectual, with her ludicrous inculcation of the alphabet, but the spectator is never sure that she is meant to be, so that the foolishness comes to seem in Ford as much as in the character. Deborah's ineffectuality is the more disappointing in that there are signs near the beginning of the film that she was partly meant to embody values that would effectively challenge those invested in the cavalry, and especially the Fordian nostalgia: she tells Widmark in the schoolhouse scene that he thinks only about the past, but she thinks of the future. Nothing in the film really fulfills the promise of radical questioning implicit in that moment.

Centrally revealing in the film is the incident involving Sergeant Wichowsky (Mike Mazurki) and his decision not to re-enlist. On the night his enlistment period expires, Wichowsky gets drunk in his tent, where he is confronted by Capt. Archer (Widmark). He tells Archer that he is a Pole, and in his country the Poles are persecuted by Cossacks; this, he now sees, is what they are doing to the Cheyenne – the cavalry are Cossacks; he won't re-enlist. Archer can give him no answer to this. The next morning, as the troop rides on to continue the persecution, Wichowsky is in his place once again. No reason is given for his change of mind: perhaps none is necessary: there is simply nothing else for the man to do. And this is precisely Ford's position. The cavalry values have become shallow and worn: nowhere in the film is the treatment of the cavalry warmed and enriched with the loving commitment that characterized the trilogy. Yet, although Ford sees this well enough, like Wichowsky he can only 'rejoin' them. Faced with the dilemma of the Cheyennes' predicament, he can only come up with the old paternalist answer, in the old paternalist figure of Edward G. Robinson. There is no more poignant moment in Ford's work than that in which Robinson in his bewilderment looks at a portrait of Lincoln and asks. 'What would you do, old man?' But the poignance derives more from our sense of Ford's identification with the character at that point and from our knowledge of his past work (particularly, of course, *Young Mr. Lincoln*, in which Fonda's performance so beautifully and convincingly incarnates the essential Fordian values) than from any success of artistic realization within the context of the film itself. The technically poor back-projection in the scene of Robinson's meeting with the Cheyenne was a misfortune necessitated, one gathers, by Robinson's unfitness to travel. But in expressive terms it has a sad appropriateness, adding the dimension of visual phoniness to the scene's general lack of conviction.

Ford's values are not really reversed; they are just disastrously weakened. His commitment to the cavalry is a commitment to the establishment; when he tries to place the Cheyenne at the center of his value-system, he merely turns them into an alternative establishment, but without the richness and complexity of the cavalry world of the earlier films. The conception remains obstinately paternalist, the Indians' stiff and boring nobility thinly concealing Ford's condescension. The Sal Mineo sub-plot seems designed to off-set this; it is said to have been severely cut by Warner Brothers in the final editing, but on the evidence of what is left one doubts whether it would ever have carried much conviction. Only an anti-establishment artist could hope to succeed with the kind of reversals Ford attempts in *Cheyenne Autumn* – as one can see if one turns from that to *Little Big Man*. Penn comes nearer than any other director to creating an Indian life and culture of genuine vitality, and this is partly because his social and psychological attitudes themselves tend to be subversive, because he is fascinated by spontaneity, by uninhibited natural responses, by the Id impulses. His presentation of white civilization in *Little Big Man*, although its obvious source is in Thomas Berger's novel, may owe something to *Cheyenne Autumn*'s Dodge City sequences. But the Dodge City interlude remains just that: it is never satisfactorily assimilated into the overall tone of the film, there is no significant give-and-take relationship between the 'civilization' shown there and the Cheyenne. *Cheyenne Autumn* is a film without any really convincing positive center that yet never quite dares take the plunge into despair.

For all its failures, *Cheyenne Autumn* is a sufficiently rich and substantial film for some sort of positive case to be made out for it, and the interested reader should be referred to the article by Victor Perkins in *Movie 12*. If I find it much harder to discuss *Donovan's Reef* and *Seven Women*, this is because I find both films so weak that I can't imagine what serious case could be argued in their defense. *Donovan's Reef* is, according to *Movie*, Ford's *Hatari!* Certainly, one can see resemblances: both films have an improvisatory feel about them, something of the loose, relaxed air of a prolonged family party; both depict what one might take for their creators' ideal societies, as imagined at that stage of their careers. *Hatari!* seems to me considerably below the level of Hawks' greatest work, but *Donovan's Reef* is sadly inferior to it. Both 'ideal' societies show a disturbing tendency towards the infantile: neither, at least, appears to encourage the development of anything one might call full human maturity. What gives *Hatari!* its organic life and formal coherence is the recurrent motif of inter-relationships between instinct and consciousness, animals and humans, the primitive and the sophisticated. *Donovan's Reef* is formally a mess: it quite lacks *Hatari!*'s relaxed but unifying rhythm. Its narrative line is hopelessly broken-backed, Amelia Ded-

ham's capitulation to the Ailakaowa way of life being so rapid
(and so perfunctorily charted) that by half-way through the film
there seems absolutely no reason why she should not simply be
Told All, and the resulting plot-maneuvers to eke out the narrative
before the final denouement become tedious and irritating in the
extreme. This may seem a superficial objection – an apparently
weak narrative line, after all, may serve (as in *Hatari!*) merely as
a pretext for a series of thematic variations. But there is a difference
between the almost unnoticeable narrative of *Hatari!* and the positive annoyance of that in *Donovan's Reef*, and the slipshod
impression the film makes on this level seems to me symptomatic
of a more general slovenliness and unconcern.

The nearest I have found to a reasoned defense of the film lies
in the few hints offered in Peter Wollen's *Signs and Meaning in the
Cinema*, where we are told that 'the *auteur* theory enables us to
reveal a whole complex of meaning in films such as *Donovan's
Reef*. . . . The 'whole complex of meaning' Mr. Wollen has in mind
is presumably outlined in this passage:

> In many of Ford's late films – *The Quiet Man, Cheyenne
> Autumn, Donovan's Reef* – the accent is placed on traditional
> authority. The island of Ailakaowa, in *Donovan's Reef*, a kind
> of Valhalla for the homeless heroes of *The Man Who Shot
> Liberty Valance*, is actually a monarchy, though complete with
> the Boston girl, wooden church and saloon, made familiar by
> *My Darling Clementine*. In fact, the character of Chihuahua,
> Doc Holliday's girl in *My Darling Clementine*, is split into
> two: Miss Lafleur and Lelani, the native princess. One
> represents the saloon entertainer, the other the non-American,
> in opposition to the respectable Bostonians, Amelia Sarah
> Dedham and Clementine Carter. In a broad sense, this is a
> part of a general movement which can be detected in Ford's
> work to equate the Irish, Indians and Polynesians as traditional
> communities, set in the past, counterposed to the march
> forward to the American future, as it has turned out in reality,
> but assimilating the values of the American future as it was
> once dreamed. [page 101; see below page 142]

The motifs to which Mr. Wollen alludes are certainly present,
more or less, in *Donovan's Reef*. The question he fails to ask –
and which the Structuralist heresy helps him to evade – is this:
how are 'the values of the American future as it was once dreamed'
realized in *Donovan's Reef*? It seems to me that, if those values
(as I take it) are equated with Ford's earlier ideals and aspirations,
they are consistently and painfully debased, all under cover of the

film's rowdy humor. The Boston girl no longer represents anything significant in the way of cultural refinement: the civilization she comes from is briefly and grotesquely caricatured (the Boston board meeting, which one would set beside the Dodge City sequences of *Cheyenne Autumn* as evidence of how Ford's faith had crumbled), and she herself brings nothing to Ailakaowa that it couldn't do without. The shift in courtship patterns from the gallant to the hearty–brutal is surely significant: Clementine wasn't subjected to crude horseplay or the ultimate indignity of a spanking to encourage her to submit to her man. The church provides the film's one good scene – the Christmas Eve celebrations – but again one finds a coarsening of the values it embodied in *Clementine*. Ford's religion has always been more social than metaphysical; when he attempts to be religious he becomes merely religiose and maudlin. The church floor in *Clementine* is, typically, the scene of a dance, not a service. Yet as a social hub it has a profoundly serious significance into which the scene's varied and delicately handled comic elements are easily assimilated without the least incongruity. The Christmas Eve sequence in *Donovan's Reef* is – in a film largely given over to the childish – touchingly childlike. But the farcical elements (Marcel Dalio's clumsy overplaying is symptomatic) are no longer safely contained within an overall seriousness of effect. The church is no longer the focal point for a society, but a place where wildly heterogeneous elements assemble for a brief lark. As for the splitting in two of poor Chihuahua, one can see well enough that Miss Lafleur is her descendant – the similarities are confirmed by the way both are unceremoniously deposited in water by the film's heroes, apparently with Ford's full approval. But Mr. Wollen would have to explain rather more fully what Chihuahua is supposed to have in common with Lelani who, although she isn't a sufficient presence in the film to count for much, clearly has more in common with Clementine, both in personality and in the treatment accorded her, and might have provided Mr. Wollen with another of his 'significant' structural reversals. The passage quoted is a good example of how the apparent 'scientific' rigors of Structuralist criticism can conceal the most extraordinary looseness of argument. In fact, *Donovan's Reef* is only interesting if one ignores the film and concentrates on its abstractable motifs; it can be defended only by a method that precludes any close reading of what is actually on the screen.

The tiresome and protracted buffoonery of *Donovan's Reef*, far from embodying any acceptable system of values, merely conceals an old man's disillusionment at the failure of his ideals to find fulfillment. The sadness inherent in Ford's situation reaches partial expression in *Seven Women*, which is why that film is so much less irritating. One can produce quite a *frisson* by cutting, mentally, across twenty years, from the moment where Clementine and Wyatt Earp walk towards developing civilization (in the form of the church) accompanied by a stately and devout rendering of 'Shall We Gather At the River?,' to the moment where Sue Lyon leads the children out of collapsing civilization (in the form of the mission) with a panicky and perfunctory singing of the same hymn. But if the film is Ford's acknowledgement of the disintegration of everything he had believed in, it is all done at several removes. He has fled not only to the other end of the world but to (for him) eccentric and partly uncongenial subject-matter. (It is surely significant that Mr. Wollen, in his structural analysis of Ford, nowhere refers to this film). The result is at best an accomplished minor work, though that is perhaps a generous estimate of a film that only intermittently transcends the schematic conventionalities of its script. There are numerous incidental felicities of *mise en scène*, but of the kind that suggests an old master skillfully applying his 'touches' rather than an artist passionately involved in his material. Anne Bancroft carries off the central role (the eighth woman? – I can never get the sum out right) with magnificent swagger and assurance, but I hardly think it will go down in film history as her subtlest or most rounded characterization. I get the impression that the actress, like the character she is playing, looked round, summed up the situation, and set her mind to doing the best she could and enjoying herself as much as possible under the somewhat discouraging circumstances.

My chief impression of *Seven Women* is of hollowness. The essence of the film is a thinly concealed nihilism. The lack of real religious feeling in Ford prevents him from finding any transcendent spiritual values in the missionaries and their work; any positive belief in the mission as a community, or as an epitome of civilization, is made nonsense of by its futility, by its inner tensions and outer ineffectuality. The only alternatives presented are barbarism and the 'tough' bitterness of Anne Bancroft. Ford's barbarians are merely brutes: he can't conceive of them as possessing any natural fineness, and their vitality is presented as exclusively destructive. They are monstrous Id-figures rising up to take revenge on the worn and faded superego values of civilization. Ford's presentation of them is very crude and simplistic, quite adequately expressed through Mike Mazurki's pantomime-giant 'Ho-ho-ho.' There are moments of quiet and touching tenderness, such as Miss

Argent's farewell and Bancroft's response to it; but on the whole Ford's sense of positive human value seems greatly enfeebled.

It would be ungenerous to end on such a note. My primary aim is not to offer gratuitous insult to the failed late works of one of the cinema's great masters, but to right an injustice; for it seems to me that sentimentally to hail films like *Donovan's Reef* and *Seven Women* as masterpieces is insulting to Ford's real achievement. That achievement depended on a commitment to ideals which the society Ford lives in has signally failed to fulfill. But that invalidates neither the ideals nor the films. One shouldn't expect Ford to be able to cope with the kind of radical reorientation the failure of those ideals within American society demanded. The late films, certainly, have their poignance, but it is the product of their failure, not of their strength.

11 · Peter Wollen (Lee Russell): 'John Ford'

New Left Review, no. 29, January / February 1965

Peter Wollen's most influential formulations on Ford appear in the extract from *Signs and Meaning in the Cinema* in the next section, and are criticized by Robin Wood in the essay which precedes this. The differences in methodology and position between Wollen and Wood in the mid-1960s are pointed up very clearly in an exchange between the two on Godard in *New Left Review*, no. 39, September–October 1966. The present essay can be read usefully both in its relationship to Wood's essay, and in relation to Wollen's subsequent, more structural, analysis of Ford.

The cinema of John Ford is rooted in history. He has steeped himself in those crucial periods of American history which have determined popular American consciousness: the colonization of the West, the waves of immigrants, the three great wars, the depression. Today America has emerged as the most prosperous and most powerful nation in the world. Yet, for Ford, something irretrievable has been lost. History for him has been a search, a long trek across hostile country towards the 'promised land' (*Grapes of Wrath*), the 'New Jerusalem' (*Three Godfathers*), the 'Crystal City' (*Wagonmaster*), 'H-O-M-E: home' (*Cheyenne Autumn*). More and more he has come to see the search as a delusion, the prospect of arrival as a cheat. In revenge, he has put back the golden age into the past; history has become tradition and hope memory. In the work of Ford we see the celebration of a vast panorama of the American past. We see the American dream as it inspired immigrants and pioneers: the dream of an ideal moral community. But we see also the renunciation of the American present, the corruption of the dream. Compare, for instance, the Wyatt Earp of *My Darling Clementine* – upright, devout, courageous – with the Wyatt Earp of *Cheyenne Autumn* – decadent, dissolute and cowardly. The drive westward, the major theme of Ford, has become the battle of Dodge City: a grotesque rabble, thrown into panic by the sight of one Indian. The victims become the heroes and the civilizers savages; when a group of starving Cheyenne, the last pathetic standard-bearers of the old West, stop and beg for food, they are shot and scalped.

Since Ford's cinema is about history, it is also about politics. During the period of the New Deal, when critical orthodoxy leant to the left, Ford was discovered and thrust forward, but badly misunderstood. Critics saw what they wanted to see: the hardships of the masses, contempt for the rich, a cinematic expression of the social realist novel. By their premature judgements and unilateral approach, they contributed to Ford's postwar critical ruin. When a new school of criticism emerged, Ford was discredited along with the orthodoxy which had extolled him. There is almost no mention of Ford, for instance, in the whole collection of *Cahiers du Cinéma*. *Cahiers*, in its polemic, concentrated, not on capturing old masters for its new methodology, but in building up new masters. Consequently Ford was completely neglected. Eventually he was abandoned even by those who used to praise him or, at best, honoured as the 'classic' of a bygone era. In recent years only Andrew Sarris has made a serious attempt to evaluate Ford's work. Today it seems likely that Ford's long career is over; he was forced by illness to leave the set of his latest project, *Young Mr Cassidy*. For almost 50 years, since *Cactus, My Pal* in 1917, Ford has been making films, over a hundred in all. The time has now come to judge his work in its entirety, to outline the continuities and transitions of its fundamental themes.

Ford's work is full of contradictions. Perhaps this is true, above all, of its politics. Ford's political thought springs from Jacksonian populism, reflecting its criss-crossing strands of liberalism and conservatism. Populism is not a system of ideas but a melange of paradoxes, vacillating and unstable: the individual and the people, the golden age and the utopian future, for private property but against big business. The peculiarly American current of Jacksonian populism has produced thinkers as diverse and antagonistic as Wright Mills and Barry Goldwater, forced as they attempt to transcend the contradictions in their thought into positions they do not fully understand. Most critics were quick to label *Cheyenne Autumn* as 'liberal'. But further reflection suggests that it might almost have been made by Barry Goldwater himself, who is, after all, a great expert in Indian lore, censor of moral decay and opponent of the crude pork-barrel interests of big business. The same contradictions emerge in the interpretation of Ford's great hero, Lincoln. The Lincoln of Neruda's *Let the Rail-Splitter Awake*? Or the Lincoln of expanding Yankee capitalism? Populism is troubled by the dilemma, but has no answer.

Ford's chief love is the old West; it is there that the roots of his populism are to be found, in the society which produced Andrew Jackson, frontiersman and Indian-fighter. (The degree of Ford's attachment to the old West can be seen from the self-portrait of a Hollywood director in *Wings of Eagles*.) The landscape of Ford's West is well-known: the gaunt rock outcrops of Monument Valley. Nature is hostile; to survive, man must be as tough as the cactus. In this barren environment Ford's protagonists are, in Sarris's words, 'champions of an agrarian order of family and community'. The community is organized around the church, the saloon, the barber's shop and the square-dance, the nodal points of social life and of a typically populist kind of local and direct democracy. The community is very tenuously linked to the outside world by the overland stage and by various itinerants: saloon entertainers, quack doctors, travelling Thespians, etc. But the real mediation between the community and the world at large is provided by the US cavalry, who both receive their orders direct from Washington and become involved and enmeshed with local issues and conditions. Thus, very often, the real transmission of the popular will and the real democratic struggles go on inside the army, between the public-spirited officer and the command-transmitting officer. Authority within the community is maintained by the sheriff; disorder comes, not from internal contradictions, but from outside disruptive forces who, typically, 'ride into town'. In his later films Ford shows an increasing gulf between moral and juridical authority: in both *Two Rode Together* and *Cheyenne Autumn* the sheriff is taking 10 per cent off gambling, girls, etc.

The role of the military is particularly important to Ford; it is one of the themes he has developed throughout his career. In *Stagecoach* the army represents, to all intents and purposes, the hand of divine providence; it has no place in society, but appears miraculously when it is needed. In this respect it resembles the ass and young colt which appear miraculously in *Three Godfathers* shortly after the exhausted Hightower has read about them in the Bible. These divine interventions are an endorsement of both the just cause and the determination of the human protagonists. In his later films, however, Ford begins to consider the responsibility of the army as part of society. Thus, in *Sergeant Rutledge*, centred around a negro troop of the US cavalry, general questions of race are raised: whether negroes should agree to fight against Indians and so forth. (This film also broaches the moral degeneration of the small village shopkeeper.) Strangely, however, one of Ford's lasting themes about the army is the theme of defeat. Consider, for instance, *Fort Apache*, a transposed Little Big Horn, the idolization of MacArthur in retreat in *They Were Expendable* or the child cadets marching out to battle in *The Horse Soldiers*. For Ford the values of military life reside not in victory (often hollow, as in *Cheyenne Autumn*) but in the opportunity it gives for decisive action, true camaraderie, etc. This attitude embodies both a critique of civilian life for its constrictions, petty competitiveness and animosity, etc., and a dangerous and somewhat thoughtless militarism, hardly mitigated by Ford's sympathy with indiscipline.

Ford's attitude to Indians is another key theme. In his earlier work, the Indians were merely the inverse of the cavalry: an undifferentiated, hostile force of nature, subhuman, almost diabolic. Gradually, however, Ford has brought the Indians more into the foreground. As the old West began to take on for him the aura of a golden age, so the Indians began to share in the aura. Ford's disenchantment with the progress of America threw into relief for him the role of the Indians as bearers of their own traditions, scarcely affected by the forces which drove America forward, fighting, like Ford, their own rearguard action. Thus the spokesman of Jacksonian Indian-fighters comes to be the spokesman of the Cheyenne, abused and cheated in defeat. His advocacy of their cause, in its criticism, for instance, of the military and financial elite, seems to converge with that of the anti-imperialist left. But it would be wise not to jump to conclusions.

Although the West has always been Ford's major preoccupation, he has made a great many films about other subjects. Before the war he directed a number of adaptations of books and plays by well-known authors, but these, because of the strong underswell of the original works, give a rather confused impression. Ford does, however, emphasize distinctive elements; thus, in *Grapes of Wrath* and *How Green Was My Valley*, he stresses the importance of holding the family together, a typical theme of his. Again, others – such as *The Informer* and *The Plough and The Stars* – fall broadly into the category of films about Ireland and Irishness. Ford himself comes from an Irish immigrant family, settled in Boston, and both Ireland and Boston are key features of his world. In *The Quiet Man*, about an American who returns to live in his ancestral home at Innisfree, he identifies home with the strength of the past. Ireland is portrayed as a land where traditions are still strong; the American, Sean Thornton, becomes involved with the observation of old marriage customs, the function of the marriage-broker, the dowry, etc. In this respect, the Irish are similar to the Cheyenne or the Polynesians of *Donovan's Reef*, who are equally tradition-bound. (The island of Ailakaowa in *Donovan's Reef* is a kind of Valhalla for two typical Ford heroes.) Another aspect of Ford's attachment to the Irish is shown in *The Last Hurrah*, about Irish Boston politics. This is one of his few films set in a city, but he conceives of the Irish in Boston as a community of their own, all known to each other. It is as though the typical Ford small town had been implanted, quite autonomously, within an irrelevant urban setting. The Irish community however, is contrasted with the Boston aristocracy of the Mayflower Club; this contrast, which recurs in *Donovan's Reef* and elsewhere, is primarily between the warmth of the small community of small independent citizens and the coldness, deadness and loneliness of the rich.

Something should be said about Ford's attitude to women. Women, for Ford, are a fundamentally lower order than men. Originally headstrong, they have to be humiliated before they learn their proper place and become devoted wives. They are repaid for this humiliation by being sentimentalized. In memory, they are blessed icons, standing on the railway platform waving; in reality, they are drudges, bringing up the children and cooking apple pie. Another important role of women, part of a loosely adapted chivalric system of pledges, missions, honour and so forth, is to be rescued from danger by the hero. Ford further distinguishes between two categories of women: those to be found in homes and those to be found in saloons. Women in saloons, though they never get to marry the man they love, have all Ford's sympathy: Lucy Lee, in *The Sun Shines Bright*, is glorified after her death and, in the person of Fanny (Dorothy Lamour), she appears in the Valhalla of *Donovan's Reef* to sing an old Western saloon song. He especially delights in routing the gaggle of town gossips and officers' wives, who disapprove of women who go in saloons or, as in *Two Rode Together*, have lived in an Indian camp. But he is silent about the strange transition from sweet young officer's wife to officious old officer's wife, from high-spirited respectability to mean-minded respectability.

Stylistically, Ford has long carried the burden of being the great pre-Wellesian master: sober, epic style; tableau groupings; static frame, carefully composed use of shadow and silhouette. At times, particularly in landscape shots, he has produced sequences as beautiful as those of the desert in, say, *The Searchers*; at other times, he lapses into vulgarity. His later films tend to have an altogether lazier, more fluid style, lingering more over stray detail, best seen in *Two Rode Together*. Ford uses a slate of stock actors who recur repeatedly in his films, right down to bit-parts, filling out the main action with light relief and highly coloured character vignettes. He even uses actors in a series of the same role; thus, Victor McLaglen plays the Irish Sergeant Quincannon in three different films. He uses stars in series too: the Henry Fonda phase (Abe Lincoln, Wyatt Earp) is quite different from that dominated by John Wayne, a much more relaxed and feckless actor, drinking, brawling and so on. And recently, he has used James Stewart to indicate the passing of the old West and as a foil to Wayne.

It is difficult, in writing about a director as prolific and contradictory as John Ford, to give more than an outline of his achievement, hinting at his principal themes. Andrew Sarris has summed up Ford as 'the American cinema's Field Marshal in charge of retreats and last stands'. But Ford is more than this. Alongside the themes of tradition and defeat are those of 'belongingness', of the search for a home, of community, of Irishness, of honour, etc. Often these elements are not consistently related; they are merely the arbitrary facets of what is nonetheless recognizably Ford's world. But often too, they spring into relationship to create images or sequences of great poignancy. Consider, for instance, the sequence in *Two Rode Together* in which a white child brought up by the Indians, but recaptured from them, is about to be lynched for killing his adoptive mother: a mother he does not recognize. Through the turmoil, he hears the Boccherini minuet played on a music-box. Suddenly, he remembers it. Too late. He is lynched. Such sequences mark the points at which the contradictions in Ford's thought, in the whole melange of his populism, are sharpened to a point where they cannot be assuaged. As Ford retreats again from them, they leave an aftertaste of regret, the prevailing mood of most of his films. Probably the best example, and his most consistent achievement, is *The Man Who Shot Liberty Valance*. It is a film centred around a paradox ('Nothing's too good for the man who shot Liberty Valance': in fact, it is the wrong man who is honoured for it) which reflects a deeper paradox: the destruction, by free will and popular consent, of the old agrarian order and the small town community and its replacement by a more prosperous future, but a future in which the sentiment of individual freedom and popular government has been lost. Doniphon, by shooting Liberty Valance, is destroying his own world, the world in which he can exist; but he cannot do otherwise. *The Man Who Shot Liberty Valance* is ambiguous in its attitudes towards legend and truth, towards the necessity of progress and the values of the past, but these are the ambiguities not of confusion or deception, but of a contradiction which Ford cannot resolve, but which is frozen. Ford's deficiencies are obvious: his many reactionary attitudes, his sentimentalism, his lapses into childishness. It would be very wrong to overlook his merits.

12 · Jean-Louis Comolli: 'Signposts on the trail'

Cahiers du Cinéma no. 164, March 1965

Comolli has been a prominent figure in *Cahiers* since the early 1960s, serving (with Jean Narboni) as editor in the late 1960s and giving formulation (also with Narboni) to the critical shifts which were taking place in the magazine around the events of May 1968 (Comolli and Narboni, 'Cinéma/idéologie/critique', *Cahiers du Cinéma*, nos 216, 217, 1969; in *Screen Reader*, 1): shifts which led, among other things, to the kind of critical analysis represented by the collective work on *Young Mr Lincoln*. This essay on *Cheyenne Autumn* was published in 1965.

It is a silly European reflex to think that every super-production must inevitably be a sub-product, and it's a sad prejudice to dismiss the quality of a work on account of the author's age. The two often occur in combination: with age as the dominant factor, the result is the inimitable and typically Parisian reception of *Gertrud*; with money in the forefront, it's the fate of *Cheyenne Autumn* (but people have been writing Ford off as senile for a good twenty years). The least prolific of veteran directors and the director who has most films and years to his credit have become companions in misfortune. It is not insignificant that in Mitchell's catalogue of Ford's work *Cheyenne Autumn* bears the number 129. That doesn't prove, you may say, that it's Ford at his best. Perhaps so.

1 Greed It is precisely the imperatives of large-scale production that come into play this time as never before, and one can say, without fearing to distort a truth which in any case is useless, that Messrs Warner and Smith (Bernard)[1] have usefully distorted what is perhaps the final mask behind which Ford has concealed his truth. Let's pass over the difficulties which arose in the course of shooting – the plethora of executives, each scene being shot twice, once for Ford and once for the public, then checked and approved at every level of the production hierarchy, E. G. Robinson being brought in half way through to replace Spencer Tracy, whence certain mattes (*transparences*) which are far from clear. It

109

was particularly at the editing stage that the film was improved on. If we are to believe Peter Bogdanovitch, Ford had planned to centre his film on the moral itinerary of Captain Archer (Widmark), who takes a certain amount of time to discover that in the West heroes are weary, that heroism has emigrated towards the North, and that the Indians he is pursuing are even more pitiful than the citizens of the Union; and on the parallel between the loves of Archer for the young Quaker girl and of Mineo for Montalban's wife.

That's too sentimental, said Mr Warner (or Mr Smith), and there's not enough action: no sooner said than they cut great chunks out of the Widmark–Baker scenes and almost the whole of young Mineo's part (it's hardly surprising if he looks so uptight now). So there's not much left by this stage except the physical itinerary of that stolid roughneck Widmark. Ask him for feelings! Ideas! But even with all the blabber weeded out in favour of *action*, it still seems a bit flat (not surprisingly – Ford intended to cut most of the horseback sequences which are nothing if not 'fantastic'[2]).

Mr Alex North[3] is brought in: make it so it's a bit more epic – you know, like vintage Ford. Mr North sticks violins and choirs all over the place. Perfect. But even so the action is a shade dispersed, thinks Mr Smith (or Mr Warner, what does it matter?). Why the hell does Jack want to cut that superb scene with the great Karl Malden: that at least has some guts. The publicity scene for the Actors Studio that Ford had thrown out is kept, intact. And what's this Dodge City episode doing here? It's funny, I suppose, but doesn't it confuse the action a little? So then the Stewart–Kennedy scenes are cut by half.

In the original version, which has the originality of no longer existing, Ford's idea wasn't at all, as the critics so justifiably supposed, to 'release the tension by a comic interlude, a guest performance'. No. Not at all. It was more a question of putting the famous 'Battle of Dodge City' into its true perspective. The peaceful citizens of this town who have long ago given up carrying guns are terrified by alarmist reports about the Cheyenne revolt. They decide they need a change of scenery. Under the wise guidance of the old hands Wyatt Earp (Stewart) and Doc Holliday (Kennedy), they pack their bags and get out. But no sooner do they catch a distant glimpse of a pitiful Cheyenne scout sitting on his old nag, than panic breaks out and they rush back to barricade themselves into their cellars. Earp and the Doc, who have seen it all before (and who aren't taken in), just go off to play a little poker. Then the sequence we were talking about begins. It's not quite the thing to poke fun like this at the heroism of our ancestors, decide Messrs Smith and Warner.

We have to understand them: they were counting on 'a good Western in the best Ford tradition', and could only really remember *My Darling Clementine*. They hadn't seen (any more than our critics have) *She Wore a Yellow Ribbon, The Searchers, The Horse Soldiers, Sergeant Rutledge, Two Rode Together, The Man Who Shot Liberty Valance*, or even *How the West Was Won*. It's not surprising if Ford greatly disappointed them: for a good twenty years he has been painstakingly dismantling the myths that he himself more or less created. Contrary to what our left-wing press all too rapidly concluded, *Cheyenne Autumn* is not the sudden realization that times have changed or the act of contrition of the great destroyer of Indians. In his last seven or eight films, Ford's heroes have been looking back over their past and revising their positions. Ford hasn't waited for Sam Peckinpah or Robert Aldrich in order to make 'anti-Westerns'. Autumn didn't start yesterday. Given that Fordians are so likely to see *Cheyenne Autumn* as regression rather than revolution, it is this continuity which must be particularly stressed.

2 Passion in the desert Of the film Ford wanted to make, there remains at most a few traces. Even so, we need to take account of these, perhaps simply because these traces are not entirely accidental, because the whole of Ford's work may ultimately consist entirely of traces and because these obvious traces at last disclose the nature of Ford's creation for what it always has been: scattered, fragmentary, disordered, haphazard, uneasy and uncertain (and that, in spite of the myth of a Ford preserver of order and rigour, defender of conventions and principles) – in short, the constantly evolving nature of a creation that may have seemed to have reached its ultimate many years ago.

Cheyenne Autumn begins the great Fordian peregrination all over again. Once more we hit the trail and, as always, neither the point of departure nor the destination is ever very close. As the itinerary unfolds, its limits are pushed back: if one leaves emptiness, it is to head for a reality that is still a long way from existing. Between what one is rejecting and what one is searching for, between negation and affirmation, one can only ever place a *hyphen*, whose extremities will always be out of range and can never be known. The Fordian adventure is a middle term, a continuing compromise; whether it's a physical or a moral journey, the heroes on Ford's long march are always caught between two poles. Between what one is not and what one wants to be there is just for a moment space and time to be oneself, that is, a little of both. What that means is that the first quality of this march is its stasis. The action is a lack of motion and the adventure is merely the chance revelation of this lack.

All Ford's films are informed in this same way; whether there is a proliferation of means of transport (*Four Men and a Prayer, Wings of Eagles*), or a restriction (*The Searchers, Cheyenne Autumn*); whether one is scouring the world and the four seasons or pacing the bridge of a ship, the fog or the streets of Dublin; whether characters proliferate (*Four Sons, The World Moves On*), or are rarefied (*The Lost Patrol*); whether the time scale is extended (*How Green Was My Valley*), or telescoped (*The Informer, Stagecoach*), everyone is going round in circles, quite patently, whether the process takes up the whole of their lives and even those of their forebears and their children or just a single night. It is of course around themselves that they are circling. Advancing along a curve always means eventually going back to where you started. Since *The Iron Horse*, all Ford's films have been flash-backs, either because the flash-back itself is the dynamic structural element, because the whole film progresses towards the past or even because it tries to escape from the past by moving backwards. Until now, this flight towards a Return was always presented as a kind of progress, and it would be wrong to speak of a Fordian 'pessimism' since, on the contrary, to reach one's self is the surest way of being able to go on. During the last ten years or so, this 'moral' perspective has deviated somewhat. Heedless, as before, of the bounds of his itinerary, the Fordian hero still always returns to himself. But he loses himself there more irrevocably than in deserts, discourses, adventures or legends. What his quest crystallizes of himself is something quite different from the reason for his taking up his gun and setting out in the first place. As the spiral of Adventure and Passion draws the hero ever closer to himself, to this centre of his being that he didn't know where to look for, it imposes itself on him as the sole objective he can attain, and he realizes not without bitterness or resignation that this truth about himself is not revealed intact because it has been dissipated along the way; worse, that in this centre is installed the desert, the desert he must now cross. The quest which appears to be a homing-in on his objective is, on the contrary, a dissipation. The effort which seems to bond the project to its realization (and to explain why Ford is so often accused of being schematic) neither joins nor controls, but scatters, disturbs, disperses its own markers. The itinerary is nothing but the mask of the labyrinth. *Cheyenne Autumn* strips off this mask (against Ford's will to an extent, but the intervention of the producers has in this instance made the admission more apparent).

3 The alphabet learned by heart and lost by reason The fragmentary nature of what has survived of the film explains perhaps why it is Ford's 'charitable' intentions and the meaning of the parable of redemption that have attracted attention rather than the very apparent, obsessive and insistent signs that are scattered along the way. The charming young Quaker is of course a schoolmistress. It is of course a European alphabet that she drums into the heads of the Cheyenne children. They know it (almost) by heart. They are even made to welcome the long-awaited mission with these halting utterances rather than with flowers. It is as much to take care of them as to instruct them that our charming Quaker accompanies the children. Even while the Indians are being routed, the alphabet continues to be recited, like a call for peace. For her part, the schoolmistress learns a few words of Cheyenne during the exodus. Insignificant details, you may say: just another recourse to that old (American?) idea of the civilizing and conquering language which breaks down barriers (cf. Daves's *Broken Arrow*) and converts, the most subtle and effective of all the ways of imperialism.

And yet the Cheyenne chiefs regard this 'civilization' with an increasingly suspicious eye. The children are forbidden to go to school. They boycott the alphabet. This tongue, say the big chiefs in perfect English, is a lying one. It is a forked tongue (an old Indian jibe). Your words are fickle, they can change their ideas as well as their meanings. The reservation is a desert. Your helpers are here to keep a watch on us. Solemn oaths [*serments*] become sermons. And promises remain as promises. In saying this, they are of course admitting in spite of themselves how much they have become part of the civilization they are rejecting. But it goes beyond that. For them to be completely integrated into the Union, they must also become aware of the duplicity of their own language: and then the buffalo is only a word, a dream, an idea; blood tricks blood; blood kills its own blood; orders are no longer obeyed; a semantic dispute divides two brothers. One could already say that *Cheyenne Autumn* is built on the power of words – by the power and the threats of words.

But there's more to come. Little by little, all signs of every possible kind are drawn into the film, all languages are involved in the same Adventure. The action turns out to be the exchange of signs, the search for signs, the substitution of signs. The epic dimension is duly brought back to the use of the word [*l'utilisation du verbe*]. The peace-pipe gives way to the cigar; the telegraph remains silent; written messages take on the force of codes of conduct; they become incarnate or else are replaced *in extremis* by a physical presence which then represents the Company. That's not all. The whole film is articulated around the fortunes of these signs which become the vectors of suspense and of drama. This uncouth Widmark declares his love for the schoolmistress in chalk on the blackboard. She goes one better in the casual way she rubs out his declaration with a duster. She indicates her departure in beautiful script on the same blackboard. Later, when the trail is lost, a pupil's exercise book is fished out of the water, a significant incident. Snow and water cover the tracks, in vain; there are enough traces left for the links between pursuers and pursued never to be broken. Deduction and logic have more effect here than horse-riding.

Overworked by the film, the signs go wild. A scout becomes an army; a flight becomes a revolt; words intoxicate the cultured German officer who lives surrounded by his books; newspapers are in their element; words take sides; rumours abound everywhere; written reports pile up unheeded; it's like an immense conspiracy of signs, there to draw the film on to its conclusion, to guide, mislead and contain it. In fact, it's as if the film is exploding in a myriad of contradictory signs, scattering its substance and its action to the winds, as if it were making a desperate attempt to gather together these swarms of traces and pointers, to impose, in spite of everything, an order on this disarray of signs which is leading it astray. The will to signify strives to unite the signs which both make and break it, to reconcile them. The *mise en scène* is trying to hold together the disintegration of a world. Not just the world that it shows or evokes, but the one that nurtures and governs it: for, as you can guess, it is not incidental that *Cheyenne Autumn* is Ford's 129th film. The alphabet once known by heart is relearned here by the very reasoning that it had itself stifled.

4 *What are yellow ribbons for?*   The law of large numbers prevents any certainty here. Who is Ford? After ten films we already begin to talk about an author. After thirty, we talk about him a lot. But past a hundred, how can we still talk about what the author is? What 'thematic' can we derive when the repetition more than a hundred times over of the *same* themes, situations, relationships, roles, must clearly have led to an infinite diversity of nuances

or, on the contrary, to a whittling away until the friction of one against the other has reduced them all to nothing? Depending on the point of view, Ford seems rich and confused, or perfunctory and narrow. But in *Cheyenne Autumn*, the two effects come together: there is on the one hand the centrifugal effect derived from the differential link between each of his films, and which projects into the latest one interferences, resonances, references from Ford to Ford; and at the same time there is the centripetal force exerted by this latest film in an attempt to appropriate to itself the figures of the round, that is to stress them, to recognize them for what they are, to render them explicit and repeat them, to condense the whole stock of Fordian material into the compass of a single film.

We can then see that, for quite a number of films, Ford has been intent on not letting himself be completely carried away, submerged or dispersed by his world, on defining himself within his own narrowest limits so that he can hold out against the onslaughts of this world, preserving the possibility of action, a creative space. This is cinema set against cinema: what has to be done must undergo the temptation and the resistance of what has already been done; the great Fordian Return is both *mise en scène* and subject-matter: as *mise en scène*, it's the expression of his mobility or fixation, of his compromises or his inflexibility; as subject-matter, it's what catches him up in a vicious circle in which movement is only the illusion of stasis. Like his heroes, once again, the director is caught between two polarities of himself which he is for ever trying to bring into a state of equilibrium or resolution. In all Ford's work before *Cheyenne Autumn*, the centrifugal force was dominant, casting each film out into ever-increasing orbits until all the films were circumscribed, but with each film somehow managing to wind back this force to its centre, where it waited, ready to spring open again.

Cheyenne Autumn also demonstrates this attempt to tighten the spring: to collect signs and traces together once more, to use them to counteract the explosive thrust as if each were a bond. Which is what they've always been. But *Cheyenne Autumn* admits the use [*usage*] (and no doubt the wearing thin [*usure*]) of all that previously was presented as characteristics or mannerisms of style, or as in-jokes: Ford's private world reveals here both its usefulness and its necessity. Exuberance makes way for the barrenness which it was concealing. The traces were misleading, the signs were false, prairies are deserts (the heroes are those skeletons or those ghosts), the yellow ribbon is worn through to the bare threads.

Translator's notes

1 Producers of *Cheyenne Autumn*.
2 'Ces chevauchées rien moins que fantastiques': a play on the French title of *Stagecoach* – *La Chevauchée fantastique*.
3 Composer.

13 · Jean Narboni: 'Casting out the eights: John Ford's *Seven Women*'

Cahiers du Cinéma, no. 182, September 1966

Narboni can be associated with Comolli not only as editor of *Cahiers*, but also as representative of the magazine's development away from the *politique*, towards a more complex view of the author as a problematic figure, the site of contradictions and repressions. *Seven Women* had been an almost universal disappointment, even to critics sympathetic to Ford (the exception being Andrew Sarris, who defends it as a 'genuinely great film': *The John Ford Movie Mystery*, p. 184). Narboni's title is 'La preuve par huit', a play on the expression *la preuve par neuf* ('casting out the nines'), a mathematical proof for checking multiplications by a process of adding together the sums of the various digits after eliminating all the nines.

If we agree to count Miss Ling as one of the members of what used to be called the 'fair sex', whose number and presence provides John Ford's latest film with its title (and the fact that we are once again dealing with an outsider would seem to be a strong incentive for us to do that), we have to admit that these seven women in fact become eight. Namely: Agatha Andrews, the woman in charge of the mission, concealing beneath an armour of excessive piety a horrific combination of repressed sensuality and deeply felt vacuity; her shadow and ghost, the impalpable Miss Russell, smoky grey and got up later on, when rebellion and disrespect win her over, in a ridiculously oversize raincoat; Emma Clark, the young missionary, the object of every kind of tenderness, even the most perturbing; Flora Peter, making the mission vibrate with her continual screaming, in which the natural nervousness of the pregnant woman is in competition with the terrifying but thrilling prospect of being attacked by Mongol marauders; Dr Cartwright (Anne Bancroft), tender, coarse, concealing her wounds, the archetype of the positive Fordian character; then two English women pursued by outlaws, Miss Bins and Jane Argent; lastly, Miss Ling.

Miss Ling is first of all the outsider, the absent one, everywhere a displaced person. Perhaps, we are told, a descendant of deposed

Chinese princes, she accompanies the two English women as far as the mission. Silent, unseeing, isolated from the seven women, she waits. When Anne Bancroft says to Sue Lyon, 'You are the only one who can get away from here', the framing brings together the blond missionary and the impassive Chinese woman who is no more concerned or animated than a table or a plate. Then the Mongols arrive – and they are even more anti-Chinese than they are anti-American. Torn away from a group of which she wasn't really – or wasn't yet – a part, she is now subjected to all kinds of humiliation, demeaned, scoffed at, mauled, reduced to the position of slave and object.

One frequently finds, you may say, in Ford's films situations like this, in which two civilizations, two hostile, or at least foreign, racial universes are in conflict, interweave or interpenetrate: whites and Indians, Europeans and Polynesians, westerners and orientals. With, between the two, a whole interplay of exchanges, of difficult adoptions, of abductions and retrievals; a whole series of transfers and transitions, from exclusions to false recognitions, from treacherous reunions to repeated captures. Whites forced to become Indians, restored to their own civilization only to be rejected by the very people who sought their release (*The Searchers, Two Rode Together*); or the free choice and adoption of another world, of a new homeland (*Donovan's Reef*). It would be inviting, and much too easy, in that case, claiming to know Ford, to label Miss Ling as the classic type of the victim of racial ostracism, banished and despised. The diabolical structuring of the film, by declaring her 'out of play', makes it impossible to allocate to her the number Eight and thus to skirt round the problem.

It is simply that, at the opposite pole, and not at the fringes but within the group of women itself, there is Anne Bancroft, representing a second known type of undesirable, for moral rather than ethnic reasons this time; all the more disturbing for being obstinately present and active: an energetic, brutal, outspoken presence, forcibly injected into the lethargic universe of the mission. Unequivocal in her tone of voice, her conduct, her language, tolerated only because of her function, fomenting a feeling of unease, made still more intolerable by her being indispensable. Within the walls of the mission house, doubly isolated by its location and the epidemic, she wreaks salutary havoc, sows healthy devastation.

What is so fundamentally new in *Seven Women*, what gives this film which seems on the surface to be so calm its 'disturbing' power, its disequilibrium and its controlled instability, its incessant and unpredictable rebounds, is, then, the confrontation of two orders, two types of conflict and situation which are usually kept separate in Ford's other films. Not focusing on one or other character, but effecting between the outsider and the intruder a series of to-ings and fro-ings, of exchanges; passing from the moral to the social order, making them subtly interact and fuse, condemning the two women to the same fate. Being excluded from one group equals being solicited and integrated by the other. Substitution replaces addition; racial discrimination and puritanism reveal the same features of hatred and taboo. Chosen by Tunga Khan – and it is with diabolical skill that Ford gradually reveals that she has been chosen not as a doctor but first and foremost as a woman – seated at the chief's right hand during the circus games, when adorned in oriental costume, Miss – and no longer Dr – Cartwright creates by her absence a lack in the group. Immediately Miss Ling is handed back. The number Seven is restored by interchangeability. The women are allowed to go free. Anne Bancroft poisons the Mongol and kills herself.

It is perhaps not an exaggeration, then, to see in this single unit, this one number too many, this superfluity that may be thought anodyne, this hardly perceptible surplus, the most developed and most dissimulated form of the excess Ford has always liked to use – and now more than ever – in order to pervert conformity and tranquillity to the extent of destroying them. Thus it is astonishing to see how perplexed, not to say disappointed, some of the most resolute Fordians have been, seeing *Seven Women* as an aberration, an untypical film, contradicting, even, the mythology of its author. No doubt it is one of those works which are at once synthesis and crowning achievement, in which the absolute project of an author is located at the borderline between the excessive and the sublime. Yet all Ford is present, though in a tranquil immoderation. Even the story is not absolutely new: it is enough to cast your mind back to a television programme in which we were told of the misfortunes of two nuns confronted by Chinese bandits. Once again it is a group of people united by the hazards of a journey or condemned to stagnation. Prisoners of the desert or of the high seas,[1] a group of men or, for the first time, of women, it all comes to the same in the end. (Ford plays all the time, moreover, on sexual ambiguity: the natural status conferred on Anne Bancroft because of her profession, then her hyperfeminization; the schoolteacher mistaken for a preacher, like the whisky drummer in *Stagecoach*; Margaret Leighton's ambivalent attraction towards Sue Lyon, etc.). Always the same enclosed cell, here unchangeable, ossified, fusty; an abandoned planet over which Margaret Leighton scurries with her curious walk, like a broken marionette, half scampering, half gliding; an artificial enclave, quite deliberately and pointedly designated as such by the set, swept by arbitrary, violent lighting and moonspots. And the outside, the hostile surroundings, oppressive, without clear features. In the muted opening shots, bristling with hostility and white-hot, an inhuman pattern of relationships reveals its unbearable intensity. A whole series of internal delapidations is brought into play, the exacerbation of desires, of hates in successive scenes in which militant atheism and blasphemy become intertwined with frigid, repressed or flagrant sexuality. From surreptitious advances to brief moments of painful separation, from violent confrontations to restrained frenzy, the plot moves along towards the resolution of the threat, the materialization of the Enemy. Abstract, archetypal enough for us to be able to acquit Ford of the charge of racism: Arabs, outlaws, Indians or Mongols, it is less the name attached to this enemy that interests him than the intervention of an external force of whatever kind which, as though secreted from the inside, seems, rather than compromising or interrupting, to bring to an almost salutary end the fraught coexistence of a group of individuals who have reached the extreme point of crisis in their confrontation. In the last scenes, finally, we see the culminating splendour of the great funereal ceremonies of the screen in which, from *The Princess Yang Kwei Fei* to *Europa 51* and from *Les Dames du bois de Boulogne* to *The Naked Kiss*, sacrifice, shame, cruelty and insanity (in this instance of the *mise en scène*) exchange their sparkling unction.

Translator's note

1 Narboni is referring to *The Searchers* (French title *La Prisonnière du désert*) and *The Long Voyage Home*.

Part Two

Auteur - structuralism

Even if the author had to be considered as a structure, by some coincidence there were always as many 'authorial structures', objectively describable, as there were names of directors, writers, etc.

Paul Willemen[1]

In fact a true analysis does not remain within its object, paraphrasing what has already been said; analysis confronts the silences, the denials and the resistance in the object – not that compliant implied discourse which offers itself to discovery, but that condition which makes the work possible, which precedes the work so absolutely that it cannot be found in the work.

. . . The goal of knowledge is not the discovery of a reason or a secret: through an indispensable sequence knowledge alludes to that radical otherness from which the object acquires an identity, that initial difference which limits and produces all reality, that constitutive absence which is behind the work. If the notion of structure has any meaning it is in so far as it designates this absence, this difference, this determinate otherness.

Pierre Macherey[2]

By means of structure, what representation provides in a confused and simultaneous form is analysed and thereby rendered suitable to the linear unwinding of language.

Michel Foucault[3]

At the beginning of his 'Critique of cine-structuralism', Brian Henderson, quoting *Tel Quel* – 'the exact value of a text lies in its integration and destruction of other texts'[4] – suggests a sequence in which each successive text integrates or destroys the text which went before. So apparent is such a pattern in this section that it begins to form a narrative – Lévi-Strauss is integrated into Nowell-Smith, who is integrated into Wollen, and the integration is destroyed by Eckert, who returns to Lévi-Strauss for a new integration. This whole complex is destroyed by Henderson, who proclaims the entry of the *Cahiers* editorial collective, which has already, behind the scenes, as it were, integrated Althusserianism via Macherey. The narrative is one of incident and confrontation, with *Cahiers* arriving, like Lincoln himself, to win the case by producing a new and magical element out of the hat. Given the fact that the various texts comment on each other to this extent, the function of these introductory comments is simply to trace a general direction, to destroy the closure which the coherence of the narrative might imply, and to question the terms of the compound, insisting on the hesitancy indicated by the quotation marks around '*auteur*-structuralism'.

As both Eckert and Henderson indicate, one of the problems of '*auteur*-structuralism' (or 'cine-structuralism') was that, though it seemed to be theoretically grounded (at least relative to the *auteurisms* which had gone before), it was always too busy 'in the field', discovering structures and meanings, to take time out to explain precisely what its theoretical relationships were to the structuralism which it invoked or to the *auteurism* which it said it pursued. The name was given to it afterwards by those who detected in the work of a group of British critics – Peter Wollen, Geoffrey Nowell-Smith, Alan Lovell, Jim Kitses, Ben Brewster – a 'movement', and who, reasonably enough, took it that references to structures and, more specifically, to Lévi-Strauss indicated that the theoretical grounding of this new *auteurism* was in the structural study of myth undertaken by Lévi-Strauss, a grounding which seemed to justify the term '*auteur*- (or cine-) structuralism'. It was only when what Henderson calls the 'scandal' of its lack of theoretical foundation was recognized that the '*auteur*-structuralists' themselves came to acknowledge that their relationship to structuralism had been less theoretical than instrumentalist – it had seemed to be a useful tool when applied to films. There is, indeed, a certain scandal in a justification which relies solely on the results which a tool produces, ignoring the possible objects which the tool may deform or obscure.

In a reply to Charles Eckert's article, Geoffrey Nowell-Smith argued that the combination of structuralism and *auteurism* represented an attempt to steer the course of film criticism between the 'Scylla and Charybdis of pro-*auteur* subjectivism and anti-*auteur* empiricism',[5] to found a 'materialist (or if you prefer, objective) basis for the concept of authorship',[6] which, by posing structures, even unconscious structures, would avoid the idealism of the concept of the *auteur* as a creating subject with intentions who was the source of all value in the text, while still being able to account for the fact that films by the same author had striking consistencies. Nowell-Smith does not claim that the attempt was wholly successful, or even that it was correctly directed, but he does suggest that it is wrong to assume that it was only the *auteurism* which was transformed by the addition of structuralism: the structuralism (in so far as it properly was one) was itself transformed in the conjunction.[7]

The operative question is whether the concepts employed in the revision of the *auteur* theory make sense in the place in which they are found, and, frankly, the more eclectic and even abusive the use of 'structuralist' concepts, the more likely they are to belong in their new location. The transfer of a 'method' from one object to another is a delicate business, but the delicacy does not consist in preserving the purity of the method but in testing its adequacy to the object and the validity of the transformations its application will produce. If any of us English film critics had really had ambitions to turn our trade into a sub-branch of structural anthropology, then one or other of the charges [of Eckert] might stick, but fortunately we did not.

By the time of this essay, 1973, Nowell-Smith and a number of the other critics identified with '*auteur*-structuralism' were themselves trying to find a way out of the conjunction. The need for such an escape is made evident here in the critique of Henderson, and in the practice of *Cahiers*, both of whom point to the limitations and inappropriateness of the structuralism which was used as a model, rather than in the critique of Eckert, who, while his essay is extremely useful in pointing to the way in which Lévi-Strauss was appropriated, remains within 'the same problematic in which the texts being criticised were imprisoned'.[8]

The attraction of some kind of structuralism for film criticism had a lot to do with its 'scientificness'. Structural linguistics, from its foundations in the work of Saussure, had been the success story of the attempt to make the social sciences more scientific. It had transformed the study of language from an evolutionary, and often prescriptive, account of language into a systematic study of the relationships between terms within language:[9]

> Structural linguistics abandoned the question of bourgeois linguistics, the question of the origin and history of language, to make its object the relational composition in the interior of language itself.

and a study of the systems by which terms and language became meaningful:[10]

> The speech act is only comprehensible on the basis of the whole system from which it gains its validity; and the system itself only exists in the multitude of individual speech acts. The structure of language is the systematicity which informs every individual speech act: it is a system which can be constructed by an analyst but has no concrete existence as such. The system only exists in the fact that the potential infinity of individual utterances is comprehensible.

Since myth seemed to function as a language, the systematization which structural linguistics gave to language seemed appropriate also to the study of myth. Through its appropriation into anthropology, structuralism entered the social sciences as a whole, with greater or lesser success, but everywhere carrying with it an apparent guarantee of 'scienticity', objectivity, materialism. Marx and Freud were adopted as structuralists in method; and to Marxism particularly, where Althusser was making the notion of science respectable (even fashionable) by opposing it to ideology, re-affirming historical materialism as, precisely, a science, structuralism seemed to offer real hope in pulling history away from teleology and social transformation away from simple economic determinism. The danger of all this was in the appropriation of precise and differentiated structuralist practices (structuralisms) into a single, undifferentiated 'structuralism' which incorporated (and gave the seal of approval to) any and every attempt to reveal underlying structures: the collapse of structuralist specificities into a homogeneity lumped together the formalist, the idealist, and the materialist. Althusser, whose terminology frequently echoes with 'structures' ('overdetermined structures', 'de-centred structures', 'structures-in-dominance'[11]), is often placed into this undifferentiated 'structuralism', despite his denials and his denunciations of the ' "structuralist" ideology'.[12] Michel Foucault, in his studies of the discourses of history, has suffered the same fate.[13]

In the late 1960s the attractions of a scientific 'structuralism' for those critics who were trying to pull criticism out of its impressionism while retaining the 'discoveries' of *auteurism* are obvious; given also the development of a 'New Left' which exposed itself to the theoretical debates in France, it was almost inevitable. Specifically, what structuralism offered as a critical practice was a way of objectively analysing a body of films, and of uncovering the thematic patterns which informed them. What it seemed to offer in theory was a way of accounting for the consistencies which it discovered, in terms of underlying and unconscious structures (social categories as much as individual – the Desert and the Garden[14]), rather than in the patently inappropriate terms of the romantic artist who intentionally and consistently expresses his own unique self.

In the area of intentionality, Sarris had already offered something of a hostage to fortune in his argument that, within the production system of films, meanings were as likely to be unconscious, produced out of tensions between personality and material, as they were to be conscious and willed. Peter Wollen, for one, saw the importance of this concession, and he made his appeal to the notion of the author as an 'unconscious catalyst',[15] an agent introduced into the ingredient mixture of industry, commerce, script, cast, etc., binding them into a unified compound. The author was the 'bearer' of the structure which emerged from the analysis, rather than its creator. (It had been foundational for structural linguistics and structural anthropology that users of language and myth were not conscious of the structures which they were reproducing.) The appeal to the 'unconscious catalyst' was a way of saying that the consistencies around which the film could be shown to be structured were the result of a particular and active set of relationships of which the author was one element – the principle of consistency which gave the compound its name – but which also included relations and conditions of production, ideology, technology, genre, etc.

The metaphor of the catalyst, however, raises questions which it does not answer: specifically, it begs the question of the extent to which the

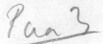

catalyst is to be privileged within the compound. What seems to emerge in practice is that the author is not simply a neutral agent, there only to facilitate the chemical process, but that it is he who individualizes the text, characterizes it and even gives it its value. The position is not clarified by an unsignalled, and apparently contradictory, shift between Wollen's 1969 text of *Signs and Meaning in the Cinema* and his 1972 postscript: in the former, John Ford appears as a structuring presence ('a great artist'), whereas in the latter he emerges as a structure which can be called 'John Ford' because that name appears on the credits of all the films which displayed that structure. In the confusion of this shift from 'artist' to '*post factum*' structure (from structuring to structured), it becomes unclear where we are to find the *auteur* in the structural relations which go to make up the text – is he still at the centre of the structure, giving it its meaning and its value, or do we have what Althusser might call a 'de-centred structure' (a structured totality without a 'God'), meaning being produced out of the interplay of structural parts?

The point is not that Wollen moves his position – it would be a much more serious weakness if he did not – but that the move is not signalled. The *auteur* theory (from Sarris through Wollen) is given credibility and stability by being made to appear complete, coherent and consistent; whereas, in fact, the undoubted progressiveness of Wollen's work, seen in retrospect, seems to lie precisely in the productivity of its contradictions. While broadly agreeing with much of Henderson's critique, it seems important to recognize the historical place of Wollen's intervention within the development of film theory. In the present context, it is clear, at least, what he was trying to do: he was trying to exploit the objectivity of structuralism to destroy the romantic idealism of creativity without simply inverting it into a mechanistic determinism. It is a real problem, and if Wollen's solution is unsatisfactory, it is, to some degree, because the notion of structuralism which was invoked was limiting in its application to film.

The inadequacies of structuralism are dealt with in some of the texts which follow, but they can be summarized here under two headings. First of all, as Robin Wood has urged continually,[16] and as Brian Henderson urges here, structuralism (this structuralism, the 'structuralist ideology') is reductive. It reduces the play of the text to its underlying structure, giving the critic no way of accounting for anything other than this structure, and tempting him or her to believe that it is only the structure which gives the text its value. Thus '*auteur*-structuralism' massively privileged the themes within the film, its methodological success and its popularity lying precisely in its capacity to give the critic a thematic base for a director's work as a whole which he/she could then use to detect or decipher the variations on a theme within a particular film. This is clearly important; but only rarely does '*auteur*-structuralism' move beyond this to a rigorous consideration of *mise en scène* and to an analysis of the film as an active relation between screen and spectator. It is largely held within the 'eureka syndrome', dominated by the search for and discovery of hidden patterns and meanings.

This leads into its second inadequacy. Structuralism, as Brian Henderson puts it, 'is an empiricism. It takes for its object the text as given'.[17] For '*auteur*-structuralism' the film is a finished thing: complete, but with a structure concealed in its depths which it is the critic's business to reveal. The '*auteur*-structuralist' critic, though he/she may have doubts about the centrality and intentionality of the *auteur*, nevertheless retains the traditional role of expositor, offering an exegesis of scripture, of an already written text. The separation, familiar to empiricism, of the 'knowing subject' (the critic and, by extension, the spectator) and the 'textual object' is founded on the assumption that both subject and object are already constituted. As against this, the decisive intervention of the *Cahiers* collective in their analysis of *Young Mr Lincoln*, and of Macherey, appears not simply as a critical reaction against structuralism, but as a challenge to the empiricist epistemology on which it is based, and to the assumption which it involves of given subjects, given objects, and a separation between them. For Henderson, as for the *Cahiers* collective and for the writing in Part Three (and, faintly and implicitly, for the best of early *auteurism*), text and spectator act upon each other. Neither the knowing subject nor the textual object are there as 'givens', already constituted. Rather than a finished and 'authorized' scripture, there is only a continual writing, producing meanings and 'meaning-effects' with each reading. Criticism does not defer to scripture or expose the secrets of its author. The *Cahiers* collective denounces 'interpretation',[18] as Macherey denounces 'commentary',[19] each preferring in their place the active reading which intricates itself with the text, attentive to its silences and repressions, making it say what it doesn't want to say. Thus Macherey:[20]

> We should question the work as to what it does not and cannot say, in those silences for which it has been made. The concealed order of the work is thus less significant than its real *determinate* disorder (its disarray). The order which it professes is merely an imagined order, projected on to disorder, the fictive resolution of ideological conflicts, a resolution so precarious that it is obvious in the very letter of the text where incoherence and incompleteness burst forth. It is no longer a question of defects but of indispensable informers.

This refusal of the authority of the text is the theoretical force of *Cahiers'* reading, and of Macherey, and behind it can be heard Althusser in his reading of *Capital*:[21]

> Such is Marx's second reading: a reading which might be called 'symptomatic' (*symptomale*) in so far as it divulges the undivulged event in the text it reads, and in the same moment relates it to *a different text*, present as a necessary absence in the first.

Whatever the subsequent revisions of opinion about the *Cahiers* collective's reading of *Young Mr Lincoln*, or about Macherey's theory of literature, or Althusser's theory of ideology, the theoretical importance of the shift which their work attempted is apparent. Its appropriation into film resulted not only in a break from *auteurism*, but a break also from empiricism and a resulting change in the way in which the function and activity of criticism is thought, particularly with respect to the position of the author. It remains for Oudart in his conclusion to the *Cahiers* collective text, and for the next section of the Reader, to re-pose the question of the author within a different conception of criticism: the criticism, referred to by Brecht, which 'transforms finished works into unfinished works'.[22]

Finally, in case the implication of all this is that '*auteur*-structuralism' was nothing more than an aberration to be buried now as quietly as possible, there has to be some recognition of the extent to which the appeal to a more scientific model did, importantly, initiate a new conception of film criticism, exposing the impressionism and self-expressiveness of most other *auteurisms*. More than that, we have to recognize that, however much distance we might wish to take from the theoretical premises and the practical reductiveness of '*auteur*-structuralism', nevertheless, in criticism and in spectating, the structures and consistencies with which '*auteur*-structuralism' concerned itself are used (and are useful) in defining our expectations of a work and in activating our recognitions. Recognition and expectation give the spectator a specific relation to the text, and, potentially, to the figure of the author. At the very least, the laying out of the structures which inform an author's work establishes a base line from which the theory and analysis of authorship can proceed.

Notes

1 Paul Willemen, 'Notes on subjectivity: on reading Edward Branigan's "Subjectivity under siege" ', *Screen*, vol. 19, no. 1, Spring 1978, p. 78.

2 Pierre Macherey, *A Theory of Literary Production* (1966), trans. Wall, London, Routledge & Kegan Paul, 1978, p. 150.

3 Michel Foucault, *The Order of Things* (1966), London, Tavistock, 1970, p. 136.

4 Below, p. 166.

5 Geoffrey Nowell-Smith, 'I was a star*struck structuralist', *Screen*, vol. 14, no. 3, Autumn 1973, p. 96.

6 ibid.

7 ibid., pp. 97–8.

8 ibid., p. 99.

9 Rosalind Coward and John Ellis, *Language and Materialism*, London, Routledge & Kegan Paul, 1977, p. 14.

10 ibid.

11 See Ben Brewster's glossary to his translation of Louis Althusser and Etienne Balibar, *Reading Capital* (1968), London, New Left Books, 1975.

12 In Althusser's foreword to the Italian edition of *Reading Capital*, p. 7.

13 See Michel Foucault, *The Archaeology of Knowledge*, trans. Sheridan Smith, London, Tavistock, 1974; particularly his introduction and conclusion.

14 See Peter Wollen, below; see also Jim Kitses, *Horizons West*, London, Secker & Warburg, 1969.

15 Peter Wollen, below p. 147; see also pp. 144–5.

16 See particularly 'Hawks de-Wollenized', in *Personal Views*, London, Gordon Fraser, 1976. See also above, pp. 98–9.

17 See below, p. 179.

18 See the opening methodological explication in the Editors of *Cahiers du Cinéma*, 'John Ford's *Young Mr Lincoln*', *Cahiers du Cinéma*, no. 223, August 1970; Translated in *Screen*, vol. 13, no. 3, Autumn 1972; in *Screen Reader I*, Nichols, Mast and Cohen.

19 See Macherey, op. cit., p. 149 – 'Can there be a criticism which would not be a commentary . . .?'

20 See below, p. 194.

21 Althusser, op. cit., p. 28.

22 Brecht, *Gesammelte Werke*, vol. 18, Frankfurt, Suhrkamp Verlag, 1967, pp. 85–6; quoted by Stephen Heath, 'From Brecht to film: theses, problems', *Screen*, vol. 16, no. 4, Winter 1975–6, p. 44.

15 · Claude Lévi-Strauss: 'The structural study of myth' (extract)

From *Structural Anthropology*, vol. I, Allen Lane, London, 1969; first published Paris, 1958

The importance of Lévi-Strauss for contemporary thought, and the dissemination of Lévi-Straussian structuralism through most of the cultural and social discourses, needs very little comment. His work, or at least his method, is referred to in most of the articles in this section, is elaborated by Eckert, and is criticized by both Henderson and Macherey. This short extract is intended to give some minimal, but concrete, focus for these references and critiques, and to indicate something of the temptation which Lévi-Strauss's structuralism held out to those critics who sought a less impressionistic, more scientific (more materialist) method of film analysis. In particular, here, it's worth noting Lévi-Strauss's insistence that the structural analysis of a myth has to take account of all its variants. ✴

Now for a concrete example of the method we propose. We shall use the Oedipus myth, which is well known to everyone. I am well aware that the Oedipus myth has only reached us under late forms and through literary transmutations concerned more with esthetic and moral preoccupations than with religious or ritual ones, whatever these may have been. But we shall not interpret the Oedipus myth in literal terms, much less offer an explanation acceptable to the specialist. We simply wish to illustrate – and without reaching any conclusions with respect to it – a certain technique, whose use is probably not legitimate in this particular instance, owing to the problematic elements indicated above. The 'demonstration' should therefore be conceived, not in terms of what the scientist means by this term, but at best in terms of what is meant by the street peddler, whose aim is not to achieve a concrete result, but to explain, as succinctly as possible, the functioning of the mechanical toy which he is trying to sell to the onlookers.

The myth will be treated as an orchestra score would be if it were unwittingly considered as a unilinear series; our task is to re-establish the correct arrangement. Say, for instance, we were confronted with a sequence of the type: 1,2,4,7,8,2,3,4,6,8,1,4,5,

7,8,1,2,5,7,3,4,5,6,8 . . ., the assignment being to put all the 1's together, all the 2's, the 3's, etc.; the result is a chart:

```
1 2     4       7 8
  2 3 4     6     8
1       4 5     7 8
1 2       5     7
    3 4 5 6     8
```

We shall attempt to perform the same kind of operation on the Oedipus myth, trying out several arrangements of the mythemes until we find one which is in harmony with the principles enumerated above. Let us suppose, for the sake of argument, that the best arrangement is the following (although it might certainly be improved with the help of a specialist in Greek mythology):

Cadmos seeks
his sister
Europa,
ravished by
Zeus

Cadmos kills
the dragon

The Spartoi kill
one another

Labdacos
(Laios' father)
= *lame (?)*

Oedipus kills
his father, Laios

Laios (Oedipus'
father) =
left-sided (?)

Oedipus kills
the Sphinx

Oedipus =
swollen-foot (?)

Oedipus marries
his mother,
Jocasta

Eteocles kills his
brother,
Polynices

Antigone buries
her brother,
Polynices,
despite
prohibition

We thus find ourselves confronted with four vertical columns, each of which includes several relations belonging to the same bundle. Were we to *tell* the myth, we would disregard the columns and read the rows from left to right and from top to bottom. But if we want to *understand* the myth, then we will have to disregard one half of the diachronic dimension (top to bottom) and read from left to right, column after column, each one being considered as a unit.

All the relations belonging to the same column exhibit one common feature which it is our task to discover. For instance, all the events grouped in the first column on the left have something to do with blood relations which are overemphasized, that is, are more intimate than they should be. Let us say, then, that the first column has as its common feature the *overrating of blood relations*. It is obvious that the second column expresses the same thing, but inverted: *underrating of blood relations*. The third column refers to monsters being slain. As to the fourth, a few words of clarification are needed. The remarkable connotation of the surnames in Oedipus' father-line has often been noticed. However, linguists usually disregard it, since to them the only way to define the meaning of a term is to investigate all the contexts in which it appears, and personal names, precisely because they are used as such, are not accompanied by any context. With the method we propose to follow the objection disappears, since the myth itself provides its own context. The significance is no longer to be sought in the eventual meaning of each name, but in the fact that all the names have a common feature. All the hypothetical meanings (which may well remain hypothetical) refer to *difficulties in walking straight and standing upright*.

What then is the relationship between the two columns on the right? Column three refers to monsters. The dragon is a chthonian being which has to be killed in order that mankind be born from the Earth; the Sphinx is a monster unwilling to permit men to live. The last unit reproduces the first one, which has to do with the *autochthonous origin* of mankind. Since the monsters are overcome by men, we may thus say that the common feature of the third column is *denial of the autochthonous origin of man*.

This immediately helps us to understand the meaning of the fourth column. In mythology it is a universal characteristic of men born from the Earth that at the moment they emerge from the depth they either cannot walk or they walk clumsily. This is the case of the chthonian beings in the mythology of the Pueblo: Muyingwu, who leads the emergence, and the chthonian Shumaikoli are lame ('bleeding-foot,' 'sore-foot'). The same happens to the Koskimo of the Kwakiutl after they have been swallowed by the chthonian monster, Tsiakish: When they returned to the surface of the earth 'they limped forward or tripped sideways.' Thus the common feature of the fourth column is *the persistence of the autochthonous origin of man*. It follows that column four is to column three as column one is to column two. The inability to connect two kinds of relationships is overcome (or rather replaced) by the assertion that contradictory relationships are identical inasmuch as they are both self-contradictory in a similar way. Although this is still a provisional formulation of the structure of mythical thought, it is sufficient at this stage.

Turning back to the Oedipus myth, we may now see what it means. The myth has to do with the inability, for a culture which holds the belief that mankind is autochthonous (see, for instance, Pausanias, VIII, xxix, 4: plants provide a *model* for humans), to find a satisfactory transition between this theory and the knowledge that human beings are actually born from the union of man and woman. Although the problem obviously cannot be solved, the Oedipus myth provides a kind of logical tool which relates the original problem – born from one or born from two? – to the derivative problem: born from different or born from same? By a correlation of this type, the overrating of blood relations is to the underrating of blood relations as the attempt to escape autochthony is to the impossibility to succeed in it. Although experience contradicts theory, social life validates cosmology by its similarity of structure. Hence cosmology is true.

Two remarks should be made at this stage.

In order to interpret the myth, we left aside a point which has worried the specialists until now, namely, that in the earlier (Homeric) versions of the Oedipus myth some basic elements are lacking, such as Jocasta killing herself and Oedipus piercing his own eyes. These events do not alter the substance of the myth although they can easily be integrated, the first one as a new case of auto-destruction (column three) and the second as another case of crippledness (column four). At the same time there is something significant in these additions, since the shift from foot to head is to be correlated with the shift from autochthonous origin to self-destruction.

Our method thus eliminates a problem which has, so far, been one of the main obstacles to the progress of mythological studies, namely, the quest for the *true* version, or the *earlier* one. On the contrary, we define the myth as consisting of all its versions; or, to put it otherwise, a myth remains the same as long as it is felt as such. A striking example is offered by the fact that our interpretation may take into account the Freudian use of the Oedipus myth and is certainly applicable to it. Although the Freudian problem has ceased to be that of autochthony *versus* bisexual reproduction, it is still the problem of understanding how *one* can be born from *two*: How is it that we do not have only one procreator, but a mother plus a father? Therefore, not only Sophocles, but Freud himself, should be included among the recorded versions of the Oedipus myth on a par with earlier or seemingly more 'authentic' versions.

16 · Geoffrey Nowell-Smith: *Visconti* (extract)

From *Visconti*, Secker & Warburg, London, 1967

This very short extract from the introduction to Nowell-Smith's book on Visconti places very concisely the relationship of the *auteur* theory to structuralism, and indicates some of the strengths and limitations of the structuralist approach. The book itself was the first to appear in English film criticism containing an explicit reference to a structuralist method; though as Nowell-Smith makes clear elsewhere ('I was a star*struck structuralist' *Screen*, vol. 14, no. 3) in answer to Charles Eckert's 'history of ideas' account of '*auteur*-structuralism', it's a mistake to rely on the empirical evidence of the chronology of publication as a way of showing 'who started it' (p. 94):

> In this particular case other texts, e.g. BFI Education Department seminars papers, could be brought in to show that the order of semi-public diffusion of the ideas was different from the one that emerges from a study of the published texts. Worse, the practice could be extended to cover all the private conversations through which ideas were passed from one person to another.

For the history of authorship theory, the point of interest is that most of the critics who introduced structuralism to English-speaking film criticism (Nowell-Smith, Peter Wollen, Jim Kitses, Alan Lovell, Ben Brewster, Paul Willemen) were in fairly close contact, each being associated, in some way or another, with the British Film Institute (BFI) and/or the Society for Education in Film and Television (SEFT) in London; and most of them, at some time, wrote in *Screen*.

It is necessary, at this point, to make clear certain assumptions about the concepts of authorship and of structure which have guided me in this work. The so-called *auteur* theory can be understood in three ways: as a set of empirical assertions to the effect that every detail of a film is the direct and sole responsibility of its author, who is the director; as a standard of value, according to which every film that is a *film d'auteur* is good, and every film that is not is bad; and as a principle of method, which provides a basis for a more scientific form of criticism than has existed hitherto.

136

The first interpretation is manifestly absurd. Any proponent of the theory who puts it forward uncompromisingly in that form both trivialises the theory and commits himself to a statement that is demonstrably untrue. The second is simply gratuitous and leads only to a purposeless and anti-critical aesthetic dogmatism. It is only in the third interpretation that the theory has any validity. As a principle of method the theory requires the critic to recognize one basic fact, which is that the author exists, and to organize his analysis of the work round that fact. Whether one is trying to get to grips with a particular film or to understand the cinema in general, let alone when one is studying the development of an individual director, the concept of authorship provides a necessary dimension without which the picture cannot be complete.

But the principle of authorship does not stop short here. If it were simply a recommendation to look at films in terms of their directors it would hardly be an advance on what we know already. However, one essential corollary of the theory as it has been developed is the discovery that the defining characteristics of an author's work are not always those that are most readily apparent. The purpose of criticism becomes therefore to uncover behind the superficial contrasts of subject and treatment a structural hard core of basic and often recondite motifs. The pattern formed by these motifs, which may be stylistic or thematic, is what gives an author's work its particular structure, both defining it internally and distinguishing one body of work from another.

The structural approach, which has evolved, by a kind of necessary accident, out of the applications of the *auteur* theory and resolves many of the difficulties of the theory as originally put forward, brings with it, however, problems of its own. It narrows down the field of inquiry almost too radically, making the internal (formal and thematic) analysis of the body of works as a whole the only valid object of criticism. In so doing it is in danger of neglecting two other equally basic factors. One is the possibility of an author's work changing over time and of the structures being variable and not constant: the other is the importance of the non-thematic subject-matter and of sub-stylistic features of the visual treatment.

17 · Peter Wollen: 'The *auteur* theory' (extract)

From *Signs and Meaning in The Cinema*, Secker & Warburg, London, 1967 and 1972

The importance of the book from which this extract is drawn has been recognized both in America by Charles Eckert – '*Signs and Meaning in the Cinema* must be, after *Film Form* and *What is Cinema?*, the most widely read work on film theory among present-day film students' (see p. 154 below) – and in Britain by Robin Wood – 'Peter Wollen's *Signs and Meaning in the Cinema* is probably the most influential book on film in English of the past decade' ('Hawks de-Wollenized', in *Personal Views*, p. 193). The central importance of its chapter on the *auteur* theory is apparent in the number of times it is included in general anthologies. Wollen's reformulation of *auteurism* provided a focus not only for the development of a more systematic, 'scientific' or materialist critical practice, but was also influential, as Wood testifies (p. 193), within the more pragmatic criticism practised by *Movie*.

I have attempted to highlight the unmarked shift in Wollen's position, noted by Henderson and in my introduction to this section, by placing together an extract from the 1969 chapter and an extract from the 1972 postscript.

1969

Something further needs to be said about the theoretical basis of the kind of schematic exposition of Hawks's work which I have outlined. The 'structural approach' which underlies it, the definition of a core of repeated motifs, has evident affinities with methods which have been developed for the study of folklore and mythology. In the work of Olrik and others, it was noted that in different folk-tales the same motifs reappeared time and time again. It became possible to build up a lexicon of these motifs. Eventually Propp showed how a whole cycle of Russian fairy-tales could be analysed into variations of a very limited set of basic motifs (or moves, as he called them). Underlying the different, individual tales was an archi-tale, of which they were all variants. One important point needs to be made about this type of structural analysis. There is a danger, as Lévi-Strauss has pointed out, that by simply noting and mapping resemblances, all the texts which are studied (whether Russian fairy-tales or American movies) will be reduced to one, abstract and impoverished. There must be a moment of synthesis as well as a moment of analysis: otherwise, the method is formalist, rather than truly structuralist. Structuralist criticism cannot rest at the perception of resemblances or repetitions (redundancies, in fact), but must also comprehend a system of differences and oppositions. In this way, texts can be studied not only in their universality (what they all have in common) but also in their singularity (what differentiates them from each other). This means of course that the test of a structural analysis lies not in the orthodox canon of a director's work, where resemblances are clustered, but in films which at first sight may seem eccentricities.

In the films of Howard Hawks a systematic series of oppositions can be seen very near the surface, in the contrast between the adventure dramas and the crazy comedies. If we take the adventure dramas alone it would seem that Hawks's work is flaccid, lacking in dynamism; it is only when we consider the crazy comedies that it becomes rich, begins to ferment: alongside every dramatic hero we are aware of a phantom, stripped of mastery, humiliated, inverted. With other directors, the system of oppositions is much more complex: instead of there being two broad strata of films there are a whole series of shifting variations. In these cases, we need to analyse the roles of the protagonists themselves, rather than simply the worlds in which they operate. The protagonists of fairy-tales or myths, as Lévi-Strauss has pointed out, can be dissolved into bundles of differential elements, pairs of opposites. Thus the difference between the prince and the goose-girl can be reduced to two antinomic pairs: one natural, male versus female, and the other cultural, high versus low. We can proceed with the same kind of operation in the study of films, though, as we shall see, we shall find them more complex than fairy-tales.

It is instructive, for example, to consider three films of John Ford and compare their heroes: Wyatt Earp in *My Darling Clementine*, Ethan Edwards in *The Searchers* and Tom Doniphon in *The Man Who Shot Liberty Valance*. They all act within the recognizable Ford world, governed by a set of oppositions, but their *loci* within that world are very different. The relevant pairs of opposites overlap; different pairs are foregrounded in different movies. The most relevant are garden versus wilderness, plough-share versus sabre, settler versus nomad, European versus Indian, civilised versus savage, book versus gun, married versus unmarried, East versus West.

These antinomies can often be broken down further. The East, for instance, can be defined either as Boston or Washington and, in *The Last Hurrah*, Boston itself is broken down into the antipodes of Irish immigrants versus Plymouth Club, themselves bundles of such differential elements as Celtic versus Anglo-Saxon, poor versus rich, Catholic versus Protestant, Democrat versus Republican, and so on. At first sight, it might seem that the oppositions listed above overlap to the extent that they become practically synonymous, but this is by no means the case. As we shall see, part of the development of Ford's career has been the shift from an identity between civilised versus savage and European versus Indian to their separation and final reversal, so that in *Cheyenne Autumn* it is the Europeans who are savage, the victims who are heroes.

The master antinomy in Ford's films is that between the wilderness and the garden. As Henry Nash Smith has demonstrated, in his magisterial book *Virgin Land*, the contrast between the image of America as a desert and as a garden is one which has dominated American thought and literature, recurring in countless novels, tracts, political speeches and magazine stories. In Ford's films it is crystallised in a number of striking images. *The Man Who Shot Liberty Valance*, for instance, contains the image of the cactus rose, which encapsulates the antinomy between desert and garden which pervades the whole film. Compare with this the famous scene in *My Darling Clementine*, after Wyatt Earp has gone to the barber (who civilises the unkempt), where the scent of honeysuckle is twice remarked upon: an artificial perfume, cultural rather than natural. This moment marks the turning-point in Wyatt Earp's transition from wandering cowboy, nomadic, savage, bent on personal revenge, unmarried, to married man, settled, civilised, the sheriff who administers the law.

Earp, in *My Darling Clementine*, is structurally the most simple of the three protagonists I have mentioned: his progress is an uncomplicated passage from nature to culture, from the wilderness left in the past to the garden anticipated in the future. Ethan Edwards, in *The Searchers*, is more complex. He must be defined not in terms of past versus future or wilderness versus garden compounded in himself, but in relation to two other protagonists: Scar, the Indian chief, and the family of homesteaders. Ethan Edwards, unlike Earp, remains a nomad throughout the film. At the start, he rides in from the desert to enter the log-house; at the end, with perfect symmetry, he leaves the house again to return to the desert, to vagrancy. In many respects, he is similar to Scar; he is a wanderer, a savage, outside the law: he scalps his enemy. But, like the homesteaders, of course, he is a European, the mortal foe of the Indian. Thus Edwards is ambiguous; the antinomies invade the personality of the protagonist himself. The oppositions tear Edwards in two; he is a tragic hero. His companion, Martin Pawley, however, is able to resolve the duality; for him, the period of nomadism is only an episode, which has meaning as the restitution of the family, a necessary link between his old home and his new home.

Ethan Edwards's wandering is, like that of many other Ford protagonists, a quest, a search. A number of Ford films are built round the theme of the quest for the Promised Land, an American re-enactment of the Biblical exodus, the journey through the desert to the land of milk and honey, the New Jerusalem. This theme is built on the combination of the two pairs: wilderness versus garden and nomad versus settler; the first pair precedes the second in time. Thus, in *Wagonmaster*, the Mormons cross the desert in search of their future home; in *How Green Was My Valley* and *The Informer*, the protagonists want to cross the Atlantic to a future home in the United States. But, during Ford's career, the situation of home is reversed in time. In *Cheyenne Autumn* the Indians journey in search of the home they once had in the past; in *The Quiet Man*, the American Sean Thornton returns to his ancestral home in Ireland. Ethan Edwards's journey is a kind of parody of this theme: his object is not constructive, to found a home, but destructive, to find and scalp Scar. Nevertheless, the weight of the film remains orientated to the future: Scar has burned down the home of the settlers, but it is replaced and we are confident that the homesteader's wife, Mrs Jorgensen, is right when she says: 'Some day this country's going to be a fine place to live.' The wilderness will, in the end, be turned into a garden.

The Man Who Shot Liberty Valance has many similarities with *The Searchers*. We may note three: the wilderness becomes a garden – this is made quite explicit, for Senator Stoddart has wrung from Washington the funds necessary to build a dam which will irrigate the desert and bring real roses, not cactus roses; Tom Doniphon shoots Liberty Valance as Ethan Edwards scalped Scar; a log-home is burned to the ground. But the differences are equally clear: the log-home is burned after the death of Liberty Valance; it is destroyed by Doniphon himself; it is his own home. The burning marks the realisation that he will never enter the Promised Land, that to him it means nothing; that he has doomed himself to be a creature of the past, insignificant in the world of the future. By shooting Liberty Valance he has destroyed the only world in which he himself can exist, the world of the gun rather than the book; it is as though Ethan Edwards had perceived that by scalping Scar, he was in reality committing suicide. It might be mentioned too that, in *The Man Who Shot Liberty Valance*, the woman who loves Doniphon marries Senator Stoddart. Doniphon when he destroys his log-house (his last words before doing so are 'Home, sweet home!') also destroys the possibility of marriage.

The themes of *The Man Who Shot Liberty Valance* can be expressed in another way. Ransom Stoddart represents rational–legal authority, Tom Doniphon represents charismatic authority. Doniphon abandons his charisma and cedes it, under what amount to false pretences, to Stoddart. In this way charismatic and rational–legal authority are combined in the person of Stoddart and stability thus assured. In *The Searchers* this transfer does not take place; the two kinds of authority remain separated. In *My Darling Clementine* they are combined naturally in Wyatt Earp, without any transfer being necessary. In many of Ford's late films – *The Quiet Man, Cheyenne Autumn, Donovan's Reef* – the accent is placed on traditional authority. The island of Ailakaowa, in *Donovan's Reef*, a kind of Valhalla for the homeless heroes of *The Man Who Shot Liberty Valance*, is actually a monarchy, though complete with the Boston girl, wooden church and saloon made familiar by *My Darling Clementine*. In fact, the character of Chihuahua, Doc Holliday's girl in *My Darling Clementine*, is split into two: Miss Lafleur and Lelani, the native princess. One represents the saloon entertainer, the other the non-American in opposition to the respectable Bostonians, Amelia Sarah Dedham and Clementine Carter. In a broad sense, this is a part of a general movement which can be detected in Ford's work to equate the Irish, Indians and Polynesians as traditional communities, set in the past, counterposed to the march forward to the American future, as it has turned out in reality, but assimilating the values of the American future as it was once dreamed.

It would be possible, I have no doubt, to elaborate on Ford's career, as defined by pairs of contrasts and similarities, in very great detail, though – as always with film criticism – the impossibility of quotation is a severe handicap. My own view is that Ford's work is much richer than that of Hawks and that this is revealed by a structural analysis; it is the richness of the shifting relations between antinomies in Ford's work that makes him a great artist, beyond being simply an undoubted *auteur*. Moreover, the *auteur* theory enables us to reveal a whole complex of meaning in films such as *Donovan's Reef*, which a recent filmography sums up as just 'a couple of Navy men who have retired to a South Sea island now spend most of their time raising hell'. Similarly, it throws a completely new light on a film like *Wings of Eagles*, which revolves, like *The Searchers*, round the vagrancy versus home antinomy, with the difference that when the hero does come home, after flying round the world, he trips over a child's toy, falls down the stairs and is completely paralysed so that he cannot move at all, not even his toes. This is the macabre *reductio ad absurdum* of the settled.

Perhaps it would be true to say that it is the lesser *auteurs* who can be defined, as Nowell-Smith put it, by a core of basic motifs which remain constant, without variation. The great directors must be defined in terms of shifting relations, in their singularity as well as their uniformity. Renoir once remarked that a director spends his whole life making one film; this film, which it is the task of the critic to construct, consists not only of the typical features of its variants, which are merely its redundancies, but of the principle of variation which governs it, that is its esoteric structure, which can only manifest itself or 'seep to the surface', in Lévi-Strauss's phrase, 'through the repetition process'. Thus Renoir's 'film' is in reality a 'kind of permutation group, the two variants placed at the far ends being in a symmetrical, though inverted, relationship to each other'. In practice, we will not find perfect symmetry, though as we have seen, in the case of Ford, some antinomies are completely reversed. Instead, there will be a kind of torsion within the permutation group, within the matrix, a kind of exploration of certain possibilities, in which some antinomies are foregrounded, discarded or even inverted, whereas others remain stable and constant. The important thing to stress, however, is that it is only the analysis of the whole *corpus* which permits the moment of synthesis when the critic returns to the individual film.

Of course, the director does not have full control over his work; this explains why the *auteur* theory involves a kind of decipherment, decryptment. A great many features of films analysed have to be dismissed as indecipherable because of 'noise' from the producer, the cameraman or even the actors. This concept of 'noise' needs further elaboration. It is often said that a film is the result of a multiplicity of factors, the sum total of a number of different contributions. The contribution of the director – the 'directorial factor', as it were – is only one of these, though perhaps the one which carries the most weight. I do not need to emphasise that this view is quite the contrary of the *auteur* theory and has nothing in common with it at all. What the *auteur* theory does is to take a group of films – the work of one director – and analyse their structure. Everything irrelevant to this, everything non-pertinent, is considered logically secondary, contingent, to be discarded. Of course, it is possible to approach films by studying some other feature; by an effort of critical ascesis we could see films, as Von Sternberg sometimes urged, as abstract light-show or as histrionic feasts. Sometimes these separate texts – those of the cameraman or the actors – may force themselves into prominence so that the film becomes an indecipherable palimpsest. This does not mean, of course, that it ceases to exist or to sway us or please us or intrigue us; it simply means that it is inaccessible to criticism. We can merely record our momentary and subjective impressions.

Myths, as Lévi-Strauss has pointed out, exist independently of style, the syntax of the sentence or musical sound, euphony or cacophony. The myth functions 'on an especially high level where meaning succeeds practically in *"taking off"* from the linguistic ground on which it keeps rolling'. *Mutatis mutandis*, the same is true of the *auteur* film. 'When a mythical schema is transmitted from one population to another, and there exist differences of language, social organization or way of life which make the myth difficult to communicate, it begins to become impoverished and confused.' The same kind of impoverishment and confusion takes place in the film studio, where difficulties of communication abound. But none the less the film can usually be discerned, even if it was a quickie made in a fortnight without the actors or the crews that the director might have liked, with an intrusive producer and even, perhaps, a censor's scissors cutting away vital sequences. It is as though a film is a musical composition rather than a musical performance, although, whereas a musical composition exists *a priori* (like a scenario), an *auteur* film is constructed *a posteriori*. Imagine the situation if the critic had to construct a musical composition from a number of fragmentary, distorted versions of it, all with improvised passages or passages missing. . . .

What the *auteur* theory demonstrates is that the director is not simply in command of a performance of a pre-existing text; he is not, or need not be, only a *metteur en scène*. Don Siegel was recently asked on television what he took from Hemingway's short story for his film, *The Killers*; Siegel replied that 'the only thing taken from it was the catalyst that a man has been killed by somebody and he did not try to run away'. The word Siegel chose – 'catalyst' – could not be bettered. Incidents and episodes in the original screenplay or novel can act as catalysts; they are the agents which are introduced into the mind (conscious or unconscious) of the *auteur* and react there with the motifs and themes characteristic of his work. The director does not subordinate himself to another author; his source is only a pretext, which provides catalysts, scenes which fuse with his own preoccupations to produce a radically new work. Thus the manifest process of performance, the treatment of a subject, conceals the latent production of a quite new text, the production of the director as an *auteur*.

Of course, it is possible to value performances as such, to agree with André Bazin that Olivier's *Henry V* was a great film, a great rendering, transposition into the cinema, of Shakespeare's original play. The great *metteurs en scène* should not be discounted simply because they are not *auteurs*: Vincente Minnelli, perhaps, or Stanley Donen. And, further than that, the same kind of process can take place that occurred in painting: the director can deliberately concentrate entirely on the stylistic and expressive dimensions of the cinema. He can say, as Josef Von Sternberg did about *Morocco*, that he purposely chose a fatuous story so that people would not be distracted from the play of light and shade in the photography. Some of Busby Berkeley's extraordinary sequences are equally detached from any kind of dependence on the screenplay: indeed, more often than not, some other director was entrusted with the job of putting the actors through the plot and dialogue. Moreover, there is no doubt that the greatest films will be not simply *auteur* films but marvellous expressively and stylistically as well: *Lola Montès, Shinheike Monogatari, La Règle du Jeu, La Signora di Tutti, Sansho Dayu, Le Carrosse d'Or*.

The *auteur* theory leaves us, as every theory does, with possibilities and questions. We need to develop much further a theory of performance, of the stylistic, of graded rather than coded modes of communication. We need to investigate and define, to construct critically the work of enormous numbers of directors who up to now have only been incompletely comprehended. We need to begin the task of comparing author with author. There are any number of specific problems which stand out: Donen's relationship to Kelly and Arthur Freed, Boetticher's films outside the Ranown cycle, Welles's relationship to Toland (and – perhaps more important – Wyler's), Sirk's films outside the Ross Hunter cycle, the exact identity of Walsh or Wellman, the decipherment of Anthony Mann. Moreover there is no reason why the *auteur* theory should not be applied to the English cinema, which is still utterly amorphous, unclassified, unperceived. We need not two or three books on Hitchcock and Ford, but many, many more. We need comparisons with authors in the other arts: Ford with Fenimore Cooper, for example, or Hawks with Faulkner. The task which the critics of *Cahiers du Cinéma* embarked on is still far from completed.

1972

At this point, it is necessary to say something about the *auteur* theory since this has often been seen as a way of introducing the idea of the creative personality into the Hollywood cinema. Indeed, it is true that many protagonists of the *auteur* theory do argue in this way. However, I do not hold this view and I think it is important to detach the *auteur* theory from any suspicion that it simply represents a 'cult of personality' or apotheosis of the director. To my mind, the *auteur* theory actually represents a radical break with the idea of an 'art' cinema, not the transplant of traditional ideas about 'art' into Hollywood. The 'art' cinema is rooted in the idea of creativity and the film as the expression of an individual vision. What the *auteur* theory argues is that any film, certainly a Hollywood film, is a network of different statements, crossing and contradicting each other, elaborated into a final 'coherent' version. Like a dream, the film the spectator sees is, so to speak, the 'film façade', the end-product of 'secondary revision', which hides and masks the process which remains latent in the film 'unconscious'. Sometimes this 'façade' is so worked over, so smoothed out, or else so clotted with disparate elements, that it is impossible to see beyond it, or rather to see anything in it except the characters, the dialogue, the plot, and so on. But in other cases, by a process of comparison with other films, it is possible to decipher, not a coherent message or world-view, but a structure which underlies the film and shapes it, gives it a certain pattern of energy cathexis. It is this structure which *auteur* analysis disengages from the film.

The structure is associated with a single director, an individual, not because he has played the role of artist, expressing himself or his own vision in the film, but because it is through the force of his preoccupations that an unconscious, unintended meaning can be decoded in the film, usually to the surprise of the individual involved. The film is not a communication, but an artefact which is unconsciously structured in a certain way. *Auteur* analysis does not consist of re-tracing a film to its origins, to its creative source. It consists of tracing a structure (not a message) within the work, which can then *post factum* be assigned to an individual, the director, on empirical grounds. It is wrong, in the name of a denial of the traditional idea of creative subjectivity, to deny any status to individuals at all. But Fuller or Hawks or Hitchcock, the directors, are quite separate from 'Fuller' or 'Hawks' or 'Hitchcock', the structures named after them, and should not be methodologically confused. There can be no doubt that the presence of a structure in the text can often be connected with the presence of a director on the set, but the situation in the cinema, where the director's primary task is often one of co-ordination and rationalisation, is very different from that in the other arts, where there is a much more direct relationship between artist and work. It is in this sense that it is possible to speak of a film *auteur* as an unconscious catalyst.

However, the structures discerned in the text are often attacked in another way. Robin Wood, for example, has argued that the '*auteur*' film is something like a Platonic Idea. It posits a 'real' film, of which the actual film is only a flawed transcript, while the archi-film itself exists only in the mind of the critic. This attack rests on a misunderstanding. The main point about the Platonic Idea is that it pre-dates the empirical reality, as an archetype. But the '*auteur*' film (or structure) is not an archi-film at all in this sense. It is an explanatory device which specifies partially how any individual film works. Some films it can say nothing or next-to-nothing about at all. *Auteur* theory cannot simply be applied indiscriminately. Nor does an *auteur* analysis exhaust what can be said about any single film. It does no more than provide one way of decoding a film, by specifying what its mechanics are at one level. There are other kinds of code which could be proposed, and whether they are of any value or not will have to be settled by reference to the text, to the films in question.

Underlying the anti-Platonic argument, however, there is often a hostility towards any kind of explanation which involves a degree of distancing from the 'lived experience' of watching the film itself. Yet clearly any kind of serious critical work – I would say scientific, though I know this drives some people into transports of rage – must involve a distance, a gap between the film and the criticism, the text and the meta-text. It is as though meteorologists were reproached for getting away from the 'lived experience' of walking in the rain or sun-bathing. Once again, we are back with the myth of transparency, the idea that the mark of a good film is that it conveys a rich meaning, an important truth, in a way which can be grasped immediately. If this is the case, then clearly all the critic has to do is to describe the experience of watching the film, reception of a signal, in such a way as to clear up any little confusions or enigmas which still remain. The most that the critic can do is to put the spectator on the right wavelength so that he can see for himself as clearly as the critic, who is already tuned in.

The *auteur* theory, as I conceive it, insists that the spectator has to work at reading the text. With some films this work is wasted, unproductive. But with others it is not. In these cases, in a certain sense, the film changes, it becomes another film — as far as experience of it is concerned. It is no longer possible to look at it 'with the same eyes'. There is no integral, genuine experience which the critic enjoys and which he tries to guide others towards. Above all, the critic's experience is not essentially grounded in or guaranteed by the essence of the film itself. The critic is not at the heart of the matter. The critic is someone who persists in learning to see the film differently and is able to specify the mechanisms which make this possible. This is not a question of 'reading in' or projecting the critic's own concerns in to the film; any reading of a film has to be justified by an explanation of how the film itself works to make this reading possible. Nor is it the single reading, the one which gives us the true meaning of the film; it is simply a reading which produces more meaning.

Again, it is necessary to insist that since there is no true, essential meaning there can therefore be no exhaustive criticism, which settles the interpretation of a film once and for all. Moreover, since the meaning is not contained integrally in any film, any decoding may not apply over the whole area of it. Traditional criticism is always seeking for the comprehensive code which will give the complete interpretation, covering every detail. This is a wild goose chase, in the cinema, above all, which is a collective form. Both Classical and Romantic aesthetics hold to the belief that every detail should have a meaning — Classical aesthetics because of its belief in a common, universal code; Romantic aesthetics because of its belief in an organic unity in which every detail reflects the essence of the whole. The *auteur* theory argues that any single decoding has to compete, certainly in the cinema, with noise from signals coded differently. Beyond that, it is an illusion to think of any work as complete in itself, an isolated unity whose intercourse with other films, other texts, is carefully controlled to avoid contamination. Different codes may run across the frontiers of texts at liberty, meet and conflict within them. This is how language itself is structured, and the failure of linguistics, for instance, to deal with the problem of semantics, is exemplified in the idea that to the unitary code of grammar (the syntactic component of language) there must correspond a unitary semantic code, which would give a correct semantic interpretation of any sentence. Thus the idea of 'grammaticality' is wrongly extended to include a quite false notion of 'semanticity'. In fact, no headway can be made in semantics until this myth is dispelled.

The *auteur* theory has important implications for the problem of evaluation. Orthodox aesthetics sees the problem in predictable terms. The 'good' work is one which has both a rich meaning and a correspondingly complex form, wedded together in a unity (Romantic) or isomorphic with each other (Classical). Thus the critic, to demonstrate the value of a work, must be able to identify the 'content', establish its truth, profundity, and so forth, and then demonstrate how it is expressed with minimum loss or leakage in the signals of the text itself, which are patterned in a way which gives coherence to the work as a whole. 'Truth' of content is not envisaged as being like scientific truth, but more like 'human' truth, a distillation of the world of human experience, particularly inter-personal experience. The world itself is an untidy place, full of loose ends, but the artefact can tie all these loose ends together and thus convey to us a meaningful truth, an insight, which enables us to go back to the real world with a re-ordered and re-cycled experience which will enable us to cope better, live more fully and so on. In this way art is given a humanistic function, which guarantees its value.

All this is overthrown when we begin to see loose ends in works of art, to refuse to acknowledge organic unity or integral content. Moreover, we have to revise our whole idea of criteria, of judgement. The notion behind criteria is that they are timeless and universal. They are then applied to a particular work and it is judged accordingly. This rigid view is varied to the extent that different criteria may apply to different kinds of works or that slightly different criteria may reflect different points of view or kinds of experience, though all are rooted in a common humanity. But almost all current theories of evaluation depend on identifying the work first and then confronting it with criteria. The work is then criticised for falling short on one score or another. It is blemished in some way. Evidently, if we reject the idea of an exhaustive interpretation, we have to reject this kind of evaluation. Instead, we should concentrate on the *productivity* of the work. This is what the 'modern movement' is about. The text, in Octavio Paz's words, is something like a machine for producing meaning. Moreover, its meaning is not neutral, something to be simply absorbed by the consumer.

The meaning of texts can be destructive – of the codes used in other texts, which may be the codes used by the spectator or the reader, who thus finds his own habitual codes threatened, the battle opening up in his own reading. In one sense, everybody knows this. We know that *Don Quixote* was destructive of the chivalric romance. We know that *Ulysses* or *Finnegans Wake* are destructive of the nineteenth-century novel. But it seems difficult to admit this destructiveness into court when judgements are to be made. We have to. To go to the cinema, to read books or to listen to music is to be a partisan. Evaluation cannot be impartial. We cannot divorce the problem of codes from the problem of criteria. We cannot be passive consumers of films who then stand back to make judgements from above the fray. Judgements are made in the process of looking or reading. There is a sense in which to reject something as unintelligible is to make a judgement. It is to refuse to use a code. This may be right or wrong, but it is not the same thing as decoding a work before applying criteria. A valuable work, a powerful work at least, is one which challenges codes, overthrows established ways of reading or looking, not simply to establish new ones, but to compel an unending dialogue, not at random but productively.

This brings us back to Godard. The hostility felt towards Godard expresses precisely a reluctance to embark on this dialogue, a satisfaction with the cinema as it is. When, in *East Wind*, Godard criticises not only the work of other film-makers, but his own practice in the first part of the same film, he is at the same time asking us to criticise our own practice of watching his film. At the same time as he interrogates himself, we are interrogating ourselves. The place of his interrogation is the film, the text. This is not simply a question of self-consciousness. It is consciousness, first and foremost, of a text and the effect of this text is like the effect of an active intruder. It is this intrusion which sets up conflict, which cannot be settled by one (rational) part of consciousness surveying another part of its own past and then bringing it back into line. It is only natural that people should want to drive the intruder out, though it is difficult to see how a critic could justify this.

Godard represents the second wave of impact of the 'modern movement' on the cinema – the movement represented elsewhere by Duchamp, Joyce, and so on. During the twenties, Russian film-makers like Eisenstein and Vertov make up the first wave. It remains to be seen whether Godard will have any greater short-term effect than they had. But it is necessary to take a stand on the question and to take most seriously directors like Godard himself,

Makavejev, Straub, Marker, Rocha, some underground directors. As I have suggested, they are not all doing the same thing, and it may be that a director like Makavejev is not really in the same camp as Godard at all. This remains to be seen. For this reason, I do not believe that development of *auteur* analyses of Hollywood films is any longer a first priority. This does not mean that the real advances of *auteur* criticism should not be defended and safeguarded. Nor does it mean that Hollywood should be dismissed out of hand as 'unwatchable'. Any theory of the cinema, any film-making must take Hollywood into account. It provides the dominant codes with which films are read and will continue to do so for the foreseeable future. No theorist, no *avant-garde* director can simply turn their back on Hollywood. It is only in confrontation with Hollywood that anything new can be produced. Moreover, while Hollywood is an implacable foe, it is not monolithic. It contains contradictions within itself, different kinds of conflicts and fissures. Hollywood cannot be smashed semiologically in a day, any more than it can economically. In this sense, there may be an aspect of 'adventurism' or Utopianism in Godard. There certainly is in a number of underground film-makers.

18 · Charles Eckert: 'The English cine-structuralists'

Film Comment, vol. 9, no. 3, May/June 1973

Eckert's essay came under fairly heavy attack. Not only is it subjected to a critical reading by Henderson in the essay which follows, but its point of attack is seriously blunted by Geoffrey Nowell-Smith's blithe confession that Lévi-Strauss's method was indeed abused, and that, within film theory, it was the better for it. In a letter to *Film Quarterly*, Eckert recanted: 'Perhaps I shouldn't bother to respond, but I fear that if I don't, my article will continue to stand in opposition to their criticisms; and I would like to rise in my pew and acknowledge this Rosemary's baby' ('Shall we deport Lévi-Strauss?' *Film Quarterly*, Spring 1974, p. 63). At the same time, what Eckert calls his 'fetishistic attachment to Lévi-Strauss's method' leads him to flush out '*auteur*-structuralism' from behind its scientific cover, forcing it to take seriously its structuralist name-dropping, questioning the easy identification of film with myth.

In the late 1960s, just when the *politique des auteurs* began to look shopworn and foxed at the edges, a group of English critics gave it a hard inspection, stripped it to its framework, and refurbished it with a bright new critical material called structuralism. In its new habit, and viewed from a distance, auteurism might pass as the creation of Claude Lévi-Strauss, or Roland Barthes, or Christian Metz – or even such un-structuralists as Freud and Jung – though certainly it bears little resemblance to Truffaut and Sarris. But seen close up it quickly proves to have few distinctive features, to pertain, in fact, to all its fathers – or to none of them – like a ragamuffin promiscuously conceived in the streets and dropped on the nearest doorstep.

The English critics in question are Geoffrey Nowell-Smith, Peter Wollen, Jim Kitses, Alan Lovell, and Ben Brewster. An assessment of their work would seem in order before discussing the future of the method they have developed. But before assessing it, we must define the major forms of criticism which are today called structuralist and with which their work is easily confused. Although structural insights have always underpinned conceptual thinking in philosophy and the sciences (Aristotle, Hegel, Marx, Jung), their wide modern vogue derives from the structural linguists. The basic insights of de Saussure, Jacobson, and others have been ramified into three forms of structural criticism of special interest to film critics: the study of linguistic structures in narrative, mainly by Todorov and Barthes; the semiological study of the 'language' of cinema by Metz, Pasolini, Eco and others (really an attempt to determine how cinema signifies and whether it can be analyzed like a language); and Lévi-Strauss's study of the underlying structures of thought and of the codes employed in the dialectical systems which operate in mythic thought.

The last form of structural study most closely approximates that used by the English critics, and is the one I shall concentrate upon. The study of narrative structure in film employing purely linguistic analogues does not look promising; in fact, Barthes has said as much and, more importantly, has professed to find little that is intellectually interesting in the cinema (certainly a comment on his method rather than the cinema). Metz, the most thorough of the semiologists, seems satisfied that the study of film as a language is limited in scope and in the applicability of the insights it achieves. But we have not as yet seen any *thorough* attempt to apply Lévi-Strauss's study of mythic thought and codes to film. I emphasize the word *thorough* because Lévi-Strauss's name and his method are frequently alluded to by the English auteur-structuralists.

Perhaps the best way to elaborate these complex matters is, first, to assess the work of this group of critics and to compare their methods with those formulated by Lévi-Strauss, and then to define both the achievements and the promise of auteur-structuralism, and of structuralism in general. From this point on, any reference I make to structuralism should be considered a reference to Lévi-Strauss's method. (For those interested in the recent *Cahiers* disparagement of structural study as opposed to a Marxist-ideological analysis I have appended a brief note.[1]) The first influential work – indeed, the generative locus for the auteur-structuralist criticism we are considering – was Geoffrey Nowell-Smith's *Luchino Visconti* (1967). This work influenced Peter Wollen, whose *Signs and Meaning in the Cinema* (1969) in turn gave rise to a series of articles concerned with structuralism in *Screen*. Nowell-Smith moved from the assertions that authorship is a necessary dimension for the study of films, and that 'the defining characteristics of an author's work are not those that are most readily apparent,' to his main thesis: 'the purpose of criticism becomes therefore to uncover behind the superficial contrasts of subject and treatment a structural hard core of basic and often recondite motifs.'[2] The principal drawbacks to this approach, he found, were a radical narrowing of the field of inquiry, the 'possibility of an author's work changing over time and of the structures being variable and not constant', and the temptation to neglect the myriad aspects of a film's production and aesthetic effect that a study of motifs does not impinge upon. In Visconti's films Nowell-Smith did not find a 'single and comprehensive structure,' largely because Visconti has developed with the years and has adopted many styles of filmmaking.

As a structuralist approach this is tentative and qualified indeed. And Nowell-Smith's entire study of Visconti brings under analysis many aspects of production, history, and stylistic influence that have no bearing upon structure, yet are considered indispensable for understanding the films. Yet the dominant impression one receives from this thoughtful, independent analysis is that structured themes are indeed at the heart of Visconti's enterprise and Nowell-Smith's critical interest. In the later discussion of Lévi-Strauss I will attempt to position and to assess Nowell-Smith's method. For the moment let us consider Peter Wollen's use of his conceptions.

Signs and Meaning in the Cinema must be, after *Film Form* and *What is Cinema?*, the most widely read work on film theory among present-day film students. Its faults are many, but they have proven to be seminal faults, spawning as many ideas and thoughtful reactions as the Bazin–Eisenstein controversies. The centrality of this work makes its views on auteur-structuralism especially important. Wollen begins with quotations from Nowell-Smith's study, then chooses the films of Howard Hawks as a test case for the 'structural approach.' He first dichotomizes Hawks's films into two categories: the adventure drama and the crazy comedy (he here follows Robin Wood, who also has structuralist affinities). These types 'express inverse views of the world, the positive and negative poles of the Hawksian vision.'[3] An awareness of 'differences and oppositions,' he continues, must be cultivated along with the awareness of 'resemblances and repetitions' usually found in thematic or motif-seeking criticism. He then cites main sets of antinomies in Hawks's work and notes how they break down into lesser sets – any of which may overlap or be 'foregrounded in different movies.'

But Wollen's most intensive criticism is saved for John Ford, in whose work he finds the 'master antinomy' of wilderness and garden (the terms are derived by Wollen from Henry Nash Smith's *The Virgin Land*). The entire analysis of Ford reaches its principal conclusion in this statement: 'Ford's work is much richer than that of Hawks and . . . this is revealed by a structural analysis; it is the richness of the shifting relations between antinomies in Ford's work that makes him a great artist, beyond being simply an undoubted auteur'. This statement captures the essence of Wollen's species of structuralism, just as the search for a 'hard core of basic and often recondite motifs' defines Nowell-Smith's.

Both of these definitions were harmonious with the intentions of a work appearing in the same year as Wollen's – Jim Kitses's *Horizons West*. Kitses began, 'But I should make clear what I mean by auteur theory. In my view the term describes a basic principle and a method: the idea of personal authorship in the cinema and – of key importance – the concomitant responsibility to honour all of a director's works by a systematic examination in order to trace characteristic themes, structures and formal qualities.'[4] Kitses also draws upon Smith's *The Virgin Land* for the insight that the image of the West has a dialectical form: 'Thus central to the form we have a philosophical dialectic, an ambiguous cluster of meanings and attitudes that provide the traditional thematic structure of the genre.' Kitses provides a chart listing the principal antinomies, and notes that polar terms may be transposed in the course of an auteur's development. His study of individual auteurs is very subtle, yet, as I will show later, not as close in spirit to Lévi-Strauss as Wollen's.

The works of Nowell-Smith, Wollen and Kitses, all produced in the late Sixties, might have represented a mere eddy in the current of auteur criticism had their methods and their cause not been taken up by other English critics. In the March/April 1969 issue of *Screen* Alan Lovell published a strongly dissenting criticism of the work of Robin Wood, finding it deficient in analytic method and concerned with gaining assent rather than giving proof as it measured films and directors against an established system of beliefs and values. As an antidote, Lovell proposed an auteur-structuralist method strongly resembling those already discussed: 'any director creates his films on the basis of a central structure and . . . all of his films can be seen as variations or developments of it.'[5] To illustrate his method he analyzed a pattern found in Arthur Penn's work consisting of a polarity between social groups and heroes, and a father-figure who mediates between the two (both the groups and heroes are prone to violence; the fathers mediate the violent camps much as the Prince does in *Romeo and Juliet*). Lovell's article began a chain-reaction of response including an attack on Lovell's structuralism by Robin Wood, a reply by Lovell, an independent defense of Wood by John C. Murray, and a well-informed discussion of the structural contributions of Barthes, Metz and others by Ben Brewster.[6]

Although much of the discussion is contentious, when one pares away the *ad hominem* forensics and the quite pointless debates over the 'value' of totally divergent critical methods, one finds both the intentions and the limitations of auteur-structuralist criticism clarified. Both Wood and Murray note that Kitses, Wollen, and Lovell are making judgements of the worth of directors on such bases as the clarity of the antinomic structures or the complexity of their interrelations (Wollen on Ford; Lovell on Penn). Structuralism, Wood and Murray contend, is not used as a mere analytic tool, but as a measure of a director's maturity or artistic stature. And they find its discoveries – the pairs of opposites, the patterns of interchange – banal, of no great significance, mere critical jargon that cannot help us distinguish between a great film and a highly polarized and structured cartoon by Tex Avery or Chuck Jones (Murray).

There is so much oversimplification, obtuseness, and downright unfairness running through the whole debate that one must resist the temptation to leap in. But what one principally feels is the need for a re-truing of terms, for a fresh look at the notion of structuralism, and at the suitability of a structural study of a director's body of work – or of films in general. We must begin with the writings of the doyen of structuralism, Claude Lévi-Strauss. There are two indispensable essays, both of them attempts to formulate and delimit the uses of structuralism. 'The Structural Study of Myth' (1958),[7] and the 'Overture' to *The Raw and the Cooked* (1964).[8] The essays are so broad-ranging, especially the latter, that we would do best to define our interests before approaching them. We might express these interests as a series of questions directly bearing upon film: Has a truly Lévi-Straussian study of a director been made? In what would it consist? Should structural study be limited to directors, or has it promise for genres of film, the output of individual studios, or more specialized aspects of films such as visuals and sound tracks? Or is film too syncretic and complex an art form to yield anything of value to such an approach?

We should begin with a definition of Lévi-Strauss's object (myth) and the analytic method he devised to comprehend it. Lévi-Strauss's object is relatively simple and uniform: a body of myth (usually short narratives) collected by ethnographers and anthropologists in a given region of the world. It is immaterial whether one has all the available versions of a myth or is able to assess the 'reliability' of one's sources: myths are interminable and have no definitive or 'ur' form. All versions of a given myth constitute the myth; and one can begin the task of analysis with any of the versions. The myths are analyzed sequentially, each 'gross unit' of the analysis consisting of a term and a relation which are one half of an antinomic pair: Oedipus kills his father – the Sphinx's death gives life to Thebes. A given term may enter into many relations: the sun, for instance, may figure in the first relation in the pairs. It gives light – darkens; burns – freezes; causes growth – causes death. Or it may be ambivalent and represent both relations: causes drought – gives new life. Its value at any moment in a myth must, therefore, be determined through careful assessment of its function in (usually) a number of polarized relations. It is the next analytic step, however, that is most unique in Lévi-Strauss's method: 'The true constituent units of a myth are not the isolated relations but *bundles of such relations*, and it is only as bundles that these relations can be put to use and combined so as to produce a meaning.'[9] Lévi-Strauss's brilliance resides in his ability to discern central 'bundles' of relations in myths and to suggest *why* they are meaningful – a task that requires more intelligence and discernment than analytic rigor. One cannot, without extended quotation from Lévi-Strauss's work, show how the analysis proceeds. I can only refer the reader to specific passages and to commentaries on the method by interpreters.[10] The entire task is additionally complicated by the possibilities for permutation among the relations one is analyzing: 'two opposite terms with no intermediary always tend to be replaced by two equivalent terms which admit of a third one as mediator; then one of the polar terms and the mediator becomes replaced by a new triad, and so on.'[11] These 'transformations' of the myth usually express the same opposition(s) by working through a variety of similarly structured taxonomies – in primitive societies, taxonomies of plants, animals, stones, heavenly bodies, and so forth. The opposition sun–moon may carry the same meaning as the opposition eagle–bear, even though the terms are drawn from separate taxonomies.

Again and again, Lévi-Strauss emphasizes the importance of *polarized* thought ('myth works from an awareness of oppositions to their progressive mediation') and the *dynamic, fluctuating nature* of this thought. Polarization is basic to all processes of thought and language, as a form of clarification and ordering of the world about us; dynamism reflects both the ongoing process of thought and – this is *most* crucial – the essential nature of myth: an obsessive, repetitive conceptualizing of a dilemma or contradiction, the meaning of which is hidden from the narrator who rather compulsively tells and retells versions of the myth.

Structural study consists, then, in breaking down many versions of a myth into significant elements, arranging these in the polarized patterns natural to myth, and noting clusters of relations. One discovers the core of the myth only upon an examination of all of the individual analyses. What the myth is 'about' usually proves to be something quite different from its surface meaning. If its content were not hidden from the narrators, they would have no reason to obsessively reshape it, retell it, and accord it such significance in their lives. Once a myth has been penetrated and understood, it dies; it no longer functions as an expression of a dilemma or contradiction. The nonliving mythologies of the world are fossilized dynamic thought which has been discarded because it was resolved, outgrown, or made irrelevant by events or cultural evolution. The analyst begins his task on the same footing with the creator of myth – in a condition of ignorance. If he is assiduous he can read the riddle at the center of the myth and see how all of its versions are related.

This is all general and abstruse and can only be clarified through specific applications to film. I will take up the most provocative of Lévi-Strauss's insights in the general order of their importance and breadth of application. We will then be in a position to assess the achievements of current auteur-structural studies and to suggest further uses that might be made of the structural approach.

Before films can be equated with myths they must fulfil one fundamental condition: they must originate in a community possessed of a 'common conception of the world.' Only in such a community can the sort of dialectical system typical of myth be coherent. Given this criterion, myth may be 'any manifestation of the mental or social activities of the communities under consideration.'[12] Let us measure film against this primary criterion. Film history is usually written as an analysis of communal blocks of art, defined as national schools or styles (German expressionism, Italian neo-realism), as international movements (Surrealism, the New Wave) or as studio-centered styles (Biograph, Ufa, Warner Brothers). Such tidy bins always do violence to the dynamic, creative interplay of art history, but they are probably no less arbitrary than the 'communities' that Lévi-Strauss defines for study. And they do reflect the fact that films are generally produced as communal efforts. Hollywood at its zenith resembled a complex social structure not unlike the family-clan-village structures that Lévi-Strauss works with. Within the larger community called Hollywood there existed the distinctive cultures of Warners, MGM, Paramount, Republic, and others, and within these, units made up of given production teams or devoted to creating certain genres of film (topical, comedy, epic, serial).

Whether Warner Brothers or Ufa or the Russian experimentalists were possessed of 'a common conception of the world' is a matter for research and study, not for arbitrary pronouncement. But if one can draw upon the kind of intuitive judgment built up from seeing films, this criterion seems likely to be met. One would have to allow for the syncretic forces that affect all communities in the modern world (Lang travels to Hollywood, Kubrick to England), but the gestalt ambiance of a community is more frequently reflected in films than not. Before leaving this topic it is worth underlining Lévi-Strauss's statement that a myth may be 'any manifestation' of the social or mental activities of a community. By this token, the publicity and life-style of a film community (say Hollywood in the Twenties) would qualify as versions of its myth or myths.

A second major criterion that films would have to answer in order to qualify as bona fide myths is that they must arise out of a 'dialectical system of contrasts and correlations' that is logical, consistent, and demonstrably typical of the community under study. Such systems in the myths Lévi-Strauss analyzes are usually zoological, botanical, or made up of tangible qualities (the raw and the cooked). Lévi-Strauss's major contribution to myth may be the insight that abstract ideas can be conveyed through the manipulation of such 'empirical categories.' Modern societies no longer employ taxonomic schemes made up of plants and animals, but we do employ comparable schemes of many sorts. Films are especially rich in schemes constructed of physical objects (clothing, parts of the body, furnishings, topography) or of qualities (beauty–ugliness, darkness–light). These systems function in myths as codes: one must discover, frequently through interview or research, the meaning or significance accorded a land tortoise by a primitive community before one can 'read' a myth in which it appears; similarly one must discover the significance accorded a monocle in Hollywood in the late Twenties or a black shirt in the early Thirties to 'read' the appropriate character traits of Von Stroheim or Tim McCoy. Certainly films, with their almost compulsive and fetishistic attachment to physical objects, reveal many codified schemes upon even casual analysis. And such schemes can, with discernment, be found in lighting, camera, editing, and acting styles, as well as musical scores (the codification of music begins early with the Kinotheks).

Whether these codes are part of a careful, logical system can only be established through research. My own preliminary attempts at analysis suggest that they are – but that they are affected by many more contingencies than appear in Lévi-Strauss's myths. With myths one must contend with the abilities of narrators, lapses of memory, all sorts of disruptive cultural forces (although Lévi-Strauss virtually negates all of these by treating individual myths as 'found objects'); whereas with films one must consider physical as well as artistic and cultural forces – that is, accidents that affect the achievement of the screen image (casting, change of script, censorship, loss of a shot, and so forth) and of the conceptual schemes of the writer and/or director. Perhaps these problems are no more inhibiting for structuralism than for any form of film criticism; but we cannot treat films as found objects, because we know too much about how they are made.

The study of codes central to periods of film, studios, genres, even individual directors could also illuminate the logical systems of directors who react against traditional codified systems or work subversively within them (Truffaut, Godard, Buñuel, Sirk). I am not implying something as simple as a study of how Hollywood thugs wear hats in order to footnote the image of the hired killers in *Shoot the Piano Player* (we don't need analysis of what is already an implicit analysis), but rather a study that would help us comprehend the ambiguous tensions Truffaut maintains between traditional and novel images, gestures, or musical effects – those details of the film which may lead us to the central myth that Truffaut expresses. If the meaning of a myth is hidden from its creator, Truffaut's film is neither an homage to nor a satire on Hollywood (even if – or especially if – these definitions satisfy Truffaut). The myth it embodies will be discovered through analysis of the 'bundle of relations' that constitute the entire film, and comparison with analyses of other French New Wave films.

Before leaving the subject of the codes that constitute the 'dialectical system of contrasts and correlations' in films, we should note one important distinction between films and the narratives that Lévi-Strauss analyzes. To put the distinction aphoristically: anyone in a community can tell a myth, but only MGM can make a movie. The codes found in films are closely linked to the creative processes behind the film: they are narrative, visual, and aural codes of great variety originating often in individual minds, often evolved as part of a studio or production team style, or even derived from the larger community that surrounds the filmmakers (documentary, locale shooting, exposé). Even when evolved within a film community, they are related to the codes of the larger community of filmgoers – or else audiences would find the films incomprehensible. The most accessible film codes, I would suggest, are those intrinsic in the script, in the visuals, and in the music, especially when it is through-composed or thoroughly cut to the film (as were the best Kinothek scores for silent films). Films seem to meet the criteria discussed so far, although the analyst's task is undeniably complex.

The next requirement, that the meaning of a myth be hidden from its narrator, seems less problematical. Perhaps no other major art form is so characteristically opaque to its creators and consumers as is the cinema. The dominant metaphor for the film experience from Méliès to Fellini has been a 'dream,' and like dreams, films perform magical psychic functions. They are also endlessly repetitive and compulsively consumed ('they're showing four Clint Eastwoods at the Drive-In'). This dreamlike repetitiveness points unerringly to their mythic character. In Lévi-Strauss's terms, a myth is the embodiment of a dilemma or contradiction; and its repetitiveness, which grows out of its compulsive nature, functions to make its structure apparent. Or to make the same point in applied terms, the hero who is central to the detective action film is an embodied dilemma: if this dilemma were resolved by filmmakers and viewers the hero would cease to attract them. That is, I believe, an extremely seminal insight. It can be applied to individual character types, to entire plots, to genres of film, to series or 'runs' (Andy Hardy, motorcycle films) and so forth. The dioscuric union of filmmakers and their audience produces a strange Janus of art – myths made by mythmakers that are only certified as true or untrue after they have been created. Perhaps the best index to authentically mythic films, then, is the yearly box-office ratings.

Two more of Lévi-Strauss's stipulations deserve brief consideration. The first is that every myth is only a limited application of the pattern that emerges as the analysis of a body of myths proceeds. This means, quite simply, that many films must be analyzed before a valid structure can be discerned. Presumably, one must analyze a substantial quantity of De Mille epics or Republic Westerns before substantive discoveries will be made. Or if one is focusing upon a given studio or era, one would have to consider films of many genres.

The second stipulation brings us to the end of this discussion and can serve as a bridge back to the subject of auteur-structuralism. It is that figures in myths have meanings only in relation to other figures. They cannot be assigned set meanings, as is typically done in an archetypal or Freudian analysis, nor should they be expected to maintain the same meaning in so dynamic a thought-form as myth. Again we can illustrate the argument better than we can paraphrase it. Jane Darwell is Jung's archetype of the 'Good Mother' as certainly as Joan Collins is an 'Evil Anima.' The Jungian system also allows for mixed archetypes, but one way or another the meaning tends to get fixed. For a structuralist, Jane Darwell's 'meaning' in, say, *The Grapes of Wrath* would be expressed as a series of relations – to other characters, to ideas if she functions allegorically, or expressed in terms of contrasting camera treatments, musical leit motifs, or mimetic styles. The search is not for what she resembles or for what she symbolizes, but rather for the meaning of the myth in which she is one figure entering into many relations.

The issue of how figures are to be interpreted takes us to the heart of the whole enterprise I have characterized as auteur-structuralism. Each of the authors mentioned earlier employs a unique critical method, although each is nominally a structuralist. Which of them most closely approximates the method elaborated by Lévi-Strauss? Nowell-Smith makes a careful analysis of relationships in individual films, and is especially attentive to the shifting nature of these relationships and to dialectical progressions. But his initial premise is that Visconti developed too much as an artist to make a comparative study of his films possible. He prefers to 'consider the film singly, attempting in the analysis of each to bring out its relationship, hidden or overt, to the rest of Visconti's work.' The absence of a thoroughly comparative method not only qualifies his structuralism, it raises the profound issue of whether or not the body of films produced by an individual director over a period of years can qualify as a 'set' of myths. Let us return to this question at the end of the discussion.

Kitses does analyze the canon of a director's works as a single body of myth, but his individual figures are defined in archetypal and iconic terms; their meanings are traditional rather than dependent upon relationships within each film. Only his emphasis upon the dynamic interaction of the figures and their tendency to form antinomic pairs resembles Lévi-Strauss's analysis. Lovell's method is extremely close to Kitses, employing a mixture of archetypal and structural insights.

Of all the critics, Peter Wollen shows the closest familiarity with Lévi-Strauss's writings. His analysis of Hawks and Ford, though only intended to be exploratory and suggestive, is less attuned to archetypes, is thoroughly directed at 'bundles of relations' and is founded on the premise that 'it is only the analysis of the whole *corpus* which permits the moment of synthesis when the critic returns to the individual film'.

It would seem then, that there are two *bêtes noires* roaming the domain of the current auteur-structuralists: the questions of how figures are to be interpreted, and of the degree to which an auteur's works possess the same unity to a communal body of myth. The laying of the first beast was Lévi-Strauss's primary task in 'The Structural Study of Myth': 'If there is a meaning to be found in mythology, it cannot reside in the isolated elements which enter into the composition of a myth, but only in the way those elements are combined'. So much, it appears, for father-figures, traditional icons, and Henry Nash Smith's wilderness and garden. The acceptance of such set meanings may not only blind us to important shifts of relationship, it may also commit us to the surface meaning of the myth – to the narrator's rationalized account of what his story is about, or the critic's overlay of fossilized myth upon a living structure. Of course, traditional meanings may well emerge from the process of analysis; but the point is that they will be *discovered* rather than established *a priori*.

The question of the degree of unity in an auteur's work is less easily resolved, although two reflections come to mind: Renoir's opinion that a director spends his life making one film; and Elizabeth Sewell's contention that every artist creates the myth by which he is to be interpreted. Both buttress the main premise that is implicit in the auteur theory: that a director's body of work possesses unity. The alternative notion, that an artist evolves through disparate stages of thought and technique, is a more nineteenth-century conception, attuned to the belief in purposive evolution. The modern study of myth has attacked or militated against evolutionary schemes and has substituted synchronic studies of motifs, types, and forms. The reaction has undoubtedly been extreme. We must use judgment in deciding to what degree a director conforms to Renoir's definition and invites a mythic analysis; and we must anticipate that an apparent evolution in style and theme may only mask what is recurrent in a body of work.

The structuralist method, considered in all of its potential applications, will probably be productive in proportion to the discretion and intelligence with which it is applied. Its promise, however, is undeniable: the cinema, after sensationalist and arty beginnings, took over the communal myth-making functions of a variety of dramatic, literary and oral forms – and all but supplanted them.

And it came to serve as a vehicle for more private mythologies, like those of Cocteau, Buñuel, and Bergman. What is more problematical is the pursuing of studies that depend upon long-term access to or possession of large numbers of films. My own experience is that only third, fourth and fifth viewings of films bring the intimate familiarity required for structural analysis. But for those who can surmount this obstacle, there remains much to be done beyond what current auteur-structuralism has suggested.

Notes

1 *Screen* has recently published a translation of *Cahiers'* very important collective analysis of Ford's *Young Mr Lincoln*. In the introductory remarks *Cahiers* characterizes structural analysis as the 'dissection of an object conceived of as a closed structure, the cataloguing of progressively smaller and more "discreet" units,' ignoring their use by the filmmaker and 'the dynamic of the inscription' (*Screen*, 13, no. 3, p. 6). This reflects early attitudes of Althusser, *Cahiers'* principal mentor, toward all forms of intellectual effort conceived within bourgeois ideologies which show little or no consciousness of their own premises and restrictions. But in his 1968 essay, 'Lenin and Philosophy,' Althusser acknowledged that philosophy in the future has a true object – 'pure thought,' and then added: 'what else is Lévi-Strauss up to today, on his own admission, and by appeal to Engels' authority? He, too, is studying the laws, let us say the structures *of thought*' (*Lenin and Philosophy and Other Essays*, trans. Ben Brewster, London, New Left Books, 1971, p. 59). I interpret this as a validation of Lévi-Strauss's objectives and his method: a Marxist reading of myth must also comprehend the structures that the mind creates and imposes upon all art; it will simply see more and different structures (see Althusser's reading of the temporal structures of Bertolazzi and Brecht in *For Marx*).
2 G. Nowell-Smith, *Luchino Visconti* (1967), New York, Doubleday, 1968, p. 10. [See above, p. 137]
3 P. Wollen, *Signs and Meaning in the Cinema*, Indiana University Press, 1969, p. 81.
4 J. Kitses, *Horizons West* (1969), Indiana University Press, 1970, p. 7.
5 A. Lovell, 'Robin Wood – a dissenting view,' *Screen*, 10, no. 2, March/April 1969, pp. 47–8.
6 Robin Wood, 'Ghostly paradigm and H.C.F.: an answer to Alan Lovell,' *Screen*, 10, no. 3, May/June 1969, pp. 35–47; Alan Lovell, 'The common pursuit of true judgement,' *Screen*, 11, no. 4/5, August/September, 1970, pp. 76–88; John C. Murray, 'Robin Wood and the structural critics,' *Screen* 12, no. 3, Summer 1971, pp. 101–10; Ben Brewster, 'Structuralism in film criticism,' *Screen*, 12, no. 1, Spring, 1971, pp. 49–58.
7 'The structural study of myth', in *Structural Anthropology*, trans.

Claire Jacobson and Brook Schoepf (1958), New York, Doubleday, 1963. See extract above.

8 'Overture' to *The Raw and the Cooked*, trans. John and Doreen Weightman (1964), New York, Harper and Row, 1970, pp. 1–32.

9 'Structural study,' p. 207.

10 See Lévi-Strauss's analysis of the Oedipus and 'Zuni emergence' myths in 'Structural study,' and his article 'Le Triangle culinaire,' *L'Arc*, no. 26, Aix-en-Provence, 1965, pp. 19–29. The latter serves as an introduction to the analysis employed throughout the three published volumes of *Mythologiques*. The best interpretation is that of Edmund Leach, *Claude Lévi-Strauss*, New York, Viking Press, 1970.

11 'Structural study,' p. 221.

12 'Overture,' p. 8.

19 · Brian Henderson: 'Critique of cine-structuralism' (part I)

Film Quarterly, vol. 27, no. 1, Fall 1973

Brian Henderson's critique appeared in two parts, only the first of which, addressing itself to the essays by Nowell-Smith, Wollen and Eckert, is included here. The second part is concerned with the 'post-*auteurism*' of *Cahiers*' reading of *Young Mr Lincoln*, and with Ben Brewster's attempt ('Notes on the text "John Ford's *Young Mr Lincoln*" ' *Screen*, vol. 14, no. 3, Autumn 1973) to re-articulate the problem of the author with Metz's concept of codes and sub-codes. The movement described in Henderson's critique is a movement away from the retention of 'the subject as producer of unique or distinctive meanings', towards the theory of the subject called for in Part Three below by Stephen Heath, and associated by Henderson with the work of Derrida, Kristeva and Lacan.

Several recent texts put the question of structuralist study of cinema back on the agenda: Charles W. Eckert's *Film Comment* article, 'The English Cine-Structuralists'; the new edition of Peter Wollen's *Signs and Meaning in the Cinema*, which reconsiders aspects of the 1969 original; and the *Screen* translation of the *Cahiers du Cinéma* collective text on *Young Mr Lincoln*.[1] The latter is explicitly a critique of structuralism and itself a post-structuralist work. It appears in English with an afterword by Peter Wollen, which provides the occasion for a specific confrontation. These critical texts are more readily comparable in that they all deal, directly or indirectly, with a common object, the films of John Ford. According to *Tel Quel*, 'the exact value of a text lies in its integration and destruction of other texts.'[2] The texts we are concerned with have value by this test. Wollen's book destroyed and/or integrated in whole or part many previous film-critical texts. Eckert partially destroys the auteur-structuralist texts, even as he seeks to valorize them. The *Young Mr Lincoln* text lays waste four entire areas of film study. The present text seeks to integrate and destroy these texts in turn; more precisely, it inaugurates this task. This is its only praise, for most film-critical texts are not worth destroying and are certainly not to be integrated.[3]

Eckert's article concerns those English critics who refurbished the *politique des auteurs* with the critical apparatus of structuralism in the late sixties: Geoffrey Nowell-Smith, Peter Wollen, Jim Kitses, Alan Lovell, and Ben Brewster. He distinguishes three forms of structural criticism of special interest to film critics: (1) the study of linguistic structures in narrative (Todorov and Barthes); (2) the semiological study of the language of cinema (Metz, Pasolini, Eco), which attempts to determine how cinema signifies and whether it can be analyzed like a language; and (3) Lévi-Strauss's study of the underlying structures of thought and of the codes employed in the dialectical systems which operate in mythic thought. The last form of structural study most closely approximates that used by the auteur-structuralists and is the one Eckert concentrates on. (He finds the other two studies 'unpromising' and 'limited in scope and in the applicability of the insights they achieve.') Eckert proposes to assess the work of these critics by comparing their methods with those formulated by Lévi-Strauss and then to define the achievements and the promise of auteur-structuralism and of structuralism in general.

The first influental work in English cine-structuralism was Nowell-Smith's *Luchino Visconti* (1967).[4] The purpose of criticism, according to it, is to uncover behind the superficial contrasts of subject and treatment in a director's work a structural hard core of basic and often recondite motifs. The drawbacks to this approach, noted by Nowell-Smith, were the possibility of variable structures due to changes in an author's work over time and the temptation to neglect the myriad aspects of a film's production and aesthetic effect that a study of motifs does not impinge upon. Indeed in his own study, Nowell-Smith does not find a simple and comprehensive Visconti structure because the latter developed over the years and adopted many styles of film-making. His book also studies many aspects of production, history, and stylistic influence that have no bearing upon structure. Nevertheless, Eckert's dominant impression of the book is that structural themes are indeed at the core of Visconti's enterprise and of Nowell-Smith's critical interest.

Wollen's *Signs and Meaning* quotes Nowell-Smith's theory of criticism then takes up the films of Howard Hawks as a test case for the structural approach. He dichotomizes Hawks's films into two categories, the adventure drama and the crazy comedy. These types express inverse views of the world, the positive and negative poles of the Hawksian vision. Wollen cautions that an awareness of differences and oppositions must be cultivated along with the awareness of resemblances and repetitions usually found in thematic or motif-seeking criticism. He then cites the main sets of antinomies in Hawks's work and notes how they break down into lesser sets, any of which may overlap or be foregrounded in different movies. But Wollen's 'most intensive criticism' is saved for John Ford, in whose work he finds the master antinomy of wilderness and garden (terms derived from Henry Nash Smith). His analysis of Ford reaches its principal conclusion in this statement: 'Ford's work is much richer than that of Hawks and . . . this is revealed by a structural analysis; it is the richness of the shifting relations between antinomies in Ford's work that makes him a great artist, beyond being simply an undoubted auteur.' For Eckert, this statement captures the essence of Wollen's species of structuralism, just as the search for a hard core of basic and recondite motifs defines Nowell-Smith's.

Both definitions were harmonious with the intentions of Jim Kitses's *Horizons West*.[5] To him, the auteur theory meant the idea of personal authorship in cinema and the concomitant critical responsibility to systematically examine all of a director's work, in order to trace characteristic themes, structures, and formal qualities. Kitses also takes from Henry Nash Smith the insight that the image of the West has a dialectical form. Central to the form of the Western is a philosophical dialectic, an ambiguous cluster of meanings and attitudes that provide the traditional thematic structure of the genre. Kitses lists the principal antinomies involved and notes that polar terms may be transposed in the course of an auteur's development. (These three books led to articles by other English critics, some favorable to structuralism (Alan Lovell and Ben Brewster), some unfavorable (Robin Wood).)

Following his review of these texts, Eckert does not proceed immediately to the promised evaluation of the auteur-structuralists. Instead he returns to Lévi-Strauss, nominally to derive the principles with which to conduct this assessment. 'I will take up the most provocative of Lévi-Strauss's insights in the general order of their importance and breadth of application.' The oddity of this long section is that Eckert uses only two of the many points it develops in his subsequent return to the auteur-structuralists. These are: that every myth is only a limited application of the pattern that emerges as the analysis of a body of myths proceeds, hence many myths must be analyzed before a valid structure can be discerned; and that figures in myths have meanings only in relation to other figures in that myth; they cannot be assigned set meanings.

Nowell-Smith makes a careful analysis of relationships in individual films and is especially attentive to the shifting nature of these relationships and to dialectical progressions, but his initial premise is that Visconti developed too much as an artist to make a comparative study of his films possible. Hence he considers each film singly, attempting to bring out its relationship, hidden or overt, to the rest of Visconti's work. The absence of a thoroughly comparative method not only qualifies Nowell-Smith's structuralism, it raises the issue whether or not the body of films produced by a director can qualify as a set of myths. Kitses does analyze a director's work as a single body of myth, but his individual figures are defined in archetypal and iconic terms; their meanings are traditional rather than dependent upon relationships within each film. Only his emphasis on the dynamic interaction of the figures and their tendency to form antinomic pairs resembles Lévi-Strauss's analysis. (Lovell's method is very close to Kitses's, employing a mixture of archetypal and structural insights.) Peter Wollen shows the closest familiarity with Lévi-Strauss's writings. His analysis of Hawks and Ford, though only intended to be exploratory and suggestive, (1) is less attuned to archetypes and is thoroughly directed at bundles of relations, and (2) is founded on the premise that it is only the analysis of the whole corpus which permits the moment of synthesis when the critic returns to the individual film.

Eckert enlarges upon the two principles before concluding. Lévi-Strauss's 'The Structural Study of Myth' settled that meaning in mythology cannot be found in the isolated elements which enter into the composition of the myth, but only in the way those elements are combined. So much (Eckert adds) for father figures, traditional icons, and wilderness and garden. Accepting such set meanings may blind us to important shifts of relationship and commit us to the surface meaning of the myth. Traditional meanings may well emerge from the process of analysis, but the point is that they will be discovered rather than established *a priori*. The question of the degree of unity in an auteur's work is less easily resolved. The main premise implicit in the auteur theory is that a director's body of work possesses unity. The alternative notion, that an artist evolves through stages of thought and technique, is a nineteenth-century conception, attuned to purposive evolution. The modern study of myth has attacked evolutionary schemes in favor of synchronic studies of motifs, types, and forms. We must use judgment in deciding to what degree a director conforms to unity and invites a mythic analysis; and we must anticipate that an apparent evolution in style and theme may only mask what is recurrent in a body of work. Eckert concludes overall that the structural method will probably be productive in proportion to the discretion and intelligence with which it is applied. Its promise, however, is undeniable. 'There remains much to be done beyond what current auteur-structuralism has suggested.'

Why does Eckert return to basic Lévi-Strauss between his review and his evaluation of auteur-structuralism, when so much of what he develops seems non-operative in relation to that project? Why, in defending auteur-structuralism, does Eckert begin again from zero by asking whether 'film can be equated with myths' and questioning 'the suitability of a structural study of a director's body of work – or of films in general'? Either the auteur-structuralists have covered this ground before or they haven't. If they have, then Eckert's reconsideration is either repetitious or it is a critique of their foundational work, apparently a covert critique, as this section makes no reference to their texts. If they have not covered this ground, then Eckert's defense of the auteur-structuralists uncovers an absence vastly more important than the virtues he finds in their work – their failure to found their criticism theoretically, the absence of an auteur-structuralist epistemology. In activating these texts, Eckert has activated the scandal of their lack of foundation. Attempting to integrate them, they have come apart in his hands. The middle section of his article is then a kind of glue or bricolage which attempts to put them back together.

Eckert's text provides a cue, in the form of a speech against itself, which turns us back to the original texts. Neither Kitses nor Nowell-Smith discusses Lévi-Strauss. Wollen does, to be sure, but in ways which avoid rather than confront the problem of founding the method he proposes. This avoidance is inscribed in the rhetoric of Wollen's second chapter, 'The Auteur Theory.' The latter begins with the historical origins of the auteur theory, then quotes Nowell-Smith and applies the structural method to Hawks. It is only then that it discusses foundations – in two paragraphs squeezed between Hawks and Ford, a foundational discourse in the form of a transition between main headings and delivered on the run.

Something further needs to be said about the theoretical basis of the kind of schematic exposition of Hawks's work which I have outlined. The 'structural approach' which underlies it, the definition of a core of repeated motifs, has evident affinities with methods which have been developed for the study of folklore and mythology.

There is a danger, as Lévi-Strauss has pointed out, that by

simply noting and mapping resemblances, all the texts which are studied (whether Russian fairy-tales or American movies) will be reduced to one, abstract and impoverished.

This means of course that the test of a structural analysis lies not in the orthodox canon of a director's work, where resemblances are clustered, but in films which at first sight may seem eccentricities.

The protagonists of fairy-tales or myths, as Lévi-Strauss has pointed out, can be dissolved into bundles of differential elements, pairs of opposites. . . . We can proceed with the same kind of operation in the study of films, though, as we shall see, we shall find them more complex than fairy-tales. It is instructive, for example, to consider three films of John Ford and compare their heroes. . . .[6]

In the four passages quoted, Wollen's text proceeds from a notation of similarities to a tenuous equation to an achieved integration to a wholesale importation which moreover cautions itself to proceed carefully. Needless to say, each of these stages is unearned, including the first, a notation of affinities at the phenomenal level which asserts its own evidence. The apparent progress of the passage is a feat of rhetoric. The fundamental questions – whether films are like myths, whether modes of myth study are applicable to film study, and whether the auteur theory is compatible with Lévi-Straussian structuralism – are avoided by Wollen, elided by a skillful rhetoric which seems to answer them.

There are some theoretical passages following the discussion of Ford but they do not return to the problem of foundations. Here Wollen discusses the 'noise' of camera style and acting, arguing that films, like myths, exist independently of style. Hence, despite noise, 'the film can usually be discerned,' 'film' here meaning auteur-structure. Pivoting on the sentence: 'It is as though a film is a musical composition rather than a musical performance. . . .', Wollen then launches into a dazzling essay on the distinction between composition and performance in music, painting, and theater as they developed over several centuries.* Following this he concludes that the director is not simply in command of a performance of a pre-existing text, but himself a composer also. The incidents and episodes of the original screenplay or novel are:

the agents which are introduced into the mind (conscious or unconscious) of the auteur and react there with the motifs and themes characteristic of his work. The director does not

---

* This section is not included in the extract above. [Ed.]

subordinate himself to another author; his source is only a pretext, which provides catalysts, scenes which fuse with his own preoccupations to produce a radically new work. Thus the manifest process of performance, the treatment of a subject, conceals the latent production of a quite new text, the production of the director as an auteur.[7]

The chapter concludes with a reminder that the task begun by the original auteur critics is still far from completed.

Founding auteur-structuralism would mean beginning with structuralism and its foundations and moving from it to film study, specifically to the study of auteurs, deriving the principles of the latter study from structuralism. As has been seen, Wollen does not do this. Instead he begins with auteurism, establishes it as an ongoing activity, then turns to structuralism as another ongoing activity, and then discovers affinities and similarities between the two.

Let us look more closely at these 'affinities' and at the text's 'discovery' of them. We note first that at least four different senses of 'the auteur theory' may be distinguished in Wollen: the French original, Nowell-Smith's transformation, Wollen's transformation (1969), Wollen's transformation (1972). Yet Wollen refuses to differentiate these senses, speaking at all times of 'the auteur theory,' as though it were one thing now and had always been one thing. Besides blurring the first two senses, Wollen himself redefines the auteur theory, even as he affirms its singularity of meaning. Most readers may be aware that Wollen is transforming the auteur theory, not merely expositing it; but they may not be aware of how this device affects his argument, precisely because the rhetoric which this collapse of multiple meanings permits is so persuasive. So we ask – why does Wollen's text deny that it is altering the auteur theory as originally developed? Why does it pass off its transformation as a 'discovery' of what already exists? That is, *why does it deny its own work*? The collapse of multiple meanings takes place in several stages. First, by presenting Nowell-Smith's definition of the auteur theory as a 'summary' of it 'as it is normally presented today,'[8] Wollen denies the latter's transformation of the auteur theory even as he imports it into his own discourse. Not long after this Wollen discovers affinities between the auteur theory and structuralism. Since it is obvious that Nowell-Smith's 1967 book was already influenced by Lévi-Strauss and his followers, this 'discovery' is less than fortuitous. Wollen has already imported a basic structuralism on the 'auteur theory' side of his exposition. As the essay proceeds, he brings this structuralism more specifically into line with the Lévi-Strauss original, though still under cover of expositing a singular and constant auteur theory. What Wollen's assertion of constancy entails, at this point, is not only that auteurism and structuralism are literally the same thing, but that *they have always been the same*. It is only this impossible contention which relieves Wollen from having to provide foundations for auteur-structuralism. If he admitted that he was transforming the auteur theory, specifically that he was seeking to merge the auteur theory with structuralism, then he would have had to found or justify his action theoretically.

Wollen says at one point:

There are other kinds of code which could be proposed [besides that of auteur-structure], and whether they are of any value or not will have to be settled by reference to the text, to the films in question.[9]

Several other passages put the emphasis on results. There is a way of reading Chapter Two which says: all questions of logic and foundation aside, auteur-structuralism is justified because it works – that is, because it produces (excellent, true) results when applied to films. This reading of Wollen's text is supported by its rhetorical organization. Auteurism is established by the Hawks discussion before Lévi-Strauss and structuralism are introduced; then, after two paragraphs, it turns to an even longer discussion of Ford. (Auteur-structuralism is happier in the field than in the theoretical laboratory.) The organization of the chapter makes these critical discussions carry the principal weight of its argument. To a considerable degree, they *are* its argument. Leaving aside the merits of Wollen's results, let us look at this argument itself. What can be said against the argument of good results? Marxist theory, philosophy, and semiology have operated singly and conjointly to dismantle the ideological, conceptual, and linguistic foundations of empiricism. Any system of interpretation *generates* its own results. Every system of interpretation will produce 'results' which are in full accordance with its methods. Hence justification by results is circular. As Roland Barthes says in an early text,

One seeks, and naturally one finds. . . . We must not complain about this – the demonstration of a coherence is always a fine critical spectacle – but is it not evident that, though the episodic content of the proof may be objective, the postulate that justifies looking for it is utterly systematic?[10]

Even more importantly, any system which simply produces results as a kind of spectacle, that is, without dismantling and questioning its own foundations, assumptions, problematic, and operations (the means by which it produces results), is necessarily and entirely ideological.

The explanation of Eckert's middle section, too long and wandering for the project proposed in the first section and concluded in the third section, is that it attempts to provide for auteur-structuralism those foundations which the latter does not provide for itself. In doing so, it answers a question which it does not ask, which it cannot ask without calling attention to the scandal of its absence in the work of the auteur-structuralists, thereby undermining their work and possibly itself also. What of Eckert's foundational attempt? In fact it is no more than a sketch, far from the systematic and thorough study that would have been needed to carry its project. Still, it is interesting in several respects. It is genuinely foundational in that it grounds itself in Lévi-Strauss and attempts to move forward toward auteurism. It proceeds in this task only by constructing a highly fragile latticework of premises, inferences, evidences, and connections, many of which are questionable yet each one of which is necessary to make the link which Eckert seeks.

> Whether these codes [of physical objects and of qualities in films] are part of a careful, logical system can only be established through research. My own preliminary attempts at analysis suggest that they are.[11]

The most interesting aspect of the section is that it moves in a direction nearly opposite to that of auteur-structuralism, toward a criticism of the *many* codes of cinema (most of which Wollen dismisses as 'noise,' 'inaccessible to criticism'[12]) rather than the single code of auteur-structure, and toward an understanding of cinema as myth very different from that of auteur-structuralism:

> The dioscuric union of film-makers and their audience produces a strange Janus of art – myths made by mythmakers that are only certified as true or untrue after they have been created. Perhaps the best index to authentically mythic films, then, is the yearly box-office ratings.[13]

This is very nearly the antithesis of auteur-structuralism. Having reached this point, how does Eckert rearrive at auteur-structuralism, as promised in the first section? He does so only by an authorial *coup de force* – through an abrupt discontinuation of the foundational discourse, which amounts to its abandonment if not its repeal, and an arbitrary jump back to the original discourse. All of which constitutes an extreme and uncharacteristic scriptural violence and the second major way in which Eckert's text criticizes itself, effectively demonstrating the impossibility of arriving at auteurism through a Lévi-Straussian discourse. Immediately follow-ing the 'box-office' statement Eckert says, 'Two more of Lévi-Strauss's stipulations deserve brief consideration,' whereupon he adduces the two principles discussed above, which have no con-nection with his foundational discourse nor with the point at which he arrived in considering the box-office, but which provide the occasion for a none-too-smooth return to the auteur-structuralists.

The issue of how figures are to be interpreted takes us to the heart of the whole enterprise I have characterized as auteur-structuralism.[14] *

We have let the auteur-structuralist texts speak for themselves and in speaking, through their gaps, omissions, rhetorical strat-egies, and contradictions, destroy themselves. We have seen not only that the auteur-structuralist texts have no theoretical foun-dations, but also that what is present in these texts, their specific traces, can only be understood in relation to this absence. That is, these texts as they exist constitute themselves as an ersatz built over and in relation to this absence, which nevertheless warps them from the inside. We have not asserted positively that auteurism and structuralism are incompatible, that they *can not* be combined. Nor do we intend to do so, for that would involve first constructing such a foundation as we have demanded and then destroying it, a useless operation. Nor do we suppose that we would do a better job at this than the auteur-structuralists. On the contrary. In re-lation to the practical problem of directing film critical energies, however, we will consider briefly the problems faced by anyone attempting to do this. This will also help explain the failure of the auteur-structuralists, for they are clearly not unintelligent. The difficulty lies in the contradictory project of auteur-structuralism

---

* Eckert's text criticizes itself only covertly and unconsciously. At this point we are reminded of Nowell-Smith's book, which (as Eckert himself presents it) contains an explicit critique of structuralism even as it seeks to apply the method. Nowell-Smith's text is demoted by Eckert for its failed structuralism; but when we move outside of the Wollen and Eckert problematic (based on commitment to auteur-structuralism and, in Eckert's case, on the question of which auteur-structuralism most closely resembles Lévi-Strauss's method) and raise our own questions, we are not bound by Eckert's evaluation (which is consistent with his premises). Then we are free to reconsider Nowell-Smith's text and perhaps find it the most interesting of the three, in part for its explicit critique of structuralism, both theoretical and practical. To another problematic it is considerably less disappointing that Nowell-Smith found himself unable to exclude 'many aspects of production, history, and stylistic influence that have no bearing upon struc-ture'[15] in considering Visconti's films.

itself, which exists in its purest form in Wollen: the attempt to merge auteurism with structuralism *without altering either in the process*. But, as Eckert's middle section indirectly reminds us, for Lévi-Strauss myths have no origins, no centers, no subjects, and no authors. Bodies of films organized by auteur signature are obviously defined by their origin, which is a subject and an author as well as a definitive center. Wollen attempts to deny this or at least he considers it important when he says, in the 1972 edition of *Signs and Meaning*, that the auteur is not a conscious creator but an unconscious catalyst and even (revising his theory of 'noise') that the auteur-structure is only one code among many which are discernible.

What the auteur theory argues is that any film, certainly a Hollywood film, is a network of different statements, crossing and contradicting each other, elaborated into a final 'coherent' version. Like a dream, the film the spectator sees is, so to speak, the 'film facade,' the end-product of 'secondary revision,' which hides and masks the process which remains latent in the film 'unconscious.' Sometimes this 'facade' is so worked over, so smoothed out, or else so clotted with disparate elements, that it is impossible to see beyond it, or rather to see anything in it except the characters, the dialogue, the plot, and so on. But in other cases, by a process of comparison with other films, it is possible to decipher, not a coherent message or world-view, but a structure which underlies the film and shapes it, gives it a certain pattern of energy cathexis. It is this structure which auteur analysis disengages from the film.

The structure is associated with a single director, an individual, not because he has played the role of artist, expressing himself or his vision in the film, but because it is through the force of his preoccupations that an unconscious, unintended meaning can be decoded in the film, usually to the surprise of the individual involved. The film is not a communication, but an artefact which is unconsciously structured in a certain way. Auteur analysis does not consist of re-tracing a film to its origins, to its creative source. It consists of tracing a structure (not a message) within the work, which can then *post factum* be assigned to an individual, the director, on empirical grounds.[16]

Wollen twists and turns and makes vocabularic concessions to recent theoretical work, but he does not escape the criticisms he is aware of because he retains the subject as producer of unique or distinctive meaning. In the passage above, Wollen confuses a methodological point with a foundational one. Since auteur-structuralism works empirically (from the works to the director, rather than *a priori*, from the director to the works) and since it is not interested in the person of the director (his condition as actual subject – biography, psychoanalysis, personal ideology) but only with the structures which are labelled with his name, Wollen supposes that he has solved the foundational problems of auteur-structuralism outlined above. But he has not. To do so, he would have to explain how it can be that individual subjects produce unique or distinctive meanings (structures), which moreover have the integrity and constancy of mythic meanings and can be studied in the same way. In short, he would have to provide that theory of the subject which Lévi-Strauss deliberately and systematically omits, because his work is founded upon the interchangeability of subjects in the production of meaning. The contention that (some) individual directors can and do stamp their films with a distinctive or unique meaning (structure) cannot be grounded in Lévi-Strauss. Nor is the problem overcome if it is stipulated that the auteur-structure is only one meaning among many, for the problem of accounting for the production of this meaning remains.

Wollen is, in any case, ambiguous about his opening out to other codes and the implications of this opening for his method. The greatest source of ambiguity is that the 1972 edition of *Signs and Meaning* reprints chapters 1–3 *without change* but adds a new conclusion which seems to reconsider several issues, yet explicitly retracts nothing bearing on auteur-structuralism, neither critical discussions nor theoretical formulations. Wollen continues to speak of 'the auteur theory,' even though he makes a few changes of emphasis. Now the director's structuring activity is unconscious whereas before it was 'conscious or unconscious.' Before it was the script or novel which acted as catalyst to the director, now it is the director who acts as catalyst to his materials. As noted, however, Wollen retains auteur-structure, nominally as one code among many, but really in a privileged position as he continues to identify structure with auteur-meaning and therefore meaning with auteur-structure. Above all, there is nothing in the 1972 edition which recants or revises the fundamentals of auteur-structuralism or overcomes the latter's foundational lack – its disconnection with Lévi-Strauss. The latter's name is not mentioned in the new chapter. Wollen wishes to retain his critical achievements and his critical method, though he is willing to change his vocabulary to facilitate this. Hence the long reaffirmation of the auteur theory (pp. 167–

73), which is not at all retracted in his remark that chapters 1 and 3 (not 2) are 'the most valuable sections' and his remark that 'I do not believe that development of auteur-analyses of Hollywood films is any longer a first priority.' This does not mean abandonment of his previous auteur studies, indeed it freezes them in the eternity of a completed auteurism. As he says in the next sentence, 'This does not mean that the real advances of auteur criticism should not be defended and safeguarded.'

The questions, Can modes of myth study be applied to film study? and Can structuralism be merged with auteurism? are *not identical*. Both Wollen and Eckert assume this identity, though Eckert strains against the assumption and his text cracks on it. Auteur-structuralism treats the two questions as one; specifically, it reduces the first question to the second. It thereby makes the study of films as myths dependent upon the fusion of auteurism and structuralism and effectively rules out other modes of study. In this way it seeks to take over and occupy this field of study entirely. In English-language studies so far, it has actually done so; the auteur-structuralists have succeeded in identifying their methods and concerns with the very notion of a study of films as myths. Having critiqued auteur-structuralism, we are in a position to reconsider this relationship and to disentangle these questions. When auteur-structuralism is destroyed, it is by no means the case that the study of films as myths is destroyed also. Indeed, it would seem that *only* the destruction of auteur-structuralism *liberates* the other question, that is, allows it to be asked and answered.* Since prospects for the merger of auteurism and structuralism are not promising, it seems that film criticism would do better to look for other possibilities. Eckert's aberrant middle section suggests a non-auteurist structuralism, one neither dependent upon auteurist epistemology nor organizing its materials by auteur signature. It also suggests, apparently reinstating Metz, Eco, *et al.*, semiological study of cinematic codes of expression.

But before embarking on such studies, we should consider certain important criticisms of structuralism, which also apply to some practices of semiology. These criticisms derive from the wide-ranging theoretical developments inscribed in the texts of Derrida, Kristeva, Lacan, and many others. These criticisms have shaken

---

* The problematic of a text is not only the questions which it asks, but the questions which it does not ask. Specifically it is the relationship between these, for a text raises certain questions only at the price of not asking others. The relationship between questions asked and questions suppressed is always ideological.

structuralism to its foundations, or rather, shaken it *at* its foundations (and therefore everywhere), for it is a specifically foundational and epistemological critique. Of course the texts concerned are far from complete agreement with each other, even in regard to the defects of structuralism. This polyphony, which includes repetition as well as discord, relieves the present text from the need to speak for or from any other particular text, which would in any case be foolhardy. Its list of criticisms of structuralism will therefore be partial, sketchy, and highly general.*

The foundational defects of structuralism are interrelated. First of all, it is an empiricism. It takes for its object the text as given. This given, the textual object, is its horizon and absolute. Secondly, structuralism posits the object as other. It is based upon the separation of subject and object, that is, upon empiricist epistemology, which in turn is based upon traditional Western (dualist) metaphysics. This epistemology determines the practice of structuralism as a species of representation, itself locatable as concept and method within the historical ideologies of the West. (Michel Foucault identifies representation as the episteme of the seventeenth and eighteenth centuries.[17]) The structuralist work represents or reproduces the structure of the object; so that the two are related to each other as mirror-images. The structuralist text is a simulacrum of its object. (See Barthes, 'The Structuralist Activity.')

The critique of structuralism transforms this model in every respect. On the one hand, the text is no longer seen as an object, given and achieved (essentially a product), but as a process, as itself a production, specifically as a collocation of mechanisms for the production of meaning. Thus it is necessary to speak of the *work* of the text if one is to avoid reifying it à la the consumerist ideology of capitalism. This collocation of mechanisms for pro-

---

* Of course, 'structuralism' refers to a great number of discourses and to a great number of texts combining these discourses in various ways. It is perhaps too early to say that structuralism has been definitely replaced by a subsequent movement, let alone to differentiate the structuralist from the non-structuralist constituents of the new constellation. The critique of structuralism outlined here may even be read as structuralism's critique of itself. The critique is then a purge of the empiricist wing of structuralism and of the empiricist elements which have figured in it more generally. In such a critique-purge, 'structuralism' – constituted as a sum of defects, as that which is critiqued – becomes the virtual object of structuralism, the theoretical activity, in the latter's clarification and transformation of itself. Such an object need not have hard edges, still less need it correspond to actual objects. What is important is the theoretical activity which it permits.

ducing meaning is itself not a given but is determined by material conditions which must be examined in analyzing the text. Thus the text cannot be understood by examination of the text alone. Similarly, indeed identically, the discourse which studies the text is productive. It does not represent the structure of the text, it does not study an object over a gap that divides subject from object, knower from known. It mixes with the text studied. The productivity of the text studied and that of the discourse which studies merge and interact to form a new text.

Related to the productivity of the text is the principle of intertextuality. This means, over-simply, that no text is isolated, discrete, unique, and that none is self-originating. Every text is a combination of other texts and discourses, which it 'knots' in a certain way and from a certain ideological position. (Thus the notion of anthropology, of a universality of studies addressing culture as a whole, disappears. The latter denies its own signifying practice, which is always ideological.) Thus description of the structure of a text impoverishes and distorts it and, indeed, mistakes the nature of textuality itself.

Empiricism is overthrown not only because the productivity of the text replaces the static object, intertextuality replaces structure, and the conjoined productivity of critical practice replaces the subject—object split and representation, but also because inquiry is no longer limited to the object itself, the given, but addresses what is there in light of what is not there. This includes questioning the problematic of the text: not just the answers the text gives, but the questions it asks, and not just the questions it asks, but the questions which it does not ask. Why are certain discourses included in the text and others left out? Why does the text combine these and accent them in a certain way? By subordinating itself to the object and its problematic, empiricism is necessarily ideological in function. It reproduces the ideology of the object and above all its own ideology, by constituting itself as a discourse which does not ask fundamental and foundational questions, above all of itself.

The relation of this theoretical work to film study may not be immediately apparent, except for the immense shadow it throws on the entire project of cine-structuralism, by which we mean here not only auteur-structuralism but other kinds as well. There exists in English, however, a film-critical text which seeks to build itself upon this theoretical foundation, the *Cahiers* collective text, '*Young Mr Lincoln.*' As mentioned above, the entirety of '*Young Mr Lincoln*' may be read as a critique of structuralism and as a realization of the theoretical critique of structuralism in the area of film criticism.

Notes

This text owes much to conversations and collaborations with Daniel Dayan over the past year.

1 *Film Comment*, 9, no. 3, May/June, 1973, pp. 46–51 [see above]; *Signs and Meaning in the Cinema*, Indiana University Press, 1972 [see extract above]; *Screen*, 13, no. 3 Autumn 1972, pp. 5–47.

2 *Théorie d'ensemble*, Paris: Seuil, 1968, p. 75.

3 This text very nearly reverses Eckert's findings, concluding that (3) is not promising, at least as pursued so far. For reasons not fully developed here, we find (1) – perhaps more along the lines of Oudart than of Metz – and (2) of considerable promise. See Alan Williams's piece in this issue [of *Film Quarterly*] for a study of narrative mechanisms in *La Ronde*. Such study does not reduce the text to 'underlying structures.' It works on the traces of the film, it does not bypass the inscription in favor of systems which allegedly underlie it. It not only works on the signifiers, whereas auteur-structuralism bypasses the signifiers to get to the signifieds; it studies the *production* of signifiers, specifically those mechanisms which generate narrative. If this is not comprehensive study of inscription, as in the *Cahiers* 'Young Mr Lincoln,' it is necessary preparation for such study.

4 *Luchino Visconti* (1967), New York, Doubleday, 1968. [See extract above]

5 *Horizons West* (1969), Indiana University Press, 1970.

6 *Signs and Meaning*, pp. 93–4. [See above, p. 139]

7 ibid., p. 113. [See above, pp. 144–5]

8 Note the crucial repetition of the word 'indispensable,' before and after the Nowell-Smith quote, on p. 80. Two things equal to the same thing are equal to each other.

9 *Signs and Meaning*, p. 168. Wollen's ambiguous use of the word 'code' confuses his text at several points. Many of these confusions are carried over into Eckert's text where they generate new ones. One can argue that codes function at the level of meaning analyzed by Lévi-Strauss, but these must be differentiated from the other codes referred to by Wollen. Lévi-Strauss isolates what Hjelmslev would call the form of content. It is perhaps preferable to refer to structure at this level and to reserve 'code' for the levels of expression. Thus structuralism, concerned with form of content, indeed – positing many layers of content – with a deep structure within the form of content, may be distinguished from semiology, which is concerned with moving from the level of expression to the level of content via codes. But, as noted in the text, structuralism is often used globally to refer to all work influenced by Lévi-Strauss and structural linguistics.

Wollen consistently confuses codes of expression with form of content, according them an equal status, perhaps in an attempt to make his 'structures' seem more legitimate. Asking whether particular codes are of value or not compounds the confusion. It is evident that all codes have value in the production of meaning in film. The question can only embody a preference for certain types of meaning and methods of analysis over others. The answer depends on the principle of pertinence chosen and the results desired by the analyst. [See above, p. 147]

10 *On Racine* (1960), New York, Hill and Wang, 1964, p. 170.

11 'The English cine-structuralists,' p. 49. Again, a confusion regarding codes. To the extent that a film produces meaning at all, one must assume the operation of codes at the level of expression. Codes are by definition logical in that they are constructed by a logical system of analysis. [See above, p. 160]

12 *Signs and Meaning*, pp. 104–5. 'Noise' for Wollen has quite a different meaning than for most semiologists. He seems to consider as noise anything deriving from the level of expression. If camera style and acting were the noise which Wollen suggests, that is, if they resisted codification, then no form of content could emerge from film at all. Hjelmslev would argue that one must posit a total parallel (not identity) between expression and form for the process of signification in cinema to be conceivable at all. Wollen revises his theory of noise in the 1972 edition, but, as argued in the text, with considerable ambiguity regarding the question of codes. [See above, pp. 143–4]

13 'The English cine-structuralists,' p. 50. [See above, p. 161]

14 ibid.

15 ibid., p. 47. [See above, p. 154]

16 *Signs and Meaning*, pp. 167–8. [See above, p. 146]

17 *The Order of Things* (1966), London, Tavistock, 1970, pp. 46–217.

18 *Collected Essays* (1964), Evanston, Northwestern University Press, 1972, pp. 213–20.

20 · Jean-Pierre Oudart: 'Conclusion to Cahiers du Cinéma editors' "John Ford's Young Mr Lincoln" ' (extract)

Cahiers du Cinéma, no. 223, August 1970, translated in Screen, vol. 13, no. 3, Autumn 1972. In Nichols, Mast and Cohen and Screen Reader I

The collective text on Young Mr Lincoln by the editors of Cahiers du Cinéma in 1970 is a crucial text for film theory precisely in the sense of marking a turning point. For Cahiers it can be seen in the context of a reassessment of political and critical practice in the light of the events of May 1968. In their editorial article, 'Cinema/ideology/criticism', written in 1969, Comolli and Narboni defined a category of films 'which seem at first sight to belong firmly within the ideology and to be completely under its sway, but which turn out to be so only in an ambiguous manner' (Cahiers, no. 216 pp. 13–14). Cahiers' response to such films was 'to show the process in action', a project which was carried out most successfully in the analysis of Young Mr Lincoln.

In the opening section of the essay the collective defines its methodology, a methodology which the following quotation may clarify:

What will be attempted here through a re-scansion of these films in a process of active reading, is to make them say what they have to say within what they leave unsaid, to reveal their constituent lacks; these are neither faults in the work (since these films, as Jean-Pierre Oudart has clearly demonstrated – see the preceding issue – are the work of extremely skilled film-makers) nor a deception on the part of the author (for why should he practise deception?); they are structuring absences, always displaced – an overdetermination which is the only possible basis from which these discourses could be realized, the unsaid included in the said and necessary to its constitution. In short, to use Althusser's expression – 'the internal shadows of exclusion'.

The films we will be studying do not need filling out, they do not demand a teleological reading, nor do we require them to account for their external shadows (except purely and simply to dismiss them); all that is involved is traversing their statement to locate what sets it in place, to double their writing with an active reading to reveal what is already there, but silent (cf. the notion of palimpsest in Barthes and Daney), to make them say not only 'what this says, but what it doesn't say because it doesn't want to say it' (J. A. Miller; and we would add: what, while intending to leave unsaid, it is nevertheless obliged to say).

What is the use of such a work? We would be obliged if the reader didn't envisage this as a 'Hollywood revisited'. Anyone so tempted is advised to give up the reading with the very next paragraph. To the rest we say: that the structuring absences mentioned above and the establishment of an ersatz which this dictates have some connection with the sexual *other scene*,* and that 'other scene' which is politics; that the double repression – politics and eroticism – which our reading will bring out (a repression which cannot be indicated once and for all and left at that but rather has to be written into the constantly renewed process of its repression) allows the answer to be deduced; and this is an answer whose very question would not have been possible without the two discourses of over-determination, the Marxist and the Freudian. This is why we will not choose films for their value as 'external masterpieces' but rather because the negatory force of their writing provides enough *scope* for a reading – because they can be re-written.

The extract which follows assumes some familiarity with a readily available text. The point of breaking into the collective work and extracting Oudart's conclusion (a conclusion which is identified in the text as 'the point of departure for our study') is not simply to pay tribute to an important text which is too long and too available to include in full; rather, it is to draw attention to the particular part of the analysis which seems to focus the problems which the analysis as a whole raises for theories of authorship. In an important essay on the *Cahiers* text ('Notes on the text "John Ford's *Young Mr Lincoln*" '*Screen*, vol.14, no.3, Autumn 1973; and *Screen Reader 1*), Ben Brewster relates the *Cahiers* reading to the Metzian concepts of 'code', 'sub-code', and 'singular textual systems'. (See Christian Metz, *Language and Cinema*, particularly chapter 7.) Distinguishing certain codes and sub-codes at work in *Young Mr Lincoln*, Brewster concludes (p. 41):

the generic code (the youth of the hero) and its specific ideological motivation in this film text (the ideology of the Hayes–Tilden compromise)** are much less specific to the text and probably to the political conjuncture than the *Cahiers* analysis suggests. Inversely,

---

* 'Freud named the locus of the unconscious by a term that had struck him in Fechner . . ., namely, *ein anderer Schauplatz*, another scene . . .' Lacan, *Ecrits*, London, Tavistock, 1977, p. 193. [Ed.]

** Brewster had already referred to the Radical Republican movement and the Reconstruction of the South which followed the Civil War as 'certainly the most revolutionary government and governmental strategy there has ever been in the USA'. He continues, 'The ideology of Ford and Griffith, combining Lincoln worship with Southern nostalgia, might be called the ideology of the Hayes–Tilden compromise which ended Reconstruction in 1876' (p. 40). [Ed.]

the 'cracks' – the inverse motivations – are due to the interaction of these very broad sub-codes with the Fordian sub-code – the textual system constituted by Ford's films – and hence this system/code is of more importance than the *Cahiers* analysis implies. '*Young Mr Lincoln*' thus seems to confirm the intuition, if not the theory and method, of author criticism. The authorial system/code remains a crucial element in the analysis of the American cinema.

In the second part of his 'Critique of cine-structuralism' Brian Henderson is dismayed by the 'return of the author' in Brewster's conclusion, which he dismisses as a 'misrecognition' and a 'misreading' of *Cahiers* (*Film Quarterly*, vol. 27 no. 2, p. 45):

it seems that Brewster's analysis has weakened *both* the Metzian position and that of '*Young Mr Lincoln*' and that the surprise beneficiary of this double collapse is – the author. . . . In this light, Brewster's text plays agent provocateur or just plain saboteur.

This is the problematic which the extract from Oudart attempts to focus: what are the implications of Oudart's use of the notion of a 'Fordian inscription' as a source of tension in the text? Is this 'inscription' adequated by the concept of sub-code and textual system? Despite Henderson's dismay, it seems clear that the '*Young Mr Lincoln*' text, at least in its conclusion, can still be brought to bear productively on the theory of authorship.

(The complete text of 'John Ford's *Young Mr Lincoln*' appears in Nichols, Mast and Cohen and *Screen Reader* I; see bibliography.)

---

25 Violence and Law[1]

I A discourse on the Law produced in a society which can only represent it as the statement and practice of a moralist prohibition of all violence, Ford's film could only reassert all the idealist representations which have been given it. Thus it is not very difficult to extract from it an ideological statement which seems to valorise in all innocence the ascetic rigour of its agent, making it into the unalterable value which circulates throughout the film from scene to scene; it is also easy to observe that this cliché, presented as such in the film and systematically accentuated, is not there merely to ensure the acceptability of the Fordian inscription.[2] Without this cliché which provides the fiction with a kind of metonymic continuity (the same constantly re-asserted figure) – whose necessity is moreover overdetermined, its function being more than simply setting up a character whose 'idealism' can most conveniently be signified by the external signs of the very puritan sense of election – the film would appear, in fact does appear in spite of it, to be a text of disquieting unintelligibility; through its constant disconnections, it places us in a forced position for the reading and in fact its comprehension demands:

(1) That one first take no account of this at once insistent and fixed statement;

(2) That one listens carefully to what is stated in the succession of so obviously 'Fordian' scenes which support this statement, and in the relations between the figures, all more or less part of the Fordian fiction, which constitute these scenes;

(3) That one tries to determine how all these are involved; i.e. to discover what the operation by which Ford inscribes this character into his fiction consists of, insofar as, despite appearances, it is not superimposed on Ford's 'world', does not traverse it like a foreign body, but finds through this inscription into his fiction a designated place as representative of his Law; for the film-maker promotes the character to the role to which his (legendary) historical referent destines him only at the price of his subjection to the (Fordian) fictional logic. This determined his entry there in advance insofar as his role was already written and his place already set out in Ford's fiction. The work of Ford's *écriture* only becomes apparent in this film through the problem involved in producing the character in this role, in that he took a place which was already occupied.

II It is the character of the mother that incarnates the idealised figure of Ideal Law in Ford's fiction. Moreover, it is often, as in *Young Mr Lincoln*, the widowed mother, guardian of the deceased father's law. It is for her that the men (the regiment) sacrifice the cause of their desire, and under her presidency that the Fordian celebration takes place; this in fact consists in a simulacrum of sexual relations from which all effective desire is banned. But it is in the constantly renewed relationship of this group with another (the Indians), in the dualism of Ford's universe that the inscription of the structural imperative of Law which dictates the deferment of desire and imposes exchange and alliance is realised, in violence, guided by the mediating action of the hero (often a bastard) who is placed at its intersection.

III In *Young Mr Lincoln* one of the results of using a single character for both roles is that he will have both their functions, which will inevitably create, by their interference and their incompatibility (insofar as one secures the taboo on the violence of desire, the other is agent of its inscription), disturbances, actions which oppose the order of Ford's world, and it is remarkable that each comical effect always shows them up (there is no film in which laughter is so precisely a sign of a constant disorder of the universe). The compression of their functions will in fact be used only on the one level of the castration of the character (signified at the ideological level by its puritan cliché, and at the same time written, in the unconscious of the text, as the effect of the fictional logic on the structural determination of the character) and of his castrating action, in a fiction ruled by Ideal Law alone since the dualism of Ford's world is abandoned in favour of the mass–individual opposition. (In fact the political conflict intervenes only as a secondary determination of the fiction and literally only acts backstage.) In fact, we see that:

(1) The character's calling originates in his renouncing the pleasures of love, it is strengthened because he resists its attraction: Lincoln becomes so well integrated in the fiction and is so vigilant against the violences and plots which take place there only because he refuses to give in to the advances constantly made to him by women, affected by a charm which is due only to the prestige of his castration.

(2) This extreme postponement of the hero's desire soon becomes meaningful since it permits him to become the restorer of Ideal Law, whose order has been perturbed by a crime which the Mother has not been able to prevent but which she will attempt to stifle.

This shows that:

(1) The puritan cliché which Ford emphasizes has the very precise function of promoting the character to his role as mediator, insofar as the pleasure which he rejects allows him to thwart any attempt at sexual and political corruption; it thus simultaneously guarantees the credibility of the figure of Lincoln and the position of the character as the figure of Ideal Law in Ford's fiction. At the obvious price of installing him within a castration, whose comical aspects Ford uses sufficiently to indicate how indifferent he is to producing an edifying figure, and how much more attentive he is to the disturbing results of its presence in the fiction: for example in the dance scene in which his character perturbs the harmony, where the agent of Law behaves like a kill-joy, thus making visible what the harmony of the Fordian celebration would conceal.

(2) The fact that the character literally takes the place of the Mother, i.e. takes on simultaneously her ideal position and her function (since he assumes responsibility for her children, and

promises to feed them well in the new home which the prison becomes), gives rise to a curious transformation of the figure, as this repetition of roles is effected under the sign of a secret which the Mother must (believes she does) keep to try to prevent any violence – even, inconceivably, that of the Ideal Law which she incarnates – against her children; and by thus incubating the crime she projects her role into a quasi-erotic (almost Hitchcockian) dimension never presented as such by Ford, since usually the fiction protects her from any relationship with the crime (since it is part of her function to be ignorant of violence). This is comically re-introduced in the final scene of the trial, when the real proof (an almanac on a sheet of which should have been written the letter of love which Lincoln was planning to write for her, only to lull her attention and extract confessions from her) is pulled out of Lincoln's hat; it was necessary for the re-establishment of Law that by the end of the trial a signifier (the proof of the crime) be produced whose very occultation renders it erotic; and that it must necessarily be produced by the figure of Law to fit into the fictional logic since it is from this ideal Law that originated the cancellation of the criminal act in the fiction, the statement of the taboo on violence (on pleasure), the position of the Mother as the figure of forbidden violence (pleasure), the possession of the phallus by this figure (as a signifier of this pleasure) and the production of the proof of the crime as if it were a phallic signifier obviously pro-ceeding from the same statement. In such fictions this usually means, either that the weapon, the trace of the crime, acts like a letter which Law must decipher, since its very proscription has written it, or that the confession be produced by the criminal as a return of the repressed in an erotic form. The two results are here compressed, Law producing the proof of the crime (the writing which reveals the murderer) as if it were a phallic object which Ford's comedy presents like the rabbit pulled out of the conjuror's hat; the improbable levity with which Ford brings the trial to its close really can only be read as a masking effect which conceals to the end the 'human' context, thus allowing the logic of the inscrip-tion to produce this gag as its ultimate effect, a final consequence of Lincoln's re-enactment of the Mother's role, a fantastic return of the mask.

IV The fact that the overdetermination of this inscription of the Lincoln figure, as agent of the Law, in Ford's fiction by all the idealised representations of Law and its effects produced by the bourgeoisie, far from having been erased by Ford, has been declared by his writing and emphasised by his comedy, shows what a strange ideological balancing act the film-maker has insisted on performing, and what strange scriptural incongruities he has insisted on exploiting; to the extent that by the fictional constraints he gave himself, by giving up the usual bisection of his fiction and the sometimes truly epic inscription of Law thereby articulated (which recalls Eisenstein in *The General Line*) he could only produce the Law as a pure prohibition of violence, whose result is only a permanent indictment of the castrating effects of its discourse. Indeed to what is the action of his character reduced if not hitting his opponents at their weakest point – weaknesses which Ford always perversely presents as being capable of provoking a deadly laughter? So that the sole but extreme violence of the film consists of verbal repression of violence which, in certain scenes (the unsuccessful lynching) is indicated as really being a death sentence, a mortal interdict which has no equivalent except maybe in Lang and which shows the distance Ford, or rather his writing, keeps between himself and the idealist propositions which he uses.

V For, with a kind of absolute indifference to the reception given to his stylistic effects, the film-maker ends by practising stubbornly a scriptural perversion which is implied by the fact that, paradoxically, in a film meant to be the Apology of the Word, the last word is always given to the iconic signifier, entrusted by Ford with the production of the determining effects of meaning. And as in this film what is to be signified is always either the (erotic, social, ideological) separation of the hero relative to his surroundings, or the immeasurable distance between him and his actions, or the absence of any common denominator between the results he obtains and the means he uses, and those obtained by his opponents (insofar as he holds the privilege of the castrating speech) Ford succeeds, by the economy of means which he uses to that effect – his style forbidding him the use of effects of implicit valorisation of the character which he could have drawn from an 'interiorised' writing – in simultaneously producing the same signifier in completely different statements: (for example in the moonlight scene, where the moonlight on the river indicates at the same time the attempted seduction, the past idyll, and the hero's 'idealist' vocation); or even in renewing the same effect of meaning in totally different contexts (the same spatial disconnections of the character used in the dance scene and the murder scene). So that the intention of always making sense, of closing the door to any implicit effect of meaning, of constantly re-asserting these same meanings, in fact results – since to produce them the film-maker always actualises the same signifiers, sets up the same stylistic effects – in constantly undermining them, turning them into parodies of themselves. (With Ford parody always proceeds from a denunciation of the writing by its own effects.) The film's ideological project thus finds itself led astray by the worst means it could have been given to realise itself (Ford's style, the inflexible logic of his fiction) mainly to the benefit of a properly scriptural projection (obtained not by the valorisation after the event of previously constituted effects of meaning, but proceeding directly from the inscription, produced anew and resolved in each scene, of the character in Ford's fiction) of the effects of the repression of violence: a violence whose repression, written thus turns into exorcism, and gives to its signifiers, in the murder and the lynching scenes, a fantastic contrast which contributes considerably to the subversion of the deceptively calm surface of the text.

Notes

1 The collective analysis is in twenty-five sections. This conclusion is attributed in the immediately preceding section to Jean-Pierre Oudart, and is identified as 'the point of departure of our study'. [Editor's note]

2 This usage of inscription (*l'inscription*) refers to work done by Jacques Derrida on the concept of *écriture* in *Théorie d'ensemble* (Collection Tel Quel, 1968). *Cahiers'* point here is that all individual texts are part of and inscribe themselves into one historically determined 'text' (*l'histoire textuelle*) within which they are produced; a reading of the individual text therefore requires examining both its dynamic relationship with this general text and the relationship between the general text and specific historical events. [*Screen* editors' note]

21 · Pierre Macherey: 'Literary analysis: the tomb of structures' (extract)

From *A Theory of Literary Production*, Routledge & Kegan Paul, London, 1978; first published Paris, 1966

The inclusion of this short extract from Macherey is intended, first, to provide a context for *Cahiers'* practice of 'active reading', particularly the reading of texts through their 'determinate absences'; second, to round off the critique of structuralism by returning it to Lévi-Strauss; and third, and most importantly, to establish the connection between this practice and this critique on the one hand, and the work of Louis Althusser on the other. Macherey, who is a lecturer in philosophy at the University of Paris I, was part of the group (which also included Althusser, Etienne Balibar, Roger Establet and Jacques Rancière) which produced the first edition of *Lire le Capital* (see Althusser and Balibar, *Reading Capital*, 1970), his contribution appearing in volume IV ('A propos du processus d'exposition du *Capital'*). The reading of literature which Macherey proposes has much in common with Althusser's reading of Marx, and with Marx's reading (according to Althusser) of earlier economists: that is to say, he is less concerned with the intentions of a creative intelligence than with the conditions which determine what is present, and, crucially, what is absent in the work. Macherey operates broadly within Althusser's conception of ideology (see Althusser's 'Ideology and Ideological Apparatuses' in *Lenin and Philosophy*, 1971). For literary theory, he poses the work of the text as the resolution of contradiction; the work of the materialist literary critic is to re-trace, through a reading of gaps and silences, the contradictions which the text is there to resolve. The foundational importance of this for the *Cahiers* collective text is apparent, as is its relevance for the Reader. The author having been de-centred, robbed of his unifying function and placed within ideology and within the relations of the text, it is for Part Three of the Reader to try to specify his function and his functioning there.

A totality: a certain relation links the parts and thus *makes* them into a whole. The work succeeds in so far as it realises this convergence: otherwise it is merely the shadow of a work, a failure. This is how the privileges of form are represented: the form is that which gives body, which endows the work with its organic existence. The work is held together by the internal necessity of these relations: it owes it to itself to exist. It is full of itself: those elements which are the object of analysis only enter into its composition in so far as they find *their* place in the work. This representation of literary space is entirely borrowed from Aristotelian physics, an aesthetic physics in which objects are identified by their qualities. The diversity of elements is relative, a prior material, necessary to the realisation of order but with no existence independent of it. Thus literature is easily reinserted in the series of the arts: on condition that these arts are defined as *the activity of producing imaginary organisms*. The organic unity which constructs the work from a formal exigency also endows it with a meaning, a content. Criticism is consequently *interpretative*: it elucidates the principle of this unity, the rationality of this whole.

This is exactly Lévi-Strauss's procedure when he interprets or analyses (for him the two operations go together) the story of Asdiwal, which is successively divided and reassembled. First he defines the different levels in relation to a '*subjacent* structure, common to all the levels'. The myth is constructed like a 'musical score': its apparent diversity supposedly conceals a unity. Elements of the myth, horizontal sequences and vertical schemes are combined to form the text of a *message*:

> All the paradoxes conceived by the native mind, on the most
> diverse planes – geographical, economic, sociological, and even
> cosmological – are, when all is said and done, assimilated to
> that less obvious yet so real paradox, the dilemma which
> marriage with the matrilateral cousin attempts but fails to
> resolve. But the failure is *admitted* in our myths, and there
> precisely lies their function.[1]

The myth only lends itself to analysis in so far as analysis can identify an intention in the myth; inversely, we ascertain what the myth has to say by constituting its 'structure'. The myth resolves the contradictions of the real which are necessarily diverse and scattered; in this sense it belongs to the domain of the imaginary. The myth presents reality by means of a number of deformations; but the whole constituted by these deformations is structured: it is thus significant.

We are dealing with an exemplary positive analysis: Lévi-Strauss articulates what is *in* the myth. But, at least in this specific case, he does not see what is not in the myth, without which the myth might not perhaps exist. The structure is construed in relation to an intention (whether the intention produces the myth or vice versa), and the intention is thus the object of a *psychology* but not of a true *logic*. Logic precisely enables us to grasp how a relation between two such terms can establish itself on the basis of their difference: if unity is postulated from the beginning (in the *intention*, for example) there is no further problem. In reality, the structure is the very space of difference: in principle, then, it is absent from the relation which it helps to explain. In this text of Lévi-Strauss, the structure is ineluctably *present*: even though it is temporarily silent. In so far as it contributes to the imaginary resolution of a contradiction, it affirms the permanence of that contradiction. Such a contradiction could only be imaginary: it is impossible to think the real presence of a contradiction; it can only be conceived as an absence. It will then be claimed that the myth exists to give *form* (rather than body) to this absence.

Even if the conception of structure proposed by Lévi-Strauss (the presence of an absence, not a true absence) is an appropriate solution to the problem of analysing myths, the question must still be asked whether it can be used as it stands in literary analysis.

The concepts of order and totality produce satisfying *descriptions* of literary works; they pose the problem of the interpretation of their object; above all, they establish a certain peculiar rigour in the work, a certain tenacity and solidity; it produces itself rather than being produced. Thus, as we have seen, is eliminated the problematic of creation. But this rigour is necessary only because it is also totally imaginary: thus described, the work differs from all others in that it might not have existed. (This distinction is also a certain form of resemblance. In relation to the question, What is literature? all works are similar.) This necessity is thus gratuitous, precarious. The entire description is based on a logical fallacy: the work is all of a piece, like a solid body in a literary space; the analysis strives to establish precisely this self-presence of the work.

A different hypothesis, more fruitful though hardly ever used, might be offered: the work exists above all by its determinate absences, by what it does not say, in its relation to what it is not. Not that it can conceal anything: this meaning is not buried in its depths, masked or disguised; it is not a question of hunting it down with interpretations. It is not in the work but by its side: on its margins, at that limit where it ceases to be what it claims to be because it has reached back to the very conditions of its possibility. It is then no longer constituted by a factitious necessity, the product of a conscious or unconscious intention.

To take up a vocabulary well known to novices of philosophy, structural criticism or metaphysical criticism is only a variant of theological aesthetics. In both cases the aim is a causal explanation:

a personal intention in the case of the aesthetics of creation; an abstract intention, presented in the form of an entity, in the case of structural analysis. Perhaps the time has come to elaborate a positive criticism which would deal with laws rather than causes. The critical question would then be: *In what relation to that which is other than itself is the work produced?* Positive is, as we know, also opposed to negative: and Comte opposes the 'demystification' of metaphysics to that positive knowledge which is uniquely equipped to define real relations. We also know that metaphysical ideologies and positive science are not just different answers to the same question: positive science requires a different question. Indeed, the structural method is content to give a new answer to the old question of aesthetics, just as the writers themselves have asked it. The real critical question is not: What is literature? (What does *one* do when *one* writes, or reads?) The question is: What kind of necessity determines the work? What is it really made from? The critical question should concern the material being used and the implements so employed.

From without, then, structure is that which dispossesses the work of its false interiority, its secret cause, revealing that basic defect without which it would not exist. At this point the treaty with linguistics and psychoanalysis takes on its full significance. The literary work is also doubly articulated: at the initial level of sequences (the fable) and themes (the forms) which establish an illusory order; this is the level of organicist aesthetic theories. At another level, the work is articulated in relation to the reality from the ground of which it emerges: not a 'natural' empirical reality, but that intricate reality in which men – both writers and readers – live, that reality which is *their ideology.* The work is made on the ground of this ideology, that tacit and original language: not to speak, reveal, translate or make explicit this language, but to make possible that absence of words without which there would be nothing to say.

We should question the work as to what it does not and cannot say, in those silences for which it has been made. The concealed order of the work is thus less significant than its real *determinate* disorder (its disarray). The order which it professes is merely an imagined order, projected on to disorder, the fictive resolution of ideological conflicts, a resolution so precarious that it is obvious in the very letter of the text where incoherence and incompleteness burst forth. It is no longer a question of defects but of indispensable informers. This distance which separates the work from the ideology which it transforms is rediscovered in the very letter of the work: it is fissured, unmade even in its making. A new kind of necessity can be defined: by an absence, by a lack. The disorder that permeates the work is related to the disorder of ideology (which cannot be organised as a system). The work derives its form from this incompleteness which enables us to identify the active presence of a conflict at its borders. In the defect of the work is articulated a new truth: for those who seek to know this truth it establishes an original relation to the real, it establishes the revealing form of a knowledge.

Note

1 Claude Lévi-Strauss, *Structural Anthropology*, vol. 2 (trans. M. Layton), London, Allen Lane, 1977, p. 170.

Part Three

Fiction of the author/ author of the fiction

The text is a fetish object, and *this fetish desires me*. The text chooses me, by a whole disposition of invisible screens, selective baffles: vocabulary, references, readability, etc.; and, lost in the midst of a text (not *behind* it, like a *deus ex machina*) there is always the other, the author.

As institution, the author is dead, his civil status, his biographical person have disappeared; dispossessed, they no longer exercise over his work the formidable paternity whose account literary history, teaching, and public opinion had the responsibility of establishing and renewing; but in the text, in a way, *I desire* the author: I need his figure (which is neither his representation nor his projection), as he needs mine (except when 'prattling'[1]).

Roland Barthes[2]

Then perhaps the subject returns, not as illusion, but as *fiction*. A certain pleasure is derived from a way of imagining oneself as *individual*, of inventing a final rarest fiction: the fictive identity.

Roland Barthes[3]

So the subject of the statement should not be regarded as identical with the author of the formulation – either in substance, or in function. He is not in fact the cause, origin, or starting-point of the phenomenon of the written or spoken articulation of a sentence; nor is it that meaningful intention which, silently anticipating words, orders them like the visible body of its intuition; it is not the constant, motionless, unchanging focus of a series of operations that are manifested, in turn, on the surface of discourse through the statements. It is a particular vacant place that may in fact be filled by different individuals; but, instead of being defined once and for all, and maintaining itself as such throughout a text, a book, or an *oeuvre*, this place varies – or rather it is variable enough to be able either to persevere, unchanging, through several sentences, or to alter with each one. It is a dimension that characterizes a whole formulation *qua* statement. It is one of the characteristics proper to the enunciative function and enables one to describe it. If a proposition, a sentence, a group of signs can be called a 'statement', it is not therefore because, one day, someone happened to speak them or put them into some concrete form of writing; it is because

199

the position of the subject can be assigned. To describe a formulation *qua* statement does not consist in analysing the relations between the author and what he says (or wanted to say, or said without wanting to); but in determining what position can and must be occupied by any individual if he is to be the subject of it.

Michel Foucault[4]

It seems to me . . . that the 'fiction' of the author enables us to locate an *author of the fiction* who is by no means dispersed but who in 'his' notional coherence provides the means for us to grasp the text in the moment of its production before us.

Geoffrey Nowell-Smith[5]

The intervention of semiotics and psychoanalysis into the field of film theory has tended to shatter the unity of the author, scattering fragments over the whole terrain, calling into question the possibility of a theory of the author which is not also a theory of ideologies, of discourses, of commodities and, crucially, of the subject. If the *politique* and the theory of the *auteur* had seemed to hold out the promise of a coherency which would resolve the debate about authorship by explaining the role of the author as someone exterior and prior to the text, the present section is more concerned with how the text itself works, and with the author's place within a textual process which involves a shifting relationship with the spectator. The author, rather than standing behind the text as a source, becomes a term in the process of reading or spectating. At the same time, there is a reluctance to situate this new attention as a simple devaluation of the author (hence the hesitation implied by the title of this section). Rather, the attempt is to give the theory of authorship a context within a theory of textuality, of the subject, and of film as a discourse. There are two 'pulls' which have to be taken into account: on the one hand, there is 'John Ford', the author-function, the subject constituted in language; on the other hand, there is the insistence of the pleasure (and seduction) of the films identified by Ford's name and marked by his recognizable thematic and stylistic presence (we go to see John Ford movies). This section tries to hold the two pulls together.

At a certain level, it can seem that the shift within criticism and theory from the concept of the artist as a self-expressive personality to the concept of subject positions within the text is simply a strategy, a ploy to institute a materialist aesthetic, a decision by someone to replace an untidy humanism with the 'scientific' concept of an impersonal, non-individual subject. While it is true that the development of a theory of how subjects are constructed is closely bound up with developments in recent materialist and Marxist theory, it would nevertheless be wrong to see this as a simple voluntarist decision to re-adjust priorities. What a theory of the subject pursues is an account of the determinations and pressures which operate on individuals in terms of the places they come to occupy within the formations (social, textual, sexual, familial, discursive) which provide the sites of their activity. Such a theory is called for by the view that individuals are neither merely 'economic agents' nor simply 'free agents', but are formed as social, sexual, political subjects by a whole range of often contradictory discourses. Within film, a theory of the constructed spectating subject is called for by the quite generally held belief that film has ideological effects (that is to say, it positions its spectators as ideological subjects). But simply to produce a theory of the spectating subject is to suggest a stable, fixed relation, a one-way process in which the spectator is simply acted upon. What the conjunction of articles in this section is intended to suggest is the need for a theory of the subject of enunciation in film which involves an understanding of the shifting relation between enunciating subject and spectating subject, the subject of the enunciation being a position which can be occupied by either. Such a theory is in no way co-extensive with a theory of authorship; but, at the same time, such a theory cannot do without an understanding of the way in which the author-figure functions in the shifting relation. Much of the basis of this project was laid in work on language, and in the theorization (reinforced by Lacanian psychoanalysis) of the ways in which the subject was constituted within language.

The development of semiotics in France, principally in the writing of Barthes, Kristeva and the *Tel Quel* group,[6] offered a mode of analysis of signifying practices which was both precise and specific, opening itself, from its basis in Saussure's systematization of the sign, and his separation of the signifier and the signified,[7] to the specific operations by which literary language signified and was understood, and to the specificities of modes of signification other than spoken or written language. The introduction of semiotics to the analysis of film, broadly speaking, took two forms, which are at least methodologically separable. First, semiological work was concerned with the structures, codes and conventions by which film signified. The focus here was on the codes of narrative, it found its most developed form in the early work of Christian Metz,[8] and was inserted into English-speaking film theory largely, and controversially, through a special issue of *Screen* in 1973.[9] When semiology is referred to casually it tends to be a reference to this area of work: work, that is, which was considerably marked by linguistic formalism (if that can be said without in any way dismissing the conjunctural and theoretical importance of the work).

Second (and in a sense necessarily – filling in the hole left by the formalism of a purely structural concentration), semiotics, as the science of specific signifying *practices*, was concerned with film as discourse; with the analysis, that is, of film not simply as a statement (something already formulated, 'given'), but also as an enunciating practice, an 'utterance' (something in process at the moment of projection). The distinction of 'statement' and 'enunciation' (product and producing activity) corresponds to the distinction in linguistics between *énoncé* and *énonciation*, which is elaborated here by Metz and Nowell-Smith in the context of Emile Benveniste's related distinction of *histoire* (history, story) and *discours* (discourse).[10] For such a distinction the functioning of the enunciating subject in the text is crucial: who is it who says 'I'? or what is the relationship of a concealed 'I' to the revealed 'he/she/it'? The position of the narrator, or the 'implied author' in the novel, and the relation of narrator to reader have been long-standing issues for literary theory.[11] For film, lacking the clearly marked 'persons' (first, second and third) which can indicate the terms of a novel's address, the issue is particularly difficult: how does a film say 'I', 'you', or 'dear reader'? The absence of those clear marks which Jakobson calls 'shifters',[12] which immediately show up the presence of someone speaking (the apparent absence in film of those incursions and digressions by the narrator, which, in the novel, continually play on our relation to the text), encourages the impression that film is simply narrative (the art of the story), offering a fixed and passive position to the spectator. The focus of a theory of authorship (almost, of narratorship) in this context becomes to retrace the marks of the enunciating subject, the marks which constitute the film as a discourse, an ideological address rather than 'just a story', and which determine the shifting positions and relations of the spectating subject within and to the text.

The distinction of discourse and story, or, in a way more appropriately, of discourse and history (the translation of '*histoire*' as 'history' being justified by the importance of the distinction between the 'presentness' of discourse and the 'pastness' of the story) is central to this section. It has to be insisted, though, that the distinction is not a mutual exclusion, with the text as either one or the other, but that it refers to two terms which continually jostle each other in the text, both, even, present at the same moment, the one masked by the other, or, more precisely, masquerading as the other. The object of the analysis is, in Metz's sense here of 'breaking open the toy to see how it works',[13] to open up the history to discover the terms of its discourse, to break the story as something which is already finished in order to discover the operation of its address and its relation to the spectator in the present. Metz's playful metaphor should not conceal the seriousness of such an analysis for an understanding of the production of ideology in films since it is precisely the masquerade of discourse in the form of story which allows the ideological and the historically specific to masquerade in the form of the natural and the everlasting. The film, since it is not 'authored', seems to proceed from nowhere, taking its 'truth' only from the 'real world'. The removal or suppression of the clear marks of 'authored discourse' transforms ideology from something produced out of a locatable, historical, determined position into something natural to the world. The strategies, techniques and rules of classical film-making are there to conceal construction and enunciation (invisible editing at natural points, eyeline match, camera movement justified by movement in the frame). The film seems to have an organic relation to the world: a story of what happened, rather than a discourse on it.

If on the contrary, we consider a film such as the Godard/Gorin *Letter to Jane*,[14] where the film is presented as an explicit discourse (precisely, a letter, addressed and signed), we find a text which not only admits an authorial position, but, more importantly, in the same moment renders itself problematic as ideology by constituting a subject outside the text (Jane Fonda, and, in her place, the spectator) who can object, forcing the spectating subject into a critical position ('critical' in every sense – the finding of a position in relation to what is being said becomes urgent). In the face of a discourse which *identifies itself*, which announces a subject of its enunciation, identification is made difficult, or impossible, for the spectator, and he/she is given a distance from the text. This is part of the strategy of Brecht, which is exemplified in didactic form in *Letter to Jane*.

Letter to Jane is an exceptional case, but a useful illustration. The contrary effect, in narrative, of the story's suppression of an authorial discourse is to leave a vacant space within the text, a vacant subject position into which the spectator can fall, identifying with (that is to say, finding his/her identity in) the coherent world of the fiction and its characters. In the absence of an enunciating subject the spectator becomes the subject of the enunciation, giving it its coherence.

But this only begins the question. What is frequently left insufficiently explicit is the extent to which films are not frozen as *either* discourse *or* history, but move continually between the two, filling and emptying the subject positions with enunciating subjects and spectating subjects, the spectators continually moving in and out of identification with the fictive world. More precisely, what is left inexplicit is the extent to which this movement of positions is not the exclusive privilege of the Brechtian film which has learned the lessons of distanciation, but is a movement characteristic also of classic narrative; the extent, that is, to which this movement in and out of the fictional space is involved as much in the pleasure of the text as in its disruption. Attention to film as a text has, perhaps, produced a lack of attention to film as a performance.

In a sense, performance is always an enunciation, and in so far as film is both a text and a performance of a text it can be seen as moving between statement and enunciation, activating a play of subjectivity. In those sequences of a film where the story seems to be suspended in a moment of pure performance, of visual delight, of an excess of style, one is aware of nothing so much as of spectating, of looking on. Think of Ophuls, or Sternberg, or Minnelli. There is an admiration of skill. In those moments, equally, where the film finds an image which contains and represents its dramas and its tensions, we are aware of being spoken to, of having things made clear. Geoffrey Nowell-Smith refers to the moment in *All That Heaven Allows* when Jane Wyman finds herself reflected back in the blank screen of her new television set. We are being addressed in the discourse of the film; we are aware of ourselves as spectators at a performance; the conception of a perpetually passive spectator, his/her identity helplessly given over to the unfolding of the story, has to be qualified.

This is not at all to say that such moments of enunciative performance constitute their films as in some way 'Brechtian'. Where the interruptions of the Brechtian performance work as dislocations, a discourse never entirely recuperated into the story, the play of subjectivity in the classic narrative is a play of relocations, most typically intensifying our pleasure in a moment of admiration and delight in performance. The argument which I am conducting here is with the view which sees the 'classic realist text' as a stability of subject positions from which enunciation can be discovered only by force. Such a view can understand the incursion of the enunciative instance into the smooth flow of the history only as a moment of 'disturbance' or 'threat' to the narrative, a break in the continuity of the spectator's identification, a crack in the coherence of the fictive world. Given enough cracks in the representation of the bourgeois world, the text is reconstituted for progressive criticism as radical. While stylistic excess can be disruptive, there is a danger of neglecting the ways in which disruptions are recuperated, and the extent to which performance and the play of positions which it involves is pleasurable.

Within this concept of the film as performance, the figure of the author seems to function in a complex but important way. It seems frequently to be the recognition of the marks of a supposed (or real) author which allows the spectator, in a moment of admiration (or, indeed, in an awareness of clumsiness), to give up his/her position within the fiction without losing possession of it. I admire (or criticize) from outside the fiction. The moment of admiration, in a sense, is one of dispossession. Paradoxically, by identifying with the fiction, by accepting the subject position which it gives me, by agreeing to forget my individual separateness in favour of the identity which the film has constructed for me, I seem to possess the film: it shows me what I want to see, it is my fantasy, I am at its centre, in the position of the subject. But in the moment of performance and admiration, someone else is performing the film: I am dislodged from the centre, a looker-on, and my pure possession of the film is challenged. This dispossession, however, is not experienced as a loss of pleasure, because it is accompanied by a recognition – a recognition of the figure of the author which I construct precisely to fill the subject position of the film's performance. The appearance of this new subject of the enunciation establishes me outside the fiction, but still within the textual space, still within a certain possession of the film (the performance is for me), and, where the performance is expert or familiar, my pleasure is intensified from a new position. In those films where the director does not operate as a recognizable figure, the 'performer' is as likely to be identified as the actor, the designer, or simply the film itself. In those films, on the other hand, where the director has a 'signature', my admiration and my pleasure is focused on the recognition of the author, whom I place, at least momentarily, as subject of the film's discourse. It's in this way that the presence or absence (presence *and* absence) of the marks of the enunciative authorial figure activates the play of subject positions.

Not to acknowledge the functioning of this recognition and the position which can be given to the author-figure in the film's performance is to leave out of account part of the movement of our pleasure and to leave a gap in any theory of subjectivity in the cinema. This question overlaps with questions of ideology. What is the relation between film's production of ideology and its production of pleasurable recognition? Given that I am a social subject with a very different ideological formation from John Ford, what is the relation between my pleasure (and emotional involvement) in Ford's films (in the scene, say, of John Wayne's retiral from the army in *She Wore a Yellow Ribbon*), and my recognition of the marks of a Fordian discourse? Where a film is so authored (and few are) it seems more important to account for the seductiveness of its pleasure than to deny that that pleasure had something to do with John Ford, the *auteur*.

Equally, in our reading of the film and in our construction of its sense, it seems clear that there are indeed continuities and consistencies in the films of certain directors, and that an awareness of these in the films in general comes into play as we watch a film in particular. While it is true that, as a critical term, the author is a figure constructed out of his films, and while it can be argued that he does not have an existence prior to those films, it does not follow that the figure does not have an existence prior to each individual film. In a sense, the continuities and consistencies which can be recognized in, and which identify, an authorial code or sub-code constitute another text which has to be read into the single film, determining our expectations and recognitions, breaking the pure self-containment of the singular, autonomous text, producing a kind of authorial intertextuality,[15] one text finding its meaning and effect in its relation to other texts. We are left happily conceding certain assumptions of *auteurism* – that there are consistencies – but instead of celebrating them as demonstrations of creativity, or finding in them the expression and values of a personality, we return them to the question of discourse, of how they produce an authorial subject for the discourse, and of how that production relates to the production, positioning and continual repositioning of spectating subjects.

The recognition of intertextuality is important. We are no longer dealing with a pure text which inhabits a 'noiseless' space, containing all its meanings and effects within its own edges, or with an ideal spectator who comes to the text innocently, cleansed of the contagion of other films and other practices. The crack in the singular text's self-containment is opened wider by questions of subjects other than the purely textual subject – social subjects, sexual subjects, historical subjects – subjects who are constituted in a plurality of discourses (in an intertextuality of other texts) of which the single text is only one moment. For authorship, just as the ideal spectator existing outside history and sociality is an illusory figure, so also the ideal author, existing only inside the text, will have to be questioned. Both of these figments have allowed theory to confront some problems by side-stepping others; but it is becoming increasingly clear that those other problems are now pressing. Feminist criticism, in particular, has to question the priorities which allowed the ideal author to be removed from sexuality, separated from a sexual look. This question is raised here by Sandy Flitterman;[16] and in his essay on Bresson, Oudart raises the question of the traces of the director's desire and its repression, and of his status as a social subject producing his discourse within and for a specific social group. Such questions are important if theory is to be related to different and specific practices, rather than to a monolithically conceived 'Cinema', and they are crucial for the understanding and development of alternative practices with different terms of address. Theory and analysis which remains within a pure semiotics, while it offers a theorization of the negotiation of subject positions within the textual process, and while it produces a rhetoric of the textual disposition, nevertheless finds it difficult to escape formalism. It's precisely this limitation which produces the need for semiotics (theory of the textual subject) to be joined with psychoanalysis (theory of the sexual, specular, divided subject) and historical materialism (theory of the social, political, historical subject, and the economic subject of exchange).

The author, then, both as a possible subject of the enunciation and as a sexual, social, historical subject, does indeed have a place within theory. The insistence on holding together the notion of the author as a subject position constructed in the film's performance, the notion of the authorial code as another text determining our reading and our recognition and the notion of the author as a subject of other practices and formations – that is to say, 'the fiction of the author' and 'the author of the fiction' – is precisely to break the autonomous coherence of each: to break the coherence of the text as a pure 'inside' (producing itself, for an empty spectator, out of its own internal operations), or as a pure 'outside' (given by an originating source), and to attempt to formulate the text, and its subjects, as a movement between the two, or as the involvement of the one in the other, destroying the purity of each.

Notes

1 '*Sauf à "babiller"* ', 'except to "prattle" ': I have altered the translation a little: Barthes has earlier referred to the 'prattle' of a text which is boring, which only satisfies the writer's desire to write, but carries no satisfaction for the reader.

2 Roland Barthes, *The Pleasure of the Text* (1973) (trans. R. Miller), New York, Hill & Wang, 1975, p. 27.

3 ibid., p. 62.

4 Michel Foucault, *The Archaeology of Knowledge* (1969) (trans. Sheridan Smith), London, Tavistock, 1972, pp. 95–6.

5 Geoffrey Nowell-Smith, 'Six authors in pursuit of *The Searchers*', see below, p. 223.

6 There is a useful introduction to the work of this group in Rosalind Coward and John Ellis, *Language and Materialism*, London, Routledge & Kegan Paul, 1977. The work is also represented in a collection of essays, *Théorie d'ensemble*, Paris, Editions du Seuil (collection *Tel Quel*), 1968.

7 See Appendix I, 'Notes on terms'.

8 Christian Metz, *Film Language*, New York/London, Oxford University Press, 1974; and *Language and Cinema*, Paris/The Hague, Mouton, 1974.

9 Double issue, 'Cinema semiotics and the work of Christian Metz', *Screen*, vol. 14, nos 1–2, Spring–Summer 1973; to be reprinted in *Screen Reader 2*.

10 Emile Benveniste, *Problems of General Linguistics*, Coral Gables, Florida, University of Miami Press, 1971; see also Appendix I, 'Notes on terms'.

11 Discussed particularly in Wayne Booth, *The Rhetoric of Fiction*, Chicago/London, University of Chicago Press, 1961; and in Gérard Genette, *Figures III*, Paris, Editions du Seuil, 1972.

12 See Appendix I, 'Notes on terms'.

13 Below, p. 227.

14 The film takes the form of a spoken letter, addressed to Jane Fonda, following her role in the Godard/Gorin *Tout va bien*. The 'writers' of the letter question the way in which the film star allows her image (specifically, a photograph of her talking to a group of Vietcong) to be appropriated by the media.

15 For Kristeva's use of the notion of intertextuality, see 'Problèmes de la structuration du texte', in *Théorie d'ensemble*, pp. 311ff. See also Coward and Ellis, op. cit., pp. 52–3.

16 The question is also raised in Laura Mulvey, 'Visual pleasure and narrative cinema', *Screen*, vol. 16, no. 3, Autumn 1975, pp. 6–18; in Pam Cook and Claire Johnston, 'The place of women in the cinema of Raoul Walsh', in *Raoul Walsh*, ed. Phil Hardy, Edinburgh Film Festival, 1974, pp. 93–109; and in Constance Penley, 'The avant-garde and its imaginary', *Camera Obscura*, no. 2, Fall 1977.

23 · Roland Barthes: 'The death of the author'

From *Image-Music-Text*, Fontana, London, 1977; first published Paris, 1968

Barthes, both from his position on the editorial board of *Tel Quel* and from his position as a director of studies in the École Pratique des Hautes Études, has been a central figure in the development of a semiotically based 'modernist criticism'; that is to say, a criticism which is founded on writing as a practice (rather than simply as a transmitter of messages), and on criticism as another form of writing practice, standing alongside the literary (or filmic) text, opening it up to the play of its meanings, rather than tying it down to an authorized interpretation of closed meanings (see particularly *S/Z*, an account of Balzac's novella, *Sarrasine*). Such a view of the text inevitably dislodges the author from the seat of authority.

In his story *Sarrasine* Balzac, describing a castrato disguised as a woman, writes the following sentence: '*This was woman herself, with her sudden fears, her irrational whims, her instinctive worries, her impetuous boldness, her fussings, and her delicious sensibility.*' Who is speaking thus? Is it the hero of the story bent on remaining ignorant of the castrato hidden beneath the woman? Is it Balzac the individual, furnished by his personal experience with a philosophy of Woman? Is it Balzac the author professing 'literary' ideas on femininity? Is it universal wisdom? Romantic psychology? We shall never know, for the good reason that writing is the destruction of every voice, of every point of origin. Writing is that neutral, composite, oblique space where our subject slips away, the negative where all identity is lost, starting with the very identity of the body writing.

No doubt it has always been that way. As soon as a fact is *narrated* no longer with a view to acting directly on reality but intransitively, that is to say, finally outside of any function other than that of the very practice of the symbol itself, this disconnection occurs, the voice loses its origin, the author enters into his own death, writing begins. The sense of this phenomenon, however, has varied; in ethnographic societies the responsibility for a narrative is never assumed by a person but by a mediator, shaman or relator whose 'performance' – the mastery of the narrative code – may possibly be admired but never his 'genius'. The author is a modern figure, a product of our society insofar as, emerging from the Middle Ages with English empiricism, French rationalism and the personal faith of the Reformation, it discovered the prestige of the individual, of, as it is more nobly put, the 'human person'. It is thus logical that in literature it should be this positivism, the epitome and culmination of capitalist ideology, which has attached the greatest importance to the 'person' of the author. The *author* still reigns in histories of literature, biographies of writers, interviews, magazines, as in the very consciousness of men of letters anxious to unite their person and their work through diaries and memoirs. The image of literature to be found in ordinary culture is tyrannically centred on the author, his person, his life, his tastes, his passions, while criticism still consists for the most part in saying that Baudelaire's work is the failure of Baudelaire the man, Van Gogh's his madness, Tchaikovsky's his vice. The *explanation* of a work is always sought in the man or woman who produced it, as if it were always in the end, through the more or less transparent allegory of the fiction, the voice of a single person, the *author* 'confiding' in us.

Though the sway of the Author remains powerful (the new criticism has often done no more than consolidate it), it goes without saying that certain writers have long since attempted to loosen it. In France, Mallarmé was doubtless the first to see and to foresee in its full extent the necessity to substitute language itself for the person who until then had been supposed to be its owner. For him, for us too, it is language which speaks, not the author; to write is, through a prerequisite impersonality (not at all to be confused with the castrating objectivity of the realist novelist), to reach that point where only language acts, 'performs', and not 'me'. Mallarmé's entire poetics consists in suppressing the author in the interests of writing (which is, as will be seen, to restore the place of the reader). Valéry, encumbered by a psychology of the Ego, considerably diluted Mallarmé's theory but, his taste for classicism leading him to turn to the lessons of rhetoric, he never stopped calling into question and deriding the Author; he stressed the linguistic and, as it were, 'hazardous' nature of his activity, and throughout his prose works he militated in favour of the essentially verbal condition of literature, in the face of which all recourse to the writer's interiority seemed to him pure superstition. Proust himself, despite the apparently psychological character of what are called his *analyses*, was visibly concerned with the task of inexorably blurring, by an extreme subtilization, the relation between the writer and his characters; by making of the narrator not he who has seen and felt nor even he who is writing, but he who *is going to write* (the young man in the novel – but, in fact, how old is he and who is he? – wants to write but cannot; the novel ends when writing at last becomes possible), Proust gave modern writing its epic. By a radical reversal, instead of putting his life into his novel, as is so often maintained, he made of his very life a work for which his own book was the model; so that it is clear to us that Charlus does not imitate Montesquiou but that Montesquiou – in his anecdotal, historical reality – is no more than a secondary fragment, derived from Charlus. Lastly, to go no further than this prehistory of modernity, Surrealism, though unable to accord language a supreme place (language being system and the aim of the movement being, romantically, a direct subversion of codes – itself moreover illusory: a code cannot be destroyed, only 'played off'), contributed to the desacrilization of the image of the Author by ceaselessly recommending the abrupt disappointment of expectations of meaning (the famous surrealist 'jolt'), by entrusting the hand with the task of writing as quickly as possible what the head itself is unaware of (automatic writing), by accepting the principle and the experience of several people writing together. Leaving aside literature itself (such distinctions really becoming invalid), linguistics has recently provided the destruction of the Author with a valuable analytical tool by showing that the whole of the enunciation is an empty process, functioning perfectly without there being any need for it to be filled with the person of the interlocutor. Linguistically, the author is never more than the instance writing, just as *I* is nothing other than the instance saying *I*: language knows a 'subject', not a 'person', and this subject, empty outside of the very enunciation which defines it, suffices to make language 'hold together', suffices, that is to say, to exhaust it.

The removal of the Author (one could talk here with Brecht of a veritable 'distancing', the Author diminishing like a figurine at the far end of the literary stage) is not merely an historical fact or an act of writing; it utterly transforms the modern text (or – which is the same thing – the text is henceforth made and read in such a way that at all its levels the author is absent). The temporality is different. The Author, when believed in, is always conceived of as the past of his own book: book and author stand automatically on a single line divided into a *before* and an *after*. The Author is thought to *nourish* the book, which is to say that he exists before it, thinks, suffers, lives for it, is in the same relation of antecedence to his work as a father to his child. In complete contrast, the modern scriptor is born simultaneously with the text, is in no way equipped with a being preceding or exceeding the writing, is not the subject with the book as predicate; there is no other time than that of the enunciation and every text is eternally written *here and now*. The fact is (or, it follows) that *writing* can no longer designate an operation of recording, notation, representation, 'depiction' (as the Classics would say); rather, it designates exactly what linguists, referring to Oxford philosophy, call a performative, a rare verbal form (exclusively given in the first person and in the present tense) in which the enunciation has no other content (contains no other proposition) than the act by which it is uttered – something like the *I declare* of kings or the *I sing* of very ancient poets. Having buried the Author, the modern scriptor can thus no longer believe, as according to the pathetic view of his predecessors, that this hand is too slow for his thought or passion and that consequently, making a law of necessity, he must emphasize this delay and in- definitely 'polish' his form. For him, on the contrary, the hand, cut off from any voice, borne by a pure gesture of inscription (and not of expression), traces a field without origin – or which, at least, has no other origin than language itself, language which ceaselessly calls into question all origins.

We know now that a text is not a line of words releasing a single 'theological' meaning (the 'message' of the Author-God) but a multi-dimensional space in which a variety of writings, none of them original, blend and clash. The text is a tissue of quotations drawn from the innumerable centres of culture. Similar to Bouvard and Pécuchet,[1] those eternal copyists, at once sublime and comic and whose profound ridiculousness indicates precisely the truth of writing, the writer can only imitate a gesture that is always anterior, never original. His only power is to mix writings, to counter the ones with the others, in such a way as never to rest on any one of them. Did he wish to *express himself*, he ought at least to know that the inner 'thing' he thinks to 'translate' is itself only a ready- formed dictionary, its words only explainable through other words, and so on indefinitely; something experienced in exemplary fashion by the young Thomas de Quincey, he who was so good at Greek that in order to translate absolutely modern ideas and images into that dead language, he had, so Baudelaire tells us (in *Paradis Artificiels*), 'created for himself an unfailing dictionary, vastly more extensive and complex than those resulting from the ordinary pa- tience of purely literary themes'. Succeeding the Author, the scriptor no longer bears within him passions, humours, feelings, impressions, but rather this immense dictionary from which he draws a writing that can know no halt: life never does more than imitate the book, and the book itself is only a tissue of signs, an imitation that is lost, infinitely deferred.

Once the Author is removed, the claim to decipher a text becomes quite futile. To give a text an Author is to impose a limit on that text, to furnish it with a final signified, to close the writing. Such a conception suits criticism very well, the latter then allotting itself the important task of discovering the Author (or its hypostases: society, history, psyché, liberty) beneath the work: when the Author has been found, the text is 'explained' – victory to the critic. Hence there is no surprise in the fact that, historically, the reign of the Author has also been that of the Critic, nor again in the fact that criticism (be it new) is today undermined along with the Author. In the multiplicity of writing, everything is to be *disentangled*, nothing *deciphered*; the structure can be followed, 'run' (like the thread of a stocking) at every point and at every level, but there is nothing beneath: the space of writing is to be ranged over, not pierced; writing ceaselessly posits meaning ceaselessly to evaporate it, carrying out a systematic exemption of meaning. In precisely this way literature (it would be better from now on to say *writing*), by refusing to assign a 'secret', an ultimate meaning, to the text (and to the world as text), liberates what may be called an anti-theological activity, an activity that is truly revolutionary since to refuse to fix meaning is, in the end, to refuse God and his hypostases – reason, science, law.

Let us come back to the Balzac sentence. No one, no 'person', says it: its source, its voice, is not the true place of the writing, which is reading. Another – very precise – example will help to make this clear: recent research (J.-P. Vernant[2]) has demonstrated the constitutively ambiguous nature of Greek tragedy, its texts being woven from words with double meanings that each character understands unilaterally (this perpetual misunderstanding is exactly the 'tragic'); there is, however, someone who understands each word in its duplicity and who, in addition, hears the very deafness of the characters speaking in front of him – this someone being precisely the reader (or here, the listener). Thus is revealed the total existence of writing: a text is made of multiple writings, drawn from many cultures and entering into mutual relations of dialogue, parody, contestation, but there is one place where this multiplicity is focused and that place is the reader, not, as was hitherto said, the author. The reader is the space on which all the quotations that make up a writing are inscribed without any of them being lost; a text's unity lies not in its origin but in its destination. Yet this destination cannot any longer be personal: the reader is without history, biography, psychology; he is simply that *someone* who holds together in a single field all the traces by which the written text is constituted. Which is why it is derisory to condemn the new writing in the name of a humanism hypocritically turned champion of the reader's rights. Classic criticism has never paid any attention to the reader; for it, the writer is the only person in literature. We are now beginning to let ourselves be fooled no longer by the arrogant antiphrastical recriminations of good society in favour of the very thing it sets aside, ignores, smothers, or destroys; we know that to give writing its future, it is necessary to overthrow the myth: the birth of the reader must be at the cost of the death of the Author.

Notes

1 Bouvard and Pécuchet are characters in Flaubert's last unfinished novel, titled *Bouvard et Pécuchet*, who spend their retirement vainly seeking to master, in succession, all the areas of human knowledge and activity, acquiring in the process (and subsequently discarding) a heteroclite collection of objects vaguely associated with each successive phase of their interest. [Editor's note]
2 Cf. Jean-Pierre Vernant (with Pierre Vidal-Naquet), *Mythe et tragédie en Grèce ancienne*, Paris, 1972, esp. pp. 19–40, 99–131. [Translator's note]

24 · Stephen Heath: 'Comment on "The idea of authorship"'

Screen, vol. 14, no. 3, Autumn 1973

Stephen Heath's article appeared first in *Screen* bracketed on the one side by Edward Buscombe's article on which it comments, and on the other side by Geoffrey Nowell-Smith's response to Eckert's article on the English 'cine-structuralists'. Within the development of a critique of *auteurism* in Britain, the conjunction of the three has a considerable strategic importance (especially if we add Ben Brewster's notes on the *Young Mr Lincoln* text which appeared in the same issue). Buscombe provided a careful criticism of *auteurist* practice, Nowell-Smith took a critical distance from '*auteur*-structuralism'; and Heath initiated the production of a theory of the subject 'with regard to the specific signifying practice of film'.

Heath's comments are based on a paper presented by Edward Buscombe at a BFI/SEFT seminar, a revised version of which titled 'Ideas of Authorship' appears in this Reader. References to passages in the seminar paper not included in the revised article are indicated by an asterisk.

Edward Buscombe's paper outlines clearly the issues raised by the development of the *auteur* theory in the *Cahiers du Cinéma* and in subsequent extensions (Sarris) and considerations (Wollen). This comment is intended simply to raise one or two further questions and to shift the perspective a little by offering something of a different articulation of the elements of Buscombe's conclusion. The idea of authorship carries within it some assumption of the author as originator of discourse: it is as its source that the author is given as a unity of discourse. Immediately, certain qualifications impose themselves. Not all discourse has an author; nor do we demand it, surrounded as we are in our everyday living by a whole tissue of discourse to the varying interweaving strands of which we would not even know how to begin to pose the demands of authorship. These demands are, indeed, limited in relation to film; leaving aside the mass of material presented by television, think merely in this respect of the range of documentary, educational,

214

medical, newsreel works for which only exceptionally do we bring
into play any notion of the author. Even within the very area of
the book (to which the assumptions and models of authorship are
so closely connected), similar kinds of limitation can be seen to
apply. Many scientists, for example, produce books; only a very
few (a Heisenberg or a Bronowski), however, achieve the accepted
status of an author: the validity of science, in fact, is that it is
assumed as being without author, nowise particular but a clear
and general demonstration of reality (something of the same
assumption lies behind conventional conceptions of film documentary, though film also knows a convention of personal documentary, the cineast as witness – Marker on Cuba). Where the
idea of authorship is firmly established, doubts and limitations still
persist: how are we to deal with films on which a director – an
author – may have been involved in some other capacity (scenarist,
assistant director) or which he may have realised in collaboration
or to which he may have contributed no more than a brief sequence
(Resnais's contribution to *L'an 01*)? What of the problem of
control which the *auteur* theory confronted in its applications to
Hollywood directors? (Similar questions arise with regard to the
idea of authorship in literature.)

Such questions confirm the assumption of the author as originator, as source, and these ideas are then traditionally theorised,
more or less sophisticatedly, through notions of the 'creative imagination', of 'personality', 'spontaneity', 'originality', or whatever.
As source, the author produces 'works', closed units of discourse
from without himself, the series of which will have a further unity
that will be available for discussion in terms of the author's development, his 'maturity' and so on. It is these emphases that Buscombe sums up in his complex of genius, originality and organic
unity.

What can it mean, however, to speak of the author as a source
of discourse? The author is constituted only in language and a
language is by definition social, beyond any particular individuality
and, as Saussure put it in respect of natural language, 'to be accepted such as it is'. One can see how the question and the objection
are, in fact, answered in the distinction between language and
discourse, between general *langue* and singular usage. There is
support for this in linguistics in the recognition formulated by
Jakobson of increased freedom in individual language use propor-
tionate to the increased size of the linguistic unit: in the combination of distinctive traits into phonemes, the user's liberty is nil;
in the combination of phonemes into words, his liberty is heavily

circumscribed; in the formation of sentences, he is much less constrained, though his 'creativity' depends on the formal constraint
of the set of syntactic structures that transformational generative
grammar seeks to describe in its model of competence; in the
combination of sentences into blocks of discourse, finally, his liberty grows very substantially indeed and so the sentence becomes
the upper limit of linguistics as a science, the threshold beyond
which lies the individual and hence the unformalisable.

The dangers of this account can be readily seen: it tends to
instrumentalise language and it is precisely this instrumentalisation
that supports the idea of authorship in its conventional terms;
consciousness and language are confused as an immediate unity in
the flow of expression (this immediacy of consciousness is that
bourgeois conception of 'man' as the punctual subject of history
which Marx attacked in, for example, the *German Ideology*; 'man'
and 'author' go hand in hand, the latter a particular instance of
the former). In connection with cinema, an account of this kind is
especially tempting since the straight application of the *langue/
parole* model to film has led to the idea of cinema as a realm of
pure performance, as being a language without a *langue*, the perfect
expressive medium. (Critical discussion of this can be found in
various of the articles included in the special issue of *Screen*, vol.
14, nos. 1/2, on cinesemiotics). Many intuitive accounts of cinema
as language depend exactly on this equation of consciousness and
instrument in direct expression – Astruc's *caméra-stylo*, as Buscombe points out, is one instance of this. Classically, the *auteur*
theory cannot but confirm this expressionism; the author is constituted *at the expense of* language, of the orders of discourse (he
is what the texts can be stripped away to reveal). The effect of this
confirmation can be seen at its clearest when the theory functions
– and it seems inevitably always finally so to function – as a mode
of evaluation.

To combat this, Edward Buscombe proposes other ways of looking at the cinema: '(a) the examination of the effects of the cinema
on society (mass media research, etc.); (b) the effects of society on
the cinema (the influence of ideology, of economics, of history,
etc.); (c) a sub-division of (b), the effects of films on other films'.
There will probably be an overall agreement with these as general
emphases of areas with which reflection on cinema should be
concerned. What is perhaps limiting is the formulation of these
emphases in terms of a simple process of addition, as so many
approaches that can be added to *auteur* theory. It would seem
rather that the development of these emphases must constitute a

radical criticism of *auteur* theory; one cannot merely consider the 'influence of ideology' alongside that theory, retaining both as different 'approaches', for the notion of the author is itself a major ideological construction (like, for example, the 'realism' of film) and any attention to cinema as ideological articulation must come back on that notion and its assumptions. The force of Buscombe's proposals cannot be limited to a plea for a variety of independent and pacific approaches the sum of which will give a better insight into film (better because the disposition of a quantitatively greater number of separate insights); what is in question is the production, through the development of these proposals, of new objects the formalisation of which will provide not so much an insight as a theoretical grasp of film as signifying practice, a new problematic in which traditional notions are radically displaced.

Buscombe's paper effectively recognises the necessity of such a displacement. In relation to the idea of authorship, the theoretical object that the development of such a recognition entails is the *subject*; the need is for the construction of a theory of the subject with regard to the specific signifying practice of film. It is just such a theory that the notion of the author forecloses, determining a history of the cinema (how that history is conceived and written) and the history of cinema (operating an effective determination). Thus, for instance, the liberation of the camera is the evolution of its instrumental perfection (Balzac could declare an exactly similar view towards language); constructed to reproduce the centrality of the subject as punctual source (to sustain the ignorance of his subjection), it is given more and more as the point of his expression: the subject-author expresses himself in an immediate independence.

One or two elements of the displacement that a theory of the subject would operate may be worth briefly mentioning here. The function of the author (the effect of the idea of authorship) is a function of unity; the use of the notion of the author involves the organisation of the film (as 'work') and, in so doing, it avoids – this is indeed its function – the thinking of the articulation of the film text in relation to ideology. A theory of the subject represents precisely an attempt, at one level, to grasp the constructions of the subject in ideology (the modes of subject-ivity); it thus allows at once the articulation of contradictions in the film text other than in relation to an englobing consciousness, in relation now, that is, to a specific historico-social process, and the recognition of a heterogeneity of structures, codes, languages at work in the film and of the particular positions of the subject they impose. (It is evident that a theory of the subject will then question the simple use of the *langue/parole* model.)

A theory of the subject would provide a way of recasting the problem posed by Buscombe, in the paragraphs immediately preceding his original conclusion,* concerning the 'either/or choice', conscious or unconscious, 'creative artist' or 'unconscious catalyst' (note that 'unconscious' is here loosely used, with no precise analytical reference). Buscombe writes:

> It's quite* possible to do an *auteur* analysis of, say, Dickens, which would detect the presence of unconscious themes in his work, yet Dickens was far more independent of outside pressures than any Hollywood director has ever been. At the same time, a great deal of Dickens' 'meaning' was conscious (as the notes for his novels show). The either/or situation has arisen, it would seem, because traditionally it has been felt that for there to be meaning in a work there must be someone who deliberately put the meaning there. Wollen is no doubt quite right to resist this notion. But need we throw out the baby with the bath-water? Can't we say that the films of a director may reveal both an unconscious structure *and* a meaning which he has put there?

The equation of unconscious themes and outside pressures (with its corollary of conscious intention and independence as the alternative) seems especially significant in the emphases and developments of *auteur* theory. On the one hand, we find ideas of personality, free-wheeling creativity, independent intention; on the other, those of unconscious structures, constraints, effects from 'outside'. In theory, one might assign different procedures to these two emphases: stylistic analysis and structural analysis (of the kind developed by Lévi-Strauss). In practice, *auteur* theory seems to mix the two (the proportions vary as Buscombe shows in his account) in a confused strategy that generally refuses to develop theoretically the results it produces. The themes and shifting antinomies which *auteur* theory so often traces – think, for example, of Wollen's description of Ford and Hawks in the second chapter of *Signs and Meaning* – are ideological formations; it determines, in other words, the particular inscriptions of ideology by a corpus of films (the principle of pertinence for the corpus being that of authorship). If this recognition is held, new problems arise which it becomes increasingly important to consider. One such problem is that of the inscription of the subject in ideological formations and this cannot be formulated simply as the question of 'outside pressures'. Indeed, if we look at the work of Dickens, Buscombe's example* of a relative freedom from 'outside pressures', it can be seen that it responds to almost every ideological pressure of the age, so much so that it reads as a massive *dispositif* of the ideological formations then current (no form of discourse that is not somewhere assumed, even when this leads to what is defined as 'contradiction' and finally, in the later texts, overspills the given assumptions of representation to produce something of a frantic – the theme of negation, of endless circulation, of disorigination – dramatisation of the discursive orders of these formations). What is crucial is the focus on the languages, codes, orders of discourse that 'cross' the text and the analysis of the activity it brings to bear on them. The *text*, the new object that provides the necessity for a theory of the subject in relation to film, is precisely the space of the breakdown of the opposition between 'inside' and 'outside', 'dependent' and 'independent' and so on. (For discussion of the notion of *text*, see the first section of Ben Brewster's contribution to the present issue of *Screen* [vol. 14, no. 3, Autumn 1973, pp. 29– 43].) Another problem is that of the construction of the ideological subject, the production of the subject as support for ideological formations, and it is here that psychoanalysis plays a fundamental theoretical role as description of the setting in position of the individual subject. As far as the specific practice of film is concerned, it would seem that the psychoanalytical intervention in a general theory of the subject needs at once to be focused as a critical perspective on the use of the idea of authorship and its assumptions and to be employed to disengage within that idea, and hence to operate its methodological displacement, 'individual' and 'person'; where the latter is the ideological construction of the author, the former marks a configuration of elements, the subject in his particularity the determination of which, its 'history', is the task of psychoanalysis. The interrogation of a group of films within this history is not the revelation of the author but the tracing in the series of texts of the insistence of the unconscious (in the Freudian sense of the term). Such an interrogation meets difficulties similar to those encountered by the attempt to place literary texts in this perspective – absence of analytical situation, associations, transference, etc. – and it seems clear that the work that needs to be done at the moment is the close analysis of the systems of particular texts ('textual systems' in Metz's terminology) in relation to the ideological formations they reflect or articulate and the positions in which they inscribe the subject and, overall, to the whole process of subject and sense in the text. (We need, for example, to begin to reflect on the modes of relation and displacement between subject of *énonciation* and subject of *énoncé* in film.)

The list of problems could be extended and their consideration, together with that of those mentioned, is the development of that new problematic to which Edward Buscombe's proposals point and within which the question of the *auteur* theory is recast. What then remains, if anything, of that theory? The passage quoted by Buscombe from Wollen's postscript to the revised edition of *Signs and Meaning* perhaps provides one answer, though preceding formulations there tend to pull it back into rather traditional terms, in its distinction of Fuller and 'Fuller': 'But Fuller or Hawks, or Hitchcock, the directors, are quite separate from "Fuller" or "Hawks" or "Hitchcock" the structures named after them, and should not be methodologically confused'. The author, that is, may return as a *fiction*, figure – fan of elements – of a certain pleasure which begins to turn the film, or series of films the ones over the others, into a plurality, a play of assemblage and dispersion. Grasped thus, the author, like its corollary the reader as passive receiver, now becomes part of an activity of writing–reading; we come back once again, in other words, to the new object of the text, space of the process of sense and subject.

25 · Geoffrey Nowell-Smith: 'Six authors in pursuit of *The Searchers'* (extract)

Screen, vol. 17, no. 1, Spring 1976

The article from which this extract is taken was written as a critique of an issue of *Screen Education* (no. 17, Winter 1975–6) which was wholly devoted to outlining a variety of critical approaches (authorship, genre, images, industry) as they might be applied in teaching Ford's film, *The Searchers*. The extract opens up issues which are not made explicit elsewhere – the fascination and denial of the author, the hesitation between 'fiction of the author' and 'author of the fiction', and the insistence of the author as a function of the consumption and possession of 'his' text. I have opened the extract with a specific critique which Nowell-Smith offers of the '*Screen Education* team' since the point which he makes seems to be an important one for education.

My quarrel with the *Screen Education* team can best be expressed by saying that, having themselves travelled the auteurist route towards *The Searchers*, they then turn round and bar access to that route to anyone who would follow them. For both the theoretical position set out in the issue and the related educational strategies are resolutely anti-auteurist. Thus not only are students likely to find themselves stuck with watching a film that they have no particular reason for liking, though their mentors apparently do, but (more seriously) there is an unexplained disjunction between two modes of presence of the text: a mode (accessible to the writers) in which subjective processes are recognised; and another (for public consumption) in which the film text is objectified as commodity.

The objectification of the film-text is the outcome of a critical practice, widespread in the last few years, which was in struggle against subjectivist tendencies in criticism – on the one hand the inscription of the values of the critic into the account of the film, and on the other hand the ascription of the values of the film to an originating source, the mind of the author. (These tendencies might be called '*Sight and Sound*' and '*Movie*' respectively.) The struggle was, however, conducted in a partial and one-sided manner. The new criticism ('*Screen*'?) tended, among other things, to confuse subjectivism (the affirmation of the 'full' subject) with the processes of the subject as such. It also conceded too readily the commodity character of films, while stopping short of a recognition of the contradictions of the commodity form. In denouncing one mystification, it succumbed to another. Meanwhile semiotics was appropriated in its positivistic (pre-Kristeva) form as a science of signifying systems rather than as a process of production of knowledge of other signifying processes.

One particular effect of this critical operation has been to give currency to the naturalisation of the author as a sub-code. The author (external to the text) records his presence through the signs of this sub-code, to which the reader (also external to the text) can then attribute codic pertinence, or not, as the case may be. Auteur films, on this interpretation, can then be distinguished from non-auteur films by the degree to which the authorial sub-code imposes itself as a necessary component of reading on any spectator of average or above average cinematic literacy.

Now *The Searchers* is a film in which the authorial sub-code (if that is what it is) imposes itself with particular force – through the mise-en-scène as well as in the thematic structure, and through the agency of people other than the director himself. If we adopt the distinction made by Peter Wollen in the 1972 Postscript to *Signs and Meaning in the Cinema* between John Ford the person and 'John Ford' the set of structures, then it has to be said that 'John Ford' is as much present in the work of collaborators who made the film with and for the director as in the work of the director (John Ford) in person. Conversely John Ford (as person) has left his mark more heavily on the system of the mise-en-scène than in the thematic structure, which is largely generic.

What the play with inverted commas aims to do is to distinguish the author as empirical origin (John Ford, the man with the eye-patch who isn't Raoul Walsh) from the author as effect of the text ('John Ford'). But the author as effect of the text cannot simply be objectified in the form of a sub-code. Nor can this supposed sub-code be then re-related, *tel quel*, to the author as producing subject: for a variety of reasons.

First of all, if we understand by code or sub-code a pattern of possibilities more or less formalisable as paradigms (the Fordian sub-code would contain the paradigm desert/garden but would also not contain, in significant form, the paradigm individual/group) then we should also expect to be able to situate these paradigms in relation to the non-authorial sub-codes of the text. In Ford's case there is clearly a semantic sub-code to be placed on the side of the codes of the content. But there are also other 'Fordian' textual effects which do not belong there, but on the side of expression; and in the case of other authors (Welles, Lupino, Hitchcock) there are also inscriptions of the author via his or her personal presence, as actor or actress, in the film.

Whereas many effects on the side of expression can be reduced to their signifieds (e.g. in Ford, the effects that signify reticence) and so brought on to a level with the semantic paradigms, this is not always the case. The authorial sub-code, therefore, cannot be easily situated within the other impersonal codes of the text. Either we must say that there are several authorial sub-codes (of expression and of content etc, etc) or we must see the author as criss-crossing that text and marking it at various levels, in which case it would be better to talk of the author as system. Combining the two approaches (codes and system), we can argue that the Fordian system (in Metzian terms an inter-textual sub-system) incorporates various sub-codes, at least one of which (the semantic oppositions desert/garden etc) is generic in origin. But each of these sub-codes, on their entry into the system, concurs to produce 'John Ford' as a presumed subject of the 'statement' (*énoncé*) of the film – even though John Ford may not be their empirical origin. Here it is important that the system be seen as constructed by (perhaps it would be better to say 'in') the reader. But the process of construction of the particular sub-system which is the author involves not just the reading of marks which happen to be there but the positing of one of the conditions of their coherence, a condition which holds the film in place not just as narrated facts but as discourse, and which I would call the discursive, or narrating, instance. When Stephen Heath (*Screen*, vol. 14 no. 3, Autumn 1973, p. 91), following Wollen, says that the structures 'Fuller' etc. are separate from the directors Fuller etc. and should be kept methodologically distinct, this is not in order to naturalise or objectify the marks in the text, but to insist on the intersubjectivity of the process of reading – an intersubjectivity in which the 'author' does not, however, appear as total person. But where he goes on to state that the author can return as a *fiction*, I would be more cautious. It seems to me rather that the 'fiction' of the author enables us to locate an *author of the fiction* who is by no means dispersed but who in 'his' notional coherence provides the means for us to grasp the text in the moment of its production before us.

The problem that then faces us is that the ascription of a narrating instance, in the form, say, of a speaking voice (whether or not it is taken as the voice of a named person), can easily constitute a thoroughly bourgeois mode of appropriation of the film text. Both Wollen and Heath try to avoid this danger, the former by his insistence on the fissuring of the text as against its posited coherence, and the latter by deconstructing not only the author as subject but also the receiver. But the problem cannot be suppressed that easily in terms of the textual relation itself. Another relation interposes itself, which is ideological and, in the last instance, economic, and has to do with the packaging of the text in commodity form.

Classic authorial readings (e.g. in Sarris, with his naive identification of 'Ophuls' with Ophuls) attempt to transcend the commodity form by re-instituting the author as personal subject of the text. The critic enters into dialogue with the 'artist' in a language which denies the subsumption of either one into capitalist relations of production. The modified authorial reading which I am proposing, and which locates the author only as author of the fiction, may seem contaminated in the same way, in so far as it appears to invite the reader, and the bourgeois critic in particular, to make the film the object not just of consumption but of an act of appropriation. As bourgeois critic (complete with intellectual super-ego etc.) I do not just enter into a process of dispersal and inter-mixture with the film, but perform a salvaging operation which makes the text, via its 'author', my ideological property over and above its role as object of consumption. 'John Ford' thus becomes part of my intellectual patrimony, along with 'Thomas Mann' or 'Marcel Duchamp' or whoever it may be. The possibility of making the appropriation, however, is not in fact the result of any arbitrary 'auteurist' choice on my part. The text is appropriable in any case, by virtue of its immanent coherence – as bourgeois text. All I have done extra is to have located the strongest form of this coherence – authored discourse – and given it a name.

26 · Christian Metz: 'History/discourse: a note on two voyeurisms'

Edinburgh '76 Magazine, Edinburgh Film Festival, 1976 (first published Paris, 1975)

The importance of the relationship between history and discourse for theories of subjectivity in film has already been indicated in the introduction to this section. Here, Metz, from a position identified with psychoanalysis, elaborates the implications of the relationship for film, raising the questions of the subject which are involved. Metz opens up the question of subjectivity to notions of voyeurism, and of how the voyeuristic spectator relates to the subject of the enunciation. The essay has little explicit reference to notions of authorship but its implications are considerable, particularly in its posing of the relation between history and discourse in terms of the relation between cinema as text and as institution. While it may not be that simple (the discursive cannot simply be put outside the text), the inclusion of the cinema as institution in the problematic is vitally important.

This translation of Metz's essay, along with the comments on it by Geoffrey Nowell-Smith which follow, was published in the 1976 Edinburgh Film Festival Magazine in conjunction with the Festival's special event on psychoanalysis and the cinema.

I am at the cinema. The images of the Hollywood film unfold before my eyes. One of those narrative representational films – not necessarily made in Hollywood – that we think of when we talk about 'going to the pictures'; the type of picture that it is the function of the film industry to produce. Not simply the film industry, but, more widely, the whole contemporary *cinematic institution*. For these films are not just thousands of pounds of invested capital which have to be made to pay so that they can be recovered with interest and reinvested. They presuppose (if only to ensure the circulation of the money) an audience who will pay to see them, i.e. who want to see them. The cinematic institution is much wider than that sector (or aspect) of the cinema which is described as directly commercial.

Is it a matter of ideology? The audience has the same ideology as the films that are served up to them; they fill the cinemas and

225

so the machine keeps on running. Of course. But it is also a question of desire, and so of symbolic position. In Emile Benveniste's terms, the traditional film presents itself as history, not as discourse. Yet it is a discourse if one relates it to the film-maker's intentions, to its influence on the public, etc. But its defining quality, and the secret of its efficacy as a discourse, is that it effaces all marks of enunciation, and disguises itself as a story. History, as we know, is always about already 'completed' events; in the same way, the transparent film, with a narrative that purports to tell everything, rests upon a denial that anything is absent or that anything has to be searched for. We see only the reverse (and always more or less regressive) face of those factors, the one which is completed and satisfied, the formulated accomplishment of an unformulated wish.

When we talk about political or economic 'systems' we think of a certain arrangement of forces functioning together, like the engine of a car in a certain gear. Desire too has its systems or gears: its plateaux, short and long, of economic stabilisation, its points of equilibrium in relation to the defences of the psyche and its contributory formations (for example, the history itself, i.e. the narrated without the narrator, rather like a dream or a fantasy). It is not easy to find a smooth-running arrangement and much preliminary exploration is required. (The cinema groped about a lot, from 1895 on, before it found the formula which is dominant today). The smooth-running arrangement is a socially-produced phenomenon, and one which will be unmade by the next evolution. But like a political equilibrium, it is not subject to modification every minute. There is no teeming reservoir of arrangements to be put in at will. And any one of those which function really well is a highly self-sufficient machine tending to perpetuate itself and to take over the mechanisms of its own reproduction (the memory of satisfaction derived from one film becomes the projected goal in viewing another). Such is the case with the films which occupy the screens today – the exterior screens of the cinema itself, the interior screens of the *fictional*, i.e. that Imaginary – protected, and consented-to – which is offered to us by the 'diegesis'.

How shall I place myself as subject in evoking these films? I am in the act of writing these few lines, which are also a tribute to one of those men who have seen clearest*, from the *énoncé* itself, all

---

* Metz's essay originally appeared in a volume in honour of Emile Beveniste on his retirement from the Collège de France: *Langue, discours, société*, Paris, Editions du Seuil, 1975. [Ed.]

the distantiations that may be incorporated into the act of enunciation (as a distinct instance) and all the reinvestments that may in turn take place at the level of the *énoncé*. So, for the time in which I am writing this article, I am going to adopt one of the several attitudes at my disposal, the one which will permit my 'object', the standard film, to unfold the best. In the cultural psychodrama of 'positions', I shall not today adopt the role of someone who likes that kind of film, or someone who does not. The signs I shall imprint on my page are those of someone who likes to go and see them in inverted commas, who likes to absorb them like dated quotations, or like a wine which always tastes nice however many times you drink it, with an accepted ambivalence between anachronistic affection and the knowing sadism of someone who wants to break open the toy in order to see how it works.

For the type of film I am thinking of has a strong social and analytic existence. It cannot be reduced to a money-making gadget invented by grasping producers. It exists as our work, as that of the epoch which consumes it, as an *aim of consciousness*, springing from unconscious roots, without which we cannot understand the movement of forces which underlie the institution and account for its duration. It is not enough for the studios to deliver to us a small purpose-built mechanism entitled 'fiction film', it has to fulfil its purpose, or at the very least it has to work: the film must '*happen*'. And where it happens is that economic disposition which that history modelled in all of us at the same time as it modelled cinema industry.

I am at the cinema, attending a film show. *Attending*. Like a midwife who attends at a birth, and thereby also helps the woman, I am present to the film in two (inseparable) ways: witness and helper; I watch, and I aid. In watching the film I help it to be born, I help it to live, since it is in me that it will live and it was made for that: to be seen, i.e. to come into existence only when it is seen. The film is exhibitionist, as was the nineteenth-century novel with its plot and its characters, which the cinema imitates (semiologically), of which it is the continuation (historically), and which it has replaced (sociologically, since writing today takes different forms).

The film is exhibitionist, and it is not. Or at any rate there are several kinds of exhibitionism, and several corresponding kinds of voyeurism, several possible outlets for the scopic drive, some more at peace with themselves than others, participating to a greater or lesser degree in a calm and rehabilitated perverse practice. Real exhibitionism always contains an element of triumph, and is always bilateral – in the exchange of fantasies if not in the actions themselves. It is of the order of discourse, not history, resting upon the play of crossed identifications, on a continuous voluntary exchange of 'I' and 'you'. The perverse couple (who have their equivalents in the history of cultural productions) live out, in the game of passing the ball back and forth, the desire to see in its ultimate indivisibility (an indivisibility which characterised it at source, in the narcissism of the baby) caught in perpetual revolution between its two faces: active/passive, subject/object, to see/to be seen. If there is triumph in this sort of representation, it is because what is exhibited is not the person, but through him the act of exhibition itself. The one knows he is being seen, wills it, identifies himself with the voyeur whose object he is (but who also constitutes him as subject). It is a different economic system, a different arrangement. Not that of the fiction film. But sometimes, to some degree that of the theatre, where actor and spectator are present to each other, and the *action* (of players and public) is a playful sharing of roles (of 'jobs'), consented to actively by both, a ceremony which always has a certain civic quality, engaging more than the private man, a festivity. Even at the caricatural level of the West End show with its cocktail party atmosphere, the theatre retains something of its Greek origins, its climate of citizenship, of being an activity for public holidays where a whole people assembled to look at itself. (But even then there were slaves, who did not go to the theatre, a hidden mass making possible a democracy in which they themselves did not share).

The film is not exhibitionist. I look at it, but it does not look at me looking at it. It knows what I am doing, but it does not want to know. It is this fundamental denial which has channelled all of the classic cinema into the 'history' mould, which has relentlessly erased its supporting discourse, which made of it, in the best of cases, a beautiful closed object which one can only enjoy without its knowledge, against its will, an object whose boundaries are so perfectly sealed off that it cannot be turned inside-out into a subject capable of saying 'yes'.

The film knows it is being looked at, and does not know. Here we must be a little more precise. Because the one who knows and the one who does not are in fact not completely one and the same thing (it is the property of every denial to contain a split). The one who knows is the cinema as an *institution* (and its presence in every film, i.e. the discourse that lies behind the story), and the one who does not want to know is the end product, the film as *text*: the story. During a film-show the public is present to the actor, but the actor is absent to the public, and during the shooting, when the actor was present, it was the public which was absent. So the cinema manages to be both exhibitionist and secretive. The exchange of seeing and being seen is fractured down the centre and the parts spread over different moments in time: another split. It is never my partner who I see but his photograph. That does not make me any less a voyeur, but a voyeur according to a different system, that of the primal scene and the keyhole. The rectangular screen permits every type of fetishism, encourages the sense of 'things nearly seen', its sharp vibrant edge barring our view at just the height it wants, sending us plunging into the mysterious abyss.

In this type of fetishism (which today forms a stable and well-ordered economic plateau) the mechanism of gratification rests on my knowledge that the object being looked at does not know it is being looked at. 'To see' is no longer to give something back, but to take something by surprise. That 'something' which is made to be taken by surprise has gradually become installed and organised in its function, and by a sort of institutional specialisation (like those places which cater for 'special tastes') it has become history, the 'story' of the film, the thing that one goes to see when one says 'I'm going to the pictures'.

The cinema was born much later than the theatre, at a period when social life was strongly marked by the concept of the individual – or, in its nobler version, the 'person' – when there were no longer any slaves to enable the 'free men' to form a relatively integrated group, sharing a few major emotions and thus cutting down the problem of 'communication' which presupposes an already torn and fragmented culture. The cinema belongs to the private man (as does the classical novel which, unlike the theatre, is a 'history'), and the member of the audience neither wants nor needs a spectator for his voyeurism (it is dark in the cinema – only the screen is visible) nor an object who knows, or rather who wants to know, an object/subject who shares voluntarily with him in the exercise of the partial drive. His pleasure has another, entirely specific trajectory. All that he requires – but he requires it absolutely – is that the actor should behave as though he is not being seen, and so cannot see him, the voyeur. He must carry on with his ordinary occupations, live his life as the film story ordains, play around in his locked room, taking the greatest possible care not to notice that a rectangle of glass has been let into one of the walls, that he lives in a sort of aquarium which differs from real aquaria only in that it is a bit more sparing with its 'windows' (keeping something back is part of the scopic game).

Besides, the fish are on the other side, eyes glued to the glass, like the poor of Proust's Balbec who watched the guests at the grand hotel eating. Once again, the feast is not shared; it is a furtive feast, not a festive feast. An audience of fish, absorbing everything through their eyes, and nothing through their bodies. The cinematic institution demands a viewer who is immobile and silent, a *secret* viewer, constantly in a state of sub-mobility and hyper-perception, alienated and happy, acrobatically attached to himself by the invisible wire of sight, a viewer who only retrieves himself as subject at the last moment, by a paradoxical identification with his own self, stretched to the limit in the pure act of watching. This is not the viewer's identification with the characters in the film (which is secondary) but his prior identification with the instance of seeing (which itself cannot be seen): the film itself as discourse, as an instance which *foregrounds* the story, which delivers it for us to see. If the traditional film tends to suppress all the marks of the subject of enunciation, this is in order that the viewer may have the impression of being that subject himself, but an empty, absent subject, a pure capacity for seeing (all the 'content' being on the side of the seen). The important thing is that the spectacle which is 'taken by surprise' should also be surprising, that it should (like any hallucinatory gratification) bear the mark of external reality. The 'story' as system makes it possible to reconcile all that, since history, in Emile Benveniste's terms, is always (by definition) a story from nowhere, told by nobody, but received by someone (without which it would not exist). It is therefore, in a sense, the receiver (or rather the receptacle) who tells it; while at the same time it is not told at all, since the receptacle is required merely as an empty space, within which the purity of the utterance without an utterer will resound all the better. All this totally confirms Jean-Louis Baudry's contention that the primary identification in the viewer operates at the level of the camera itself.[1]

So can we identify this process with the mirror phase[2], as Baudry does? Yes, to a large extent (we have basically been saying just that). But not entirely. For what the child sees in the mirror: the other which becomes *I*, is, nonetheless, the image of his own body, so there remains an identification (and not merely a secondary one) with the *thing seen*. In the traditional cinema, the viewer no longer identifies with anything but seeing; his image does not appear on the screen, the primary identification is no longer constructed around a subject—object, but around a pure object, all-seeing and invisible, the vanishing point of monocular perspective which the cinema took over from painting. And, conversely, all the seen is thrown on to the side of the pure object, the paradoxical object which draws its peculiar force from its confined state. The situation is one of suspended but violent explosion, in which a double denial, without which there would be no story, has to be maintained at any price: the seen does not know it is seen (in order to know, it would have to be, to a certain extent, a subject) and its ignorance permits the voyeur not to recognize himself as voyeur. All that remains is the raw fact of seeing, lawless seeing, seeing of the *Id* ungoverned by an *Ego*, seeing without marks or place, directing us into vicarious experience like the narrator-as-God or the viewer-as-God; it is the 'story' which exhibits itself, the story which reigns.

Notes

1 See Jean-Louis Baudry, 'Ideological effects of the basic cinematographic apparatus', *Film Quarterly*, vol. 28, no. 2, Winter 1974–5, pp. 39–47; translated from *Cinéthique*, nos. 7–8. [Editor's note]
2 See 'Notes on terms'. [Editor's note]

27 · Geoffrey Nowell-Smith: 'A note on "history/discourse"'

Edinburgh '76 Magazine, Edinburgh Film Festival, 1976

As well as commenting on Metz's essay, and situating it usefully within the project of psychoanalysis in the cinema, Nowell-Smith's note also problematizes Metz's position, and specifies some of the questions of subjectivity in a way in which they are relevant to questions of authorship (and 'spectatorship'). The note, as well as providing a provocative conjunction with Metz's essay, also refers back to Nowell-Smith's earlier position on authorship in relation to *The Searchers* (above), and forward to the essay by Nick Browne on the 'geography of authority' in relation to point-of-view.

Psychoanalytic study of art is as old as psychoanalysis – and in some form no doubt dates way beyond psychoanalysis proper, whether as science or as cure. But for the most part it has taken the form of a wild analysis, of pseudo-analysis, of characters and authors. Hamlet is neurotic, and so, we infer, was Shakespeare.[1] Psychoanalysis of the text, and of the intersubjective textual relation, is, however, relatively recent. Although some early analysts, including Freud himself, had certain ideas about how texts (or performances) might reproduce processes whose structure was first revealed in analysis, it is only in recent years, with the insertion of signification into the problematic of psychoanalysis, notably through the work of Jacques Lacan, that a reciprocal action has become possible and the psychoanalytic concept of the subject has become a necessary part of the study of signifying systems.

Structural linguistics – and the semiotics which followed from it – was for the most part resolutely objectivist. It studied signifying systems as objects *per se*. The system might denote relations between subjects or be used to transmit messages between persons presumed to be subjects. But the notion of the subject and its representation within language was not seriously called into question. The subject was outside the system – on the one hand as an irrelevance to objective study, but on the other hand also as foundation, negligible because taken for granted.

232

This state of affairs was challenged, initially, by the work of Lacan within the field of psychoanalysis proper. In his assault on the notion of a transcendent ego (the foundation of metaphysics as well as the implicit base of linguistic 'science' and, need one add, the source of much neurotic unhappiness) Lacan showed that the subject is constructed in and through language, though in a relation of alterity to it. This discovery (itself based, at least in part, on the linguistic theories of Saussure and Jakobson) has profound implications for linguistics and for the study of all signifying forms. For one of the properties of language then becomes the relations that the subject can have to it and within it. As well as being a system of signs related among themselves, language incarnates meaning in the form of the series of positions it offers for the subject from which to grasp itself and its relations with the real.

In such a context the distinction which Saussure made, for formal reasons, between *langue* as system and *parole* as enactment has to be seen in a new light. For on the side of *parole* it is not the words as such but the fact of speaking them – and of who is speaking them – that constitutes the decisive relation to language as system.

Within *parole* therefore (but with implications also for *langue*) another distinction suggests itself, which is that between *énonciation* and *énoncé*. Both these terms tend to be translated into English as 'utterance', thereby obliterating the distinction, but basically *énonciation* (which I shall give henceforth as 'enunciation') means the act whereby an utterance is produced, and *énoncé* (which I shall give as 'statement') means what is thereby uttered in itself. This is not a distinction between form and content, nor yet one between context and text, but a distinction within the utterance itself between two forms, two contents and, indeed, two texts. Often there is no need to distinguish sharply between the two aspects. The enunciating instance can be either a matter of indifference (it doesn't much matter who says 'The Sun shines in August' or 'The King died in 1909') or else it can appear to be fused with the statement itself (as in 'I promised'). But it becomes clear on reflection that not only are the two instances distinct but they may even be in contradiction with each other. This is particularly the case when the relation between the addresser and the addressee is brought into the statement itself, as for example with the use of the personal pronouns 'I' and 'you'. The majority of statements contain a grammatical subject and a predicate, and very often neither of these invokes either addresser or addressee directly – or if they do it is some other position than the one they occupy at the moment of enunciation. The subject of the enunciation thus regularly stands outside the enunciated statement, even if it is the same person – as in 'I borrowed five pounds from your purse'. But if we look at that last statement more closely we can see that alongside the relation expressed in the statement (*énoncé*) itself, which registers money having been borrowed by one person from another, there is also a relation expressed in which I, the speaker, now enunciate and so engage my indebtedness to you who are being spoken to. An even more extreme case is provided by such phrases as 'I lied to you', which implicates another subject than the one who recently lied, this being the subject who is now (hopefully) telling the truth.

The problem of the subject in language thus becomes one of enunciation, or rather of the relation, always potentially contradictory, between enunciation and statement, *énonciation* and *énoncé*. This leads on to a further distinction, systematised by the French linguist Emile Benveniste, between discourse and history. Discourse and history are both forms of enunciation, the difference between them lying in the fact that in the discursive form the source of the enunciation is present, whereas in the historical it is suppressed. History is always 'there' and 'then', and its protagonists are 'he', 'she' and 'it'. Discourse however, always also contains, as its points of reference, a 'here' and a 'now' and an 'I' and a 'you'.[2] Benveniste cites as examples of the historical form in language on the one hand the statements of historians proper and on the other hand passages from novels representing events.[3] What characterises statements of this type – besides certain grammatical features such as the choice of tense – is the absence in the text of a point from which the enunciation stems. 'Solon established the laws' or 'The young man looked around the room' are statements which do not specify any subject of enunciation. The existence of the historian Glotz or the novelist Balzac is announced on the title page, but they conceal themselves at some point beyond, or outside, the text.

Discourse, by contrast, is always marked by the presence of a subject of the enunciation – whether this be the author/speaker as person or not. Discursive forms (or forms with a strong discursive element) include most oral communications and also oratory (even when written down), the essay, the letter and various forms of narrated fiction. A classic example of a novel visibly constructed around both a discursive and an historical order would be Laclos' *Les Liaisons Dangereuses* in which (discounting for the moment the further problem of the relation of the author, Laclos, to the text) the events represented are always related through the discourse of the characters writing letters to each other.[4] But almost any fictional form contains discursive elements, either bracketed, as with direct speech reported in inverted commas, or integrated into the text as 'free indirect' or as the standpoint of a narrator. Arguably the ambition of certain novelists, from Flaubert onwards, has been to collapse discourse into history and to naturalise events so that they seem to exist in a space defined from nowhere, but most often the effect has been the reverse. The modern novel, since Henry James, has been discursive *par excellence*.

But what of the cinema? Although the particular marks of discursive enunciation, the shifters – personal pronouns, tense, etc. – are present in the film through its use of written or spoken language, these are hardly sufficient to mark the film as a whole as discursive. Since speech in films is mostly bracketed – as the dialogue of particular characters – there arises the problem of a superior discursive or narrating instance, marked in some way in the structure of the film. The most prevailing assumption – and the one which Metz, in the article which precedes this, uses as his starting point – has been that the film is predominantly history and that, though there may be subjects of its statements (characters who are seen to speak and to perform actions) there is no way that the film as such (particularly the classic fiction film) identifies its own enunciation as proceeding from somewhere.

One way discourse can be integrated into the film – other than through the use of written language – is by 'point of view'.[5] Film narration generally proceeds by means of a series of shots, or by movements within the shot, which alter the angle from which a set of events is viewed. These changes of angle also constitute changes of point of view in so far as they successively incorporate vantage points external or internal to the action, and along, across or against the eyelines of the characters. But while an analysis of point of view may help us to individuate different discourses proceeding from the characters or from a point outside them, it does not yet solve the problem of the discourse of the film as such. Like phrases of dialogue, points of view are usually bracketed. When it is asked what is outside the brackets, or who or what does the bracketing, the answer usually remains the same. Particular discourses are all comprised within a meta-discourse, but this meta-discourse is not strictly speaking a discourse at all, but presents itself as history – a set of statements from which a subject of enunciation is absent.

It is here that psychoanalysis enters the picture. The psychoanalytic approach cannot rest content with the observation that the internal construction of a film is one which situates the events portrayed as lacking any enunciating subject. For psychoanalysis is crucially concerned with the intersubjectivity of the construction of meaning. In the absence of a subject of enunciation on the side of the film it is hard to see what position is possible for that other subject, that of the spectator him/herself. The spectating subject requires the relation to an other in order to situate itself, and somewhere the film must provide it with that other. (The objection that the spectating subject is comfortably situated in an armchair and knows perfectly well that it is so situated is here beside the point. Unless the film sustains a discourse towards that position – which is precisely what is at issue – then the relation screen/armchair is indeed conducive to fetishism.)

Elsewhere[6] I have argued that a narrating instance can often be found in the form of the author. But the search for a 'subject' of a film cannot be traced back in this way further than the discovery of a notional subject of its statements (*énoncés*). Particularly where a film is a studio product, a 'real' subject with which the spectator might engage is simply not inscribed into the film. The engagement of the spectator, except at rare moments, is therefore always with some or other aspect of the fiction. The absence of a clearly marked superior instance – a 'John Ford is telling me this' or an 'Universal Studios' or whoever it may be – encourages the setting up of various forms of discursive relation which are not linguistically bound but are informed by other structures co-existent with cinematic-linguistic systems proper. Here we may distinguish those relations which, although not linguistically (or cine-linguistically) bound, are specific to the form of the fictional text, and those whose structure can be defined from outside the fictional network. In the former category we can include various positional identifications with the characters – 'I am who the character is looking at', 'I am she who he is looking at', 'I am looking at them from where the camera is' etc. To the latter belong various relations which are normally defined in terms redolent of psychopathology – voyeurism, exhibitionism etc.

Two things are important to note here. One is that these relations are going to be set up anyway. It is proper to any work of art to posit quite a complex set of relations through which it can be grasped (or not) by the reader/viewer. The absence of a superior instance (or the concealment of this instance in the form of history) merely affects the scope and mobility of the others. Secondly it should be noted that all the relations so far mentioned are pre-eminently discursive, whatever other connotations some of them might also have. Exhibitionism, for example, is far from being just a nasty thing that dirty old men do to little girls. Quite apart from the fact that most exhibitionism in its 'real' pathological manifestations takes place in a context of complicity (within couples, or in artistic performance) the point is that the terms of the structure are those in which a relation between subject and object, active and passive, is constructed around an axis of seeing. (The exhibitionist creates the other as subject by letting himself be seen, while at the same time alienating himself in that other, etc.) The film, therefore, can hold a discourse towards the spectator as that which exhibits itself to be seen, or for that matter, as that which enables the spectator to see (identification with the camera as voyeur) or as an alternation of the two. Not only is exhibitionism, as Metz notes, 'of the order of discourse, not history' (which incidentally means that *what* is exhibited is to some extent irrelevant). It is also discursive articulation. History becomes discourse in so far as the exhibitionist/voyeurist relation (or, more simply, the relation of seeing and showing) presides over the construction of the film.

This state of affairs – including the aspect we may call a kind of necessary perversity of filmic construction – is not in fact all that different from what prevails in other art forms. In some ways the difference is only one of complexity. There are in the cinema so many more forms of potentially discursive relations to take account of. This has to do with the fact that the film is simultaneously spectacle, reproduction and narrative, and the organisation of (say) spectacle along the axis of narrative poses enormous problems of articulation. The voyeurist/exhibitionist relation often overlays somewhat uneasily on the construction of the film as narrative sequence. Hence the frequent difficulty in deciding which axis to privilege and whether the film as a whole has a single discursive structure at all (and by and large I would argue that usually it does not). But three points, I think, should be retained from Metz's attempts to 'psychoanalyse' the filmic text and the cinematic institution, even if the actual elaboration of them needs to be questioned.

One we have already mentioned: the tendency of films to disguise themselves as history and so to split the subject of enunciation into two halves – the 'real' subject not inscribed in the film, and the fictive subjects within the textual relation with whose positionality the spectating subject engages. One important feature which we have not so far discussed is that it represents events as having been accomplished. The film is present (during viewing) to the spectator, but only as something which is already past and which has already fixed a resolution for the problems it evokes. In so far as the film is successfully contained within its historicity – both its pastness and its plenitude – it is inevitably regressive, placing the spectating subject not beyond but short of desire, in an imaginary fulfilment. (In this analysis the ideological functioning of films would be very dependent on their naturalisation as history and also on the regression that accompanies it.) It is doubtful, however, to what extent the regression is actualised. This is not because people are not prone to regressing, in the cinema as at other times and places in their daily lives, but because the notion of a totally historical film is intrinsically self-defeating. Although the film may pose itself as history – thereby invoking a complex structure of disavowals, refusals of negativity etc. – it cannot do so without laying itself open, in the course of construction of its own plenitude, to other possible appropriations by the spectator. If ultimately the spectator is led back by the filmic system to a regressive point, where the film confirms itself as identical to its own beginning (already an extreme case), the journey is one with many detours in any of which the spectator might get lost, and therefore, so to speak, refound.

A second point concerns the specific relation of filmic narrativity to the axis of viewing. In addition to the structures of voyeurism and exhibitionism already mentioned (and analysable, incidentally, in phenomenological and existentialist terms as well as in psychoanalytical)[7], there arises the question of specularity and in particular, of the mirror phase posited by Lacan as a necessary nodal point in the constitution of the subject.[8] Metz is right, I think, to emphasise, both in 'History/Discourse' and elsewhere, an essential difference between the mirror relation as such, in which the child captures its own image (or is captivated by it), and cinematic representation, in which the one thing you don't see is your own image reflected.[9] Here what is significant is the fact of the contradiction: the screen is like a mirror, and yet one in which you don't see yourself. Hence the poignancy of the moment in All that Heaven Allows where Jane Wyman looks into the blank TV screen and sees her own face reflected back at her. But hence too the importance of mirror shots generally – the mirroring within the mirror by which identity (of characters and/or spectator) is variously doubled, split and recomposed. Because film is also narrative, however, the function of specularity can rarely be grasped, or impose itself, in a pure form. Not only do mirror shots perform a variety of functions,[10] but the specularity of the projected image itself will vary according to the range of identifications available to the spectator at any given time. These identifications, as Metz points out, are secondary and in a sense may be held not to inflect a primary identification of the spectator with him/herself as pure see-er opposing the screen image as pure external seen. I am not so sure about this. First of all it goes along with a general over-valuation of perception as a datum, which is very unFreudian, and secondly the very fact that something is posited as primary should make us instantly suspicious. To say something is primary is simply to locate it further back in the psychic apparatus. It does not, or should not, invite any conclusions about its efficacy. I would argue, therefore, that the so-called secondary identifications do tend to break down the pure specularity of the screen/spectator relation in itself and to displace it on to relations which are more properly intra-textual – i.e. relations to the spectator posited from within the image and in the movement from shot to shot.[11]

Thirdly, and last, we have the problem of the cinema as institution. As Metz remarks in *The Imaginary Signifier*,[12] the cinematic institution is not just the cinema industry but also includes 'the mental machinery – another industry – which spectators "accustomed to the cinema" have internalised historically and which had adapted them to the consumption of films.' This second apparatus stands in a complementary relation to the productive apparatus proper and is linked to it (and to a possible third apparatus, more narrowly psychical in scope) in so far as the demand which the productive apparatus supplies supposes a structure of wants which are socially and psychologically instituted. As Marx observes, whether the want satisfied by the commodity 'corresponds to the belly or the fantasy' is of no consequence: in the case of the cinema it is clearly fantasy.[13] But Metz is guilty of a gross oversimplification on both economic and psychological levels when he equates the functioning of the institution with the production of films as 'good objects' for the spectator (the term is Melanie Klein's) and with a supposed desire or want of the spectators to see the films that are usually produced. Such an equation leaves the terrain of psychoanalysis for that of the utilitarian psychology of Bentham and certainly departs from the terrain of Marxist economics (if indeed it was ever there) for the long exploded castles in the air of Say's law and the necessary harmony of supply and demand. When Metz further claims that the cinematic institution by definition produces more pleasure than unpleasure, the ideological mixture becomes even more suspect. What the cinema certainly does provide for the spectator is a use value, but whether this use value corresponds to pleasure in the Freudian sense is another question, which cannot be solved by recourse to tautology. It is yet another question again whether there is a correspondence between the exchange value realised by the producer and the use value obtained by the consumer. That there is some relation between what makes money for the producer and what gives pleasure to the audience is undeniable, but the relation is not an immediate one and by no means assumes equilibrium, let alone identity.

Fortunately, however, the functionalist and utilitarian equation is by no means necessary to Metz's hypothesis of the different apparatuses, and indeed runs counter to the main thrust of the argument. What is interesting to register here is the existence of different apparatuses, different economies (in the sense in which one can talk, for example, of a 'libidinal economy') which are not homologous with each other but overlap and interfere with one another at various points. One such point of interference would be precisely the production of films as (ostensibly) history rather than discourse, which is in part guaranteed by the relative anonymity of the productive apparatus and by the production of films as marketable objects. Conversely the existence in filmic textual systems of multiple points of entry into relations which are discursive can be correlated both to the diverse inheritance of previous forms of art and entertainment assumed by the cinema and reprojected onto the world market, and to a psychoanalytic instance – the possible forms of subject position faced with the cinematic apparatus as such. The cinema is a place where a lot of cotters come to the comb. The task of film theory is to disentangle them, not just cut them all off.

Notes

1 Freud himself was not exempt from this. See J. L. Baudry, 'Freud et la "Création Littéraire" ', in *Théorie d'ensemble*, Paris, Editions du Seuil, 1968, pp. 148–74.

2 These are the terms known in linguistics (since Jakobson) as 'shifters'. Their characteristic is that they are not definable as places in a system of object relations, but only by reference to the subject of enunciation itself. As well as certain pronouns and adverbs, a number of verbal forms (in English mostly the compound tenses 'I am eating', 'I have eaten', 'I shall eat') are discursive rather than historical, since they too acquire meaning in terms of the place of enunciation. See E. Benveniste, 'Les relations de temps dans le verbe français' in *Problèmes de linguistique générale*, Paris, Gallimard, 1966, pp. 237–50.

3 Benveniste, op. cit., pp. 240–1.

4 See T. Todorov, 'Les catégories du récit littéraire' in *Communications* 8, pp. 125–51. (English translation in *Film Reader*, no. 2, Evanston Ill., 1976). For Todorov the categories of history and discourse correspond (roughly) to those of *fabula* and *syuzhet* in the Russian formalists.

5 See E. Branigan, 'Formal permutations of the point of view shot', in *Screen*, vol. 16, no. 3, Autumn 1975, pp. 54–64.

6 'Six authors in pursuit of *The Searchers*', in *Screen*, vol. 17, no. 1, Spring 1976, pp. 26–33; see extract above.

7 As for example by Sartre in *Being and Nothingness*.

8 J. Lacan, 'The mirror-phase as formative of the function of the I' (1949) in *New Left Review*, no. 51, September–October 1968, pp. 71–77; see also 'Notes on terms' below.

9 C. Metz, 'The imaginary signifier', in *Screen*, vol. 16, no. 2, Summer 1975, p. 48.

10 E.g. in Welles (*Kane, Lady from Shanghai*) a multiple splitting of the character; in Ophuls (*Letter from an Unknown Woman*) an encounter with an ideal-ego in the form of an I-that-once-was; in Sirk (*Tarnished Angels*) imprisonment in images of the self, etc. Countless variations are possible. In Hawks (*Rio Bravo*), needless to say, looking into the mirror merely means giving way to a fatal (feminine) narcissism.

11 See, for example, Nick Browne, 'The spectator-in-the-text: the rhetoric of *Stagecoach*', in *Film Quarterly*, vol. 29, no. 2, Winter 1975–6, pp. 26–38. (An alternative version of the same article entitled 'Rhétorique du texte speculaire', appeared in French in *Communications* 23, 1975); see below.

12 Metz, op. cit., p. 19.

13 In *Capital*, vol. 1, Ch. 1. The formulation is both tentative and ironic, and Marx goes on to show (in vols II and III) that there is a big difference in the roles played by commodities, according to whether or not they are wage-goods (restoring and reproducing labour power).

28 · Sandy Flitterman: 'Woman, desire, and the look: feminism and the enunciative apparatus in cinema'

Ciné-Tracts, vol. 2, no. 1, Fall 1978

Sandy Flitterman's essay works to bring into relation a number of strands from within this section, and strands from beyond the scope of the Reader: from a starting point in the history/discourse distinction elaborated here by Metz she identifies herself with the work carried out in Laura Mulvey's essay, 'Visual Pleasure and the Narrative Cinema', which analyses the constitution of the woman as object of the male gaze; and she relates this to Raymond Bellour's essay, 'Hitchcock: The Enunciator', which traces the enunciative function of the look in Hitchcock's films, and particularly in Hitchcock's participation in his own films as bearer of the look. As Flitterman suggests, the conjunction is an important one for feminist analyses of film. What it does for theories of authorship is to problematize the look of the male director, to extend the dissolution of questions of authorship into questions of enunciation and subjectivity, and to give those questions a political priority.

Recent feminist analyses of film have sought to examine the signifying mechanisms in films understood as texts, that is as specific signifying practices. As Christian Metz has said, semiotics tries to give an account of filmic facts by examining their objective conditions of production rather than their projected own image. The utilization of a semiotic methodology informed by psychoanalysis (as elaborated in contemporary French interpretations of Freud) can provide useful insights into how films are understood and how the figure of the woman-image functions in a particular way within the space of representation and the time of narration to create a specific effect in the viewing subject. The image of woman is here figured as an empty sign, which speaks the desire of men: within the filmic text as it is structured, is there even a possibility for the formulation of her own desire? In analyzing the productive mechanisms of meaning in film, a psychoanalytically oriented semiotics can be brought to bear on the signifying function of woman as an object of male fantasy and on the problematic figuration of female sexuality (the unspoken, that which cannot be figured, the ruptures in the coherence of male patriarchal discourse) in the film-text – a text generated by an apparatus which is designed to produce a specific kind of pleasure. In this light the classical narrative cinema can be seen as a repository for male fantasy in which the visual and narrative exploitation of the woman is the pivotal figure which allows the machine to operate. Psychoanalysis is instrumental in facilitating understanding of spectator/film viewer/viewed relationships, emphasizing as it does notions of fantasy, and other concepts aligned with cinematic structure as it speaks the subject (both the producer of the text and the viewer whose viewing is also a fantasmatic production).

The look is both a metaphor in films and an integral part of filmic structure. The cinematic apparatus is designed to produce the look and to create in the spectator the sensation that it is she/he who is producing the look, dreaming these images which appear on the screen. Each filmmaker appropriates and then designates the look in a specific way – that is what characterizes a particular director's system of enunciation, the way the look is organized to create the filmic discourse. The central narrative function of cinema is based on the look (the filmed image is always the result of a look on something). One of the primary ways the filmic text is organized, then, is through the disposition of views: a complex intersecting web is created by a series of looks inscribed in the cinema, catching the spectator in a net of multiple identifications which are all mediated through the eye. A series of three look-relays can be established: (1) from the camera to the pro-filmic event; (2) from the viewer to the film projected on the screen; (3) among the characters within the diegesis. Across the visual trajectories the spectator is both producer of the looks and traversed by these looks. Hence the importance of such concepts as the eyeline match and point-of-view shots when seen in the light of Freudian notions of voyeurism, exhibitionism, and scopophilia, for illuminating the positioning and re-positioning of the spectator engaged in the activity of film-viewing, and for the analysis of visual pleasure which is offered by the traditional narrative cinema.

Film viewing is structured on a system of voyeuristic pleasure, the viewer's erotic contemplation of the spectacle working in complementarity with the pleasure of the filmmaker as it is figured in the film. The textual articulation of the desire of the filmmaker across the visual field dictates a specific position and function for the woman – as image and as lost object (distance from the object is intrinsic to scopophilic satisfaction). If the film is understood as a fantasmatic production, in which desire is the motor of both the psychic and cinematic apparati, the lost object is the condition of desire, its irreparable absence generating the metonymic movement of desire from one representation to another. The cinematic apparatus designates the position of the spectator as desiring subject and producer of the discourse in a position similar to that of the dreamer as enunciator of the dream. In the cinema, the enunciative apparatus, as articulated through the look, structures a specific relation of the spectator to the screen. It is possible to consider the cinematic apparatus as defining an institutional site in which the male appropriation of the scopic drive defines the woman irrefutably as object-image of the look.

In this enunciative apparatus, the film presents itself as history (in which the source of enunciation is suppressed, the verb tense is the preterite of already completed events, and the actants are 'he', 'she', and 'it') rather than as discourse (in which the enunciative source is present, its reference point is the present tense, and the pronouns 'I' and 'you' are engaged), according to Emile Benveniste's system.[1] It does this precisely because the marks of the subject of enunciation have been effaced, but it can only succeed to the extent that it disguises itself as history. The whole purpose of the apparatus is precisely to make it possible for the real subject of the enunciation – the viewer – to enter the discourse, to inscribe her/his own enunciation. To make this possible, the discourse must appear as lacking enunciation and thus must manifest itself as history, so that the viewer may have the impression of being the subject itself – an 'absent subject', a 'pure capacity for seeing'. Since by definition the story is told by nobody, from nowhere, it is the receiver who tells it. The film must present itself as history in order for the subject-effect to operate (everything is determined for the spectator's misapprehension of control of the images), and it is this effect which characterizes the filmic enunciation. Like all other aspects of the apparatus, it conceals its operation in order to exist as an apparatus.

The problem, then, is to examine the specific modes of operation of enunciation as it constitutes the subject. A major articulation of this in film is through the system of point-of-view. Logically, a deconstruction cinema will attempt to restore the marks of the subject of enunciation, or at least undermine the concealing operation which is produced and required by the apparatus. Thus by calling attention to the operating of the absent subject, a counter-cinema would reinsert this subject in the process of production. Therefore, as Laura Mulvey has pointed out,[2] feminist film practice must endeavor to generate new spectator–text relationships by rendering problematic the voyeuristic pleasures of cinema which have historically been embodied in the image of woman. Yet, the enunciative apparatus itself is so overdetermined, that the opportunity for a true counter-cinema to develop is very difficult – and it is to this level of complexity that the effort must address itself.

In her article on visual pleasure Laura Mulvey discusses scopophilia and woman's image-creation in terms of the objectification of women: the woman is the passive, still, inactive recipient of the male gaze. Raymond Bellour (in his analysis of Hitchcock's *Marnie*[3]) extends the notion of voyeurism to the apparatus itself, saying that the image of woman is actually constituted by a look. In the dominant patriarchal system of representation the active/looking, passive/looked-at split is delineated in terms of sexual difference; men are the active bearers of the look, women are the receivers. Through the look (always aggressive) and the articulation of point-of-view, woman is implicated in a position of passivity.

Mulvey also speaks of the fetishized image of the woman freezing the look, stopping the flow of the action into moments of erotic contemplation. The strong visual erotic impact of the highly coded image of woman connotes to-be-looked-at-ness. Within the diegesis, the male character bears the look of the spectator; as protagonist he controls the events, as the spectator's surrogate he controls the erotic power of the look. Thus as erotic object both within the diegesis and for the spectator, the woman-image serves as a locus for the gaze of male characters and of viewers.

Hitchcock provides a complex example of the combination of fetishistic scopophilia (in which the erotic instinct is focused on the look alone) and voyeuristic sadism (which coincides with the requirements of narrative, demanding as it does that changes occur and that action progresses). More particularly, in *Marnie* the look is central to the plot, oscillating between voyeurism and fetishistic fascination, and the confluence of these looks on the woman-image is the central mechanism of the filmic operation. Mulvey calls for a cinematic intervention which will disrupt the gaze, free the look of the camera and destroy the fascination built into the voyeuristic activity of cinematic viewing. However, as we shall see, since the erotic power of the look is built into the apparatus of cinematic enunciation itself, this is not so readily achieved.

In his article on Alfred Hitchcock's *Marnie*, entitled 'Hitchcock, The Enunciator', Raymond Bellour analyzes the enunciative function of the look. Through detailed analysis of one specific signifying mechanism (from among the many other operations which combine to generate the film-work), Bellour attempts to elaborate a theory of the enunciative apparatus in cinema. In the article he illustrates how the director uses his privileged position to represent his own desire, concentrating on the crucial function of the look in that process. For Bellour, the 'camera's look' implies virtual control, possession of the screen object. From the outset, Bellour makes the equation, body of the woman, film body; the film-work is posited as a dialectic of pursuit and possession – an aggression on the body of the woman. The camera, as the center of signifi-cation, is carrier of the look and through scopic possession of the object, assures the viewing subject of the integrity of the object. Bellour alludes to Hitchcock's power to make the image, to give Marnie concrete existence through the look. The vision of the male is seen here to be embedded in the apparatus; it is through the enunciative function of the look that the fantasy of the director, Hitchcock's film-wish, unfolds before the viewing subject. Fantasy here is understood in the sense of one of the modes of hallucinatory satisfaction of desire.

Bellour discusses how the 'camera's look' is inscribed in the film via the male's vision: from Hitchcock (the enunciator) to Mark Rutland, Strutt and Garrod, his fictional delegates. In the analysis of the first segment of the film, Bellour shows how Hitchcock inscribes the male characters onto the 'trajectory of virtual pos-session of the object' via the chain of the look. At this point the object is the woman-image. On the assumption that this film, as a production of desire across the scopic field, enacts the process whereby cinema 'exploiting the mechanism of the lure, and through the work of enunciation in the text, becomes the condition of orgastic pleasure': the director's, and through the subject-effect (since the cine-subject is artificial and in effect created by the apparatus), the spectator's, Bellour attempts to analyse how this process takes place. The image of the woman, simultaneously of-fered and snatched away, sets up 'the irreducible gap of the scopic drive'. The absence of the object is the condition of desire; here the structure of fantasy crystallizes around desire for the woman-image. Desire is here understood not as a relation to the real object independent of a subject, but as a relation to a representation.

Bellour maintains that Hitchcock defines his place as enunciator by monitoring the modalties of the scopic relationship to the object. In illustrating this, he designates three ways in which the 'camera's look' is inscribed in the film, specifically through camera move-ment, character movement, and in the variation in the distances between the two (camera and character). This modulation of these three 'complementary codic systems' is condensed in the single initial shot of Marnie, as the camera stops following her, detaches itself and remains stationary while she continues to recede into the distance. In this action, the spectator's double identification with the camera and with the object is foregrounded: by the same movement of separation the 'two processes of identification which transfix the spectator' – identification with the camera (in which Marnie is designated as object of our gaze) and identification with the object (in which the image of Marnie is constituted as a whole body) – coalesce. Here the woman as representation embodies the two contradictory aspects of pleasurable structures of looking, the scopophilic instinct (pleasurable looking at an erotic object) and ego libido (as engaged by narcissistic identification). The condensation of the processes of object choice, 'possessing' the object via the look, and identification, which operate on the subject in the cinematic viewing situation is here rendered cinematically in the breach effected between the camera's look and the spectator's gaze on the image of the woman.

Hitchcock appears at that point in the chain of events where the 'film-wish is condensed,' that point of crystallization in the film which is like the Freudian pun. He becomes a sort of double of Mark and Strutt who contribute to the 'creation' of the image of Marnie, but who are also 'caught in' the image of themselves caught by the look of the camera. An ironic doubling, since Mark and Strutt are at the outset Hitchcock's doubles. Bellour makes the point that here Hitchcock clearly intervenes as enunciator by inscribing himself in the chain of the fantasy. He literally inserts himself into the film, becoming one point in the relay of (male) looks (from the spectator through the fictional delegates) which constitute Marnie. From the floating image of Strutt's lustful description of her, (Fig. 1) to Mark's comment on her 'looks' (that image constituted through the looks given her by men) to her image-constitution effected by the camera (Fig. 2a), as if it had materialized Mark's thoughtful look in the shot which preceded this, we can see the gradual constitution of the image of the woman.

As Hitchcock appears in the hallway of the hotel, he looks first after Marnie (Fig. 2b) and then turns to the spectator, addressing the camera and in so doing, underlining his power as image-maker (Fig. 2c). By this intervention Hitchcock makes explicit the fact that the film, as discourse, is proceeding from somewhere, that it is he who is organizing the fiction and that he has delegated the look to his fictive surrogates. In terms of the history/discourse distinction discussed earlier, in the classical model, this position of enunciation is occulted, so that it appears as if the story proceeds from nowhere. Here Hitchcock disrupts this flow momentarily in order to reassert his total control of the images. He thus calls attention to his position of enunciator, as producer of the discourse, and permits a momentary eruption of discourse into the smooth fabric of the history. This is what Bellour refers to as Hitchcock's 'signature system' – the means by which, through obligatory concrete appearances in each of his films, Hitchcock punctuates the 'logical unfolding of the fantasy originating in the conditions of enunciation,' and materializes his controlling position. Insofar as the film is the perpetually displaced means of Hitchcock's satisfaction of his own desire, the assertion of his presence as producer of the look underscores his autocratic possession of the images. In terms of the spectator's position in the film-work, this provides a radical, if fleeting, subversion of the subject-effect that the apparatus is designed to produce, and to conceal.

There are many chains of meaning to follow out in Bellour's provocative and complicated essay. Perhaps the point in the essay most crucial to an understanding of the function and position of the woman-object in the *mise-en-scène* of desire, as it is articulated in film through the operation of the look, is Bellour's discussion of the shot in which Marnie, having just rinsed away a previous identity with her hair colour, looks jubilantly into the mirror. Bellour has maintained that Marnie's answer to the sexual aggression wrought on her through image-objectification is theft and shifting identities: 'All she can offer is the surface of an image and this is precisely what is attractive in her.' She constitutes *herself* as an image of desire, desired because she is an image, and offers this to the viewer.

The dramatic effect of this moment is heightened by virtue of its being the first revelation of Marnie's face – up until this shot, she has been an enigma described, remembered, and seen from behind. Now, Marnie 'looks' at her own image in the imagined mirror before her, and we, as spectators, are positioned to receive her gaze and therefore, in a sense, to offer her back her own reflected image. However, Bellour makes the point that the camera look and Marnie's look do not coincide; the angle of the shot and the position of the camera makes it impossible for Marnie to directly address the spectator. Yet this precise thing occurs, for two frames – creating the subliminal effect of a momentary condensation, uniting in one gaze Marnie's image, the camera and the spectator (Fig. 3). What Marnie sees in the 'mirror' is the spectator's gaze, herself as image, a construction of that gaze. This minute fragment of an instance passes by the conscious attention of the spectator, permitting us to see her staring at herself without her seeing us stare at her. This exemplifies the particular kind of voyeurism of the cinematic viewing situation, in which the position of the voyeur is invisible, allowing for the kind of gratification derived from the situation in which the object being looked at does not know it is being looked at.

Bellour suggests that Marnie imagines herself in terms of her image reflected in the mirror, just as Mark, stimulated by Strutt's description and his own memories, imagines her when he glances off-screen in the initial segment of the film. Marnie's absorption in her desire for her own image here makes her an object of desire for the (male) spectator, for the source of the camera-wish-Hitchcock, and for the male characters. For the woman spectator, it can only stimulate the identificatory desire to be the image, but never to possess it. For Bellour, this shot clotures the establishment of the enunciative apparatus of the film and defines the climactic moment around which the film is structured. This shot, in its complete self-referentiality, condenses the look, production of the look, and its image-product, creating a single moment in which we gain access to the mechanism of enunciation, a mechanism which is elusive by definition. This moment crystallizes the operation by which Hitchcock's film maintains a perfect economy of pleasure, organizing it through the look, and implicating the woman-object crucially in that structure.

These have been some provisional remarks about the cinematic apparatus of enunciation and the place of woman's image within that. With reference to Raymond Bellour's article on *Marnie* I have attempted to illustrate how in this film the apparatus constructs a particular viewing subject, and how the woman-image functions in the production of Hitchcock's pleasure. Bellour's analysis is applicable to the specifically Hitchcockian system of enunciation, a structure which 'crystallizes around the desire for the woman,' and it should be emphasized that Bellour describes the way in which Hitchcock repeatedly organizes his fictions; he does not propose a grid which can simply be applied to all films on the classical narrative model. But the type of analysis Bellour proposes delineates a field of investigation in which the film-work can be understood as a fantasmatic production, as a machine of representation which produces a certain kind of pleasure and a specific function for the woman image. In his attempt to analyze the fascination of the image value generated by the film text, he charts the movement in film by which there is always an element of pleasure which is displaced. And it is for this reason that this type of theoretical elaboration is profoundly significant for feminist analyses of film.

Notes

1 Emile Benveniste, *Problems of General Linguistics*, Coral Gables, Fla., University of Miami Press, 1971.
2 Laura Mulvey, 'Visual pleasure and narrative cinema', *Screen*, vol. 16, no. 3, Autumn 1975, pp. 6–18.
3 Raymond Bellour, 'Hitchcock, the enunciator', *Camera Obscura*, no. 2, Fall 1977, pp. 69–94.

I am grateful to Bertrand Augst for his valuable comments and assistance.

Marnie

Fig. 1
Strutt describing
Marnie

Fig. 2a
Marnie walks
away from camera

Fig. 2b
Hitchcock looks
after her

Fig. 2c
Hitchcock looks at
camera

Fig. 3
Marnie looks at
the camera

Stagecoach

1 (A)

2 (B) Ringo: *Set down here, ma'am*

3a (C)

3b (C)

4a (B) Dallas: *Thank you*

4b (B)

4c (B)

5 (D)

6a (E)

6b (E)

7a (C)

7b (C)

8a (B)

8b (B)

9 (C)
Hatfield: *May I find you another place, Mrs Mallory? It's cooler by the window*

10 (B)

11a (C)

11b (C)

11c (C)

12a (F)

12b (F)

29 · Nick Browne: 'The rhetoric of the specular text with reference to *Stagecoach*'

Communications, no. 23, 1975

The articulation of spectating positions through the structure of field-reverse-field and the point-of-view shot has been the object of a considerable amount of recent theoretical work.* Most influential, and perhaps most productive in this area, has been the development by Oudart, out of its use in Lacanian psychoanalysis, of the concept of suture** (a concept which is commented on in the 'Notes on terms', p. 298). In this essay Browne mobilizes notions of field-reverse-field, point of view and suture (with its concept of the 'Absent One' who 'authorizes' the look from a position off-screen) in an attempt to establish a formal rhetoric of the text – a 'geography' of the placement of authority for the look. This rhetoric falls within the terms of history and discourse which are elaborated in previous essays, posed by Browne as a relation between the fiction and the act of enunciation, the enunciation being masked by the placement of authority for the look with the characters of the fiction – 'the enunciative authority comes from the fiction itself'. Browne's essay is concerned with authority and spectatorship within the text. Its analysis of a 'geography of authority' corresponds to the rhetoric of the order of discourse which Foucault's essay seems to call for, a rhetoric which is a crucial component of the formal analysis of the function of the author within the text.

This essay appeared, in French translation, in the highly influential special issue of *Communications* (the journal of the Centre d'Etudes Transdisciplinaires) on psychoanalysis and the cinema (no. 23, *Psychanalyse et cinéma*, Paris, Editions du Seuil, 1975). The version used here is Nick Browne's original. A revised and extended version, 'The Spectator-in-the-Text: the rhetoric of *Stagecoach*', subsequently appeared in *Film Quarterly* (vol. 29, no. 2, pp. 26–44). While the later version raises interesting questions (notably, the elusive question of

---

* See particularly, Edward Branigan, 'Formal permutations of the point-of-view shot', *Screen*, vol. 16, no. 3, Autumn 1975, pp. 54–64. Kristin Thompson and David Bordwell, 'Space and narrative in the films of Ozu', *Screen*, vol. 17, no. 2, Summer 1976, pp. 41–73.

** See 'Dossier on suture' (Miller, Oudart, Heath), *Screen*, vol. 18, no. 4, Winter 1977/8, pp. 23–76. Daniel Dayan, 'The tutor-code of classical cinema', *Film Quarterly*, vol. 28, no. 1, Fall 1974, pp. 22–31. William Rothman, 'Against "the system of the suture"', *Film Quarterly*, vol. 29, no. 1, Fall 1975, pp. 45–50. The latter two articles are also in Nichols.

sympathetic identification), I have preferred this shorter version, which seems to deal with the immediate question of rhetoric more concisely.

(A note on stills. Where different moments within the same shot are shown, the still is marked 'a', 'b', etc. with the number of the shot. Readers who are unfamiliar with the context and significance of this scene within *Stagecoach* are referred to the published screenplay in J. Ford and D. Nichols, *Stagecoach* (London, Lorimer Publishing, 1971). The text is also available as one of the frame blow-up reconstructions published by Picador in the Film Classics Library series edited by Richard Anobile.)

The sequence from John Ford's *Stagecoach* shown in the accompanying set of stills raises a little explored question of filmic narrative, the relation in a text between the saying and the said, the act of enunciation and the fiction. To begin to account for certain important formal features of these images – the framing of views, the direction of glances, the position of characters, the sequence and repetition of shots – as a set of ordered relations requires an initial organizing premise: that this set of formal relations, the filmic structures that present the action, can be understood as a structured answer to a rhetorical problem. We mean that these formal structures are linked, in a way whose complexity and integrity we are prepared to demonstrate, to a rhetorical situation – the act of showing a dramatic scene to a spectator, an act we are calling the enunciation. Because of the importance of views, glances, screens and framing, both in the relations of seeing among the depicted characters and in the presentation of those relations to an audience, we are provisionally conceiving the structure of filmic discourse, here, this set of stills from *Stagecoach*, as a product of this double and linked set of views. The structure of this 'specular text' is the object of our commentary.

The paper argues through an analysis of the stills that the requirements of a rhetorical presentation are articulated as a set of integrated structures and strategies that give form to the action of the fiction and at the same time determine the locus of the spectator in what might be called his reading of the film. The paper shows in analytical detail the way in which the two levels of views, enunciation and fiction, relate in a 'text' whose structure proceeds initially from a prohibition against a meeting of glances between spectator and actor, and secondly, from social premises implied in the relations among characters. Generally, the paper proposes to consider this short but classical text for the purpose of showing the structural importance of the rhetorical situation, the integrity and coherence of the specular structures that are articulated, the determinants that give them form, the notion of the role of the implied reader, and finally for suggesting certain critical concepts needed to account for or describe these structures.

Set-up and place

There are a number of concrete features of the stills which must be noted. Of the twelve shots, there are six different set-ups: A (1); B (2,4,8,10); C (3,7,9,11); D (5); E (6); F (12). As a camera position, each set-up is a marker of the enunciation that shows the scene from a different geographical point, constituting a view.

But each set-up relates in a complex and different way, both geographically and in the logic of its connection, to the action of the fiction. The geographical places of the characters are defined by reference to the configuration of the table. Thus B, the view showing Dallas and Ringo, is from the head of the table and is presented, in a remarkable coincidence of person and view, from the place that Lucy occupies; C, the view of Lucy and the group behind her which excludes Dallas and Ringo frame left, is from a place to the left of the table that nobody in the scene occupies; D, of Lucy, from near the middle of the table, forms a shot–reverse shot unit with E, of Dallas; A and F show the entire group. Lucy, as a body, appears either by herself or with the group in all the shots except those with Ringo and Dallas, and is shown, with a single but problematic exception, from a set-up which is not from the place of anyone in the room. Ringo and Dallas are never shown in the same frame with Lucy or the group, and whether they appear together (2,4,8,10) or alone (6), they are shown from the set-up at the head of the table associated with Lucy's place. That is, each of the twelve shots of the sequence refers to Lucy's presence either by actually showing her, or by the showing of the scene of Dallas and Ringo associated with her glance, that is, either through body or the product of her eye.

View and glance

The views shown on the screen have associations of different kinds with the glance of particular characters in the fiction. As has been pointed out, in set-up B there is a literal coincidence of view and glance, which in shot 4 is given special force by the dolly forward. By contrast, A,C and F are from locations in the room that no character literally occupies. Nobody's shot, though, is concretely located by showing a particular view, and is thus connected with the depiction of a certain kind of consciousness associated with characters in the fiction. Finally the elaborate and systematic strategy of the 'depicted glance' is articulated by the shot–reverse shot paradigm, as studied in Daniel Dayan's commentary on Oudart (*Film Quarterly*, Fall 1974). In this paradigm the shot on the screen is presented as the glance of another spectator, the 'Absent One', from an implied, complementary but invisible field, in our sense from an off-screen character. In the reverse shot, the off-screen field is shown to be occupied by this character, the owner of the glance that corresponds to the first shot. The 'Absent One', the off-screen spectator of shot 1, is transferred in shot 2 from the level of enunciation to the level of fiction. The circuit of entailment and presentation proceeds like a revolving door. Views 5 and 6, the shot–reverse shot paradigm in the sequence, is made readable by this logic and shares with set-up B a justification by reference to a literal glance from within the fiction. Reading a shot as a character's view, however, does not depend on a geographical coincidence of set-up and body. For an account of the complexity and details of the structure of the enunciation in the sequence, particularly in the matter of the presenting and framing of nobody's shot, the play of this generalized logic must be concretized and elaborated.

Though the glance can be the unacknowledged explanation of the source of a view, the glances shown within the frame, that is on the level of fiction, have a structural as well as a thematic importance. Matching of shots by eyeline is not an inconsequential feature of intelligibility. There are two shots where specular relations are enclosed within a single frame – the intimate and unmediated exchange in 4a and the group's watchful suspense in 11a. But views out of the frame, the turning around to look (3), a repelling by a glance (5), an acknowledgement of shame by averting the eyes (6b), are the central actions of the sequence. To summarize, then, the regard can be associated, as a source, with the act of enunciation – as a view – by a coincidence with the place of a character, or more indirectly as a depicted glance. On the level of fiction, the regard, charged with emotion and directed either on or off screen, can be the action.

An exchange of glances in context

The presentation of the moment of highest drama, the exchange of glances between the glowering Lucy and the uncertain Dallas, illustrates the basic rhetorical structure of the sequence. Just preceding this critical moment, the prostitute Dallas, on Ringo's invitation – 'Set down here ma'am' – has seated herself beside Lucy, the married woman in the white hat already sitting at the head of the table, thus transgressing a social code well understood by those in the room, for they turn their heads. The code, of which Lucy is the primary custodian and defender, requires the distancing and exclusion of the impure, the black. The *mise-en-scène* in which this exchange of looks is enacted thus depicts, in the terms purity/impurity, the alliances and exclusions within the social structure of the group.

The figuration of shot–reverse shot stands in a necessary structural relation to its place in the chain, and is paradigmatic of the rhetorical organization of the sequence. Its presentation (5,6) is asymmetrical in the degree of frontality of the two women – Lucy is shown nearly straight on – and corresponds to a different angle for the set-ups chosen for their depiction. The asymmetry of angle is read with particular clarity by the operation of the premise of the averted glance. Dallas is depicted as being seen by Lucy, for shot 6 is, like 2 and 4, from Lucy's place at the head of the table. But the showing of Lucy, that is the depiction of Dallas's return glance, is from a place, the center of the table, that Dallas could not actually occupy. Unlike Lucy's, Dallas's depicted glance (5) does not coincide with the place of the eye of the character, the source and authority of the enunciation. Dallas's depicted glance is, in other words, displaced. In shot 6, she is looked at directly as from Lucy's eye, but she can return the glance only by averting her eyes frame left to avoid breaking the prohibition against meeting our eye. The important difference is not on the level of the fiction – the women exchange glances simultaneously – but on the level of enunciation, in which Lucy's glance is authorized and Dallas's dispossessed.

The asymmetrical presentation of the shot–reverse shot is not arbitrary, but linked in demonstrable ways to the entire pattern of views. The shot of Dallas (6) is linked by similarity of angle, if not by scale to 2, and follows by an elliptical jump from the dolly forward shot (4a, b, c). This dolly, beginning from Lucy's place at the head of the table, emphasizes its enunciative force by a movement that corresponds to or refers to a concentration of Lucy's attention. Thus, by presenting itself as the subjectivizing force of a glance, it serves as a formal means of furthering the action by introducing a change in scale. Shot 5, as a change from 4 in scale and direction, is linked by the tightest of specular logics: it is the paradigmatic shift from a scene shown by Lucy's eye (4) to the reverse field of the originating glance (5), from enunciation to fiction. The transition from 5 to 6, and from 6 to 7, follows in different ways the same current of induction. The analysis confirms that this shot–reverse shot has internal and necessary relations to surrounding views, in that it requires, and explains, its narrative movement by the same specular logic. Of course, what is yet to be accounted for from shot to shot is the precise set-up and framing which realizes this logic.

Though Dallas, as the object of Lucy's glance in 2 and 4, is presented at a weaker angle at the moment of exchange, she is given by scale, if not by set-up, a kind of independent standing through the symmetry of a static close-up. A comparison by scale is asserted. Though the enunciation favors Lucy as a position and as a figure of authority over a diffident and dislocated outcast, the exchange is a moment of dramatic tension and illustration, because the narrator asserts on Dallas's behalf, by the emphatic effect of scale, the close-up, an image of presence (6) that is put in dramatic play. The enunciation which adopts the authority of Lucy's glance as its mask, and dispossesses Dallas's, both theatricalizes the moment by scale and juxtaposition and comments on it by an asymmetry of angle. That our sympathies in the sequence are strongly with Dallas suggests the compelling force of the situation shown in the fiction.

Invisibility and the geography of authority

The presentation of this exchange of glances depends for legibility and force on its links with views (1,2,3,) that present a complementary orientation, and particularly on its relation to the view from set-up C (3,7,9,11). Structurally, the alternation of set-up C with B places and confirms Lūcy's glance as the source of views 2,4,6 and 10. Excepting the first and last shots, C is the only set-up which is not referred, apparently, in some direct way for its authority to a glance of a character in the fiction. As the product of an enunciatory act, its geographical source and its authority seem transparent and unquestioned – it is shown to us by the narrator from the eye of the camera. But the frame of set-up C excludes in a severe way the object of the group's attention (e.g. 3a, b) – Dallas and her act of transgression. Though screened from us, the prostitute and criminal are present from this set-up by the collective glance off-screen of the audience-in-the-film. The plastics of the image, differentiated into foreground and background zones by the table, are the scenes, first, of Lucy's glance of repulsion as an actor and, in the second and deeper plane, the source of a glance which defines the group as spectators or witnesses. Thus the framing of the shot responds to an off-screen scene which to us as audience at this moment is a point of invisibility, but a point that nonetheless structures the rhetoric of the sequence.

The relation of set-ups B and C is a rotating of field–reverse field. B, from the head of the table, is the product of Lucy's glance and C, the reverse field, shows the source of that glance – Lucy at the table with Dallas excluded by the frame. This structure, like 5 and 6, is an asymmetrical presentation, for Lucy is present as eye (B) and body (C), whereas Dallas, though present in body (B), is not associated as an eye with the source of C. On the contrary, her exclusion by the frame, her invisibility as being off-screen, is not the same as Lucy's invisibility as the beholding eye. The view from set-up C, 'nobody's shot', belongs not to Dallas, and this is the remarkable feature – it is the complementary field of Lucy's glance, Lucy's person. The relation of B and C makes Dallas as a source of the enunciation, an absence, a point of invisibility, by making the field–reverse field paradigm apply to two aspects of only one person – Lucy's eye and body – corresponding in turn to first- and third-person views. The view from set-up C then, showing Lucy's support by the public and excluding Dallas, is a figuration not embodied in a single glance, but is the depiction or acknowledgment by someone of all the specular and power relations in the room. It is an image of Lucy's social self-consciousness and Dallas's invisibility.

The rhetoric of invisibility or of insufficiency extends, as has been suggested, to the presentation of the shot–reverse shot of 5, 6 through an asymmetry of frontality. The asymmetry of angle in 5, as the depiction, displaced and frontal, of Dallas's glance, acknowledges Lucy's social position and her stern defense of prerogatives, and registers Dallas's own unapproachability with respect to it. In fact, by this displacement, Lucy's presence in 5 has as much the status and effect of a self-presentation as of Dallas's depicted glance, and thus, as an enunciation, is similar to 'nobody's' viewpoint in C. The angle of Dallas's depicted view in both cases is presented as social dislocation, a correlative of the , depicted shame, in the system of differences that constitutes the authorized system of seeing in the film. Because of the first-person presentation, and the premise of the averted glance, Dallas's return glance must be a look elsewhere, out of the frame. The prohibition is put in play by the enunciation in 6 as a screen to keep Lucy's and our own glance inviolate, and to insure that Dallas remains invisible – as a social phantom. The general rhetoric of views and the way characters are made visible or invisible is motivated, the sequence implies, by differences in social standing justified by reference to a moral schema that distinguishes those inside from those outside customary law.

The structural incapacity to return a glance, Dallas's invisibility, corresponds to her position in a social milieu. It corresponds as well to a concrete geography, for authority of enunciation in this rhetoric presents itself as being derived from places, of characters in the fiction. As such Dallas is the place of incapacity that can not authorize a view. In this geography of authority there are multiple points of assertion that correspond to the position of each set-up. But there is a place on the left side of the table that the camera can not occupy, though it can be referred to by a glance (C), or looked into by others (B). The points of enunciative assertion, and of absence, are the masks of narrative authority.

The further significance then of set-up C is as a mask of full authorial presentation that locates the position of Lucy's objectified social self-consciousness, as outside and from a distance, as transcendental. The image is a figuration of a psychology based on a transparency of gesture that locates personal authority in a social role and conceives drama as the enactment of conflict of such roles.

The spectator/reader

The structured presentation of the enunciation implies a rhetorical design. The 'specular text' incorporates, in other words, the place and role of the spectator, though it acknowledges his presence only by honoring the prohibition.

The role of the spectator as a reader is structured to recognize but to close gaps – differences of scale, angle, location of presentation – asserted by the shifting views of the enunciation. The spectator/reader is required to occupy, from moment to moment, nodes of enunciation that present and define the action of the scene through establishing relations to the consciousness and perception of characters depicted in the fiction. Occupying these positions, identification, is not meant here as in the strictly Freudian sense, but rather as an enabling function that supposes a process of induction that makes an intelligible connection between the place of enunciation and the action of the fiction, a relation that we are calling the locus of the spectator's reading.

The locus, for us, is a vantage point, structured into the presentation, that permits the reader to follow the sequence of actions as a coherent chain of events. As the spectator's abstract 'position', the locus does not have a fixed or concrete location but follows the action. We have shown above that Lucy's presence both on the level of the fiction and enunciation dominates the organization of the sequence. In this sequence the locus is a centre structurally associated with Lucy, the figure of authority who is privileged by Ford's moral and social code to serve formally, as in B and C, to articulate and integrate the sequence of views that constitute the discourse. The location of the camera and the views of the action are made coherent and legible by reference to the authoritative function which Lucy performs and defines. Rhetorically, that is in terms of the locus of the spectator's reading, this center, occupied or depicted as the visual presence of a body or as a glance from an eye, is with each view constantly shifted. The spectator as reader thus follows and occupies a new view by the alternation of the 'location' of Lucy's presence between enunciation and fiction. Indeed, those characters on and off the screen, and the way they are there – the general organization of the spatial relations of the sequence – follow this centered logic of authoritative presentation.

In occupying a vantage point, the reader is engaged in a way that requires that he identify in two formal capacities – as actor and as spectator. In the shot–reverse shot, like 5, 6, he identifies formally, in terms of the enunciation, with the off-screen spectator whose glance is depicted as the view on the screen. But the primary and more strictly Freudian identification, the one which has been little discussed here, and which explains our response to Dallas as an outcast, is an emotional identification with the actor-character in the fiction. Thus the critical pair actor/spectator formulates the double capacities for audience participation structured by means of the enunciation.

In each enunciative situation, there is a competitive appeal to these two roles. 'Nobody's shot', set-up B, for example, establishes the reader's position as distanced, as pure spectator. He is present to the image in much the same way as the spectators-within-the-film. By contrast, with the dolly forward in set-up B, it is the force of the act of enunciation which predominates, an act which by its movement incorporates the reader's glance, making him an actor. In general, the reader is present, one might say identifies with or sees the views of the film in accord with the way his double role actor/spectator is structured by the rhetoric of presentation. The process of reading this sequence of views, of feeling its effects of drama, coherence and continuity is a product of following the presencing of this centered figure of authority.

This governing rhetoric depends on the premise of the averted glance and asserts by its own means an effect of fascination and continuity. Daniel Dayan's commentary on Oudart exposes the logic of continuity through the operation of the 'suture'. The logic of the prohibition is double: ontologically it proposes a boundary and asserts that the space shown on the screen is virtual, an imaginary product, and of a different order than that of the projection hall; structurally it creates an obliquity, a difference, between the spectator's view and the character's that provides the ensemble of forms, and a medium of imaginary exchange available to the enunciation. It makes it possible to occupy, fictionally, the place of another's view. It creates a kind of readable space the audience must necessarily participate in, and the asymmetries noted above correspond to the formal place of the spectator. The sequencing of views around a center, when joined with this double logic has the effect, and it is a rhetorical strategy, of creating a certain form of dramatic illusionism by suggesting that the enunciative authority comes from the fiction itself. But all the shots, the personalized forms just as much as nobody's view, are masks of authority, that is presentations of an invisible narrator–author. As a production of the reading of the text, continuity and the 'effect of the real' protects this account of the status of the discourse.

The rhetoric of the specular text, the structures of viewing that mediate the relation between film and spectator and imply his 'location' as a reader, is, we propose, a stylistic–historical form. The analysis of *Stagecoach* and the critical concepts, enunciation, fiction, center, authority, locus, etc., proposed in this paper, might be regarded then as part of a semiological study of filmic texts in the way they present themselves as spectacles.

30 · Jean-Pierre Oudart: 'The absent field of the Author'

Cahiers du Cinéma, nos. 236–7, March/April 1971

Oudart's essay, focusing on Bresson and the 'New Wave', re-installs the author as a social, ideological, sexual subject (*le sujet Bresson*') into the problematic of author-subject. More accurately, he attempts to provide an articulation of this subject (in social and productive relations) with the subject produced in the textual operations. In this sense, the essay can usefully be read as an extension of Oudart's 1969 essay, 'La suture', an essay which has been translated and extensively commented on in *Screen* ('Dossier on suture', *Screen*, vol. 18, no. 4, Winter 1977–8). Oudart, here, refuses the view that the author-subject is simply a construct of the textual operation, outside history and sociality.

Oudart's essay also provokes questions about the author in the 'art cinema': in the same way Pam Cook, in the essay which follows this, raises the question of the avant-garde. The privilege which has been given to Hollywood cinema in the debate about *auteurism* has tended to flatten out distinctions between different cinematic practices, treating the relations between author, text and spectator as if they were always the same. In fact, such relations vary considerably within, as much as between, 'art cinema', 'popular cinema', 'modernist cinema'. In this respect, it is useful to refer to an earlier essay, 'The Name-of-the-Author', written by Oudart with Serge Daney, on the relations between the social, sexual and political subject, Visconti, and his text, *Death in Venice* (Daney and Oudart, 'Le Nom-de-l'auteur', *Cahiers du Cinéma*, nos 234–5, December–February 1971–2. Translation forthcoming).

The difficulty of an unfamiliar psychoanalytic terminology is apparent, and I have tried to indicate the psychoanalytic sense of as much of it as possible in the section 'Notes on terms' at the end of the book. Those terms which are included there are marked by an asterisk on their first appearance in the essay.

I 'Quatre Nuits d'un rêveur' [Bresson, 1971]

1 The intrigue[1] which is developed in the screenplay is no different from that of any of Bresson's other films: it always consists of an

erotic relationship of an hysterical* nature. That is not to say that, even on the level of the working out of the script, Bresson inscribes in his film a clinical description of hysteria. He condenses, as before:

1 the relationship between a woman (a girl) and two men, which can be referred on the one hand to the clinical analysis of hysteria, and, on the other, to the petit-bourgeois romantic mode which constantly invests it (it isn't you that I desire but another – because I am myself another and because I desire something other);

2 directly denoted social relations and patterns of behaviour of the provincial (or marginal Parisian) bourgeoisie and of an intellectual 6th–16th *arrondissement* milieu[2] (interiors whose bareness is discreetly valorized, rhyming with an interiority of the characters which is also constantly valorized: the role of 16th *arrondissement* accents in all Bresson's films).

The social 'exterior' and the already-written (the pre-text) of Bressonian films has always consisted of that, but their overdetermination*, up until *Au Hasard Balthazar*, made the ideologemes[3] anchored in their chain insistent, producing ideological effects of writing (*écriture*) which became less apparent in the later films, and which have disappeared altogether in *Quatre Nuits d'un rêveur*. The insistence of these effects was produced by the fact that:

1 the fictive milieu in which the intrigue took place was directly oppressive, full of threats of aggression and rape. Heroes and heroines could detach themselves from it fictively and abstract themselves from it ideologically through their roles as the shifters* (*embrayeurs*) of the fiction (changing place, rushing forward in time); this role was overdetermined by conduct either in excess or in default in relation to the desire* of the others and of their norms. This surplus element indicated an otherness all the more radical in that its inscription had only a fictional consistency and made the ideological effects of this otherness insistent only in the filmic articulation of the fiction (suturing* looks, voices and gestures which were fetishized as 'more-real' [*plus-de-réel*] in images which systematically lacked the realistic appearance of classical cinema, etc.);

2 the fictive milieu, whether or not it contained denoted elements of the social 'exterior' of the subject* Bresson, was invariably inscribed in a referential position with regard to the hero of the fiction: that is, in the relationship of the fictive couple constituted by the hero or heroine and the others, it

was exclusively oppressive, aggressive, transgressive in the enclosed field of the ideological and erotic relations which directly constitute the plot; in the field, that is to say, of the idealist inscription of the internal contradictions in petit-bourgeois ideology (sex/love, power/love; power = erotic relations, economic relations = erotic relations, etc.). Even in *Une Femme douce*, the characters' economic relations are nothing but the description – and a very relevant one for psychoanalysis – of a 'neurotic'* erotic relationship.

Moreover, Bresson inscribed his social 'exterior' only with a reticence which seemed, as far as his petit-bourgeois spectators were concerned, to be the mark both of his 'nobility' (his refusal of a certain obscene vulgarity characteristic of pre-war French cinema and continuing after the war), and of his catholicism (the real conflicts don't concern the objects of this world, even if these constitute their 'matter'), and even of a certain political activism (since, after all, this catholic artist made the social 'world' the fictive place of the contradiction, and chose characters who were socially marginal to reveal this contradiction).

This means that Bresson has always known his ideology and that his neurotic culture (meaning the interest he takes in erotic intrigues which are overdetermined by an inscription of neurotic fantasies) has always been the object of a process of negation: for example, the sexual and the economic are never inscribed in accordance with the order of the subject Bresson's desires for bourgeois 'dolly girls' (sometimes disguised as working class), or with his interests in money.

2 On the basis of these points, we can now establish that in *Quatre Nuits*:

1 the world of the heroes consists solely of denoted elements of the subject Bresson's contemporary social 'exterior', and the locations are constantly marked as being Bressonian (the *quais* of the Seine, the Drugstore,[4] etc.): that is to say, the shooting – and the editing – of the film constantly produces effects which externalize the intrigue 'into' a social exterior, contemporary for both the film-maker and the spectator, and which is connoted as a privileged place for the ideological contradictions exposed by the fiction;

2 as in his previous films (*Une Femme douce*), the economic inscription, very rarified here, serves only to give consistency to the erotic intrigue;

3 this erotic intrigue is completely stripped of the ideological

effects which the 'writing' of the previous films made insistent:
it is filmed with a *mise en scène* which is completely flat; it
is the object of a description which neutralizes the ideological–
erotic surplus value of the earlier films;

4 denoted as a neurotic, marginal artist (on the brink of psy-
chosis), the character who serves as narrator (and as go-be-
tween in the relationship between the heroine and the other
man – the man who desires her and who is the object of her
desire) is the third term in this hysterical erotic intrigue; it is
this third term which allows the contradiction of the intrigue
(desire/love) to be exposed, and which is itself foreclosed*
from any economic and sexual determination (he has neither
economic status nor any real sexual desire; correlatively, his
task is fetishized, and the scenes in which he picks people up
or voyeuristically observes the sexual relations of others occupy in the fiction the position of events which are extraneous
to the development of the plot).

On this basis, the fictional system of the film can be described
as the classical triangle of petit-bourgeois erotic intrigues (husband–wife–lover), but foreclosed from any economic–sexual inscription. The fiction consists of the exposition, for an hour and a
half, of a sexual relationship which is initiated and then deferred
until the end of the film, and of a love relationship which is of no
interest for the development of the plot.

What is insistent in the fiction is simply the blind desire to insert
this exposition into an exterior which Bresson fantasizes as the
social exterior of the film, whereas it is only the fetishized locations
used in the filming, into which, symptomatically, the film-maker
introduces a series of petit-bourgeois cultural fetishes (picturesque
narrow streets contrasting with the objects of capitalist industrial
civilization: gadgets, 'dolly girls', hippies); in other words, the
displacement-condensation* of his political–sexual repression, to
which are added a few scenes where the sexual is inscribed as the
primitive exterior of the fiction.

The result is that the inscription of the desire of the subject
Bresson, repressed in the plot, is foreclosed in the fictive real
(*réel-fictif*) of its narrative development (in the previous film it
invested the camera work and the process of cutting/suturing), and
is hallucinated as a social practice taking place in the exterior of
the film, that is, at a shooting location which is merged with the
place of the social practice of the actors in the film.

One can see from this that the reference in the last instance to
social practice (or rather the referential inscription of a social

practice) is the last resort of idealist cinema, its final attempt to give itself the semblance of a political position, that is, to reproduce a discourse which – since, like Bresson's, it is no longer operative on the level of the ideological struggle (as his films were at the time of the New Wave) – passes itself off, in the here and now of the fictive-real of the *mise en scène*, as the 'making-present' *(présentification) en direct*⁵ of a social practice, deemed to reflect actively the contradictions of the film-maker's real milieu.

3 Although the Bressonian intrigue has only an idealist consistency (as much in its terms as in their articulation), its inscription in a fiction overdetermined by his insistent erotic fantasies would be worked on by these fantasies, were it not that he radically censors their inscription.

The censorship operative in Bresson's work is directed (as is that of *Death in Venice*⁶) towards a double (economic–sexual) articulation (of which Bressonian eroticism constitutes what is repressed) of the signifiers of the desire of the subject Bresson, the scene of which can be constituted through an analysis of his films taken as a whole.

In the practice of Bressonian inscription, this censorship can be analysed:

(a) on the basis of the fictive establishment of a Sadian relationship between the seducer and his victim, the former witnessing the appearance of the symptom of arousal in the other;

(b) as the repressed inscription of the relationships established between the director and his actors (actresses) while the film was being shot, literally as a prohibition against designating the perpetrator of the seduction as the director, ordering his actresses to offer him the avowal of an erotic arousal which is what constitutes the whole 'reward' (*'prix'*) of the filming (*prises de vue*) (what Bresson says about the 'surprises' encountered while making the film is Sadian nevertheless, for all that it is dressed up in psychological and mystical terminology).

Moreover, in the fiction, it is always by someone else that the avowal of the victim's pleasure is made; or rather, the Bressonian fiction is structured as the articulation of the relationship between a torturer and a victim which gives the spectator time to understand the symptom of the victim's arousal as:

(a) the object of an anticipated assertion (a signifier produced for someone's look, for the look of the absent one⁷);

(b) the shifter of the fiction, which anticipates the becoming present in the next shot of the torturer whose presence retroactively sutures the act of enunciation (*énonciation**), and finally annuls the Sadian relationship, the effect of which was produced by the systematic re-marking of the '*différance*'[8] of the suture.

The Sadian relationship between the director and his actresses, indicated by the re-marking of the suture, thus constitutes the repressed in Bressonian fiction.

It also overdetermines Bressonian narration, in which it is invariably inscribed in terms of the hysterical intrigue, in which a girl is torn between a sexual desire and a need for love which are not addressed to the same man. It is worth noting that in *Balthazar* Marie is raped almost before Jacques' very eyes and that he is the first person to see her after the rape: the rapist is the 'operator'[9] of a Sadian relationship in which the lover is the director himself. The figure of the (castrated) Bressonian lover is the product of a negation of the Sadian relationship between the director and his actresses which absolves the master, and represses his mastery in a hysterical intrigue in which he is given only as being undesired.

In *Quatre Nuits d'un rêveur*, the economic–sexual foreclosure of this character, presented as a psychotic, undoubtedly marks the extreme point of regression for the Bressonian ideological inscription, overdetermined by that Sadian fantasy which is here expelled from the film's writing: the negation, which maintained both the consistency of the hysterical intrigue and the erotic insistence of a repressed political discourse on the relationship between the director and his actresses, gives way here to a lack of desire to know anything of this repression which is the written admission of the political foreclosure of this idealist discourse: the installation of the film-maker in a marginal and debilitated 'cultural' film practice, whose product has exchange value only as the fetishized trace of the passage of the author in Parisian settings.

II Fictional contradictions and historical contradictions in the New Wave

The same kind of Sadian relationship between the director and his company of performers, the repressed eroticism of their relations of production, constantly overdetermines the writing of French New Wave cineastes: it always involves exposing a team of amateur actors, often taken out of a bourgeois milieu, in an intrigue whose elements are also directly denoted by bourgeois practices, making them formulate the avowal of what the bourgeoisie is supposed to repress, and making them act in such a way that the avowal constitutes the object of a knowledge of which the spectator is instituted as the sole beneficiary, and which is in fact paid back into the account of the spectator's ideological position. This ideological position can be deduced from the ideology and practice of *'cinéma direct'* or *'cinéma vérité'* whose scene can be described as the overdetermined relation of four terms:

(a) the implicit rendering (*implicitation*) of the social exterior of the group being filmed;

(b) the implicit rendering of the political discourse which formulates the disjunction of the class and its exterior;

(c) the statement (*énoncé**) of an ideological (moralizing, metaphysical, erotic) discourse, repressing this disjunction and exhibiting instead a contradiction within the class (the bourgeois scene and its repressed);

(d) the placing in the position of controller of the fiction (that is, of agent of the avowal of the truth) of an 'operator' who participates socially in the class being represented and ideologically in its cultural values (an 'operator' for whom, therefore, the truth will consist of the revelation of an ideological contradiction within this class).

The determining contradiction of the fictional scene of this cinema consists, therefore, of the relationship between a petit-bourgeois director and a team of (amateur) players who are similarly petit-bourgeois, a relationship in which what is at stake is the truth of the relations of these players as this is understood by the ideology of the director (who can be called a master in the sense that nothing of the truth is produced in the *mise en scène* that he doesn't already know). Bressonian *mise en scène* helps us to understand how this truth consists, by choice, of a sexual signifier*, and how it is insistent as an erotic–ideological fetish: while, in Bresson, the truth most often makes itself heard from the lips of a woman, this truth arises in the position of the fetish (eroticism and surplus of soul) of something foreclosed in the *mise en scène* of its avowal, something which is the overdetermined position of the director as economic master and as desiring subject. If there is production of a fetish, it is precisely in the sense of an *objet a** arriving in the fiction in the location of a signifier which has not been made the object of a reality judgment, and which makes the determinations of the character of the foreclosed operator, inscribed as lacking in the fiction, insistent in the mode of repression. The Bressonian fetish is not connoted as erotic merely by the fact that the signifier (mouth, eye, hand) consists of an object cut from the erotogenic bodies of his actresses, but because in Bressonian fiction (the interval of the suture) it is not denoted as sexual by another performer, and is inserted in another signifying chain, a chain which consists of the overdetermination of the fictional scene by the ideological scene of the relationship between the director and his actresses, which insists each time that the foreclosure of the position of the director is re-marked, and which consists also in the intrigue to the extent that the director has inscribed it there (*Procès de Jeanne d'Arc* in particular).

What is most fetishized in *cinéma-vérité*, that is to say in New Wave films taken as a whole, is the precise historical moment and the geographical locations used in the film: what has to be seen in this case is not just the effect of a refusal to take into account the economic relations of production and the eroticism of the director in the literal inscription of the film, but also the effect of a refusal to take into account the socio-historical exterior of these relations (the ideological illusion of this cinema consisting, in the last instance, of the confusion of the inscription of secondary effects of class struggles/conflicts – affecting a family, a small group, a cinematographic team – with that of their principal determinants). What is foreclosed by *cinéma-vérité* and re-emerges in the fetishization of '*cinéma direct*', constituting the ideological surplus of its fictional system, is the socio-historical exterior of its production.

To say that it is foreclosed means that it has been:

(a) taken into account by the film-maker in his ideological and social practice; that is, in his political practice;

(b) taken into account also in the ideology of his signifying practice, since his film is addressed to a spectator who is presumed to have thought out the principal contradictions which overdetermine those which his film exposes, and since the filmic discourse interpellates the spectator as a political subject (that is, as a subject who can recognize the fiction as being cut off from its exterior) but only gives him food for thought in ideological terms.

The fetishization of the 'direct' can, in the last instance, be understood only as the mark of a division into fictional field/socio-historical exterior of this field, where one of the terms of the division is not made the object of a literal inscription since it is ideologically implied as the precise historical moment of the shooting of the film, a moment of which the spectators are presumed to have made the political analysis: the absent field of 'direct cinema' is in effect the place of a spectator presumed to have already produced the analysis of the relations between the scene of the film and its exterior, and between this scene (as site of the production of the symptoms which affect it) and the discourse which he is supposed to hold on these symptoms.

We will need to return, in a more extensive analysis, to the history of the production of this cinema in the field of a petit-bourgeois intelligentsia. *It is not a coincidence if its discourse mimics academic discourse: the whole of New Wave cinema was produced as the surplus value – always personified by an author – of a presumed knowledge of the contradictions of bourgeois society, and all its ideological effects result from the fact that it has constantly practised the assertion of this presumed knowledge.* It is the overdetermination of this practice of assertion by the film-makers of the petit-bourgeois intelligentsia that we will now need to re-inscribe methodically.

Editor's notes

1 *L'intrigue* can mean plot, affair or intrigue, and Oudart plays on all three meanings throughout the essay. Generally the word 'intrigue' has been used in English, but it is used only in so far as it seems best to contain the other meanings; and there are a number of cases where the sense of 'plot' seems to be the dominant one.

2 The 6th *arrondissement*, adjacent to the Latin Quarter, comprises the area around the Luxembourg, Odéon and Saint-Germain-des-Prés. While preserving something of its 'intellectual atmosphere', it has attracted a concentration of 'trendy' shops, restaurants and cafés. The 16th *arrondissement*, Auteuil, Passy, and the area between the Arc de Triomphe and the Bois de Boulogne, is traditionally the most opulent part of Paris. It is frequently associated with a slightly affected upper-crust accent (*l'accent du 16ᵉ*).

3 Signifiers of ideology.

4 A late-night (and, again, 'trendy') café–restaurant–store–boutique at the top of the Champs-Elysée (with a sister establishment on the site of one of the old 'intellectual' cafés at Saint-Germain-des-Prés).

5 Filming *en direct* is filming on the basis of real locations, direct sound, minimal or no added lighting and, usually, amateur actors or non-actors. It is generally associated with narrative cinema (Renoir and Rossellini provide its pedigree, with Bresson, early Godard and Straub as its later practitioners), while *cinéma vérité*, using the same principles, is more closely associated with documentary. See Jean-Louis Comolli, 'Le détour par le direct', *Cahiers du Cinéma*, no. 209, February 1969, pp. 49–53, and no. 211, April 1969, pp. 40–5. Translation forthcoming.

6 See S. Daney and J.-F. Oudart, 'Le Nom-de-l'auteur', on the place of Visconti in *Death in Venice*; in *Cahiers du Cinéma*. nos.234–5, December–February 1971–2.

7 See note on 'suture' in 'Notes on terms' below.

8 '*Différance*' is a term introduced by Derrida, constituted by a verbal play on '*différence*' (difference) and the verb '*différer*' (to defer, postpone). The play brings together the sense of the recognition of difference which is foundational for the formation of the subject, and the sense of 'deferred action' (*Nachträglichkeit*), a

> 'term frequently used by Freud in connection with his view of psychical temporality: experiences, impressions and memory-traces may be revised at a later date to fit in with fresh experiences or with the attainment of a new stage of development. They may in that event be endowed not only with a new meaning but also with psychical effectiveness.'

> Laplanche and Pontalis, *The Language of Psychoanalysis*, p. 111

As used here it refers to the way in which meaning is produced retroactively by the effect of the suturing process, the 'pure' image becoming someone's look in the following shot.

9 'Operator' here carries the additional sense of 'symbol or function denoting an operation' in mathematics (O.E.D.).

31 · Pam Cook: 'The point of self-expression in avant-garde film'

Catalogue: British Film Institute Production Board 1977–8

Pam Cook's essay – which originally introduced a number of avant-garde films in the British Film Institute Production Board catalogue – offers a consideration of the concept of self-expression from within the area of an alternative cinematic practice, arguing that, for an artisanal mode of production, ideas of 'the personal' have to be taken seriously. Importantly, she relates the argument to the development of a feminist film-making practice; importantly, also, she recognizes contradictions in the rejection of self-expression, and stresses the need to understand the relationship between the 'self' of the film-maker and the institutional practices which surround and determine his/her work. Precisely this understanding of the relation of production and institution has been one of the substantial contributions of critical, practical and theoretical work around independent and avant-garde film-making in Britain. What the article does for the Reader is to challenge the notion of a single, universal and monolithic 'Theory of Authorship' covering all practices, and to propose instead the need to understand authorship in relation to specific practices, and within the constraints of specific institutional operations.

Film has often been thought of as an essentially collective medium, and certainly if one takes dominant commercial cinema as a model, the complexities of the processes involved, the amount of 'noise' in the system would seem to exclude any possibility of identifying a single voice as the structuring source of a film or group of films, in spite of the auteur theory. In small-scale production, however, especially in avant-garde film-making, the notion of the 'artist', and the work as the self-expression of the artist, has always been important, and technological developments in 16mm, 8mm and video, offering as they do the possibility of even more intimate conditions of production, would seem to support this idea. I want to look at the importance of the concept of 'self-expression' for avant-garde film-making: historically in terms of the tradition of personal film-making, in particular the way it was developed in the New American Cinema after the Second World War, since this

271

was the context in which the debate about the cinema of 'personal vision' and the intervention of structural/minimalist film emerged; and in terms of the implications of such a concept for any film-making practice which sets itself up in opposition to dominant cinema, not only its forms (representation) but also its system of production, distribution and exhibition.

The idea of 'self-expression' suggesting as it does the creation of a private language to convey the personal fantasies and obsessions of a single individual, has come under attack from 'structural' film-makers in America and Europe with their formalist concerns, and from Marxists for whom it is a concept based on bourgeois individualism which asserts an independence from the dominant system that can only be illusory, thus relegating itself to a politically marginal position from which it can never radically challenge the dominant ideology. Nevertheless, it is a concept which, with its emphasis on the personal, the intimate, and the domestic, has always been important to the Women's Movement, and the personal diary form, for instance, has always been a means of self-expression for women to whom other avenues were closed. The suppression of the 'personal', albeit politically correct, brings to the surface specific problems and contradictions for women, and for feminist film-makers.

The Marxist–Feminist strand within the Movement has sought to resolve the contradiction by arguing for the socialisation/politicisation of the traditionally domestic and personal and the breaking down of conventional divisions by which women remain locked within the family and men control the public sphere. While this socialisation is crucial for the establishment of social equality for women, it involves a loss of autonomy and the suppression of certain forms of discourse developed by women out of their history of oppression: some examples would be embroidery, diaries and letters. It is important to recognise the value of this submerged discourse of the domestic in the reconstruction of a feminist history. It arises out of the increasing marginalisation of the personal sphere in advanced capitalist society, and its development is similar to that of personal avant-garde film-making.

Traditionally the relationship of the avant-garde film-maker to her or his work has been artisanal, i.e. the film-maker, like a craft worker, is in control of all aspects of the process of production and distribution/exhibition, retaining rights of ownership over her or his film. The artisanal mode of production has several levels: it implies a particular mode of production which is small-scale and therefore, in a capitalist economy, lies outside the dominant system.

The 'product' does not have an immediately available market, or audience, and is not geared to profit, therefore the means of production must be as cheap as possible and labour costs kept low. In the case of film this means that access to cheap film stock, and to light, cheap equipment, is essential to enable films to be made by individuals or small groups. Historically, therefore, artisanal production stands in opposition both to the capitalist economic organisation of the film industry and to the structure of labour within the industry (in terms of its hierarchy and organisation): the struggles of the New American Cinema Group in the States in the early 1960s with the staffing regulations of the unions are an example of this oppositional stance.

The small-scale artisanal mode of production allows the filmmaker(s) to control the product at all stages, including distribution and exhibition, and enables them to retain certain rights of ownership over their work, an important factor in exhibition, where choice as to how the film is to be taken up can be crucial. However, the level of personal and financial investment on the part of the film-maker(s) is high, limiting production on the whole to a privileged minority.

In general, because of its marginal position vis-à-vis the industry, artisanal film production has been supported by the patronage of wealthy individuals, funding in the form of grants from State institutions, and by the organisation of co-operative workshops which are largely self-supporting and provide a relatively autonomous structure for the production, distribution and exhibition of films, the revenue from which is divided between film-maker(s) and co-op. The high degree of artistic autonomy which this mode of production offers to film-makers leads to an emphasis on 'self-expression' which is seen as standing in opposition to the representation of the world-view of a dominant class in commercial cinema. In fact, dominant, mainstream cinema is well able to accommodate the idea of 'self-expression', as is demonstrated by the early formulations of the auteur theory, in which the films of certain 'great' directors such as John Ford or Howard Hawks were held up as examples of 'personal vision'. 'Self-expression' in this sense meant that the films were seen as the manifestations of unique personal genius, the primary creative source of the work, replacing the world-view of a dominant class by an equally homogeneous personal world-view. The work of the French journal *Cahiers du Cinéma* on John Ford's *Young Mr Lincoln* radically shifted the simplistic notion of the *auteur*, positing instead the authorial voice as a 'sub-text', breaking through the narrative structure of the film.

Historically, therefore, in artisanal production the 'personal' statement of the artist/film-maker can be seen as in opposition to the forms of dominant cinema: the private language, or idiolect, is set against the universal stereotypes of commercial cinema, and the work becomes strongly autobiographical, poetic and/or epistolary in form.

The democratisation/humanisation of the production process in which access to the means of production is seen as an end in itself can lead to the assumption that control of the means of production is political in itself, subverting the economic base of commercial cinema (see Annette Michelson's argument in 'Film and the radical aspiration'[1]). The relationship of the film-maker/producer to her or his work is no longer alienated, but close and intimate, leading to the inscription of the material presence of the film (dust particles, sprocket holes, black leader, etc.), and the presence of the film-maker, in the film itself.

The artisanal relationship to the work derives from an ambiguous attitude towards the film industry. Avant-garde film-makers have had to create their own audience, but without the resources of the industry their ability to do this is limited. French artists of the 1920s and '30s vacillated between industry and private patronage, organising viewings and screenings with discussion in an attempt to generate an audience for their work, but without much success. Until developments in 16mm technology in the States after the Second World War made it possible for film-makers to achieve autonomy through the organisation of co-ops, production and distribution/exhibition were confined largely to art-house, campus, gallery and museum. The success of the co-ops in providing a relatively autonomous structure allowed avant-garde film-makers to create an alternative space for themselves, albeit necessarily marginal, and a new audience for their films.

The '16mm revolution' in the States resulted in great accessibility to the means of production, relatively cheaper production, and lighter equipment which could be easily handled by one or two people, thus opening up the possibility of alternative conditions of production to the dominant system. One of the developments of these alternative conditions was the emergence of the group of artist/film-makers now known as the first phase of the New American Cinema, a group characterised by their 'personal' films. Influenced by avant-garde work from France, Germany and USSR the early films of the New American Cinema in the 1940s explored new territory in poetic film-making. The psycho-dramas of Brakhage, Anger and Markopoulos, and the 'lyrical' films of Maya

Deren are typical of the beginnings of the aesthetic of 'personal vision' which was to become so influential in avant-garde film-making. The importance of the film image to this aesthetic was central, its ability to work against the linear flow of narrative and allow for an exploration of meaning in depth, rather than concentrating on the resolution of the narrative enigma: Maya Deren's advocation of 'lyrical' film in terms of the vertical and the horizontal was an attempt to theorise this emphasis on the image. Largely for economic and technological reasons at this particular conjuncture sound was excluded, and fellow-artists and friends appeared as actors in the films, with the result that they seemed overwhelmingly poetic and personal, a self-contained work of the imagination, like a dream or fantasy. *Meshes of the Afternoon* (Deren) is a good example of personal film-making. It was made independently, with the help of her husband, and Maya Deren herself plays the protagonist. The form is experimental, playing with cinematic language to create the effect of a dream which must be decoded to reveal the obsessions of the film-maker, and through the dream it explores the taboo subject of ambiguous sexuality from the female protagonist's point-of-view, her thoughts as the dreamer. Maya Deren was an active campaigner for independent distribution and exhibition for avant-garde film-makers, and at this conjuncture the notion of artisanal production had a vital polemical function in opening up the question of an alternative space for independent film-makers to work.

Brakhage, of course, developed the aesthetic of 'personal vision' even further (see 'Metaphors on Vision'[2]), becoming obsessed with the process of seeing itself, in the visionary sense, and taking the idea of the artisan to its most extreme by making his own personal scratch marks on the film itself. Lighter equipment and the greater availability of film stock, together with the growth of television, contributed to a new intimacy of subject matter, and for Brakhage the raw material of his visionary films was the personal and the domestic; from the intimate and the mundane he created new artefacts, compensating for his alienation from the 'real' world through the closeness of his relationship to the material of film itself. The development of Super-8mm and video has led Brakhage to produce even more personal film-poems, like the mysterious *Songs*, which are available for general sale.

The polemical force of this intimate diary form has not yet been explored in any depth, and should not be under-estimated.

While criticisms of the way that avant-garde film production was integrated into the tradition of high art are valid, the concern of the 'personal' film-makers with questions of point-of-view, memory and fantasy, with the material base of film, and the possibility of creating an alternative language of film, remains important.

For these film-makers the family, the home, personal and sexual relationships were the site of drama and struggle, and the relationship of film-maker to film was equally dramatic. The emphasis on the material base of film itself (which arose initially from a situation of severe limitations of resources in which these film-makers worked) is not entirely 'self-referential': it carried a system of connotation with its own history outside of film. For Brakhage, for instance, the film material represents a passive mass or body which is reorganised by the active agency of the artist into a meaningful system, a notion of the 'natural' as passive and of the artist as central figure in the world which goes back to the Renaissance. It is possible, however, to see the material base as active rather than passive, as already in the process of signifying, a 'body' in motion, the site of the intersection of a multiplicity of signifying elements.

The 'break' with the cinema of 'personal vision' came in the 1960s with the structural/minimalist cinema of Warhol, Snow, Frampton et alia, under the influence of abstract painting and sculpture and the growth of large-scale financial investment in avant-garde art, leading to an increasing professionalisation of the artist. George Landow marked the break in *Remedial Reading Comprehension* . . . 'This film is about you, not about its maker', the film tells its audience. Attention turned to film itself as subject matter, its basic structures rather than its actual physical presence, and the personal was suppressed in favour of a concern with the audience's perception of filmic structure, the need to educate, to be didactic, in some cases coercive (see *T.O.U.C.H.I.N.G.* by Sharits). Film-makers saw themselves as objective scientists, films as objective phenomena (see Sharits's 'Words per Page'.[3]).

Frampton's *Nostalgia* explodes the notion of personal expression by teasing the memory and anticipation of the spectator, setting the soundtrack which describes an image yet to appear over the photograph of a time in the film-maker's past, disrupting the idea of diary or document, since each image escapes the description which belongs to it, and memory is revealed as arbitrary. It is the measured system of the film, its material structure, which dominates, fracturing the discourse of the film-maker. Structural/minimalist film reflects a change in attitude towards the dominant system and its forms, recognising its own relative autonomy by taking account of narrative – confronting it, displacing or deconstructing it.

Snow's *Wavelength* performs a similar dispersal of the personal: as the spectator waits for the zoom to finish on the 'Walking Woman' photograph (an obsessional motif in Snow's work generally), it continues zooming relentlessly towards the photograph of water, asserting the autonomy of the zoom as a structuring element above personal discourse.

Joyce Weiland's work is interesting in this context because, while obviously influenced by the structural/minimalist school, she retains more of the artisanal in her films than they do, and invests it with a political dimension. In *Pierre Vallières* for instance, the image of the male revolutionary's mouth is interrupted by work on the image (adjustment of focus and framing etc., hand-printed English sub-titles) and on the sound track the voices of the women film-makers can be heard, words indistinguishable, off. The dominant discourse of the male revolutionary is brought into question by the breaking up of the film as the reels run out, the questions of the film-makers, and the manipulation of the gaze of the camera by them. The displaced 'I' thus becomes a questioning force, a voice 'off', disturbing the hegemony of revolutionary language.

In *Rat Life and Diet in North America* the domestic context of the political allegory is emphasised by markings on the film image which are reminiscent of embroidery, rhymed with actual embroidered titles in the film itself, calling to mind Weiland's own interest in embroidery as art, and setting up a dialectical process of critique between domestic situation (the pro-filmic event takes place in Wieland's own kitchen) and revolutionary politics (Canadian anti-imperialism, Che Guevara's death, etc.) the personal interests of the film-maker erupting apparently arbitrarily into the structure of the film to question the political 'world-view'.

In these 'structural' films the marks of the film-maker are established by the use of natural sound 'voice-off', the fixed gaze of the camera, generally identified with the 'look' of the film-maker, and work on the image and structure itself. This represents a radical shift from the position of Brakhage and the centrality of the visionary artist/film-maker to his work. While it could be argued that the marginalisation of the discourse of the artist in structural/minimalist film also reflected the romantic ideology of the artist-outsider, it nevertheless changed the emphasis of the problematic. The question of ownership, for instance, marked by Brakhage in his films by hand-writing on the surface of the film and signifying the film-maker's control over processes of production, distribution and exhibition, in structural/minimalist film becomes submerged in questions of form and structure, along with other social and political questions.

The importance of the structural/minimalist break with the romantic individualism of Brakhage is to be found in the act of splitting, or dispersal. For Brakhage, the camera is an extension of the human eye, and in a hierarchy of discourses the discourse of the artist predominates, providing the overall coherence of the work. In structural film, however, the discourse of the artist is dispersed across the film in the process of separating out basic filmic elements which have a certain autonomy in themselves. The intentions/concerns of the film-maker are subject to extraneous factors, filmic and non-filmic, which are out of her or his control: chance and random elements, the unconscious of the viewer, among other things. The discourse of the film-maker is one code among many, and this foregrounding of the coding of the personal changes the problematic from the basically defensive position of Brakhage's controlling visionary to a recognition of the artist's vulnerability in a capitalist economy where her or his autonomy is only apparent.

At its most progressive this leads to a view of film as a multi-layered system, a palimpsest or 'text'. In other cases the didactic nature of some of the films leads to a harassment of the spectator, thus tending to assume both the homogeneity and passivity of the audience.

As Peter Wollen has pointed out (in his article 'The Two Avant-Gardes'[4]), the modernist break with nineteenth century representation involved a splitting of the sign into signifier and signified, with no essential relationship between the two, opening the way to the possibility of change, since there were no longer any permanent Truths represented by fixed signs: the relation of sign to referent, signifier to signified was constantly shifting.

In painting and sculpture this shifting relationship could be seen in the concern with re-contextualising objects to give them new meaning. Marcel Duchamp, for instance, took a popular provincial print of a landscape, and by adding two spots of red and green paint and a new title, 'Pharmacie', created a new set of relationships between sign and referent and signifier and signified, and a 'personal statement' about art. Modernism shifted the problematic towards language itself as an area of struggle and change, a recognition of its importance in constructing our view of the world and our position in it.

Similarly, Freudian psychoanalytic theory made it possible to break with ego-based psychology by positing a split in the psyche between ego, id and super-ego. The human individual could no longer be seen as a coherent, totally conscious being in control of its environment and destiny, but was constituted as a subject in ideology, caught in the tension between the symbolic order and what it repressed, the unconscious, therefore profoundly divided. From this account of modernism as a process of splitting up of the imaginary coherence of language and the subject it is possible to understand the notion of 'self-expression' not as the full expression of the artist's voice, but rather in the manifestation of a fragmented discourse, polysemic and polyphonic, suggesting a partial autonomy for the film-maker which allows space for her or his unconscious and conscious concerns, without suppressing the personal, but without privileging the discourse of the artist.

Although I have stressed the polemical value of the concept of 'self-expression' in avant-garde art, the concept contains contradictions within itself and in its relationship to institutional practices, contradictions which are revealed in its own practice. The desire to create a social and cultural space to allow artists to experiment with film language is the basis for the demand for an independent base for production. At the same time the role of institutions in supporting the demand for that space must be recognised. The notion of autonomy for film-makers is crucial: however, the autonomy is not self-evident, or 'given', but paradoxically dependent upon specific institutional practices, with which it is often at odds. A funding agency like the BFI Production Board which allows avant-garde film-makers aesthetic freedom, nevertheless, because of its own place within the 'film industry', has effects on that autonomy. The relationship of avant-garde film practice to such an institutional practice is contradictory and can only be understood in terms of the specificity of both, not in terms of an ideal of autonomy for the former or a monolithic repressive function on the part of the latter.[5]

The personal/artisanal mode of production implies a high level of personal investment in the films, which is often suppressed when production is completed and the films are inserted into distribution and exhibition channels over which the film-maker may have little or no control. In terms of industrial film production this process of alienation from the work would not be surprising, but the artisanal mode struggles to overcome this alienation by asserting ownership and control of the finished product. Alienation is a real problem for avant-garde film-makers, and the problematic of artistic autonomy in relation to the institutional construction of meaning through distribution and exhibition provides one level of articulation in the films, as an aspect of the film-makers' relationship to the film material itself. In *Mirror Phase*[6] for example, Super-8mm 'amateur' gauge material documenting the development of the film-maker's daughter from a pre-linguistic age to the use of 2-word sentences at 24 months is re-worked onto 16mm for commercial distribution. The possibility of allowing space and time for film-makers to re-work material in this way is central to the artisanal/avant-garde mode of production, and *Mirror Phase* argues strongly for the value of experiment, at the same time recognising in its use of the 'voice-over' the problem of accountability to external forces.

In *Riddles of the Sphinx*[7] the process of re-working is given a political dimension. The film uses the notion of the material base of film, not as an essence, with a fixed and final meaning, but as part of the process of signification. The work of the film-makers, and the audience, on the 'body' of the film is given equal value, a point beautifully made in the acrobats sequence, which was shot in black and white and then re-worked, where the re-working of the film image displaces the classic idea of women's bodies as spectacle, as objects of the look of the spectator, into the idea of the body at work, in motion (the 'body' of the film, the 'body' of the women's movement, the female body). Re-working is a process of questioning, a questioning which comes from below, as a 'voice-off', rather than from the authority of a 'voice-over'.

The importance of questions raised by avant-garde film practice for feminists is crucial in a society where the discourse of women is suppressed, and can only return in the form of symptoms in the gaps and fissures of dominant ideology. The subordinate position of women in society means that they are generally barred from access to the means of production, but even where access is possible the question of an autonomous feminist discourse outside dominant ideology remains. The organisation of small-scale independent production and distribution/exhibition facilities, whether individual or collective, is of vital importance if women are to make any significant intervention into 'patriarchal' culture, but the question of what that intervention might be is still problematic. Recent feminist criticism, by the *Camera Obscura* collective for instance, has taken up work by women avant-garde film-makers such as Yvonne Rainer and Chantal Akerman as exemplary of a feminist cinema, arguing that their articulation of their problems as women and film-makers in the form of a divided and fractured discourse constitutes a woman's controlling viewpoint (see *Camera Obscura* no. 2[8]). The work of Rainer and Akerman, articulating as it does important questions of formal alienation and distanciation, is interesting for the way it reveals the ideology of the woman-artist, a voice suppressed and marginalised by the dominant system of representation, returning in the interstices of a fragmented or hysterical text. *Riddles of the Sphinx* poses the question another way, from the perspective of sexual politics and the women's movement, suggesting that the answer goes beyond formal problems to the question of the construction of sexual difference and the organisation of reproduction in society.

The questions that the film asks about film-makers' and spectators' relationship to the film material, about space for self-definition and exploration, about the process of signification and the role of the unconscious in creating meaning, and about film language itself, the possibility of creating an alternative symbolic order, are all central to feminist film-making, and can only be explored, I would argue, in the context of small-scale artisanal production. Significantly, *Riddles of the Sphinx* incorporates the idea of the film-maker as artisan as part of its polemic.

Editor's notes

1 Annette Michelson, 'Film and the radical aspiration', in *New Forms in Film* (Montreux catalogue), 1974.
2 Stan Brakhage, 'Metaphors on Vision', *Film Culture*, no. 30, 1963.
3 Paul Sharits, 'Words per page', *Afterimage*, no. 4, 1972.
4 Peter Wollen, 'The two avant-gardes', *Studio International*, November/ December 1975; reprinted in *Edinburgh '76 Magazine*, Edinburgh Film Festival, 1976.
5 The Production Board is a department within the British Film Institute responsible for funding low-budget, 'independent' film-making. See John Ellis, 'The BFI Production Board', *Screen*, vol. 17, no. 4, Winter 1976/ 7, and subsequent correspondence in *Screen*, vol. 18, no. 1, Spring 1977.
6 *Mirror Phase*, a film by Carola Klein, funded by the Production Board and distributed by the BFI.
7 *Riddles of the Sphinx*, a film by Laura Mulvey and Peter Wollen, funded by the Production Board and distributed by the BFI (the script appears in *Screen*, vol. 18, no. 2, 1977); Pam Cook's catalogue article introduced this film and also Carola Klein's *Mirror Phase*.
8 *Camera Obscura*, no. 2, contains articles by Janet Bergstrom on Chantal Akerman's *Jeanne Dielman*, by Elizabeth Lyon on Marguerite Duras's *La Femme du Gange*, and by Constance Penley on Babette Mangolte's *What Maisie Knew*. There is also a dossier on 'Women Working'.

From *Language, Counter-Memory, Practice*, Basil Blackwell, Oxford, 1977; (first published Paris, 1969)

In his analyses of orders of discourse as they are constituted historically and socially, Foucault's work has a particular pertinence for concepts of authorship; particularly relevant are *The Order of Things* (1966) and *The Archaeology of Knowledge* (1969). This extract focuses the specific question of the function of the author, and of his name, in discourse, drawing out the historically variable uses to which the name and concept of the author has been put.

In the opening section of the essay, Foucault had addressed himself to 'the naive and often crude fashion' in which the names of authors – Bouffon, Cuvier, Marx – had been used to identify discourses in *The Order of Things* without a proper analysis of their function. He goes on to question the interdependence of the concept '*oeuvre*' and the concept 'author', and to question critically those who proclaim the disappearance of the author into '*écriture*'. In a later section, he discusses the extended sense in which certain writers – Freud, Marx – have to be seen not only as authors, but as 'initiators of discursive practices'.

It is obviously insufficient to repeat empty slogans: the author has disappeared; God and man died a common death.[1] Rather, we should reexamine the empty space left by the author's disappearance; we should attentively observe, along its gaps and fault lines, its new demarcations, and the reapportionment of this void; we should await the fluid functions released by this disappearance. In this context we can briefly consider the problems that arise in the use of an author's name. What is the name of an author? How does it function? Far from offering a solution, I will attempt to indicate some of the difficulties related to these questions.

The name of an author poses all the problems related to the category of the proper name. (Here, I am referring to the work of John Searle,[2] among others.) Obviously not a pure and simple reference, the proper name (and the author's name as well) has other than indicative functions. It is more than a gesture, a finger pointed at someone; it is, to a certain extent, the equivalent of a description. When we say 'Aristotle,' we are using a word that means one or a series of definite descriptions of the type: 'the author of the *Analytics*,' or 'the founder of ontology,' and so forth.[3] Furthermore, a proper name has other functions than that of signification: when we discover that Rimbaud has not written *La Chasse spirituelle*, we cannot maintain that the meaning of the proper name or this author's name has been altered. The proper name and the name of an author oscillate between the poles of description and designation, and, granting that they are linked to what they name, they are not totally determined either by their descriptive or designative functions.[4] Yet – and it is here that the specific difficulties attending an author's name appear – the link between a proper name and the individual being named and the link between an author's name and that which it names are not isomorphous and do not function in the same way; and these differences require clarification.

To learn, for example, that Pierre Dupont does not have blue eyes, does not live in Paris, and is not a doctor does not invalidate the fact that the name, Pierre Dupont, continues to refer to the same person; there has been no modification of the designation that links the name to the person. With the name of an author, however, the problems are far more complex. The disclosure that Shakespeare was not born in the house that tourists now visit would not modify the functioning of the author's name, but, if it were proved that he had not written the sonnets that we attribute to him, this would constitute a significant change and affect the manner in which the author's name functions. Moreover, if we establish that Shakespeare wrote Bacon's *Organon* and that the same author was responsible for both the works of Shakespeare and those of Bacon, we would have introduced a third type of alteration which completely modifies the functioning of the author's name. Consequently, the name of an author is not precisely a proper name among others.

Many other factors sustain this paradoxical singularity of the name of an author. It is altogether different to maintain that Pierre Dupont does not exist and that Homer or Hermes Trismegistes have never existed. While the first negation merely implies that there is no one by the name of Pierre Dupont, the second indicates that several individuals have been referred to by one name or that the real author possessed none of the traits traditionally associated with Homer or Hermes. Neither is it the same thing to say that Jacques Durand, not Pierre Dupont, is the real name of X and that Stendhal's name was Henri Beyle. We could also examine the function and meaning of such statements as 'Bourbaki is this or that person,' and 'Victor Eremita, Climacus, Anticlimacus, Frater Taciturnus, Constantin Constantius, all of these are Kierkegaard.'

These differences indicate that an author's name is not simply an element of speech (as a subject, a complement, or an element that could be replaced by a pronoun or other parts of speech). Its presence is functional in that it serves as a means of classification. A name can group together a number of texts and thus differentiate them from others. A name also establishes different forms of relationships among texts. Neither Hermes not Hippocrates existed in the sense that we can say Balzac existed, but the fact that a number of texts were attached to a single name implies that relationships of homogeneity, filiation, reciprocal explanation, authentification, or of common utilization were established among them. Finally, the author's name characterizes a particular manner of existence of discourse. Discourse that possesses an author's name is not to be immediately consumed and forgotten; neither is it accorded the momentary attention given to ordinary, fleeting words. Rather, its status and its manner of reception are regulated by the culture in which it circulates.

We can conclude that, unlike a proper name, which moves from the interior of a discourse to the real person outside who produced it, the name of the author remains at the contours of texts – separating one from the other, defining their form, and characterizing their mode of existence. It points to the existence of certain groups of discourse and refers to the status of this discourse within a society and culture. The author's name is not a function of a man's civil status, nor is it fictional; it is situated in the breach, among the discontinuities, which gives rise to new groups of discourse and their singular mode of existence. Consequently, we can say that in our culture, the name of an author is a variable that accompanies only certain texts to the exclusion of others: a private letter may have a signatory, but it does not have an author; a contract can have an underwriter, but not an author; and, similarly, an anonymous poster attached to a wall may have a writer, but he cannot be an author. In this sense, the function of an author is to characterize the existence, circulation, and operation of certain discourses within a society.

In dealing with the 'author' as a function of discourse, we must consider the characteristics of a discourse that support this use and determine its difference from other discourses. If we limit our remarks to only those books or texts with authors, we can isolate four different features.

First, they are objects of appropriation; the form of property they have become is of a particular type whose legal codification was accomplished some years ago. It is important to notice, as well, that its status as property is historically secondary to the penal code controlling its appropriation. Speeches and books were assigned real authors, other than mythical or important religious figures, only when the author became subject to punishment and to the extent that his discourse was considered transgressive. In our culture – undoubtedly in others as well – discourse was not originally a thing, a product, or a possession, but an action situated in a bipolar field of sacred and profane, lawful and unlawful, religious and blasphemous. It was a gesture charged with risks long before it became a possession caught in a circuit of property values. But it was at the moment when a system of ownership and strict copyright rules were established (toward the end of the eighteenth and beginning of the nineteenth century) that the transgressive properties always intrinsic to the act of writing became the forceful imperative of literature. It is as if the author, at the moment he was accepted into the social order of property which governs our culture, was compensating for his new status by reviving the older bipolar field of discourse in a systematic practice of transgression and by restoring the danger of writing which, on another side, had been conferred the benefits of property.

Secondly, the 'author-function' is not universal or constant in all discourse. Even within our civilization, the same types of texts have not always required authors; there was a time when those texts which we now call 'literary' (stories, folk tales, epics, and tragedies) were accepted, circulated, and valorized without any question about the identity of their author. Their anonymity was ignored because their real or supposed age was a sufficient guarantee of their authenticity. Texts, however, that we now call 'scientific' (dealing with cosmology and the heavens, medicine or illness, the natural sciences or geography) were only considered truthful during the Middle Ages if the name of the author was indicated. Statements on the order of 'Hippocrates said . . .' or 'Pliny tells us that . . .' were not merely formulas for an argument based on authority; they marked a proven discourse. In the seventeenth and eighteenth centuries, a totally new conception was developed when scientific texts were accepted on their own merits and positioned within an anonymous and coherent conceptual system of established truths and methods of verification. Authentification no longer required reference to the individual who had produced them; the role of the author disappeared as an index of truthfulness and, where it remained as an inventor's name, it was merely to denote a specific theorem or proposition, a strange effect, a property, a body, a group of elements, or pathological syndrome.

At the same time, however, 'literary' discourse was acceptable only if it carried an author's name; every text of poetry or fiction was obliged to state its author and the date, place, and circumstance of its writing. The meaning and value attributed to the text depended on this information. If by accident or design a text was presented anonymously, every effort was made to locate its author. Literary anonymity was of interest only as a puzzle to be solved as, in our day, literary works are totally dominated by the sovereignty of the author. (Undoubtedly, these remarks are far too categorical. Criticism has been concerned for some time now with aspects of a text not fully dependent on the notion of an individual creator; studies of genre or the analysis of recurring textual motifs and their variations from a norm other than the author. Furthermore, where in mathematics the author has become little more than a handy reference for a particular theorem or group of propositions, the reference to an author in biology and medicine, or to the date of his research has a substantially different bearing. This latter reference, more than simply indicating the source of information, attests to the 'reliability' of the evidence, since it entails an appreciation of the techniques and experimental materials available at a given time and in a particular laboratory.)

The third point concerning this 'author-function' is that it is not formed spontaneously through the simple attribution of a discourse to an individual. It results from a complex operation whose purpose is to construct the rational entity we call an author. Undoubtedly, this construction is assigned a 'realistic' dimension as we speak of an individual's 'profundity' or 'creative' power, his intentions or the original inspiration manifested in writing. Nevertheless, these aspects of an individual, which we designate as an author (or which comprise an individual as an author), are projections, in terms always more or less psychological, of our way of handling texts: in the comparisons we make, the traits we extract as pertinent, the continuities we assign, or the exclusions we practice. In addition, all these operations vary according to the period and the form of discourse concerned. A 'philosopher' and a 'poet' are not constructed in the same manner; and the author of an eighteenth-century novel was formed differently from the modern novelist.

There are, nevertheless, transhistorical constants in the rules that govern the construction of an author.

In literary criticism, for example, the traditional methods for defining an author — or, rather, for determining the configuration of the author from existing texts — derive in large part from those used in the Christian tradition to authenticate (or to reject) the particular texts in its possession. Modern criticism, in its desire to 'recover' the author from a work, employs devices strongly reminiscent of Christian exegesis when it wished to prove the value of a text by ascertaining the holiness of its author. In *De Viris Illustribus*, Saint Jerome maintains that homonymy is not proof of the common authorship of several works, since many individuals could have the same name or someone could have perversely appropriated another's name. The name, as an individual mark, is not sufficient as it relates to a textual tradition. How, then, can several texts be attributed to an individual author? What norms, related to the function of the author, will disclose the involvement of several authors? According to Saint Jerome, there are four criteria: the texts that must be eliminated from the list of works attributed to a single author are those inferior to the others (thus, the author is defined as a standard level of quality); those whose ideas conflict with the doctrine expressed in the others (here the author is defined as a certain field of conceptual or theoretical coherence); those written in a different style and containing words and phrases not ordinarily found in the other works (the author is seen as a stylistic uniformity); and those referring to events or historical figures subsequent to the death of the author (the author is thus a definite historical figure in which a series of events converge). Although modern criticism does not appear to have these same suspicions concerning authentication, its strategies for defining the author present striking similarities. The author explains the presence of certain events within a text, as well as their transformations, distortions, and their various modifications (and this through an author's biography or by reference to his particular point of view, in the analysis of his social preferences and his position within a class or by delineating his fundamental objectives). The author also constitutes a principle of unity in writing where any unevenness of production is ascribed to changes caused by evolution, maturation, or outside influence. In addition, the author serves to neutralize the contradictions that are found in a series of texts. Governing this function is the belief that there must be — at a particular level of an author's thought, of his conscious or unconscious desire — a point where contradictions are resolved, where the incompatible elements can be shown to relate to one another or to cohere around a fundamental and originating contradiction. Finally, the author is a particular source of expression who, in more or less finished forms, is manifested equally well, and with similar validity, in a text, in letters, fragments, drafts, and so forth. Thus, even while Saint Jerome's four principles of authenticity might seem largely inadequate to modern critics, they, nevertheless, define the critical modalities now used to display the function of the author.

However, it would be false to consider the function of the author as a pure and simple reconstruction after the fact of a text given as passive material, since a text always bears a number of signs that refer to the author. Well known to grammarians, these textual signs are personal pronouns, adverbs of time and place, and the conjugation of verbs. But it is important to note that these elements have a different bearing on texts with an author and on those without one. In the latter, these 'shifters'[5] refer to a real speaker and to an actual deictic situation, with certain exceptions such as the case of indirect speech in the first person. When discourse is linked to an author, however, the role of 'shifters' is more complex and variable. It is well known that in a novel narrated in the first person, neither the first person pronoun, the present indicative tense, nor, for that matter, its signs of localization refer directly to the writer, either to the time when he wrote, or to the specific act of writing; rather, they stand for a 'second self'[6] whose similarity to the author is never fixed and undergoes considerable alteration within the course of a single book. It would be as false to seek the author in relation to the actual writer as to the fictional narrator; the 'author-function' arises out of their scission – in the division and distance of the two. One might object that this phenomenon only applies to novels or poetry, to a context of 'quasi-discourse,' but, in fact, all discourse that supports this 'author-function' is characterized by this plurality of egos. In a mathematical treatise, the ego who indicates the circumstances of composition in the preface is not identical, either in terms of his position or his function, to the 'I' who concludes a demonstration within the body of the text. The former implies a unique individual who, at a given time and place, succeeded in completing a project, whereas the latter indicates an instance and plan of demonstration that anyone could perform provided the same set of axioms, preliminary operations, and an identical set of symbols were used. It is also possible to locate a third ego: one who speaks of the goals of his investigation, the obstacles encountered, its results, and the problems yet to be solved and this 'I' would function in a field of existing or future mathematical discourses. We are not dealing with a system of dependencies where a first and essential use of the 'I' is reduplicated, as a kind of fiction, by the other two. On the contrary, the 'author-function' in such discourses operates so as to effect the simultaneous dispersion of the three egos.

Further elaboration would, of course, disclose other characteristics of the 'author-function,' but I have limited myself to the four that seemed the most obvious and important. They can be summarized in the following manner: the 'author-function' is tied to the legal and institutional systems that circumscribe, determine, and articulate the realm of discourses; it does not operate in a uniform manner in all discourses, at all times, and in any given culture; it is not defined by the spontaneous attribution of a text to its creator, but through a series of precise and complex procedures; it does not refer, purely and simply, to an actual individual insofar as it simultaneously gives rise to a variety of egos and to a series of subjective positions that individuals of any class may come to occupy. . . .

Unfortunately, there is a decided absence of positive propositions in this essay, as it applies to analytic procedures or directions for future research, but I ought at least to give the reasons why I attach such importance to a continuation of this work. Developing a similar analysis could provide the basis for a typology of discourse. A typology of this sort cannot be adequately understood in relation to the grammatical features, formal structures, and objects of discourse, because there undoubtedly exist specific discursive properties or relationships that are irreducible to the rules of grammar and logic and to the laws that govern objects. These properties require investigation if we hope to distinguish the larger categories of discourse. The different forms of relationships (or nonrelationships) that an author can assume are evidently one of these discursive properties.

This form of investigation might also permit the introduction of an historical analysis of discourse. Perhaps the time has come to study not only the expressive value and formal transformations of discourse, but its mode of existence: the modifications and variations, within any culture, of modes of circulation, valorization, attribution, and appropriation. Partially at the expense of themes and concepts that an author places in his work, the 'author-function' could also reveal the manner in which discourse is articulated on the basis of social relationships.

Is it not possible to reexamine, as a legitimate extension of this kind of analysis, the privileges of the subject? Clearly, in undertaking an internal and architectonic analysis of a work (whether it be a literary text, a philosophical system, or a scientific work) and in delimiting psychological and biographical references, suspicions arise concerning the absolute nature and creative role of the subject. But the subject should not be entirely abandoned. It should be reconsidered, not to restore the theme of an originating subject, but to seize its functions, its intervention in discourse, and its system of dependencies. We should suspend the typical questions: how does a free subject penetrate the density of things and endow them with meaning; how does it accomplish its design by animating the rules of discourse from within? Rather, we should ask: under what conditions and through what forms can an entity like the subject appear in the order of discourse; what position does it occupy; what functions does it exhibit; and what rules does it follow in each type of discourse? In short, the subject (and its substitutes) must be stripped of its creative role and analysed as a complex and variable function of discourse.

The author – or what I have called the 'author-function' – is undoubtedly only one of the possible specifications of the subject and, considering past historical transformations, it appears that the form, the complexity, and even the existence of this function are far from immutable. We can easily imagine a culture where discourse would circulate without any need for an author. Discourses, whatever their status, form, or value, and regardless of our manner of handling them, would unfold in a pervasive anonymity. No longer the tiresome repetitions:

'Who is the real author?'

'Have we proof of his authenticity and originality?'

'What has he revealed of his most profound self in his language?'

New questions will be heard:

'What are the modes of existence of this discourse?'

'Where does it come from; how is it circulated; who controls it?'

'What placements are determined for possible subjects?'

'Who can fulfil these diverse functions of the subject?'

Behind all these questions we would hear little more than the murmur of indifference:

'What matter who's speaking?'[7]

Notes

1 Nietzsche, *The Gay Science, Collected Works*, ed. O. Levy, vol. 10, Edinburgh and London, T. N. Foulis, 1909–13.
2 John Searle, *Speech Acts: an Essay in the Philosophy of Language*, Cambridge, University Press, 1969, pp. 162–74.
3 ibid., p. 169.
4 ibid., p. 172.
5 [See 'Notes on terms' below.]
6 cf. Wayne C. Booth, *The Rhetoric of Fiction*, Chicago/London, University of Chicago Press, 1961, pp. 67–77.
7 Foucault returns to the question from Beckett which he had placed at the beginning of his essay: 'What matter's who's speaking, someone said, what matter's who's speaking', *Texts for Nothing*, London, Calder & Boyars, 1974, p. 16. [Editor's note]

Notes on terms

Since the terms themselves are problematic and resist easy definition, this is not intended as a glossary, but rather as a way of suggesting the implications of using certain terms. There are two difficulties for which the notes might be useful: on the one hand, some of the terms whose use is specialized ('*langue/parole*', 'mirror phase') may be simply unfamiliar; on the other hand, the very familiarity of other terms ('subject', 'desire', 'the imaginary') may conceal difficulties which they have acquired in a specialized usage. Where reliable explications already exist I have leant on them heavily. Most of these terms are given a context within the projects of semiotics and psychoanalysis in Rosalind Coward and John Ellis's *Language and Materialism*, and psychoanalytic terms are explicated very clearly in J. Laplanche and J.-B. Pontalis, *The Language of Psychoanalysis*. Where possible I have appended bibliographical references to each term. Terms are grouped logically rather than listed alphabetically.

subject
At one level, the use of this term is to mark a distinction between an individual with a personality, and a 'place' which that individual may be called upon to occupy within a formation (social, political, textual). A further distinction has to be made, though, between, on the one hand, the subject of idealism – an active agent or mind, already constituted, gaining knowledge of already constituted objects, and, in the end, transcendental (God or God-like), unifying chaos from outside it – and, on the other hand, the subject of materialism – 'subject to' the determinations of class, history and society, constituted by and in ideology. Further still, psychoanalysis poses a subject which is divided by the fact of difference, loss and separation. This 'divided subject' is held as a unity only by the repression of the unconscious, just as the 'ideological subject' (see Althusser, 'Ideology and Ideological State Apparatuses') is held as a unity by the denial of contradiction. Only idealism, then, retains its faith in the actuality of the unified, transcendental subject (a subject which is available to *auteurism* as a free creator). At the same time, for psychoanalysis and for the materialism which has been influenced by it, an imagined unity is the space in which human individuals necessarily live. Our positioning as unified subjects gives us the coherence which makes

292

activity and discourse possible. We are given positions as subjects which allow us to make sense of the discourse: that is to say, the filling of the space of the subject allows the discourse to make sense, to cohere. In his note on the term 'subjective' in *Keywords*, Raymond Williams indicates the 'historical layering' of a root term which appears in such varied formations as 'subject-matter', 'subjectivity', 'subjection', 'subject of the sentence', 'British subject'. Here, it may help to consider three possible uses of the term: (1) the grammatical subject of the sentence; (2) a subject of the Queen; (3) 'subject to ratification'. Rather than closing down into a definition, the concept of the subject involves a play of the three: (1) it is constructed in the formation of language or discourse (the sentence and the text) as a position (not necessarily that of speaker) which gives it coherence and significance; (2) it is constituted by and in a social formation, historical (i.e. changeable) rather than natural, and is defined in terms of something other than itself (the Queen, the mother, the state, the family, the text); (3) it is uncertain, unsatisfactory, and open to division and negation. All this is to suggest the subject and its complexity as a term, rather than to define it.

– see Althusser, 'Ideology and the state', in *Lenin and Philosophy*, pp. 160–5; Coward and Ellis, *Language and Materialism*, pp. 100–21; Williams, *Keywords*, pp. 259–64.

discourse

The term has gained a certain dangerous currency within a range of recent theoretical work – political, linguistic, psychoanalytic, cinematic – which has allowed it to slip, almost unnoticed, from significance to significance. Crudely, the term refers initially to quasi-autonomous systems of coherence and consistency at the level of language – a political discourse, an institutional discourse, a scientific discourse. Ambiguously, it may be identified in terms of a theme (a political discourse would be a discourse about politics), or, more appropriately, in terms of the positions which are given to its subjects (a political discourse finds its politics in the formation of relations between address, addresser and addressee; thus it may be political unintentionally). In textual analyses, discourse has frequently, and confusingly, taken on the significance which was previously given to the notion of coding: thus, in film analyses we are liable to hear of a discourse of the *mise en scène*, or a 'camera discourse'. The confusions are multiple: 'feminine discourse' seems sometimes to mean nothing more than the way women are coded in the film (dress, lighting, etc.); on other occasions, it refers to ways in which concepts of femininity are articulated in the film as a consistency. The two overlap, but are not the same. Similarly, an 'authorial discourse' seems sometimes to refer to the author as sub-code, at other times, more appropriately, to an authorial address. This second sense of discourse as an address is the one which operates in the history/discourse distinction (*histoire/discours*) discussed here particularly by Metz and Nowell-Smith, and derived from its formulation in the work of the linguist, Benveniste. At this level, discourse involves notions of the text as a production and a productivity (rather than as the 'simply natural' which its masquerade as nothing but a story implies), with someone speaking and someone spoken to, and with the positioning of the one by the other. For authorship, to talk of the film as discourse opens it up to questions of the way in which it positions its subjects (enunciating and spectating), and to questions of rhetoric.

– see Foucault, *The Archaeology of Knowledge*; Benveniste, *Problems of General Linguistics*.

langue/parole

In Saussure's linguistics, *langue* is the system or code of language (English, say) systematized out of the jumble of social and individual language facts in English: 'As soon as we give language (*langue*) first place among the facts of speech (*langage*), we introduce a natural order' (*Course in General Linguistics*, p. 9). 'Language (*langue*) is not a function of the speaker; it is a product that is passively assimilated by the individual' (p. 14). *Parole* refers to individual speech acts rather than to a social conventional system, to utterances or messages either spoken or written, to the 'executive side' of *langue*. 'Speaking (*parole*) . . . is an individual act. It is wilful and intellectual' (p. 14). It was this distinction of *langue* and *parole* which allowed Saussure to found a linguistics which had as its object a systematic study of language and its structure.

– see Saussure, *Course in General Linguistics*.

énoncé/énonciation

Nowell-Smith indicates something of what is involved in these terms: *énoncé* (the statement) referring to what is uttered; *énonciation* (the enunciation) referring to the act of uttering, in speech, writing or whatever. The importance of this distinction lies in its implications for the position of the subject: 'Discourse and history are both forms of enunciation, the difference between them lying in the fact that in the discursive form the source of the enunciation is present, whereas in the historical it is suppressed' (Geoffrey Nowell-Smith, p. 234 above). In the light of Saussure's distinction between *langue* and *parole* it is worth adding the following from Stephen Heath's 'Translator's Note' to the collection of Barthes's essays, *Image–Music–Text*:

> This distinction (*énoncé/énonciation*) rejoins *and displaces* that between *langue/parole*: every *énoncé* is a piece of *parole*; consideration of *énonciation* involves not only the social and psychological (i.e. non-linguistic) context of *énoncés*, but also features of *langue* itself, of the ways in which it structures the possibilities of *énonciation* (symbol-indexes such as personal

pronouns, tenses, anaphores are the most obvious of these linguistic features of *énonciation*).
– see Barthes, *Image-Music-Text*, pp. 8–9.

signifier/signified
The linguistic sign unites, not a thing and a name, but a concept and a sound-image. . . . I propose to retain the word sign (*signe*) to designate the whole and to replace 'concept' and 'sound-image' respectively by 'signified' (*signifié*) and 'signifier' (*signifiant*); the last two terms have the advantage of indicating the opposition that separates them from each other and from the whole of which they are parts. [Saussure, *Course in General Linguistics*, p. 67]
The importance of this distinction is made clear by Rosalind Coward and John Ellis (*Language and Materialism*, p. 5).
The possibility of the signifier and the signified as separate in the concept of the sign had two results. On the one hand, it was responsible for the production of structuralism as the synchronic analysis of a system, that is, the analysis of structural relations. On the other hand, it had a more radical potentiality since the signifier could be seen to have an active function in creating and determining the signified. It was the concentration on the first aspect to the exclusion of the second which resulted in the failure to develop the radical potentiality of Saussure's theories, and became the central problem for semiology in its exploration of the avant-garde text.
Subsequently, semiotics and psychoanalysis have attached considerable importance to the primacy of the signifier, and to its activity in determining not only meanings, but also the shifting relations of subjects to meanings. Psychoanalysis, particularly, has drawn attention to the way in which signifiers in the unconscious throw into jeopardy any fixed relations of sign and meaning: 'The unconscious from Freud onwards is a chain of signifiers which somewhere in another place (Freud's '*eine andere Schauplatz*') repeats itself and insists so as to interfere in the breaks offered by the discourse and the thought that the discourse informs' (Lacan, *Ecrits*).
– see Saussure, *Course in General Linguistics*; Lacan, *Ecrits* (particularly, 'Agency of the letter in the unconscious'); Coward and Ellis, *Language and Materialism*, particularly pp. 1–11. See also Heath, 'Film/Text/Cinetext'.

shifters
Used here specifically by Oudart, but the term also has a relation to the explicit marks of enunciation (first- and second-person pronouns, for instance) which are said to be lacking in film, encouraging it to appear as history rather than as discourse. The term 'shifters' (in French *embrayeurs*) comes from Jakobson. In his note in *Dictionnaire encyclopé-*

dique des sciences du langage, Oswald Ducrot equates shifters with
deictics, which he defines thus (p. 323):

expressions whose referent can only be defined in relation to the
interlocutors (R. Jakobson calls them 'shifters', '*embrayeurs*'). Thus,
first and second person pronouns mark out respectively the person
who speaks and the person who is spoken to. In many languages
there are pairs of expressions of which the components are
distinguished from one another solely by the fact that only one is
deictic (the first term in the pairs which follow):
  'here' (= the place at which the dialogue takes place) vs. 'there'
  'at the moment' (= the moment at which we are speaking) vs. 'at
  that moment'
  [only two of the three examples translate into English]
E. Benveniste has shown that deictics constitute an eruption of
discourse within the language system (*langue*), since their very
meaning (the method to be used in finding their referent), although it
is picked out from the language system, can only be defined by
allusion to their use.

Literature and, particularly here, film pose problems for a strictly linguistic
usage of the term, but the problem of how an enunciating subject might
be marked is clearly important.

– see Ducrot and Todorov, *Dictionnaire encyclopédique des sciences
du langage*; R. Jakobson, 'Shifters, verbal categories and the Russian
verb', in *Selected Writings*, vol. 2.

mirror phase
Used here by Metz and Nowell Smith. This is one of the basic terms of
Lacan, and was introduced by him in a paper delivered in 1936. Colin
MacCabe describes it thus:

Around the age of six to eighteen months the small infant may be
observed in an ecstasy of delight in front of a mirror. This empirical
moment can be identified with the grasping of the body as unity, with
the stage called the mirror phase within psychoanalytic theory. The
mirror phase corresponds to a primary narcissism in which every
other is seen as the same as the subject and difference is not
recognised.

This is the moment, exemplified and concretized by the experience in
front of the mirror rather than always happening there, in which the
powerless and unco-ordinated infant grasps itself (in its image) as a
unified subject, an 'Ideal-Ego'. The correspondence between the infant
in front of the mirror and the spectator in front of the cinema screen, both
fascinated by and identifying with his/her 'ideal' image, has not escaped
film theory.

– see MacCabe, 'Presentation of "the imaginary signifier" '; Laplanche
  and Pontalis, *The Language of Psychoanalysis*, pp. 250–2; Lacan,

'The mirror stage as formative of the function of the I', *Ecrits*, pp. 1–7, also in *New Left Review*, no. 51, 1968.

the imaginary

In the theoretical discourse influenced by Lacan, the imaginary cannot simply be taken to equal the illusory. Rather it refers to that stage of the subject, guaranteed in an exemplary fashion in the mirror, when the infant constitutes itself as a unity on the basis of the image (hence 'imaginary') of its counterpart (*le semblable* – the 'specular ego'), which it sees to be unified. Thus the imaginary ('the Imaginary') allows the constitution of an Ideal Ego. For the infant, according to Lacan, this unity in the Imaginary is always threatened by absence (of the mother, of objects) and by difference (the absence or presence of the penis). Language is a way of repressing or controlling this difference and absence by putting it on the plane of representations. For Lacan, the fact of difference is in the Real, conceived as a stage of the subject rather than as an external reality, and its representation/repression/control takes place in the Symbolic. The Imaginary, the Real and the Symbolic are the three psychoanalytic fields of Lacan's theory, extending the sense of Freud's preconscious, unconscious and conscious. Each has a relevance for film theory in so far as it is also a theory of the subject. But the concept of the Imaginary in which the (spectating) subject is constituted as a unity by identifying with (finding an identity in) an image in a mirror (on a screen) which it takes to be the same as itself, has a special attraction and is widely used.

– see Laplanche and Pontalis, *The Language of Psychoanalysis*, p. 210; MacCabe, 'Presentation of "The imaginary signifier" '; Metz, 'The imaginary signifier'.

l'objet 'a'

A term from Lacan, used here by Oudart. If the Symbolic, the Imaginary and the Real constitute the structure of the subject, the Real (site of difference, absence and lack) appears in the structure as object – object small 'a'. *L'objet 'a'* is defined by Lacan in terms of partialness and lack, a lack which, in a sense, needs (and causes) the structure of the subject to contain it. 'The object 'a' is something from which the subject, in order to constitute itself, has separated as organ. It stands as symbol of the lack, i.e. of the phallus, not the phallus itself but as it lacks. Thus, necessarily, it must be an object that is, first, separable, and, second, having some relation to the lack' (Lacan, *Ecrits*; quoted by Heath, 'Anata Mo', p. 53). Lacan associates this partial object which represents lack with such separable items as the nipple, excrement and, importantly for film, with the look: 'is it not clear that the trait "partial", rightly stressed in the objects, applies not to their being part of a total object which would be the body, but to their only partially representing the function that produces them?' (Lacan, *Ecrits*, quoted by Heath, 'Anata Mo', p. 53). It is the sense of partialness – of a partial object 'standing in for' another (repressed, lost, forbidden) object – which seems important for Oudart's usage. Freud's comments on the fetish object in his 1927 essay, 'Fetishism', are also relevant here.

  – see Lacan, 'Of the gaze as *objet petit a*', *The Four Fundamental Concepts of Psychoanalysis*, pp. 67–119; Heath, 'Anata Mo'; Laplanche and Pontalis, *The Language of Psychoanalysis*, pp. 273–81; Freud, 'Fetishism'.

desire
It is worth pointing to a certain precision in the use of the term 'desire' in psychoanalysis. In the first place, the word translates the German *Wunsch* – 'wish', which has a weaker sense, and a less specifically erotic connotation than the English 'desire', or the French *désir* which is used by Lacan. It is also important to separate desire in Lacanian theory from the related concepts of need and demand. Laplanche and Pontalis:

  Jacques Lacan has attempted to re-orientate Freud's doctrine around the notion of desire, and to replace this notion in the forefront of analytic theory. This perspective has led Lacan to distinguish desire from concepts with which it is often confused, such as need and demand. Need is directed towards a specific object and is satisfied by it. Demands are formulated and addressed to others; where they are still aimed at an object, this is not essential to them, since the articulated demand is essentially a demand for love.

  Desire appears in the rift which separates need and demand; it cannot be reduced to need since, by definition, it is not a relation to a real object independent of the subject but a relation to fantasy; nor can it be reduced to demand, in that it seeks to impose itself without taking the language or the unconscious of the other into account and insists upon absolute recognition from him.

  – see Laplanche and Pontalis, *The Language of Psychoanalysis*, pp. 481–3.

suture
The term is associated with Lacanian psychoanalysis where it refers to the juncture of the Imaginary and the Symbolic. For psychoanalysis, Jacques-Alain Miller poses it thus: 'Suture names the relation of the subject to the chain of its discourse; we shall see that it figures there as the element which is lacking, in the form of a stand-in (*tenant-lieu*). For, while there lacking, it is not purely and simply absent' ('Dossier on suture', pp. 25–6). On this basis, Oudart, in his 1969 article, attempts to use the concept of suture as a way of specifying a 'logic of the cinematic' (Miller talks of the 'logic of the signifier'); that is to say, a logic of the

sequence by which cinema signifies and produces subjects for its discourse. Stephen Heath summarizes Oudart thus ('Notes on suture', pp. 57–8):

As described by Oudart, the process of reading a film goes in stages, the first of which is a moment of sheer jubilation *in* the image . . .; a moment, as it were, untroubled by screen and frame, prior to the articulation of cinema. Awareness of the frame then breaks this initial relation, the image now seen in its limits; the space which just before was the pure extent of the spectator's pleasure becomes a problem of representation, of being-there-*for* – there for an absent field, outside of the image ('the fourth wall'), for the phantom character that the spectator's imagination poses in response to the problem: 'the absent one'. Crucially, what this realisation of absence from the image at once achieves is the definition of the image as discontinuous, its production *as signifier*: the move from cinema to cinematic, cinema as discourse: 'The revelation of this absence is the key-moment in the fate of the image, since it introduces the image into the order of the signifier and the cinema into the order of discourse.' What then operates, classically, is the effacement (or filling in) of the absence, the suturing of the discourse – its movement as in a continuity of articulation – by the reappropriation of the absence within the film, a character in the film coming to take the place of the absent one posed by the spectator; suture as 'the abolition of the absent one and its resurrection in some one'; 'the pure field of absence becomes the imaginary of the film and the field of its imaginary'.

– see 'Dossier on Suture', *Screen*, vol. 18, no. 4, Winter 1977–78, pp. 23–76. The dossier includes: Jacques-Alain Miller, 'Suture (elements of the logic of the signifier)' from *Cahiers pour l'analyse*, no. 1, 1966; J.-P. Oudart, 'Cinema and suture', from *Cahiers du Cinéma*, nos 211 and 212, April and May 1969; and Stephen Heath, 'Notes on suture'. See also: Dayan, 'The tutor-code of classical cinema'; Rothman, 'Against "The system of the suture" '; Johnston, 'Towards a feminist film practice' (see Bibliography).

condensation

One of the essential modes of the functioning of the unconscious processes: a sole idea represents several associative chains at whose point of intersection it is located. From the economic point of view, what happens is that this idea is cathected [that is, roughly, 'energized'] by the sum of those energies which are concentrated upon it by virtue of the fact that they are attached to these different chains.

– Laplanche and Pontalis, *The Language of Psychoanalysis*, p. 82.

displacement
The fact that an idea's emphasis, interest or intensity is liable to be detached from it and to pass on to other ideas, which were originally of little intensity but which are related to the first idea by a chain of associations.
– Laplanche and Pontalis, *The Language of Psychoanalysis*, p. 121.

foreclosure
Term introduced by Jacques Lacan denoting a specific mechanism held to lie at the origin of the psychotic phenomenon and to consist in a primordial expulsion of a fundamental 'signifier' (e.g. the phallus as signifier of the castration complex) from the subject's 'symbolic' (q.v.) universe. Foreclosure is deemed to be distinct from repression in two senses:
   (a) Foreclosed signifiers are not integrated into the subject's unconscious,
   (b) They do not return 'from the inside' – they re-emerge, rather, in 'the Real', particularly through the phenomenon of hallucination.
– Laplanche and Pontalis, *The Language of Psychoanalysis*, p. 166.

hysteria
Class of neurosis presenting a great diversity of clinical pictures. The two best isolated forms, from the point of view of symptoms, are *conversion hysteria*, in which the psychical conflict is expressed symbolically in somatic symptoms of the most varied kinds: they may be paroxystic (e.g. emotional crises accompanied by theatricality) or more long-lasting (anaesthesias, hysterical paralyses, 'lumps in the throat', etc.); and *anxiety hysteria*, where the anxiety is attached in more or less stable fashion to a specific external object (phobias).
   Freud discovered major aetio-pathogenic characteristics in conversion hysteria. It is this development which has enabled psychoanalysis to reduce a variety of clinical types affecting the organization of the personality and the mode of existence of the subject to a single common hysterical structure – and this even where there are no phobic symptoms and no obvious conversions.
   The specificity of hysteria is to be found in the prevalence of a certain kind of identification and of certain mechanisms (particularly repression, which is often explicit) in an emergence of the Oedipal conflict occurring mainly in the phallic and oral libidinal spheres.
– Laplanche and Pontalis, *The Language of Psychoanalysis*, p. 195.

neurosis
A psychogenic affection in which the symptoms are the symbolic expression of a psychical conflict whose origins lie in the subject's

childhood history; these symptoms constitute compromises between wish and defence.
– Laplanche and Pontalis, *The Language of Psychoanalysis*, p. 266.

overdetermination
The fact that formations of the unconscious (symptoms, dreams, etc.) can be attributed to a plurality of determining factors. This can be understood in two different ways:

(a) The formation in question is the result of several causes, since one alone is not sufficient to account for it.

(b) The formation is related to a multiplicity of unconscious elements which may be organised in different meaningful sequences, each having its own specific coherence at a particular level of interpretation. This second reading is the most generally accepted one.
– Laplanche and Pontalis, *The Language of Psychoanalysis*, p. 292.

Bibliography

The bibliography is intended to be extensive, but in no way exhaustive. In a sense, it would be possible to include every director study, and every *auteurist* review. For the sake of brevity, however, and to give the bibliography some focus, I have restricted the selection to articles and books which have a specific relevance for theoretical discussion of authorship or which help to make clear its various stages and developments (texts selected for this volume are included). I have also included a selection of related material: that is to say, film writing which, though it does not refer specifically to authorship, provides a context for any work on film theory; and writing on literature, politics, culture, psychoanalysis, etc., which has been important for the development of recent film theory, or which may help to make the context, and the concepts, clearer.

Three anthologies have appeared in notes as 'Mast and Cohen', 'Nichols', and '*Screen Reader I*'. These are:

Mast, G., and Cohen, M. (eds), *Film Theory and Criticism: introductory readings*, New York/London, Oxford University Press, 1974.
Nichols, B. (ed.), *Movies and Methods*, Berkeley/London, University of California Press, 1976.
Screen Reader I, London, Society for Education in Film and Television, 1977.

Books

Cameron, I. (ed.), *Movie Reader*, London, November Books, 1972.
Corliss, R., *Talking Pictures: Screenwriters in the American Cinema*, Harmondsworth, Penguin, 1975.
Graham, P. (ed.), *The New Wave*, London, Secker & Warburg (Cinema One), 1968.
Hardy, P. (ed.), *Raoul Walsh*, Edinburgh Film Festival, 1974.
Johnston, C. (ed.), *The Work of Dorothy Arzner: towards a feminist cinema*, London, British Film Institute, 1975.
Johnston, C. and Willemen, P. (eds), *Jacques Tourneur*, Edinburgh Film Festival, 1975.
Kitses, J., *Horizons West*, London, Secker & Warburg (Cinema One), 1969.
Lovell, A., *Don Siegel: American Cinema*, London, British Film Institute, 1975.
Nash, M., *Dreyer*, London, British Film Institute, 1977.

302

Nowell-Smith, G., *Visconti*, London, Secker & Warburg (Cinema One), 1967 and 1973.

Perkins, V. F., *Film as Film*, Harmondsworth, Penguin, 1972.

Sarris, A., *The American Cinema: Directors and directions, 1929–68*, New York, E. P. Dutton, 1968.

Sarris, A., *The John Ford Movie Mystery*, London, Secker & Warburg (Cinema One), 1976.

Willemen, P. (ed.), *Ophuls*, London, British Film Institute, 1978.

Wollen, P., *Signs and Meaning in the Cinema*, London, Secker & Warburg (Cinema One), 1969 and 1972.

Wood, R., *Howard Hawks*, London, Secker & Warburg (Cinema One), 1968.

Wood, R., *Hitchcock's Films*, London/New York, Zwemmer/A. S. Barnes, 1965, 1969, 1977.

Wood, R., *Personal Views*, London, Gordon Fraser, 1976.

Artioloo

Abramson, R., 'Structure and meaning in the cinema', in Nichols, pp. 558–68.

Anderson, L., 'The director's cinema?', *Sequence*, no. 12, Autumn 1950, pp. 6–11.

Anderson, L., '*They Were Expendable* and John Ford', *Sequence*, no. 11, Summer 1950, pp. 18–31.

Anderson, L., 'The Searchers', *Sight & Sound*, vol. 26, no. 2, Autumn 1956, pp. 94–5.

Astruc, A., 'The birth of a new avant-garde: *la caméra-stylo*', in Graham, *The New Wave*, pp. 17–23; first published, *Ecran français*, no. 144, 1948.

Bazin, A., 'De l'ambiguité' (on *The Red Badge of Courage*), *Cahiers du Cinéma*, no. 27, October 1953, pp. 49–54.

Bazin, A., 'Comment peut-on être Hitchcocko-Hawksien?', *Cahiers du Cinéma*, no. 44, February 1955, pp. 17–18.

Bazin, A., 'De la politique des auteurs', *Cahiers du Cinéma*, no. 70, April 1957, pp. 2–11; translation in Graham, *The New Wave*.

Bellour, R., '*Les Oiseaux*: analyse d'une séquence', *Cahiers du Cinéma*, no. 216, October 1969. pp. 24–39.

Bellour, R., 'Hitchcock, the enunciator', *Camera Obscura*, no. 2, Fall 1977, pp. 69–94.

Benayou, R., 'Le roi est nu', *Positif*, no. 46, June 1962, pp. 1–14.

Boys, B., '*The Courtship of Eddie's Father*', *Movie*, no. 10, June 1963, pp. 29–32.

Brecht, B., 'Le procès de quat'sous: expérience sociologique', in *Sur le Cinéma*, Paris, l'Arche, 1970, pp. 148–224; first appeared in vol. 3 of Brecht's *Essays*, Berlin, Kiepenheuer, 1931; also in *Gesammelte Werke*, vol. 8, Frankfurt, Suhrkamp Verlag, 1967.

Brewster, B., 'Structuralism in film criticism', *Screen*, vol. 12, no. 1, Spring 1971, pp. 49–58.

Brewster, B., 'Notes on the text "John Ford's *Young Mr Lincoln*" by the editors of *Cahiers du Cinéma*', *Screen*, vol. 14, no. 3, Autumn 1973, pp. 29–43; in *Screen Reader I*.

Browne, N., 'Rhétorique du texte spéculaire (à propos de *Stagecoach*)', *Communications*, no. 23, Paris, Editions du Seuil, 1975, pp. 202–11.

Browne, N., 'The Spectator-in-the-Text: the rhetoric of *Stagecoach*', *Film Quarterly*, vol. 29, no. 2, Winter 1975–6, pp. 26–44.

Buscombe, E., 'Ideas of Authorship', *Screen*, vol. 14, no. 3, Autumn 1973, pp. 75–85.

Buscombe, E., 'Walsh and Warner Brothers', in Hardy, *Raoul Walsh*, pp. 51–62.

Cahiers du Cinéma editors, 'John Ford's *Young Mr Lincoln*', *Cahiers du Cinéma*, no. 223, August 1970, pp. 29–47; translated in *Screen*, vol. 13, no. 3, Autumn 1972; also in Nichols; *Screen Reader I*; Mast and Cohen (2nd edn).

Cahiers du Cinéma editors, 'Sternberg et *Morocco*', *Cahiers du Cinéma*, no. 225, November–December 1970, pp. 6–13.

Cameron, I., 'Films, Directors and Critics', *Movie*, no. 2, September 1962, pp. 4–7; also in Cameron, *Movie Reader*.

Caughie, J., 'Teaching through Authorship', *Screen Education*, no. 17, Autumn 1975, pp. 3–13.

Clayton S., and Curling, J., 'On Authorship', *Screen*, vol. 20, no. 1, Spring 1979, pp. 35–61.

Comolli, J-L., 'Signes de piste' ('Sign-posts on the Trail'), *Cahiers du Cinéma*, no. 164, March 1965, pp. 15–16.

Comolli, J-L., and Narboni, J., 'Cinéma/idéologie/critique', *Cahiers du Cinéma*, nos. 216 and 217, October and November 1969, pp. 11–15 and 7–13; translation in *Screen*, vol. 12, nos. 1 and 2, Spring and Summer 1971; in *Screen Reader I*; part I in Nichols.

Comolli, *et al.*, 'Vingt ans après: le cinéma américain et la politique des auteurs', *Cahiers du Cinéma*, no. 172, November 1965, pp. 20–30.

Cook, P., 'Approaching the work of Dorothy Arzner', in Johnston, *The Work of Dorothy Arzner*, pp. 9–18.

Cook, P., 'The point of self-expression in avant-garde film', London, British Film Institute Production Board catalogue, 1977–78.

Cook, P., and Johnston, C., 'The place of women in the cinema of Raoul Walsh', in Hardy, *Raoul Walsh*, pp. 93–110.

Daney, S., and Oudart, J-P., 'Le Nom-de-l'auteur', *Cahiers du Cinéma*, no. 234–5, December–February 1971–2, pp. 79–92.

Dayan, D., 'The tutor-code of classical cinema', *Film Quarterly*, vol. 28, no. 1, Fall 1974, pp. 22–31; in Nichols.

Eckert, C., 'The English cine-structuralists', *Film Comment*, vol. 9, no. 3, May–June 1973, pp. 46–51.

Eckert, C., 'Shall we deport Lévi-Strauss?', *Film Quarterly*, vol. 27, no. 3, Spring 1974, pp. 63–5.

Fargier, J-P., 'Le processus de production de film', *Cinéthique*, no. 6, January–February 1970, pp. 45–55.

Flitterman, S., 'Woman, desire, and the look: feminism and the enunciative apparatus in cinema', *Ciné-Tracts*, 5, vol. 2, no. 1, Fall 1978, pp. 63–8.

Heath, S., 'Comment on "The idea of authorship" ', *Screen*, vol. 14, no. 3, Autumn 1973, pp. 86–91.

Heath, S., 'Notes on suture', *Screen*, vol. 18, no. 4, Winter 1977–8, pp. 48–76; accompanies translation of Oudart's 'Suture'.

Heath, S., 'Difference', *Screen*, vol. 19, no. 3, Autumn 1978, pp. 51–112.

Henderson, B., 'Critique of cine-structuralism', *Film Quarterly*, vol. 27, nos 1 and 2, Fall and Winter 1973–4, pp. 25–34 and 37–46.

Hess, J., 'La politique des auteurs', *Jump Cut*, no. 1, pp. 19–22; no. 2, pp. 20–2, May–June and July–August 1974.

Houston, P., 'The critical question', *Sight & Sound*, vol. 29, no. 4, Autumn 1960, pp. 160–5.

Houston, P., 'The figure in the carpet', *Sight & Sound*, vol. 32, no. 4, Autumn 1963, pp. 159–64.

Hoveyda, F., 'La réponse de Nicholas Ray', *Cahiers du Cinéma*, no. 107, May 1960, pp. 13–23.

Hoveyda, F., 'Autocritique', *Cahiers du Cinéma*, no. 126, December 1961, pp. 41–6.

Johnston, C., 'Women's cinema as counter-cinema', in C. Johnston, ed., *Notes on Women's Cinema*, London, Society for Education in Film and Television, 1973; in Nichols.

Johnston, C., 'Dorothy Arzner: critical strategies', in Johnston, *The Work of Dorothy Arzner*, pp. 1–8.

Johnston, C., 'Towards a feminist film practice: some theses', *Edinburgh '76 Magazine*, Edinburgh Film Festival, 1976, pp. 50–9.

Kael, P., 'Circles and squares', *Film Quarterly*, vol. 16, no. 3, Spring 1963, pp. 12–26; extracted in Mast and Cohen.

Kast, P., 'Des confitures pour un gendarme', *Cahiers du Cinéma*, no. 2, May 1951, p. 40.

Lovell, A., 'Robin Wood: a dissenting view', *Screen*, vol. 10, no. 2, March–April 1969, pp. 47–55.

Lovell, A., 'The common pursuit of true judgement', *Screen*, vol. II, nos. 4–5, August–September 1970, pp. 76–88.

Marcorelles, L., 'Ford of the movies', *Cahiers du Cinéma*, no. 86, August 1958, pp. 32–7.

Metz, C., 'History/discourse: a note on two voyeurisms', *Edinburgh '76 Magazine*, no. I, 1976, pp. 21–5; first appeared in J. Kristeva *et al.* (eds), *Langue, Discours, Société*, Paris, Editions du Seuil, 1975.

Metz, C., 'The imaginary signifier', *Screen*, vol. 16, no. 2, Summer 1975, pp. 14–76. Also in *Communications*, no. 23, May 1975, pp. 3–55.

Moullet, L., 'Sam Fuller: sur les brisées de Marlowe', *Cahiers du Cinéma*, no. 53, March 1959, pp. 11–19.

Movie editorial discussion, '*Movie* differences', *Movie*, no. 8, April 1963, pp. 19–25; with V. F. Perkins, M. Shivas, I. Cameron, P. Mayersberg. Also in Cameron, *Movie Reader*.

Movie editorial discussion, 'The return of *Movie*', *Movie*, no. 20, Spring 1975, pp. 1–25; with I. Cameron, J. Hillier, V. F. Perkins, M. Walker, R. Wood.

Mulvey, L., 'Visual pleasure and narrative cinema', *Screen*, vol. 16, no. 3, Autumn 1975, pp. 6–18.

Murray, J. C., 'Robin Wood and the structural critics', *Screen*, vol. 12, no. 3, Autumn 1971, pp. 101–10.

Narboni, J., '*Les Sept Femmes* de John Ford: la preuve par huit' ('Casting out the eights'), *Cahiers du Cinéma*, no. 182, September 1966, pp. 20–4.

Nowell-Smith, G., 'I was a star* struck structuralist', *Screen*, vol. 14, no. 3, Autumn 1973, pp. 92–9.

Nowell-Smith, G., 'Six authors in pursuit of *The Searchers*', *Screen*, vol. 17, no. 1, Spring 1976, pp. 26–33.

Nowell-Smith, G., 'A note on "History/Discourse" ', *Edinburgh '76 Magazine*, no. 1, 1976, pp. 26–32.

Oudart, J-P., 'La suture', *Cahiers du Cinéma*, nos 211 and 212, April and May 1969; translation in *Screen*, vol. 18, no. 4, Winter 1977–8, pp. 35–47. See also Heath, 'Notes on suture'.

Oudart, J-P., 'Le hors-champ de l'Auteur', ('The absent field of the Author'), *Cahiers du Cinéma*, no. 236–7, March–April 1971, pp. 86–9.

Perkins, V. F., 'The cinema of Nicholas Ray', *Movie*, no. 9, May 1963, pp. 4–10; in Cameron, *Movie Reader*.

Petrie, G., 'Alternatives to *auteurs*', *Film Quarterly*, vol. 26, no. 3, Spring 1973, pp. 27–35.

Porter, V., 'Film copyright: film culture', *Screen*, vol. 19, no. 1, Spring 1978, pp. 90–108.

Positif editors, 'Quelques réalisateurs trop admirés', *Positif*, no. 11, September–October 1954, pp. 49–59.

Rivette, J., 'Howard Hawks', *Cahiers du Cinéma*, no. 23, May 1953; translated in *Movie*, no. 5, December 1962, pp. 19–20; in Cameron, *Movie Reader*.

Rivette, J., 'Notes sur une révolution', *Cahiers du Cinéma*, no. 54, Christmas 1955, pp. 17–21.

Rohdie, S., 'Review: *Movie Reader, Film as Film*', *Screen*, vol. 13, no. 4, Winter 1972–3, pp. 135–45.

Rohmer, E., (Schérer, M.), 'Renoir américain', *Cahiers du Cinéma*, no. 8, January 1952, pp. 33–40.

Rohmer, E., (Schérer, M.), 'A qui la faute?', *Cahiers du Cinéma*, no. 39, October 1954, pp. 6–10.

Rohmer, E. *et al*, 'Les lecteurs des *Cahiers* et la politique des auteurs', *Cahiers du Cinéma*, no. 63, October 1956, pp. 54–8.

Rothman, W., 'Against "The system of the suture" ', *Film Quarterly*, vol. 29, no. 1, Fall 1975, pp. 45–50; in Nichols.

Roud, R., 'The French line', *Sight & Sound*, vol. 29, no. 4, Autumn 1960, pp. 166–71.

Sarris, A., 'The director's game', *Film Culture*, nos 22–3, Summer 1961, pp. 68–81.

Sarris, A., 'Notes on the *auteur* theory in 1962', *Film Culture*, no. 27, Winter 1962–3, pp. 1–8; also in P. Adams Sitney (ed.), *Film Culture: an anthology*, London, Secker & Warburg, 1971, pp. 121–35 and in Mast and Cohen.

Sarris, A., 'The *auteur* theory and the perils of Pauline', *Film Quarterly*, vol. 16, no. 4, Summer 1963, pp. 26–32.

Sarris, A., 'Preminger's two periods', *Film Comment*, vol. 3, no. 3, Summer 1965, pp. 12–16.

Sarris, A., '*The Searchers*', *Film Comment*, vol. 7, no. 1, Spring 1971, pp. 58–61.

Sarris, A., 'Toward a theory of film history', in Sarris, *The American Cinema*.

Truffaut, F., 'Une certaine tendance du cinéma français', *Cahiers du Cinéma*, no. 31, January 1954, pp. 15–28; in Nichols.

Willemen, P., 'Distanciation and Douglas Sirk', *Screen*, vol. 12, no. 2, Summer 1971, pp. 63–7; also in L. Mulvey and J. Halliday (eds), *Douglas Sirk*, Edinburgh Film Festival, 1972.

Willemen, P., 'Towards an analysis of the Sirkian system', *Screen*, vol. 13, no. 4, Winter 1972–3, pp. 128–34.

Willemen, P., 'The fugitive subject', in Hardy, *Raoul Walsh*, pp. 63–89.

Willemen, P., 'Notes on subjectivity – on reading "Subjectivity under siege" ', *Screen*, vol. 19, no. 1, Spring 1978, pp. 41–69.

Wollen, P. (Russell, L.), 'John Ford', *New Left Review*, no. 29, January/February 1965.

Wollen, P. (Russell, L.), 'Jean-Luc Godard', *New Left Review*, no. 39; September/ October 1966, pp. 83–7.

Wood, R., 'Jean-Luc Godard', *New Left Review*, no. 39, September–October 1966, pp. 77–83; accompanies article by Wollen, see above.

Wood, R., 'Ghostly paradigm and HCF: an answer to Alan Lovell', *Screen*, vol. 10, no. 3, May–June 1969, pp. 35–48.

Wood, R., 'Shall we gather at the river? The late films of John Ford', *Film Comment*, vol. 7, no. 3, Fall 1971, pp. 8–17.

Wood, R., 'To have (written) and have not (directed)', *Film Comment*, vol. 9, no. 3, May–June 1973, pp. 30–5.

Wood, R., 'Smart-ass and Cutie-pie: notes towards a re-evaluation of Altman', *Movie*, no. 21, Autumn 1975, pp. 1–17.

Related material

Abrams, M. H., *The Mirror and the Lamp: romantic theory and the critical tradition*, London/New York, Oxford University Press, 1953, 1977.

Althusser, L., *Lenin and Philosophy and Other Essays*, London, New Left Books, 1971.

Althusser, L., and Balibar, E., *Reading Capital* (1968), London, New Left Books, 1972.

Barthes, R., *S/Z* (1970), London, Jonathan Cape, 1974.

Barthes, R., *The Pleasure of the Text* (1973), New York, Hill & Wang, 1975.

Barthes, R., *Image–Music–Text*, ed. S. Heath, London, Fontana/Collins, 1977.

Baudry, J-L., 'Writing, fiction, ideology' (1968), *Afterimage*, no. 5, Spring 1974, pp. 22–39; translated from *Théorie d'ensemble*, collection *Tel Quel*, Paris, Editions du Seuil, 1968.

Benjamin, W., 'The author as producer' (1934), in *Understanding Brecht*, London, New Left Books, 1973.

Benveniste, E., *Problems of General Linguistics* (1966), Coral Gables, Fla., University of Miami Press, 1971.

Communications, no. 23, *Psychanalyse et cinéma*, Paris, Editions du Seuil, 1975.

Coward, R., and Ellis, J., *Language and Materialism*, London, Routledge & Kegan Paul, 1977.

Ducrot, O. and Todorov, T., *Dictionnaire encyclopédique des sciences du langage*, Paris, Editions du Seuil, 1972.

Edinburgh '76 Magazine, *Psychoanalysis/Cinema/Avant-garde*, Edinburgh Film Festival, 1976.

Ellis, J., 'Art, culture and quality', *Screen*, vol. 19, no. 3, Autumn 1978, pp. 9–49.

Foucault, M., *The Order of Things* (1966), London, Tavistock, 1977.

Foucault, M., *The Archaeology of Knowledge* (1969), London, Tavistock, 1977.

Foucault, M., *Language, Counter-Memory, Practice*, ed. D. F. Bouchard, Oxford, Basil Blackwell, 1977. (Includes 'What is an author', originally published in the *Bulletin* of the Societé française de philosophie, 63, no. 3, 1969.)

Freud, S., 'Fetishism', *On Sexuality*, Harmondsworth, Penguin, 1977.

Genette, G, *Figures III*, Paris, Editions du Seuil, 1972.

Heath, S., *The Nouveau Roman: a study in the practice of writing*, London, Elek Books, 1972.

Heath, S., 'Film/cinetext/text', *Screen*, vol. 14, nos 1/2, Spring/Summer 1973, pp. 102–28.

Heath, S., 'Metz's semiology: a short glossary', *Screen*, vol. 14, nos 1/2, Spring/Summer 1973, pp. 214–26.

Heath, S., 'Narrative space', *Screen*, vol. 17, no. 3, Autumn 1976, pp. 68–112.

Heath, S., 'Anata Mo', *Screen*, vol. 17, no. 4, Winter 1976–7, pp. 49–66.

Hirst, P., 'Althusser and the theory of ideology', *Economy and Society*, vol. 5, no. 4, 1976, pp. 385–412.

Jakobson, R., *Selected Writings*, Paris/The Hague, Mouton, 1971.

Jakobson, R., 'Shifters, verbal categories, and the Russian verb', in *Selected Writings*, vol. 2, see above.

Kristeva, J., 'The semiotic activity', *Screen*, vol. 14, nos 1/2, Spring/Summer 1973, pp. 25–39.

Kristeva, J., 'The subject in signifying practice', *Semiotext(e)*, New York, Columbia University, vol. 1, no. 3, 1975.

Lacan, J., *Ecrits: a selection*, London, Tavistock, 1977.

Lacan, J., *The Four Fundamental Concepts of Psychoanalysis*, ed. J.-A. Miller, London, Hogarth Press, 1977.

Laplanche, J., and Pontalis, J.-B., *The Language of Psychoanalysis*, London, Hogarth Press, 1973.

Leavis, F. R., *The Common Pursuit*, London, Chatto & Windus, 1952; Peregrine Books, 1962.

Lévi-Strauss, C., *Structural Anthropology* vol. 1, translated by C. Jacobson and B. G. Schoepf, London, Allen Lane, 1968. First published Paris, 1958.

MacCabe, C., 'Presentation of "The imaginary signifier" ', *Screen*, vol. 16, no. 2, Summer 1975, pp. 7–13

Macherey, P., *A Theory of Literary Production*, translated by Geoffrey Wall, London, Routledge & Kegan Paul, 1978. First published Paris, Librairie François Maspero, 1966.

Macksey, R. and Donato, E. (eds), *The Structuralist Controversy*, Baltimore, John Hopkins University Press, 1970.

Metz, C., *Film Language: a semiotics of the cinema* (1968), New York/London, Oxford University Press, 1974.

Metz, C., *Language and Cinema*, The Hague/Paris, Mouton, 1974.

de Saussure, F., *Course in General Linguistics* (1915), London, Fontana/Collins, 1974.

Screen, double issue, *Cinema Semiotics and the Work of Christian Metz*, vol. 14, nos 1/2, Spring/Summer 1973.

collection *Tel Quel*, *Théorie d'ensemble*, Paris, Editions du Seuil, 1968.

Williams, R., *Keywords*, London, Fontana, 1976.

Index of names and titles

Index of subjects